WELCOME to Imperial Academy: a private school where trying to become SUPERIOR can make you feel INFERIOR!

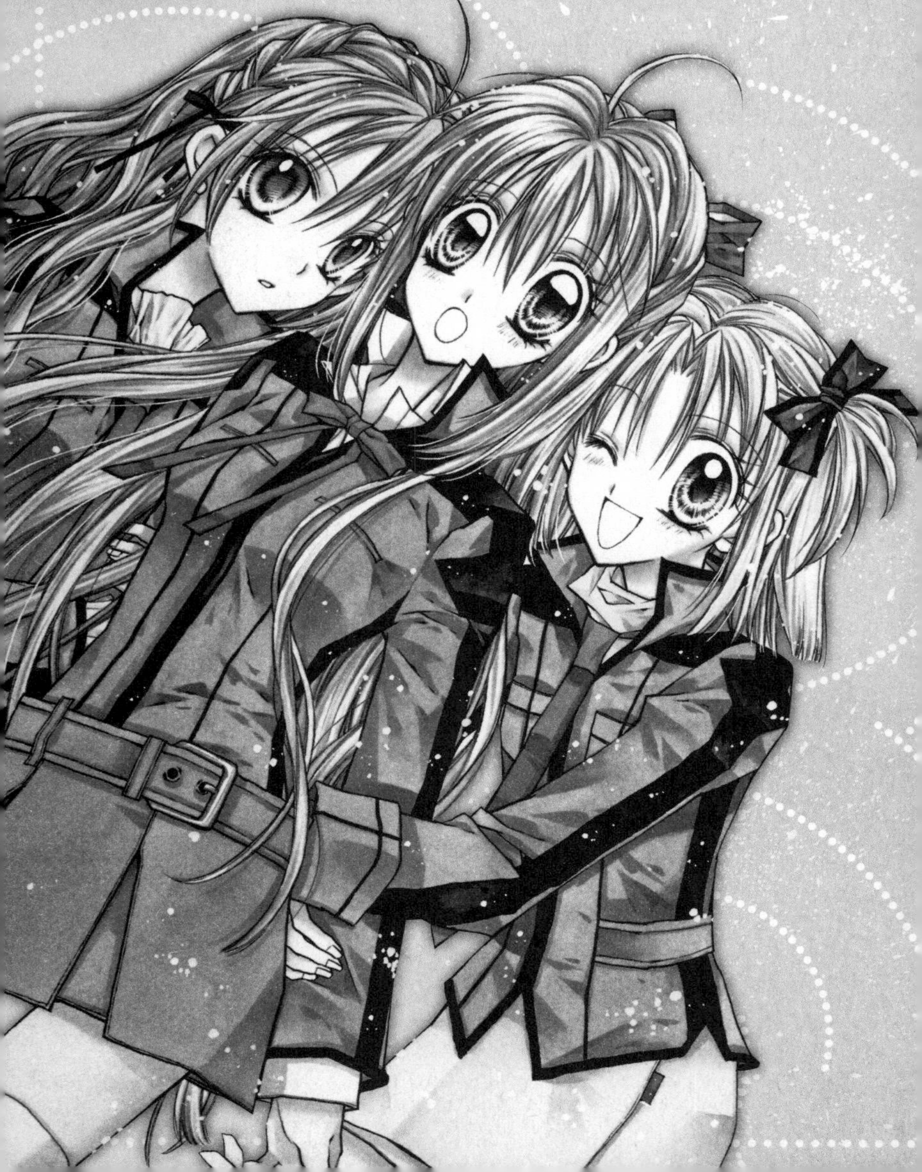

Shojo Beat

kimi ni todoke
From Me to You

Vol. 7
Story & Art by
Karuho Shiina

Volume 7

Contents

Story Thus Far

Sawako Kuronuma has always been a loner. Though not by choice, this optimistic 15-year-old can't seem to make any friends. Stuck with the unfortunate nickname "Sadako" after the haunting movie character, rumors about her summoning spirits have been greatly exaggerated. With her shy personality and scary looks, most of her classmates would barely talk to her, much less look into her eyes for more than three seconds lest they be cursed. Drawn out of her shell by her popular classmate Shota Kazehaya, Sawako is no longer an outcast in class. And with her new friends Ayane and Chizu, she's finally leading a more normal teenage life. One day Sawako, Chizu and Ayane find out that Ryu's brother Toru has a fiancée. Chizu is shocked, but her friendship with Sawako, Ayane and Ryu helps her recover. In December, Sawako is excited about sharing her first Christmas party with friends, but decides she should be at her family's party. Knowing how she feels, Sawako's father gives her a cell phone and lets her go meet her friends.

kimi ni todoke
From Me to You

Episode 25: Couple

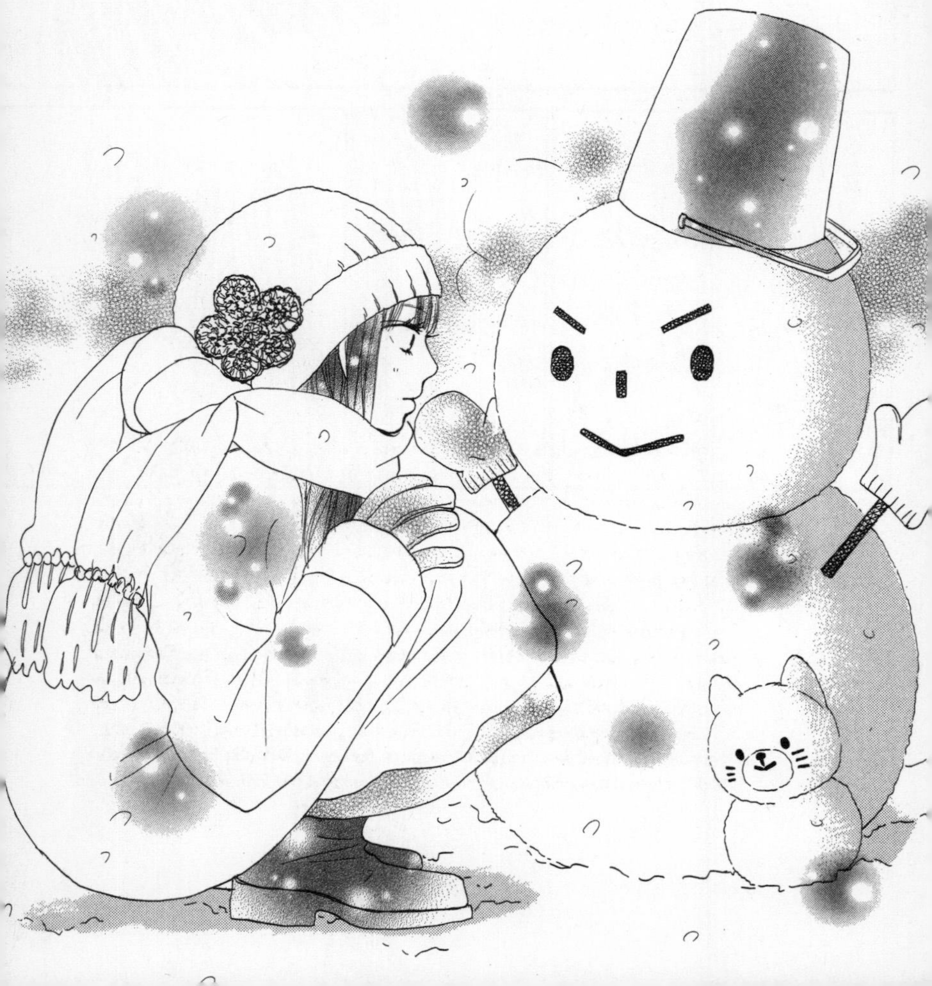

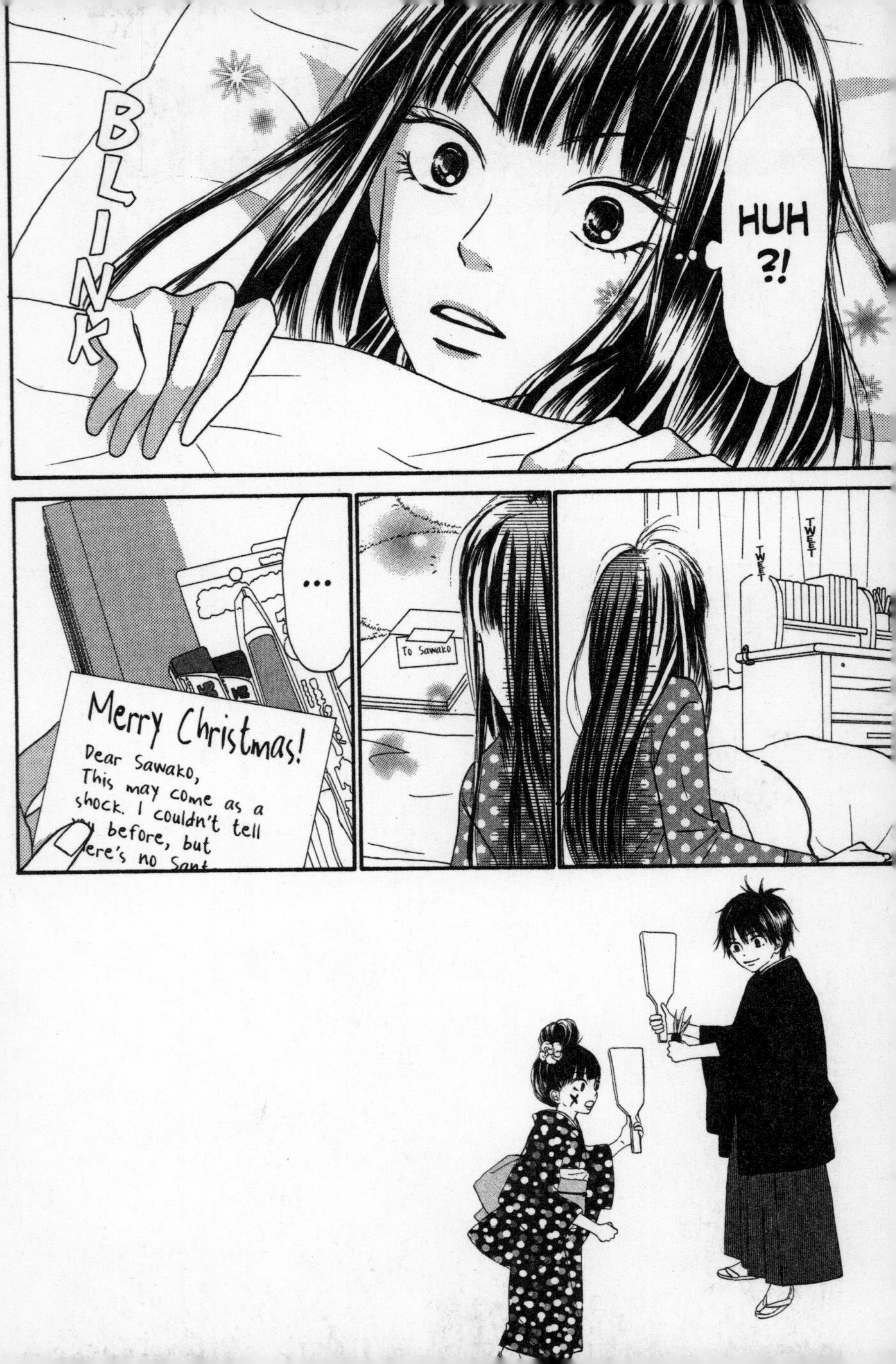

BLINK
HUH ?!
TWEET
TWEET
To Sawako
...
Merry Christmas!
Dear Sawako,
This may come as a
shock. I couldn't tell
before, but

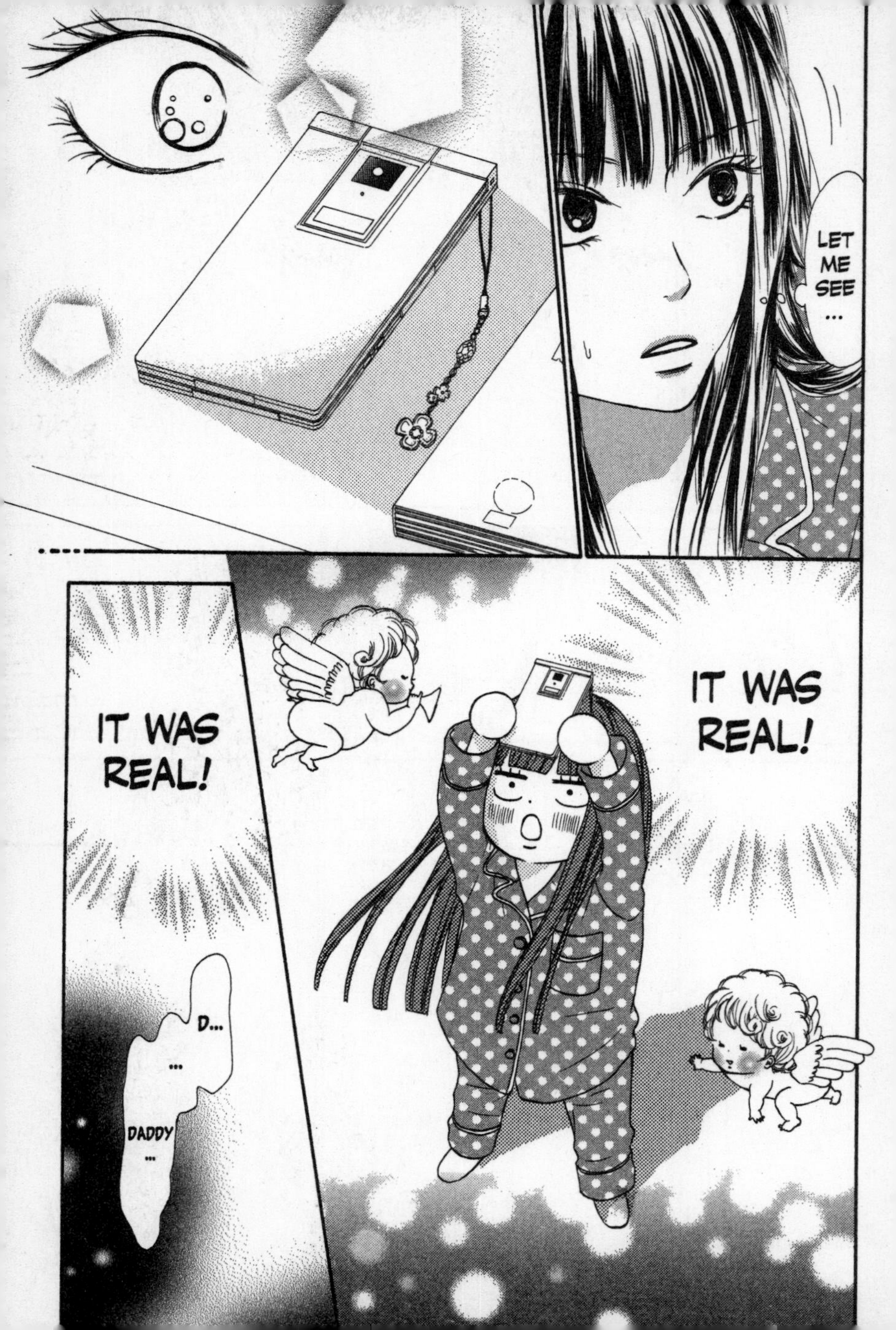
LET ME SEE ...
IT WAS REAL!
IT WAS REAL!
D... ... DADDY ...

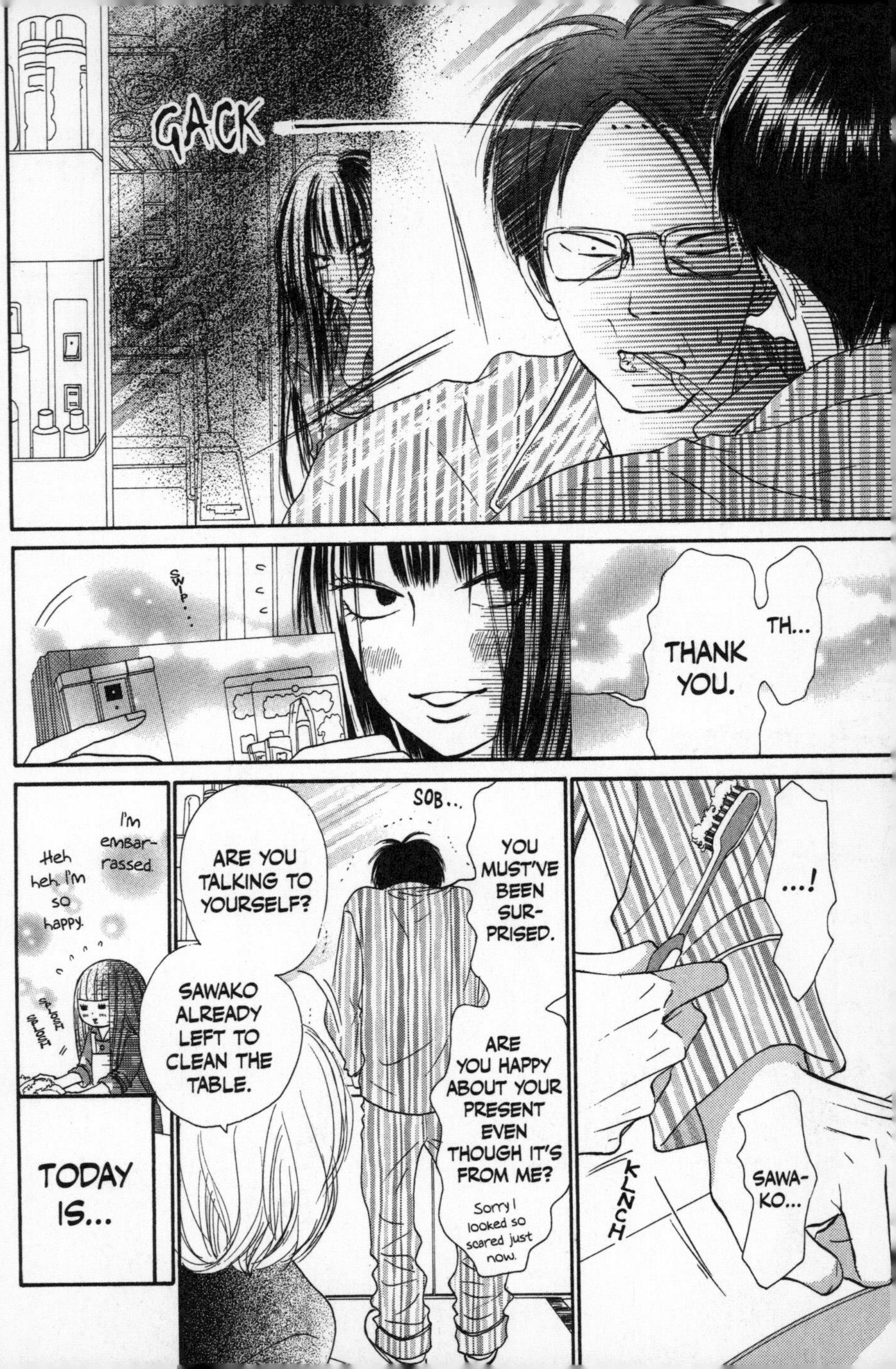
GACK
TH...
THANK YOU.
SWIP...
...!
SAWAKO...
KLNCH
SOB...
YOU MUST'VE BEEN SURPRISED.
ARE YOU HAPPY ABOUT YOUR PRESENT EVEN THOUGH IT'S FROM ME?
Sorry I looked so scared just now.
ARE YOU TALKING TO YOURSELF?
SAWAKO ALREADY LEFT TO CLEAN THE TABLE.
I'm embarrassed.
Heh heh. I'm so happy.
TODAY IS...

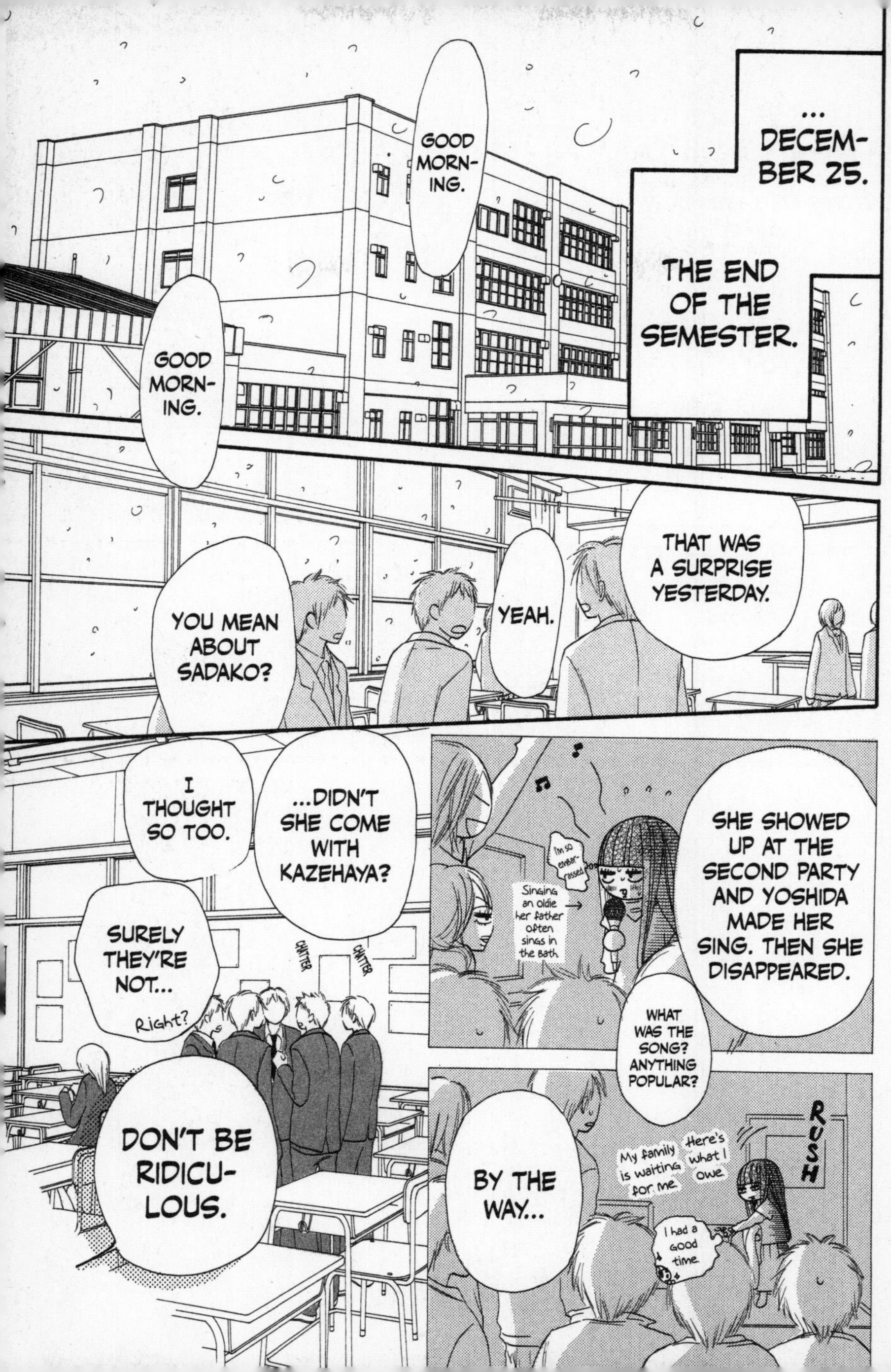
... DECEMBER 25.
THE END OF THE SEMESTER.
GOOD MORNING.
GOOD MORNING.
THAT WAS A SURPRISE YESTERDAY.
YEAH.
YOU MEAN ABOUT SADAKO?
SHE SHOWED UP AT THE SECOND PARTY AND YOSHIDA MADE HER SING. THEN SHE DISAPPEARED.
I'm so embarrassed
Singing an oldie her father often sings in the bath.
WHAT WAS THE SONG? ANYTHING POPULAR?
RUSH
Here's what I owe.
My family is waiting for me.
I had a good time.
BY THE WAY...
...DIDN'T SHE COME WITH KAZEHAYA?
I THOUGHT SO TOO.
CHATTER
CHATTER
SURELY THEY'RE NOT...
Right?
DON'T BE RIDICULOUS.

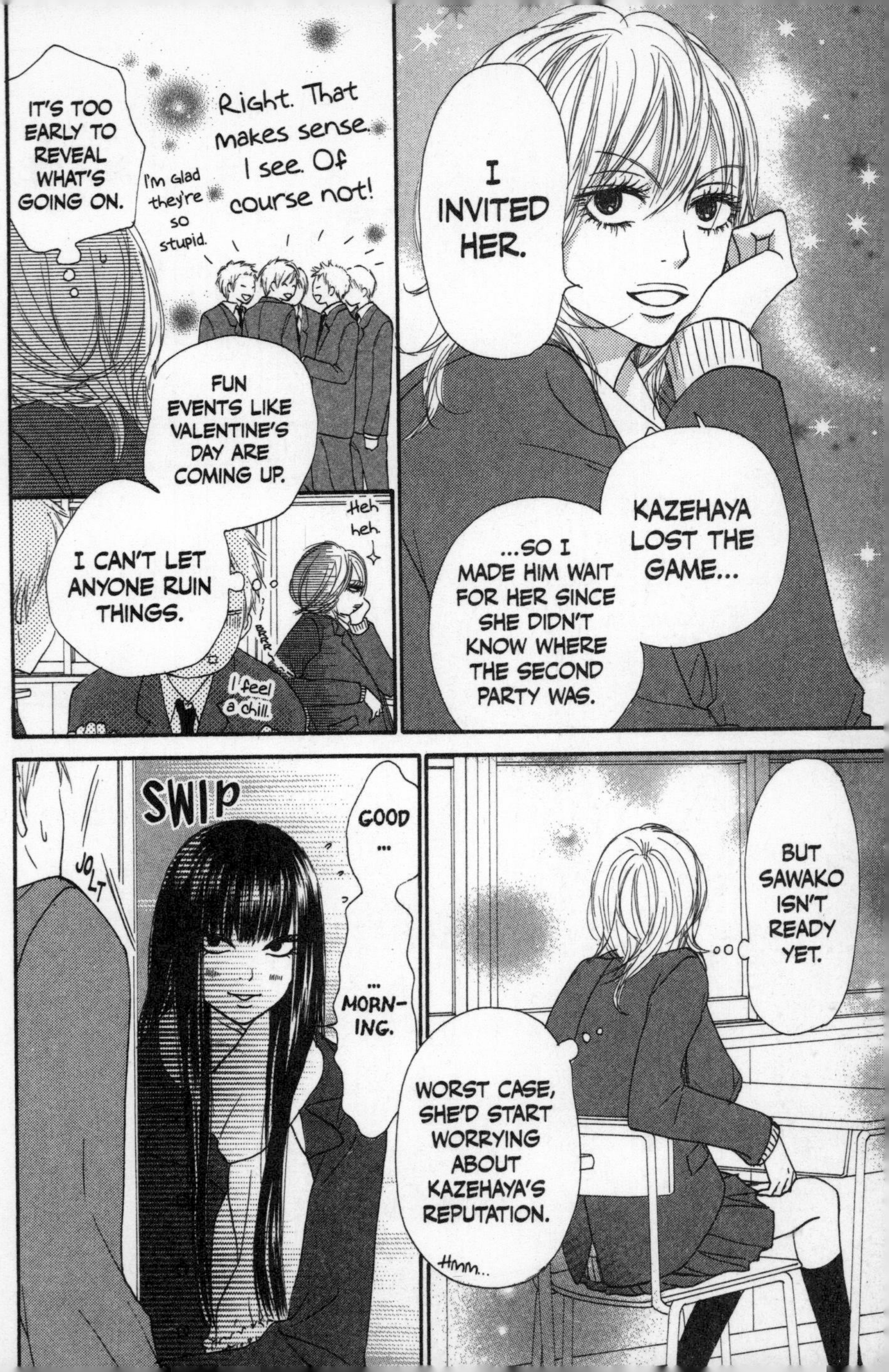
I INVITED HER.
KAZEHAYA LOST THE GAME...
...SO I MADE HIM WAIT FOR HER SINCE SHE DIDN'T KNOW WHERE THE SECOND PARTY WAS.
Right. That makes sense. I see. Of course not!
I'm Glad they're so stupid.
IT'S TOO EARLY TO REVEAL WHAT'S GOING ON.
FUN EVENTS LIKE VALENTINE'S DAY ARE COMING UP.
Heh heh.
I CAN'T LET ANYONE RUIN THINGS.
I feel a chill.
BUT SAWAKO ISN'T READY YET.
WORST CASE, SHE'D START WORRYING ABOUT KAZEHAYA'S REPUTATION.
Hmm...
SWIP
GOOD ... ...MORNING.
JOLT

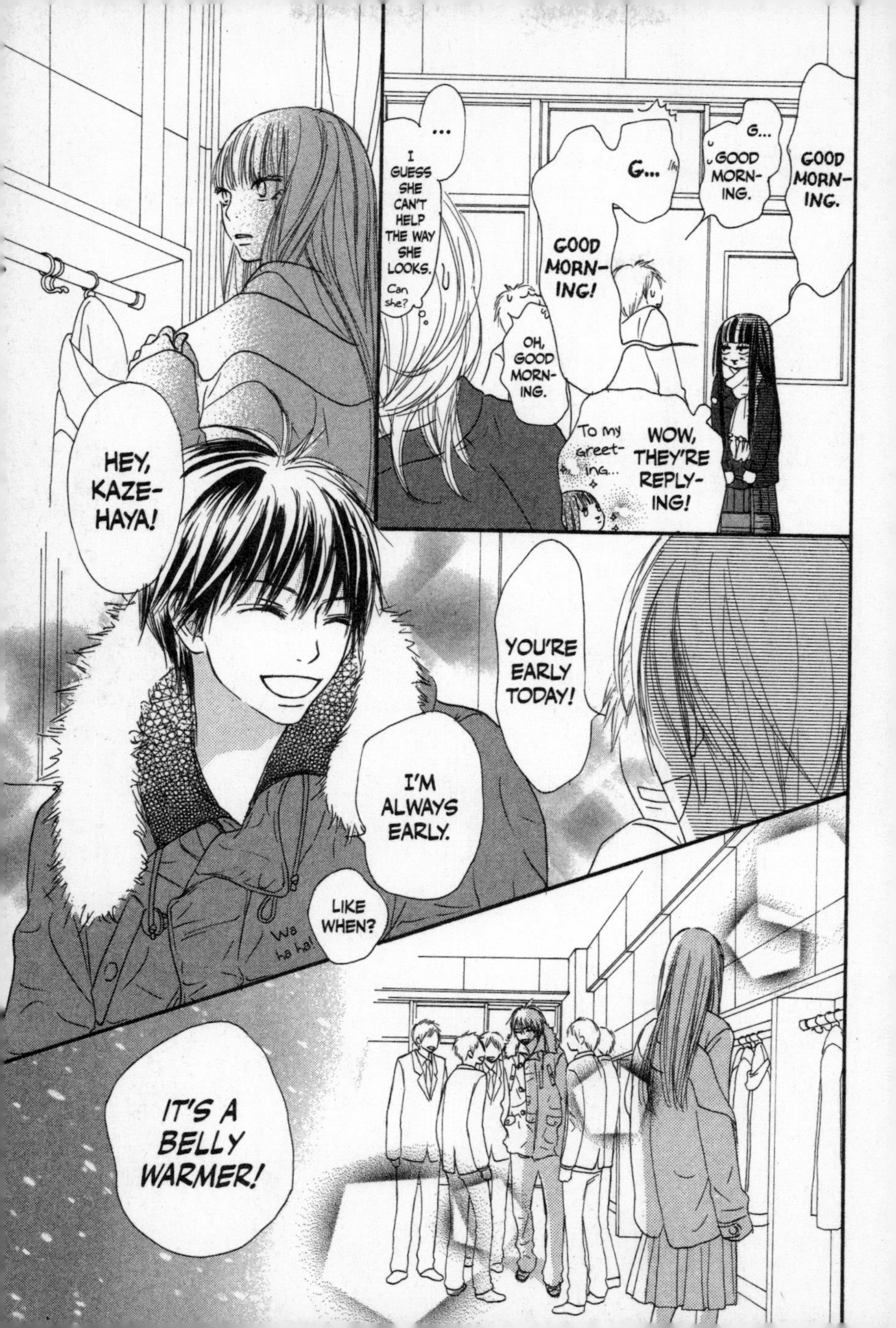
GOOD MORNING.
G... GOOD MORNING.
G...
GOOD MORNING!
OH, GOOD MORNING.
WOW, THEY'RE REPLYING!
To my greeting...
...
I GUESS SHE CAN'T HELP THE WAY SHE LOOKS.
Can she?
HEY, KAZEHAYA!
YOU'RE EARLY TODAY!
I'M ALWAYS EARLY.
LIKE WHEN?
Wa ha ha!
IT'S A BELLY WARMER!

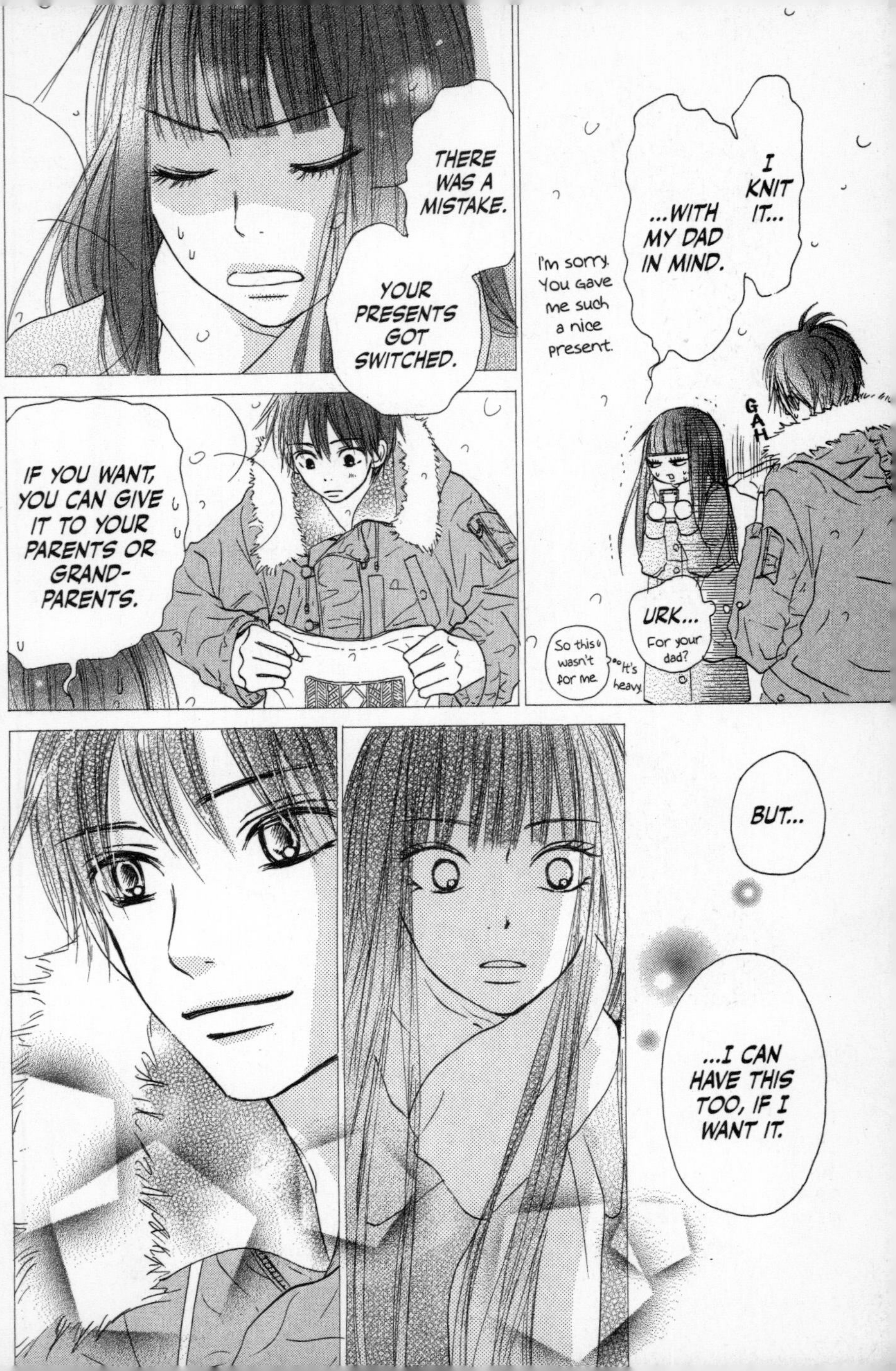
I KNIT IT...
...WITH MY DAD IN MIND.
I'm sorry. You gave me such a nice present.
GAH
URK...
For your dad?
It's heavy.
So this wasn't for me.
THERE WAS A MISTAKE.
YOUR PRESENTS GOT SWITCHED.
IF YOU WANT, YOU CAN GIVE IT TO YOUR PARENTS OR GRAND-PARENTS.
BUT...
...I CAN HAVE THIS TOO, IF I WANT IT.

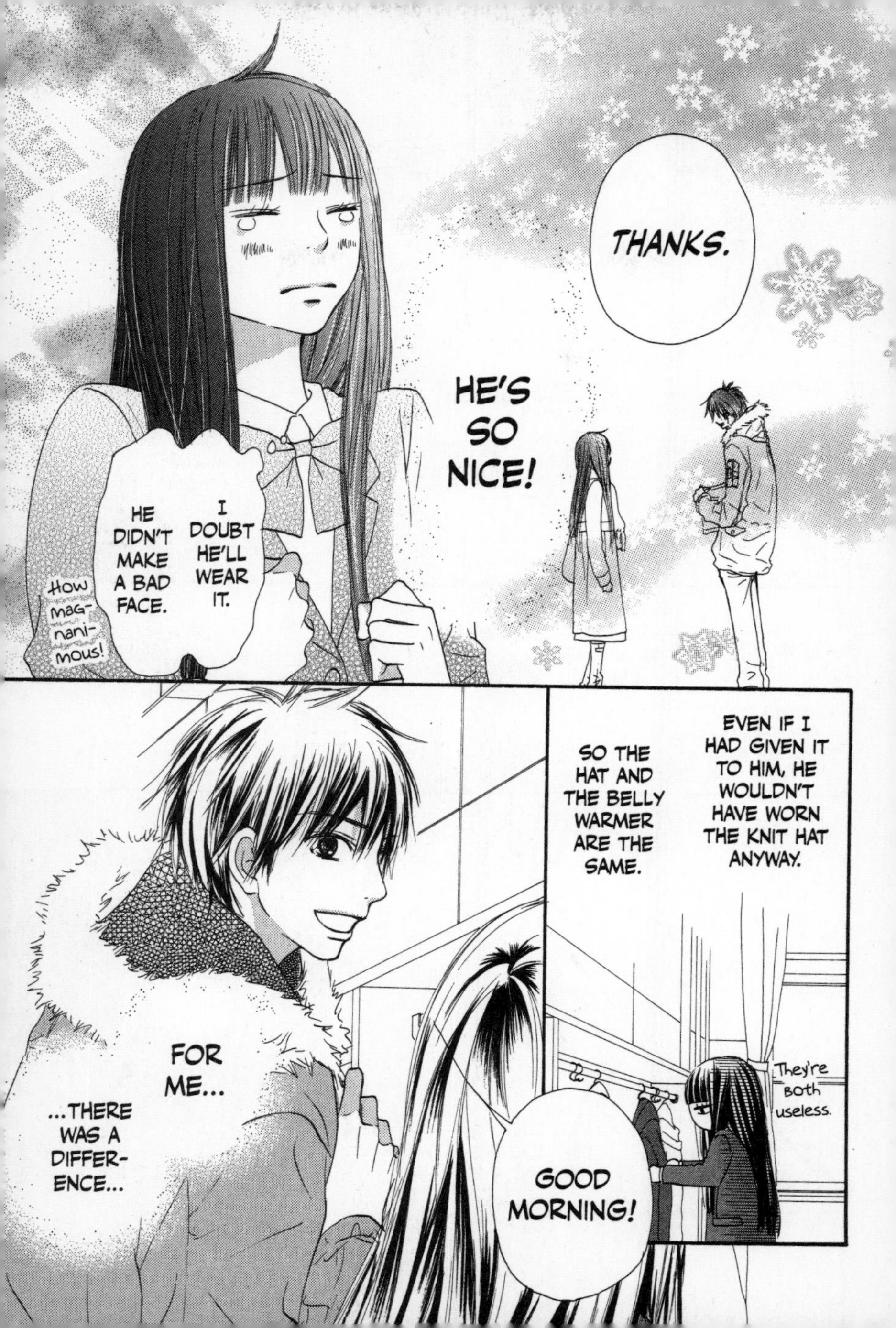
THANKS.
HE'S SO NICE!
I DOUBT HE'LL WEAR IT.
HE DIDN'T MAKE A BAD FACE.
How mag-nani-mous!
EVEN IF I HAD GIVEN IT TO HIM, HE WOULDN'T HAVE WORN THE KNIT HAT ANYWAY.
SO THE HAT AND THE BELLY WARMER ARE THE SAME.
They're both useless.
GOOD MORNING!
FOR ME...
...THERE WAS A DIFFER-ENCE...

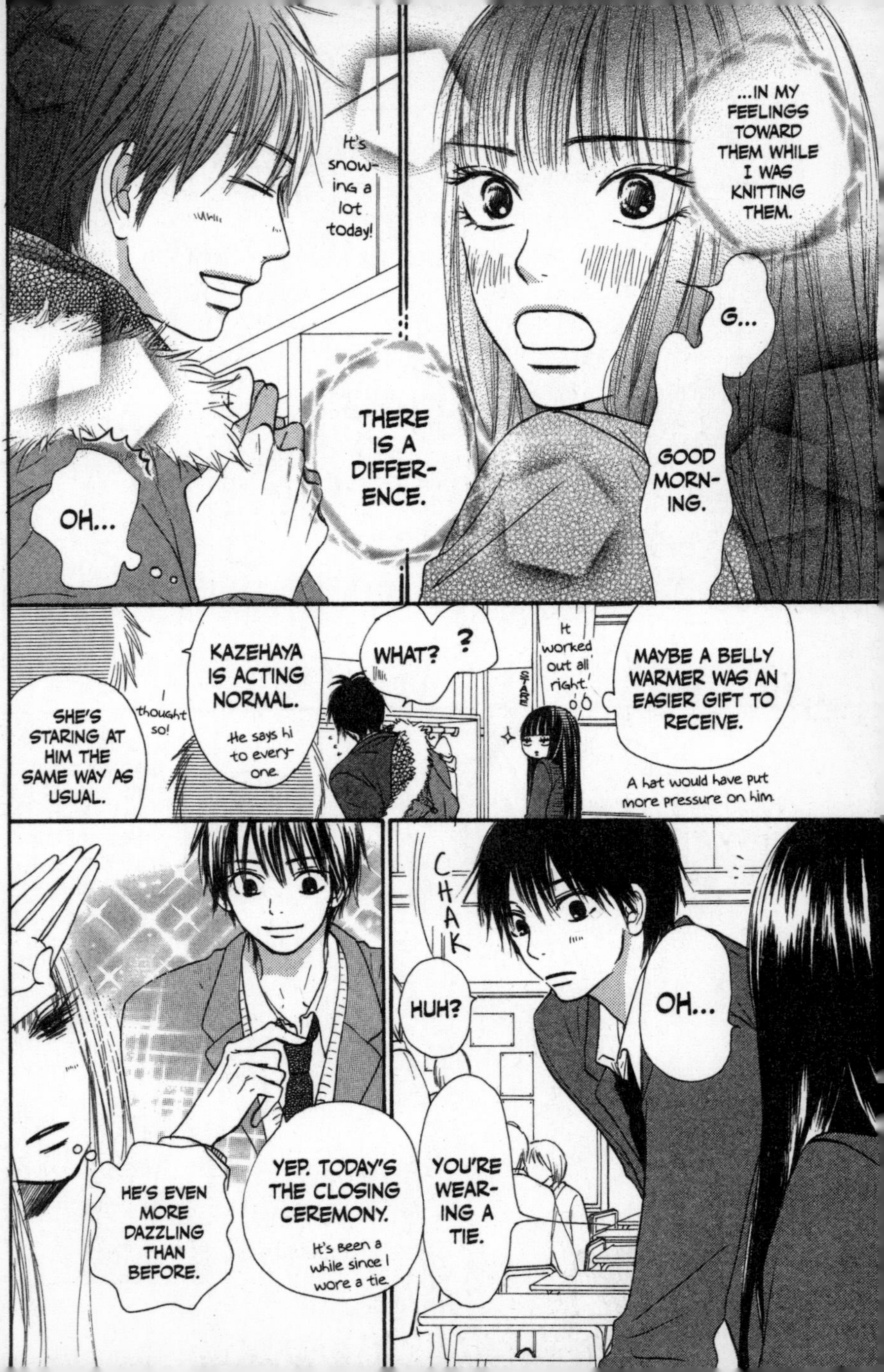
...IN MY FEELINGS TOWARD THEM WHILE I WAS KNITTING THEM.
G...
GOOD MORNING.
THERE IS A DIFFERENCE.
It's snowing a lot today!
OH...
MAYBE A BELLY WARMER WAS AN EASIER GIFT TO RECEIVE.
A hat would have put more pressure on him.
It worked out all right.
STARE
WHAT?
?
KAZEHAYA IS ACTING NORMAL.
He says hi to everyone.
I thought so!
SHE'S STARING AT HIM THE SAME WAY AS USUAL.
CHAK
OH...
HUH?
YOU'RE WEARING A TIE.
YEP. TODAY'S THE CLOSING CEREMONY.
It's been a while since I wore a tie.
HE'S EVEN MORE DAZZLING THAN BEFORE.

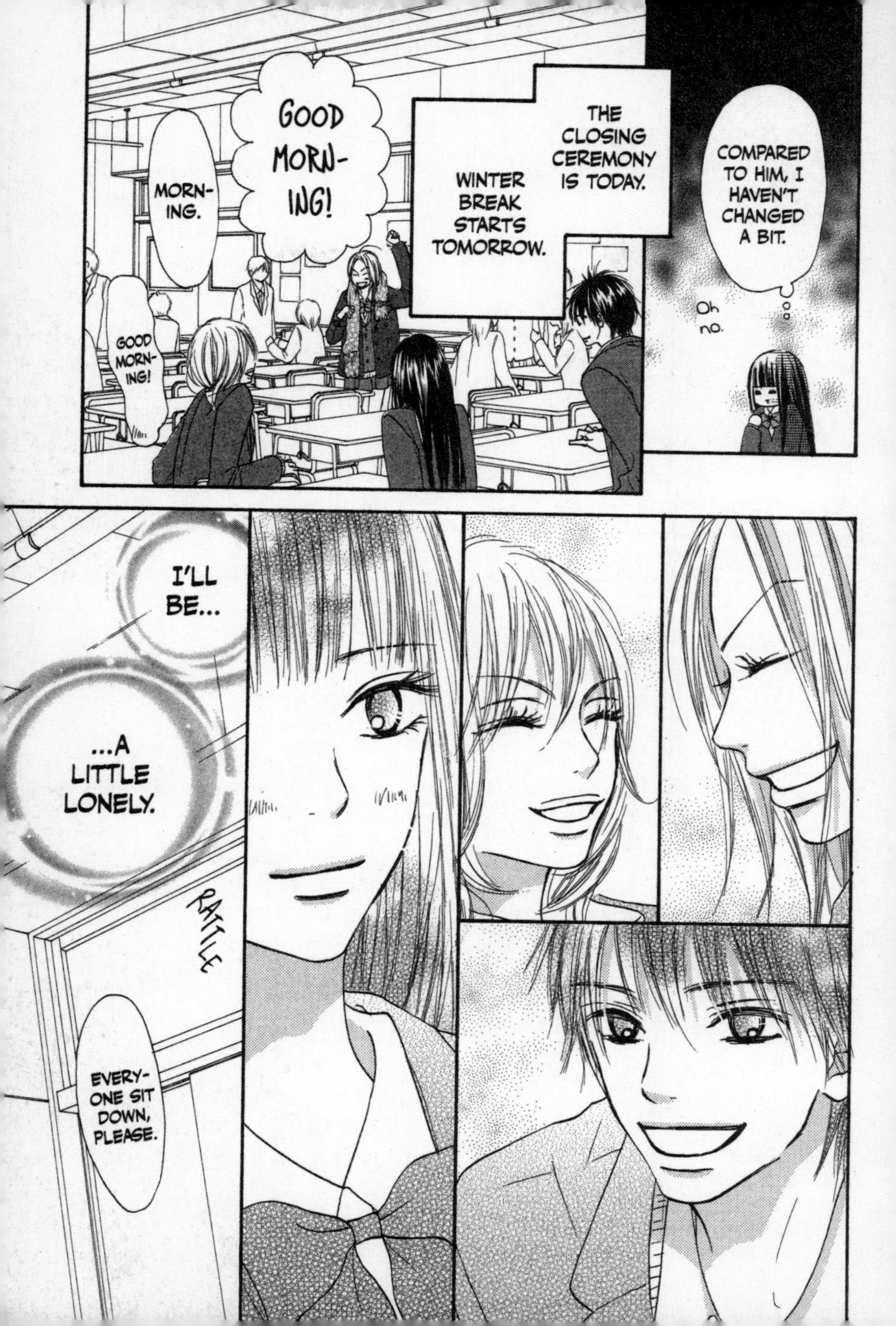
COMPARED TO HIM, I HAVEN'T CHANGED A BIT.
Oh no.
THE CLOSING CEREMONY IS TODAY.
WINTER BREAK STARTS TOMORROW.
GOOD MORN-ING!
MORN-ING.
GOOD MORN-ING!
I'LL BE...
...A LITTLE LONELY.
RATTLE
EVERY-ONE SIT DOWN, PLEASE.

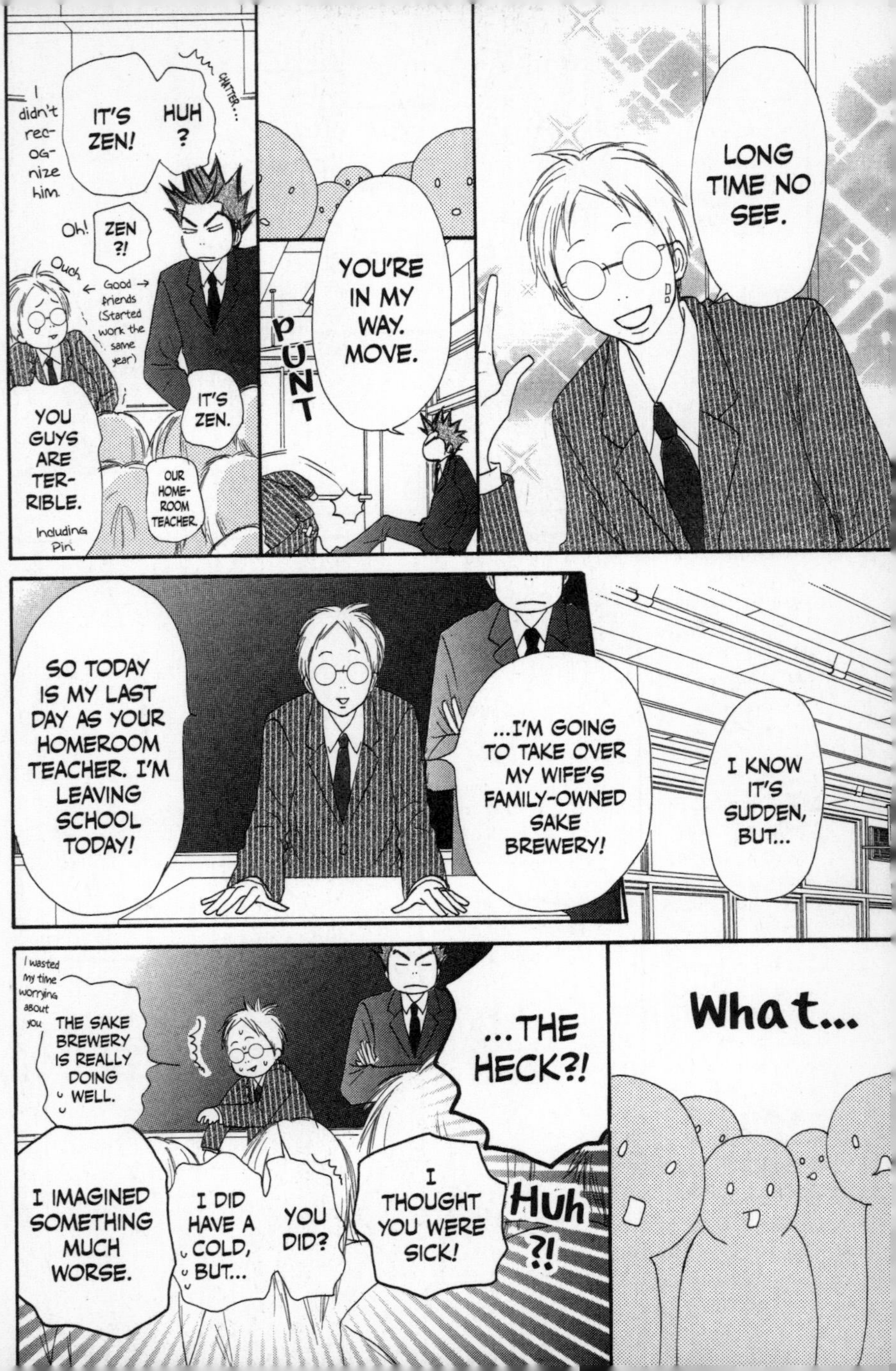
LONG TIME NO SEE.
YOU'RE IN MY WAY. MOVE.
PUNT
HUH ?
IT'S ZEN!
CHATTER...
I didn't rec-og-nize him.
ZEN ?!
Oh!
Ouch
Good friends (Started work the same year)
IT'S ZEN.
YOU GUYS ARE TER-RIBLE.
OUR HOME-ROOM TEACHER
Including Pin.
I KNOW IT'S SUDDEN, BUT...
...I'M GOING TO TAKE OVER MY WIFE'S FAMILY-OWNED SAKE BREWERY!
SO TODAY IS MY LAST DAY AS YOUR HOMEROOM TEACHER. I'M LEAVING SCHOOL TODAY!
What...
...THE HECK?!
Huh ?!
I THOUGHT YOU WERE SICK!
YOU DID?
I DID HAVE A COLD, BUT...
I IMAGINED SOMETHING MUCH WORSE.
THE SAKE BREWERY IS REALLY DOING WELL.
I wasted my time worrying about you

KARUPIN on JAPAN 1

Hi! How are you? This is Shiina. Pleased to meet you.

This is the seventh volume. In no time at all, the magazine series has appeared more than 30 times! What a surprise! When I was thinking about the cover back illustrations for volume 1 or volume 2, I thought up enough for all the way up through volume 5, but then I stopped because I wasn't sure if the series would continue that long. Because of that, now I'm scavenging the cover back illustrations from elsewhere. Oh well. Oops, I just noticed I've been writing "cover back." I mean back cover. Oh, well...

My Japanese gets worse every year. My editor told me that reading out loud is a good exercise for the brain, so I was reading a novel out loud in the bath, and my husband in the living room thought I was chanting a Buddhist sutra. Oh well.

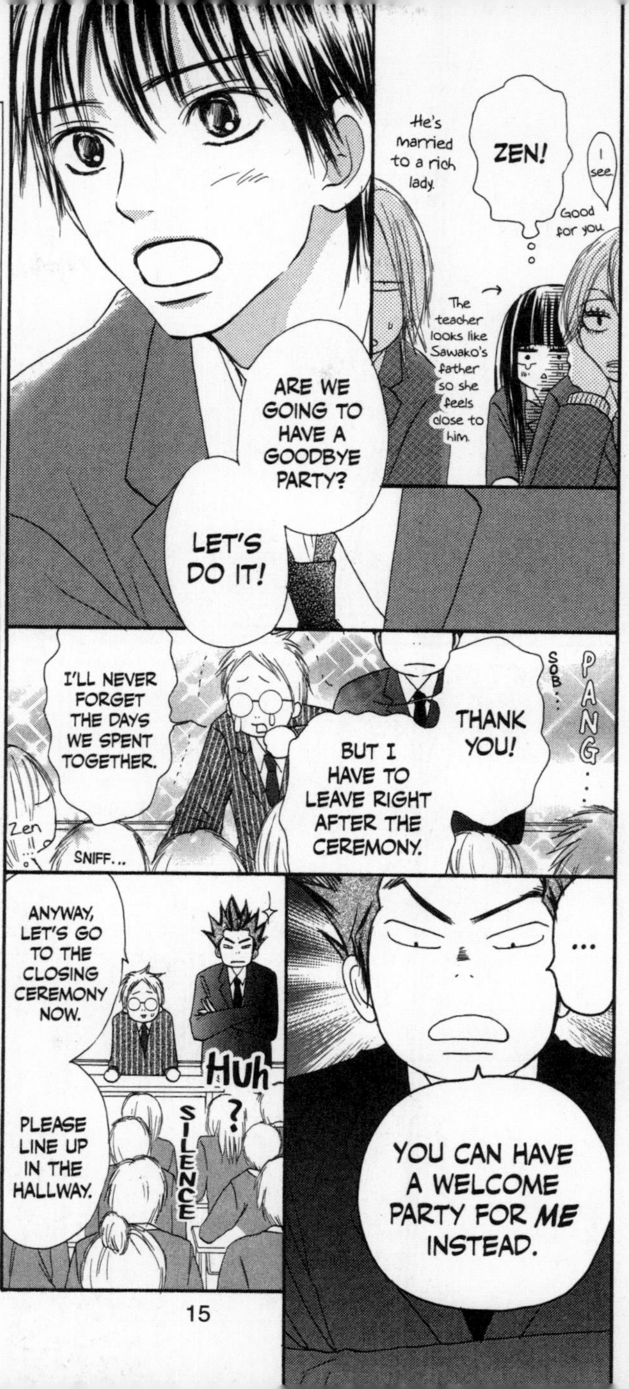
ZEN!
He's married to a rich lady.
I see.
Good for you.
The teacher looks like Sawako's father so she feels close to him.
ARE WE GOING TO HAVE A GOODBYE PARTY?
LET'S DO IT!
SOB...
PANG...
THANK YOU!
BUT I HAVE TO LEAVE RIGHT AFTER THE CEREMONY.
I'LL NEVER FORGET THE DAYS WE SPENT TOGETHER.
Zen
SNIFF...
...
YOU CAN HAVE A WELCOME PARTY FOR *ME* INSTEAD.
ANYWAY, LET'S GO TO THE CLOSING CEREMONY NOW.
Huh?
SILENCE
PLEASE LINE UP IN THE HALLWAY.

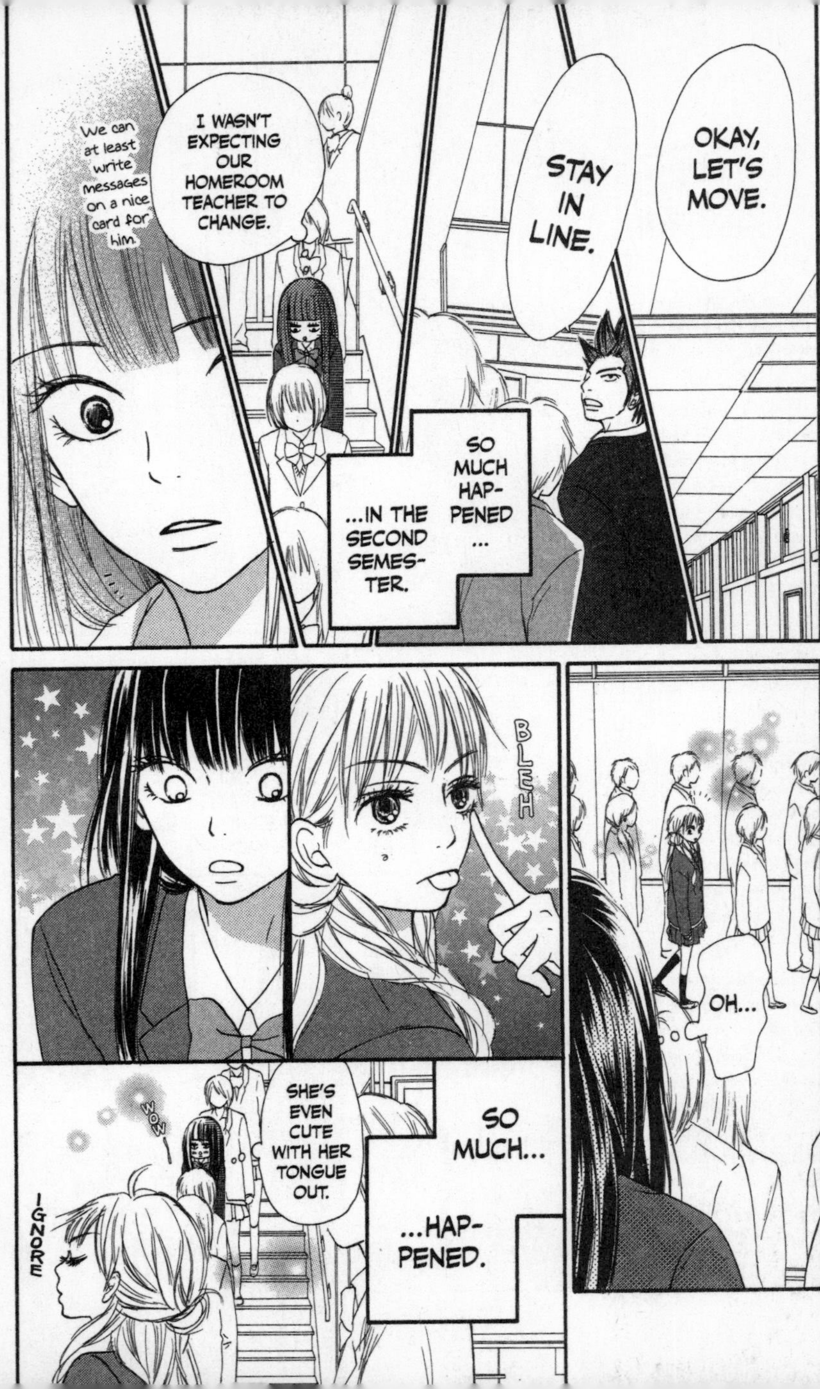
OKAY, LET'S MOVE.
STAY IN LINE.
SO MUCH HAP-PENED...
...IN THE SECOND SEMES-TER.
I WASN'T EXPECTING OUR HOMEROOM TEACHER TO CHANGE.
We can at least write messages on a nice card for him.
OH...
SO MUCH...
...HAP-PENED.
BLEH
SHE'S EVEN CUTE WITH HER TONGUE OUT.
WOW
IGNORE

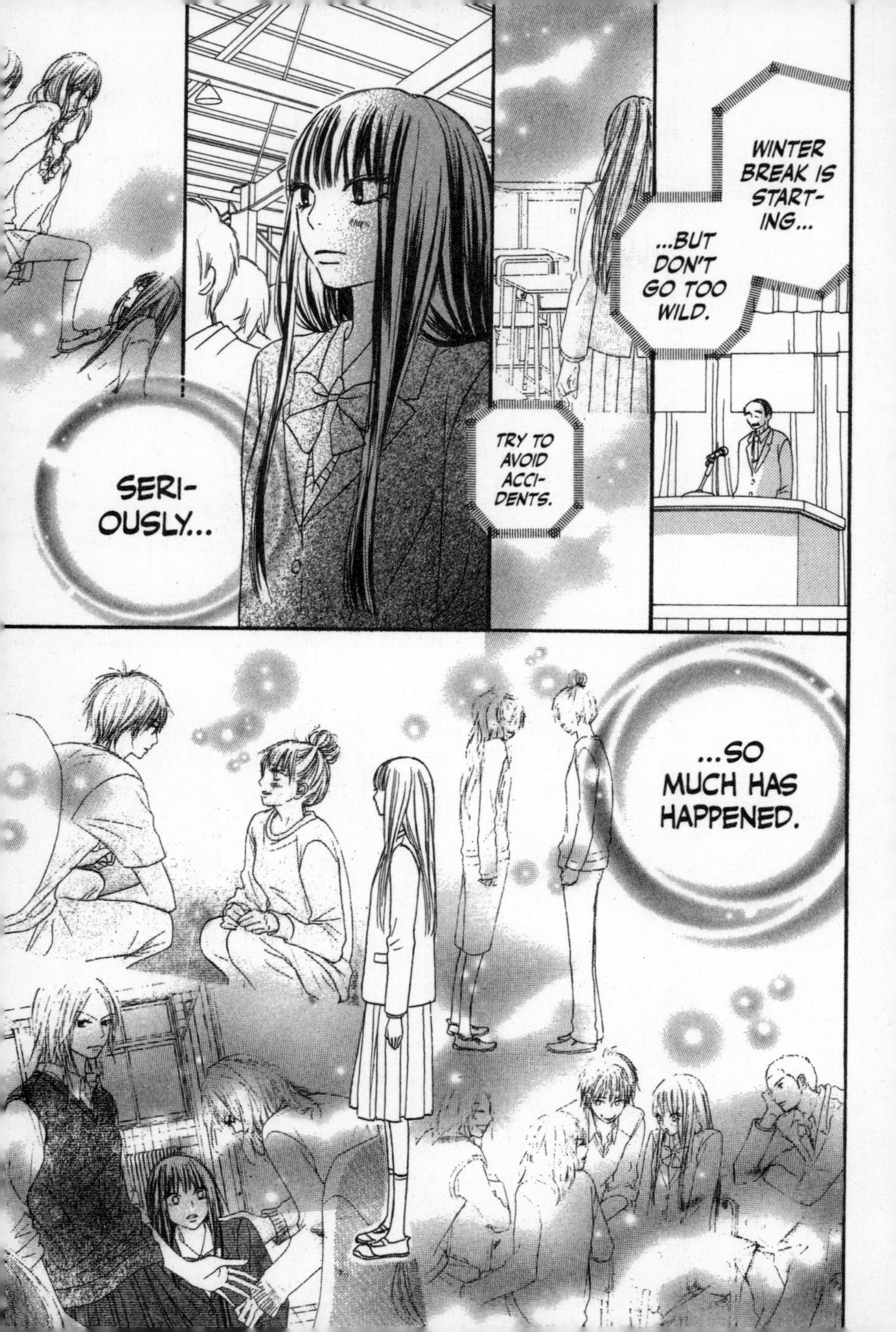
WINTER BREAK IS STARTING...
...BUT DON'T GO TOO WILD.
TRY TO AVOID ACCIDENTS.
SERIOUSLY...
...SO MUCH HAS HAPPENED.

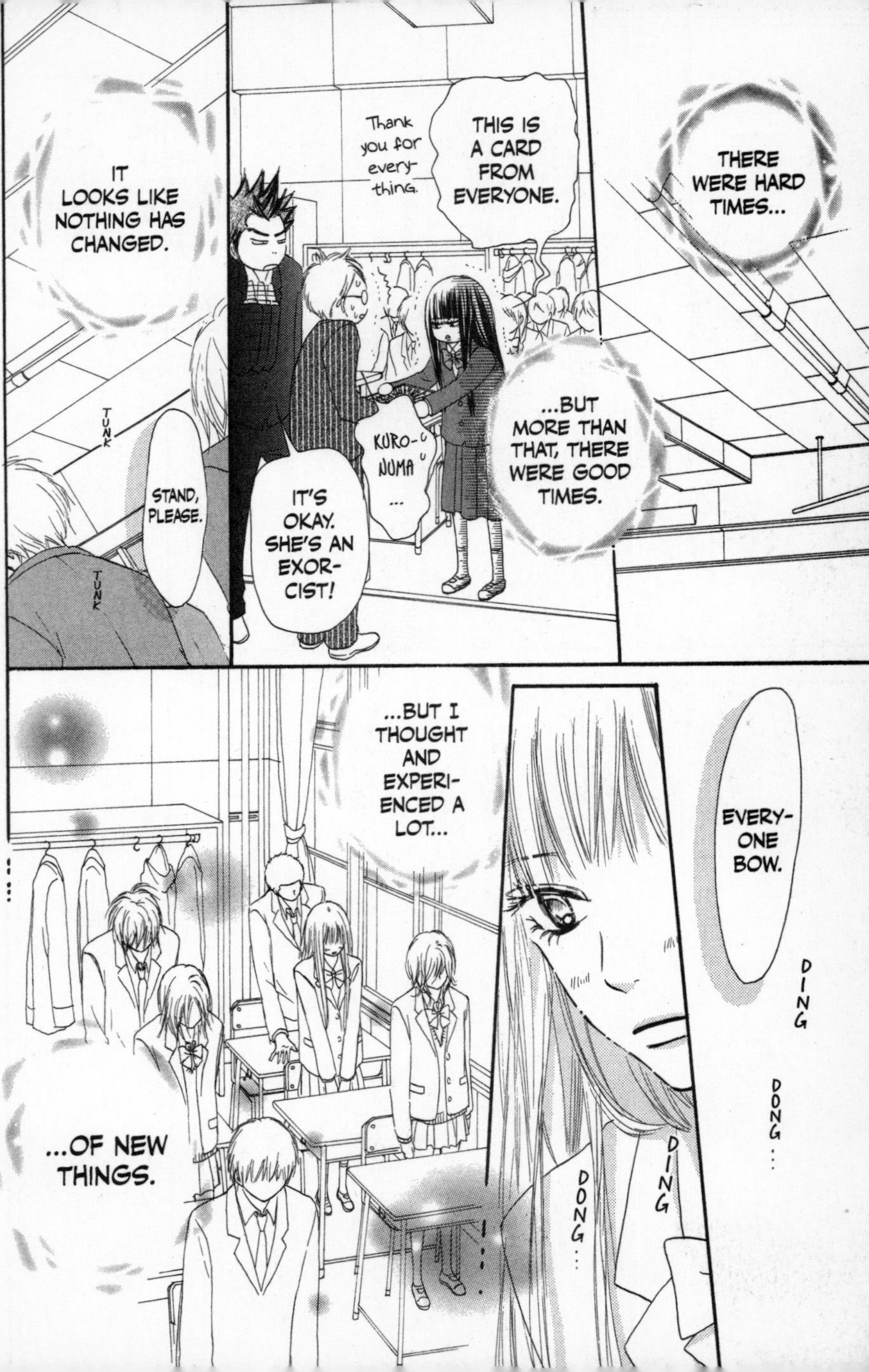
THERE WERE HARD TIMES...
...BUT MORE THAN THAT, THERE WERE GOOD TIMES.
THIS IS A CARD FROM EVERYONE.
Thank you for every-thing.
KURO-NUMA ...
IT'S OKAY. SHE'S AN EXOR-CIST!
IT LOOKS LIKE NOTHING HAS CHANGED.
TUNK
STAND, PLEASE.
TUNK
EVERY-ONE BOW.
DING DONG...
DING DONG...
...BUT I THOUGHT AND EXPERI-ENCED A LOT...
...OF NEW THINGS.

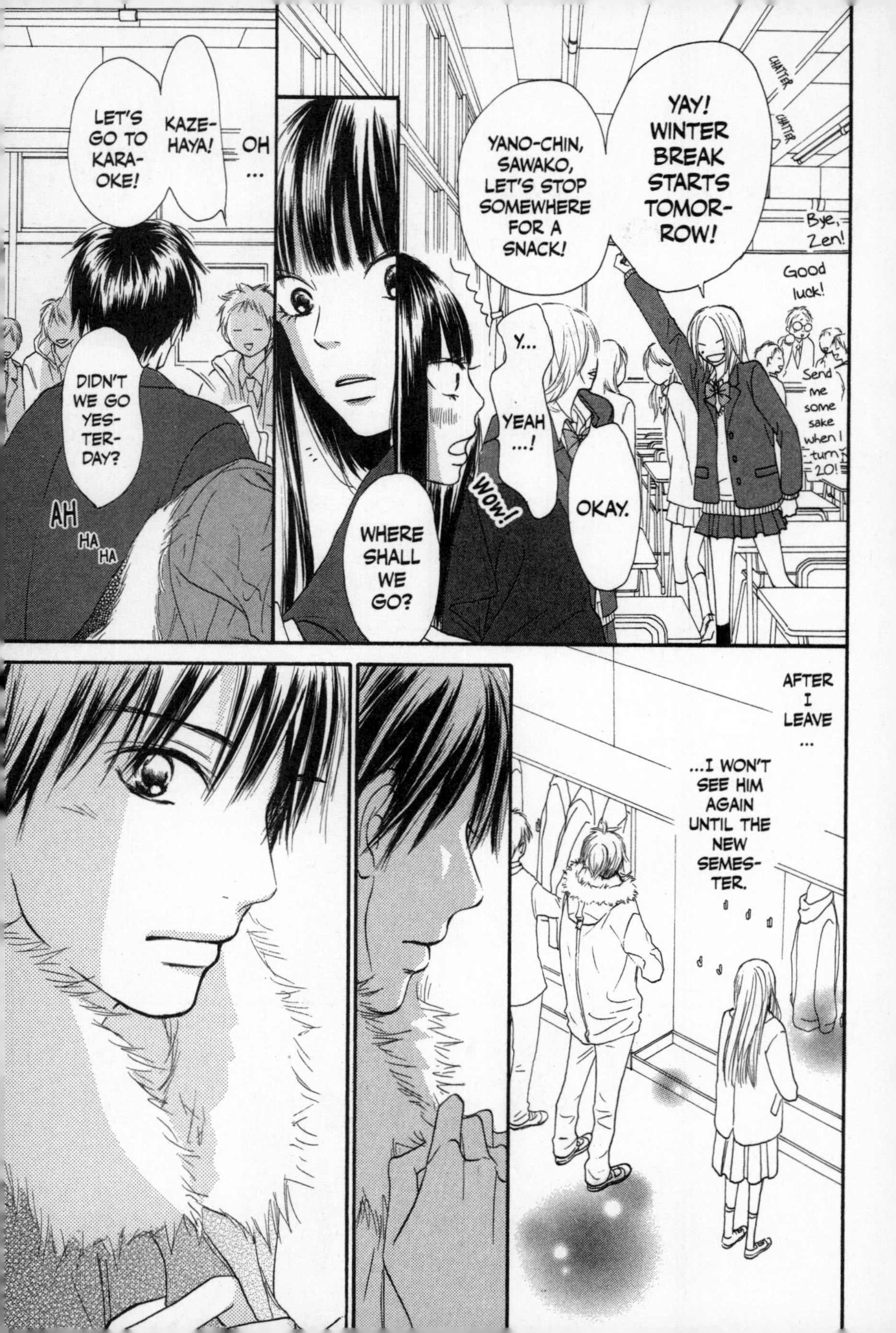
CHATTER
CHATTER
YAY! WINTER BREAK STARTS TOMORROW!
YANO-CHIN, SAWAKO, LET'S STOP SOMEWHERE FOR A SNACK!
Bye, Zen!
Good luck!
Send me some sake when I turn 20!
Y...
YEAH ...!
OKAY.
WOW!
WHERE SHALL WE GO?
OH ...
KAZE-HAYA!
LET'S GO TO KARA-OKE!
DIDN'T WE GO YES-TER-DAY?
AH HA HA
AFTER I LEAVE ...
...I WON'T SEE HIM AGAIN UNTIL THE NEW SEMES-TER.

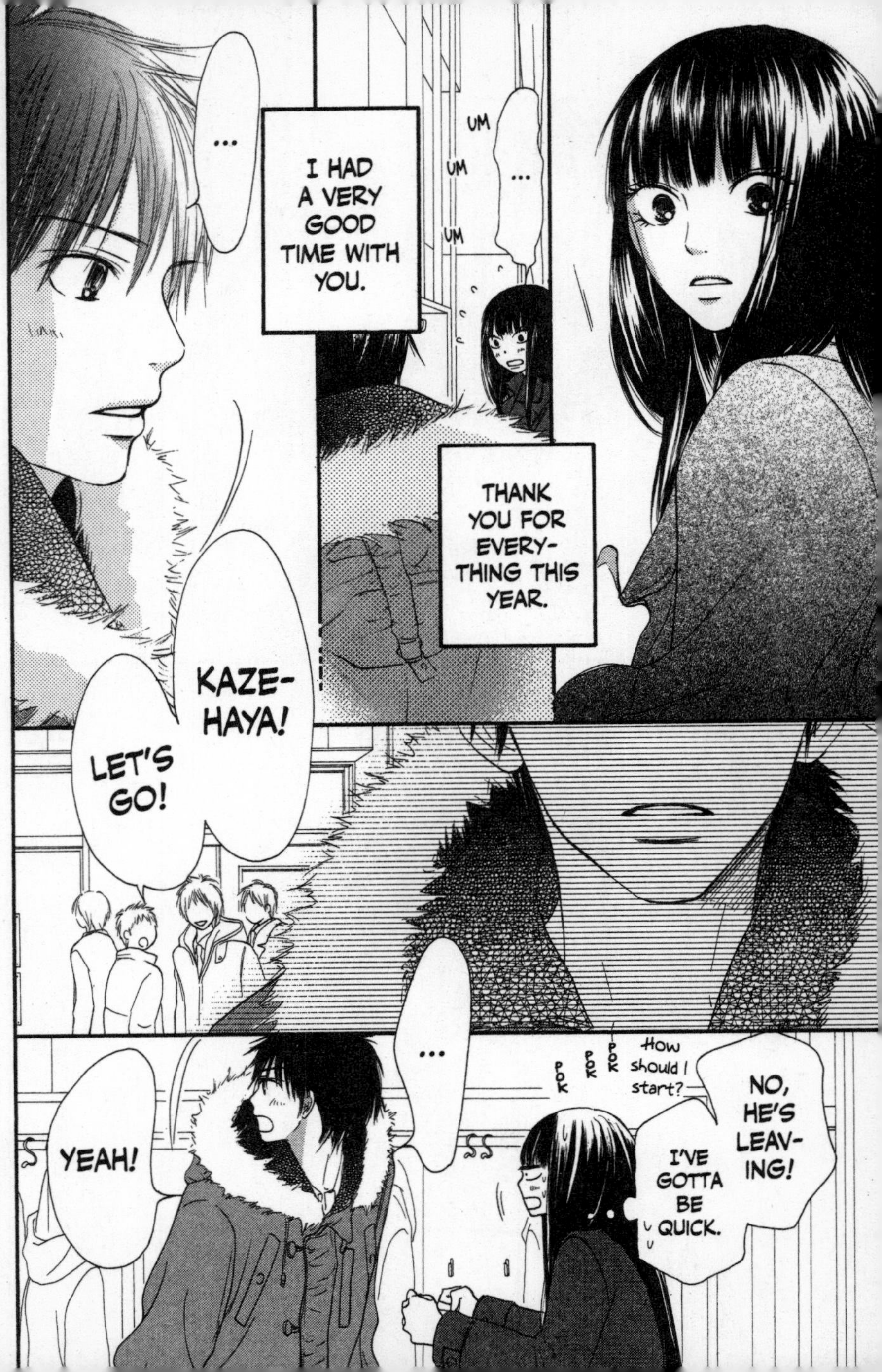
UM
UM
UM
...
I HAD A VERY GOOD TIME WITH YOU.
THANK YOU FOR EVERY-THING THIS YEAR.
...
KAZE-HAYA!
LET'S GO!
NO, HE'S LEAV-ING!
I'VE GOTTA BE QUICK.
How should I start?
POK
POK
POK
...
YEAH!

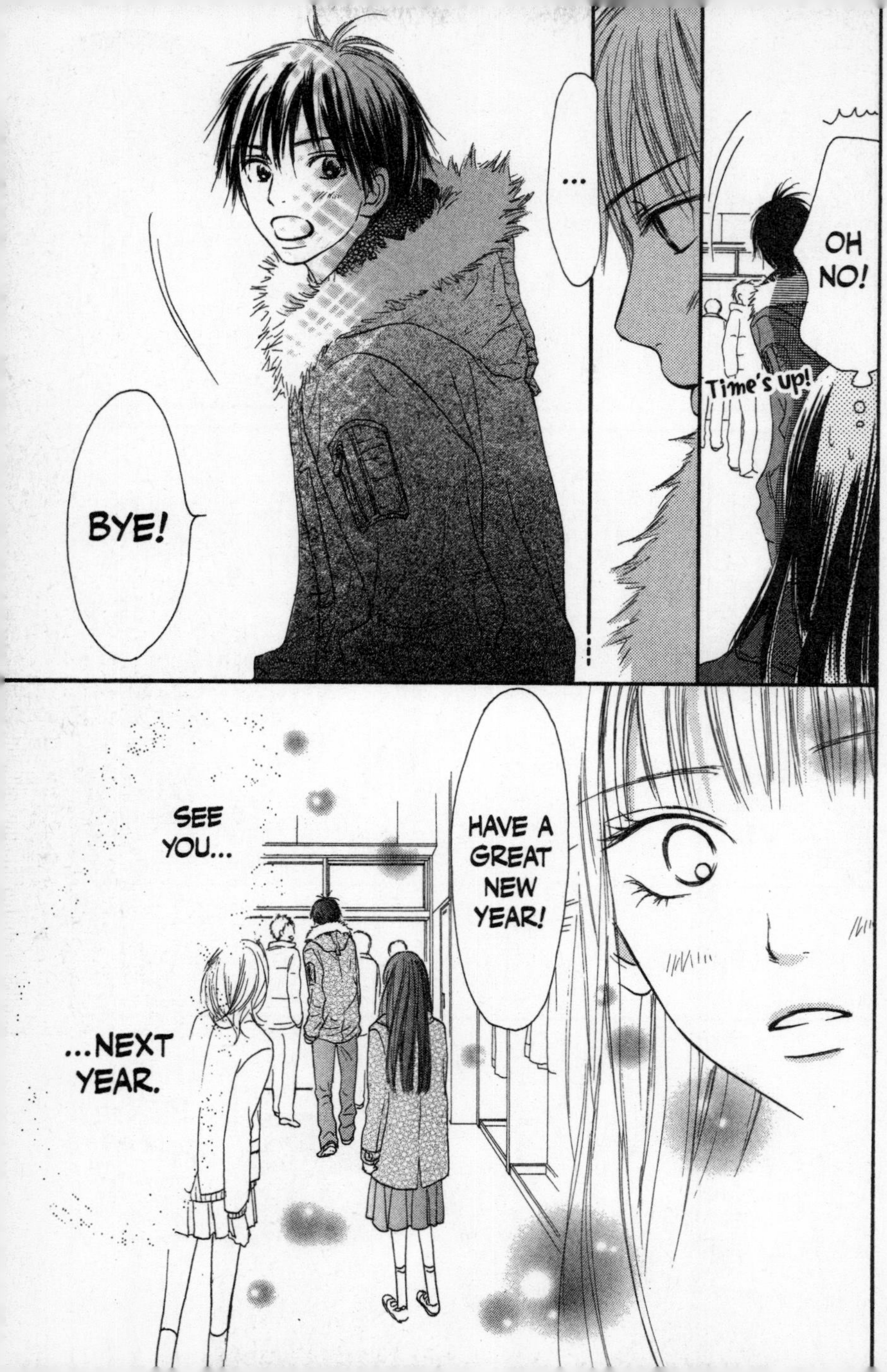
OH NO!
Time's up!
...
BYE!
HAVE A GREAT NEW YEAR!
SEE YOU...
...NEXT YEAR.

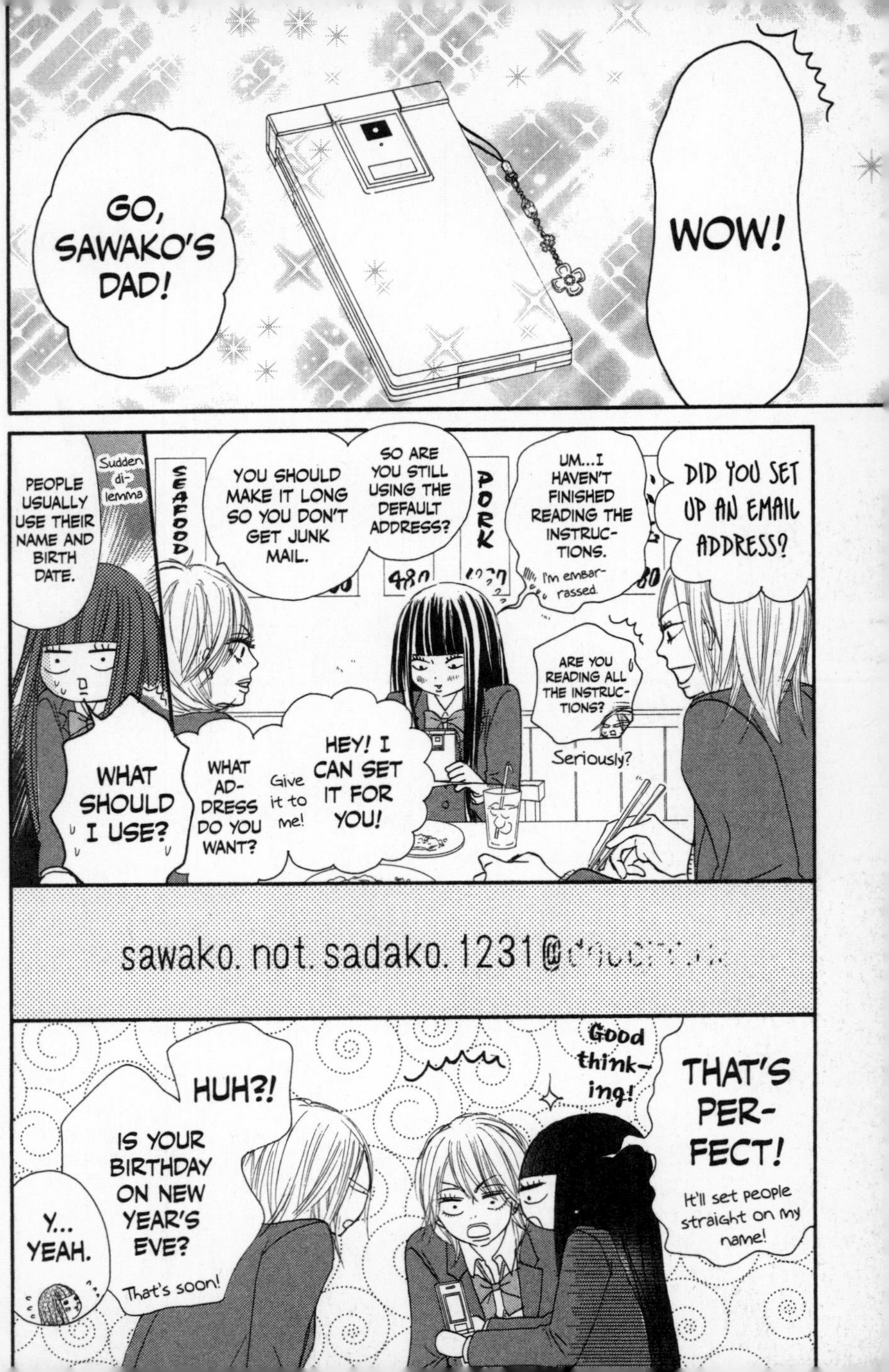
WOW!
GO, SAWAKO'S DAD!
DID YOU SET UP AN EMAIL ADDRESS?
UM...I HAVEN'T FINISHED READING THE INSTRUCTIONS.
I'm embarrassed.
ARE YOU READING ALL THE INSTRUCTIONS?
Seriously?
PORK
SO ARE YOU STILL USING THE DEFAULT ADDRESS?
YOU SHOULD MAKE IT LONG SO YOU DON'T GET JUNK MAIL.
SEAFOOD
HEY! I CAN SET IT FOR YOU!
Give it to me!
WHAT ADDRESS DO YOU WANT?
PEOPLE USUALLY USE THEIR NAME AND BIRTH DATE.
Sudden dilemma
WHAT SHOULD I USE?
sawako.not.sadako.1231@
THAT'S PERFECT!
It'll set people straight on my name!
Good thinking!
HUH?!
IS YOUR BIRTHDAY ON NEW YEAR'S EVE?
That's soon!
Y... YEAH.

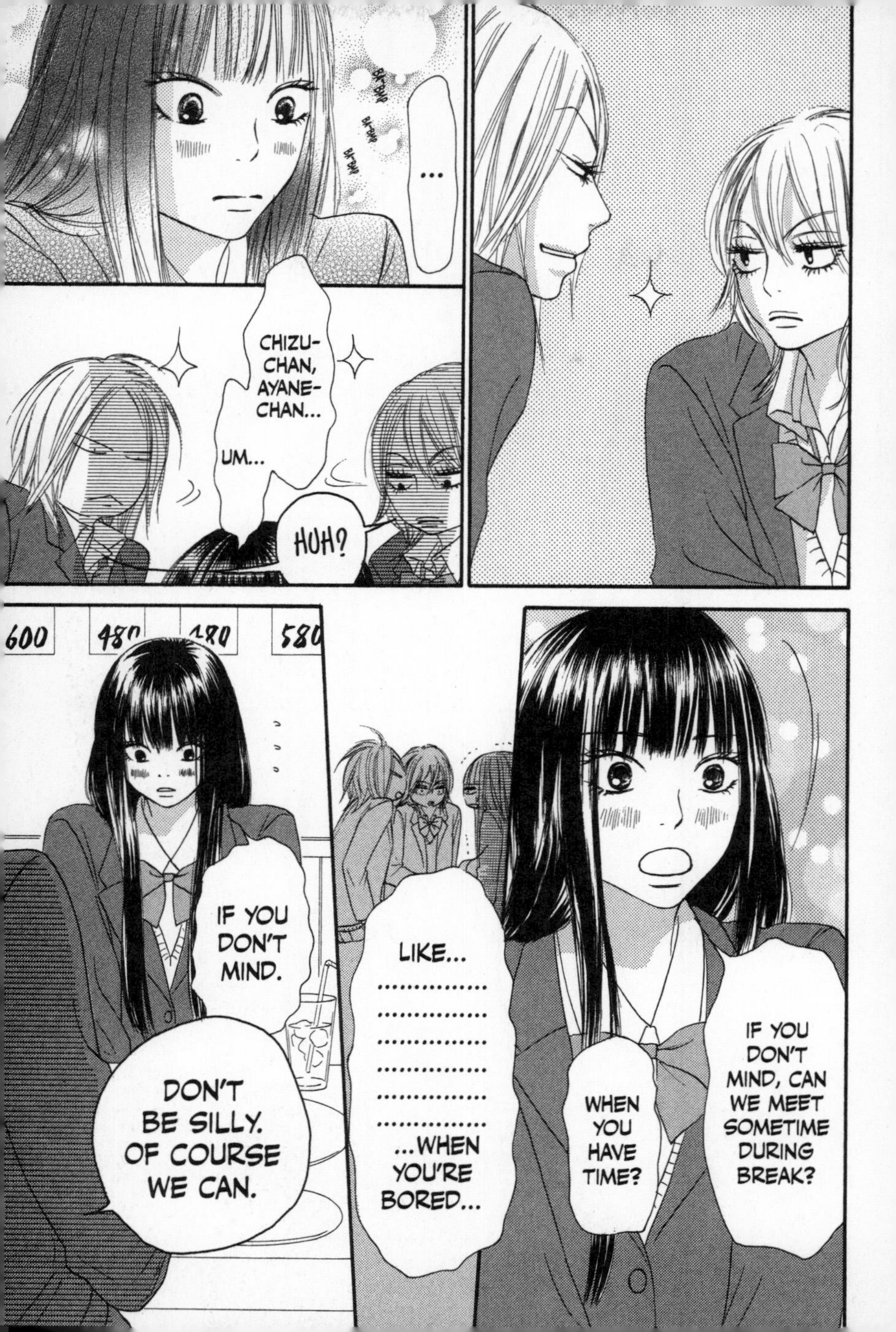

BA-BUMP
BA-BUMP
BA-BUMP
...
CHIZU-CHAN, AYANE-CHAN...
UM...
HUH?
IF YOU DON'T MIND, CAN WE MEET SOMETIME DURING BREAK?
WHEN YOU HAVE TIME?
LIKE... ....WHEN YOU'RE BORED...
600
480
480
580
IF YOU DON'T MIND.
DON'T BE SILLY. OF COURSE WE CAN.

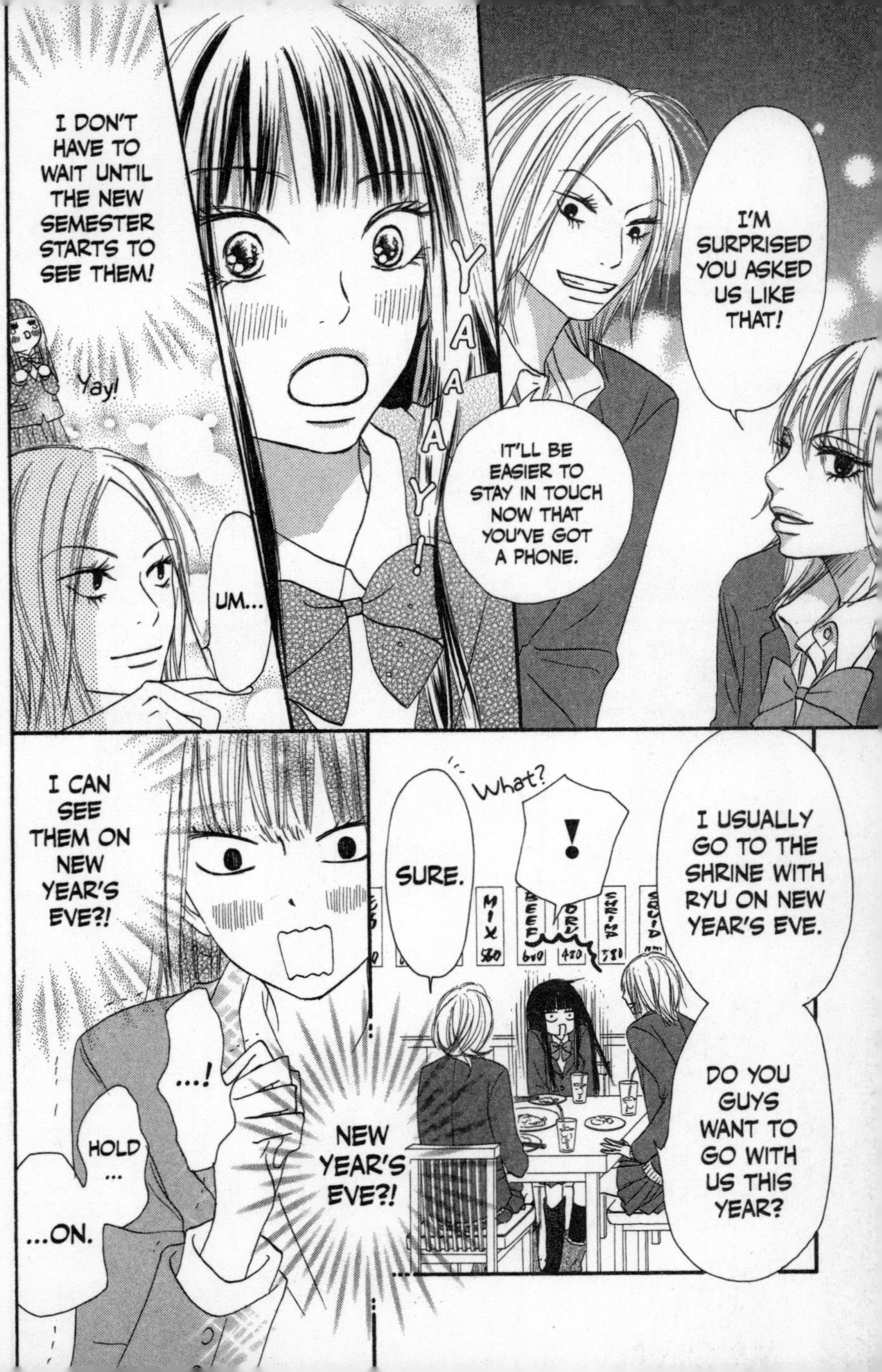
I'M SURPRISED YOU ASKED US LIKE THAT!
IT'LL BE EASIER TO STAY IN TOUCH NOW THAT YOU'VE GOT A PHONE.
YAAAAY!
UM...
I DON'T HAVE TO WAIT UNTIL THE NEW SEMESTER STARTS TO SEE THEM!
Yay!
I USUALLY GO TO THE SHRINE WITH RYU ON NEW YEAR'S EVE.
DO YOU GUYS WANT TO GO WITH US THIS YEAR?
!
What?
SURE.
MIX
BEEF
SHRIMP
SQUID
NEW YEAR'S EVE?!
...!
HOLD ...
...ON.
I CAN SEE THEM ON NEW YEAR'S EVE?!

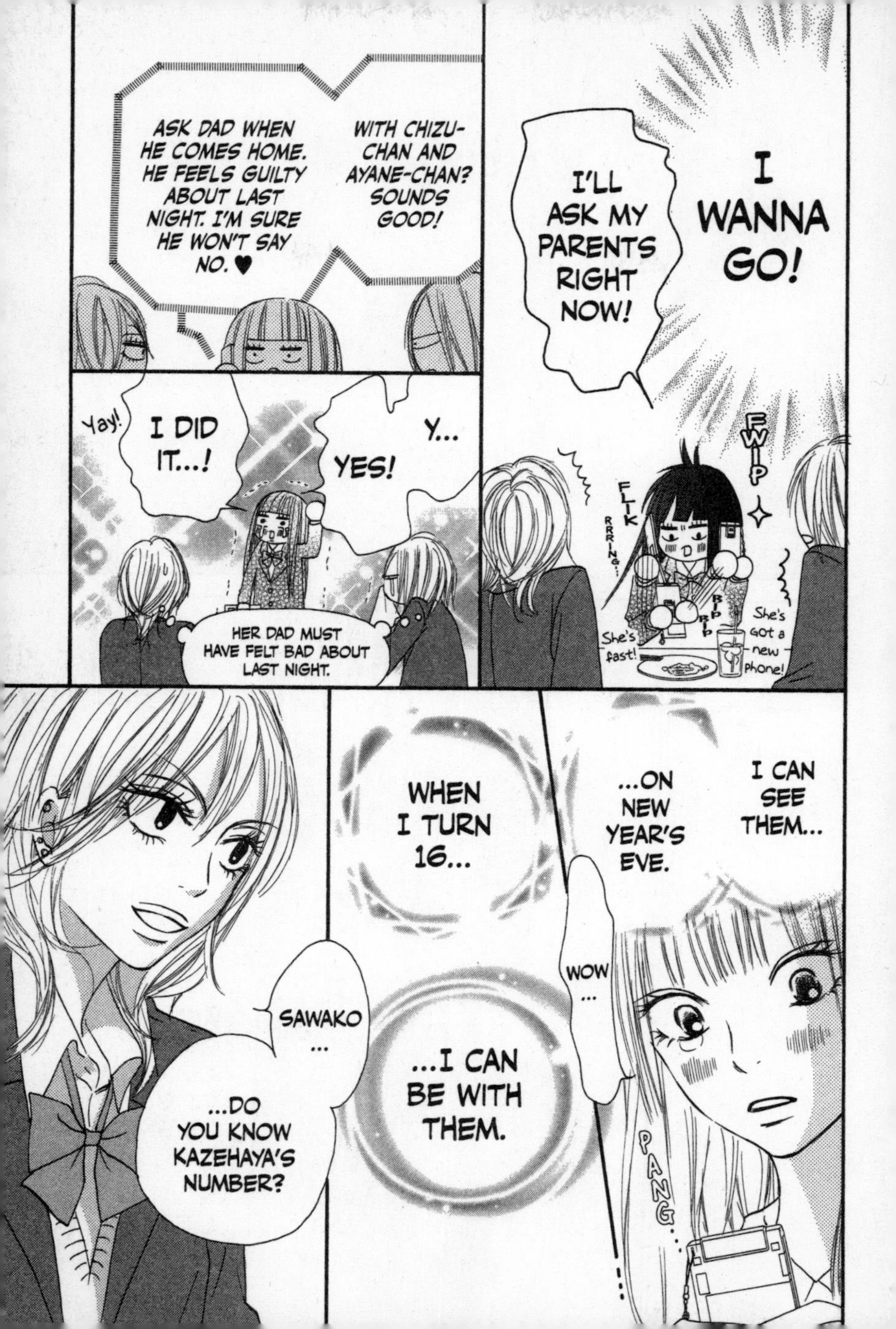
I WANNA GO!
I'LL ASK MY PARENTS RIGHT NOW!
FWIP
FLIK
RRRING...
BIP BIP
She's got a new phone!
She's fast!
WITH CHIZU-CHAN AND AYANE-CHAN? SOUNDS GOOD!
ASK DAD WHEN HE COMES HOME. HE FEELS GUILTY ABOUT LAST NIGHT. I'M SURE HE WON'T SAY NO. ♥
Y... YES!
I DID IT...!
Yay!
HER DAD MUST HAVE FELT BAD ABOUT LAST NIGHT.
I CAN SEE THEM...
...ON NEW YEAR'S EVE.
WOW...
PANG...
WHEN I TURN 16...
...I CAN BE WITH THEM.
SAWAKO...
...DO YOU KNOW KAZEHAYA'S NUMBER?

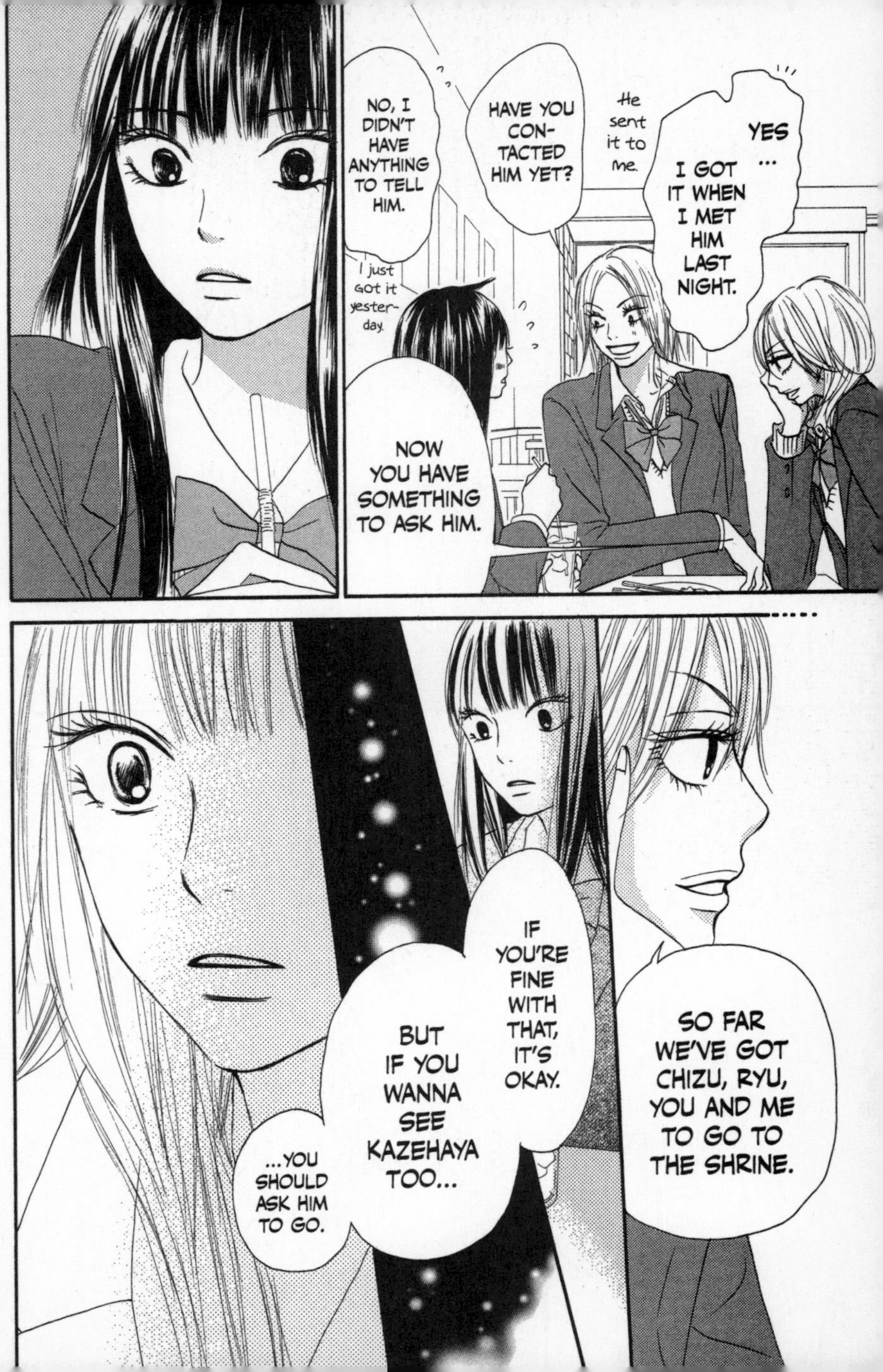
YES ... I GOT IT WHEN I MET HIM LAST NIGHT.
He sent it to me.
HAVE YOU CONTACTED HIM YET?
NO, I DIDN'T HAVE ANYTHING TO TELL HIM.
I just got it yesterday.
NOW YOU HAVE SOMETHING TO ASK HIM.
SO FAR WE'VE GOT CHIZU, RYU, YOU AND ME TO GO TO THE SHRINE.
IF YOU'RE FINE WITH THAT, IT'S OKAY.
BUT IF YOU WANNA SEE KAZEHAYA TOO...
...YOU SHOULD ASK HIM TO GO.

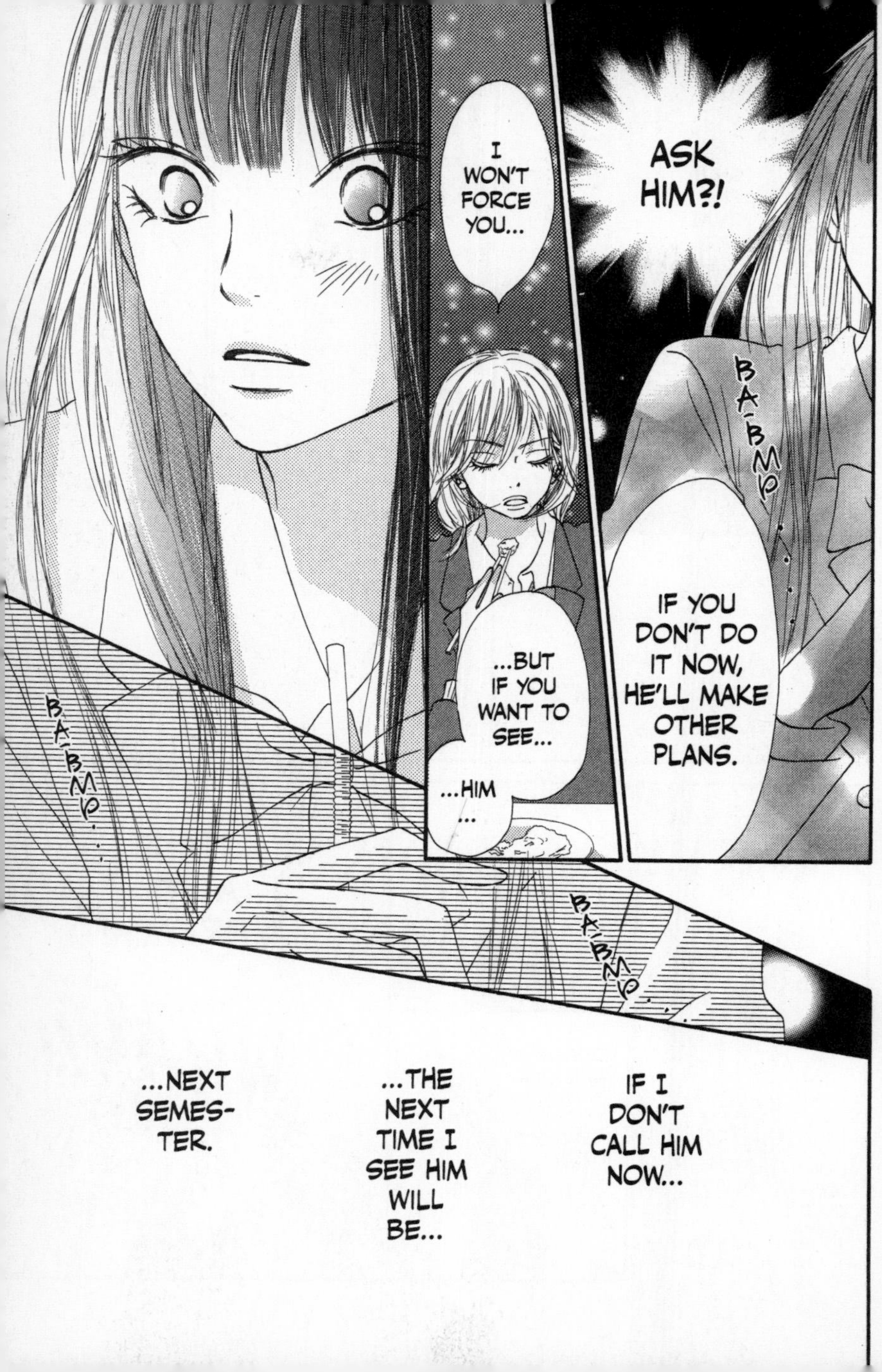
ASK HIM?!
BA-BMP
IF YOU DON'T DO IT NOW, HE'LL MAKE OTHER PLANS.
I WON'T FORCE YOU...
...BUT IF YOU WANT TO SEE...
...HIM ...
BA-BMP...
BA-BMP...
IF I DON'T CALL HIM NOW...
...THE NEXT TIME I SEE HIM WILL BE...
...NEXT SEMESTER.

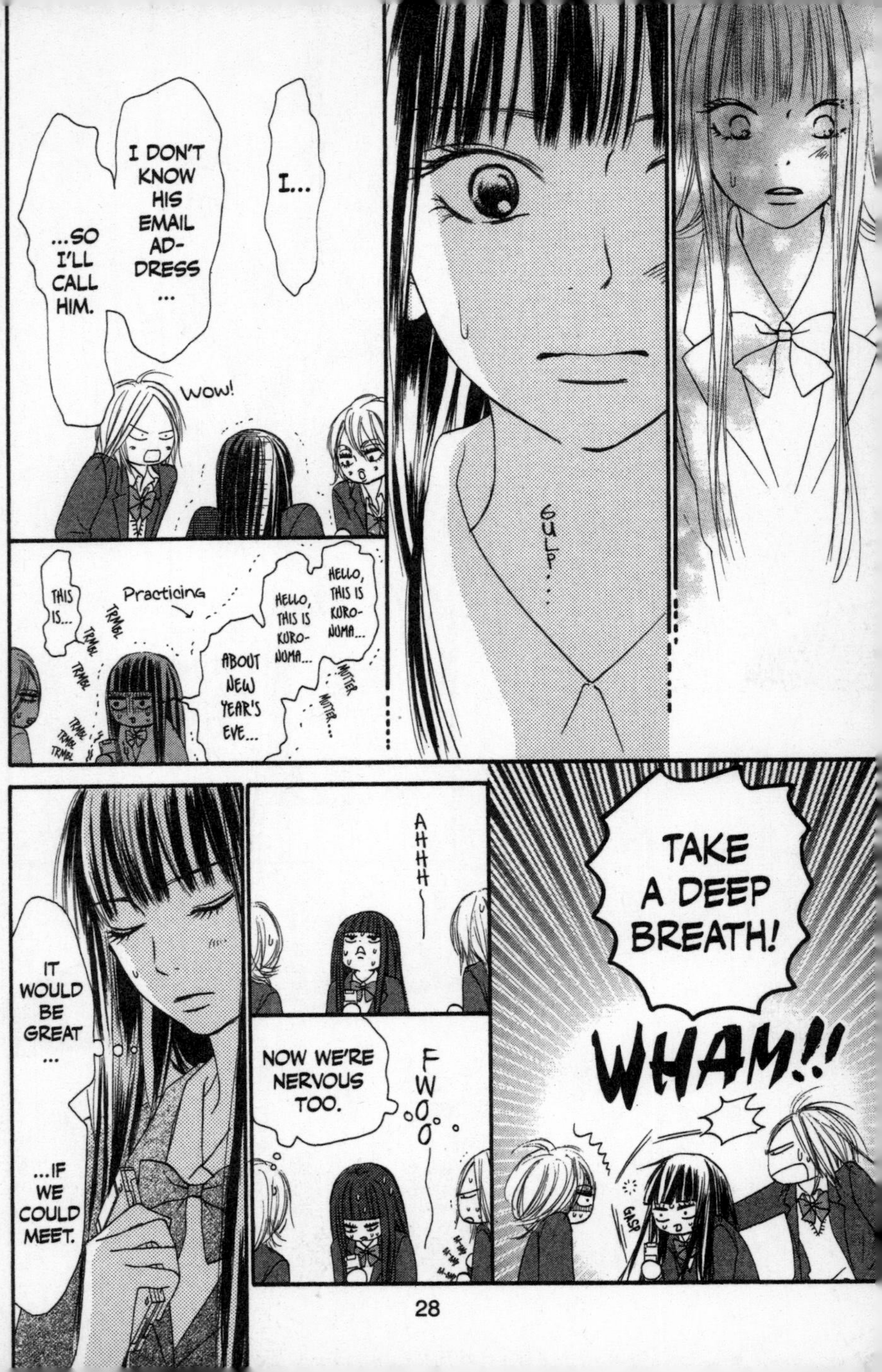
GULP...
I...
I DON'T KNOW HIS EMAIL AD-DRESS...
...SO I'LL CALL HIM.
WOW!
HELLO, THIS IS KURO-NUMA...
HELLO, THIS IS KURO-NUMA...
MUTTER MUTTER...
ABOUT NEW YEAR'S EVE...
Practicing
THIS IS...
TRMBL TRMBL TRMBL TRMBL TRMBL TRMBL
TAKE A DEEP BREATH!
WHAM!!
GASP
AHHH~
NOW WE'RE NERVOUS TOO.
FWOOO~
IT WOULD BE GREAT...
...IF WE COULD MEET.

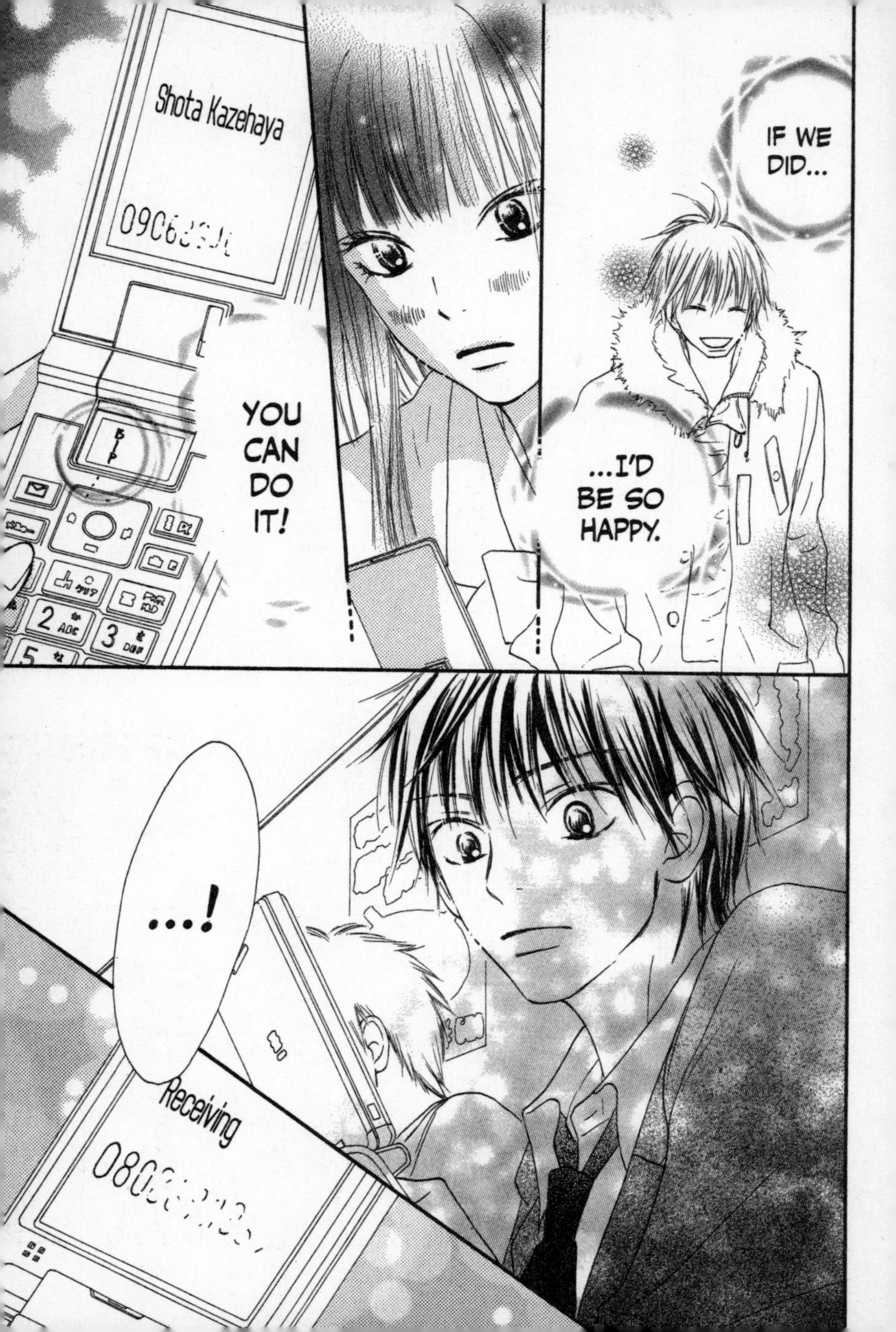
IF WE DID...
...I'D BE SO HAPPY.
Shota Kazehaya
BIP
YOU CAN DO IT!
...!
Receiving

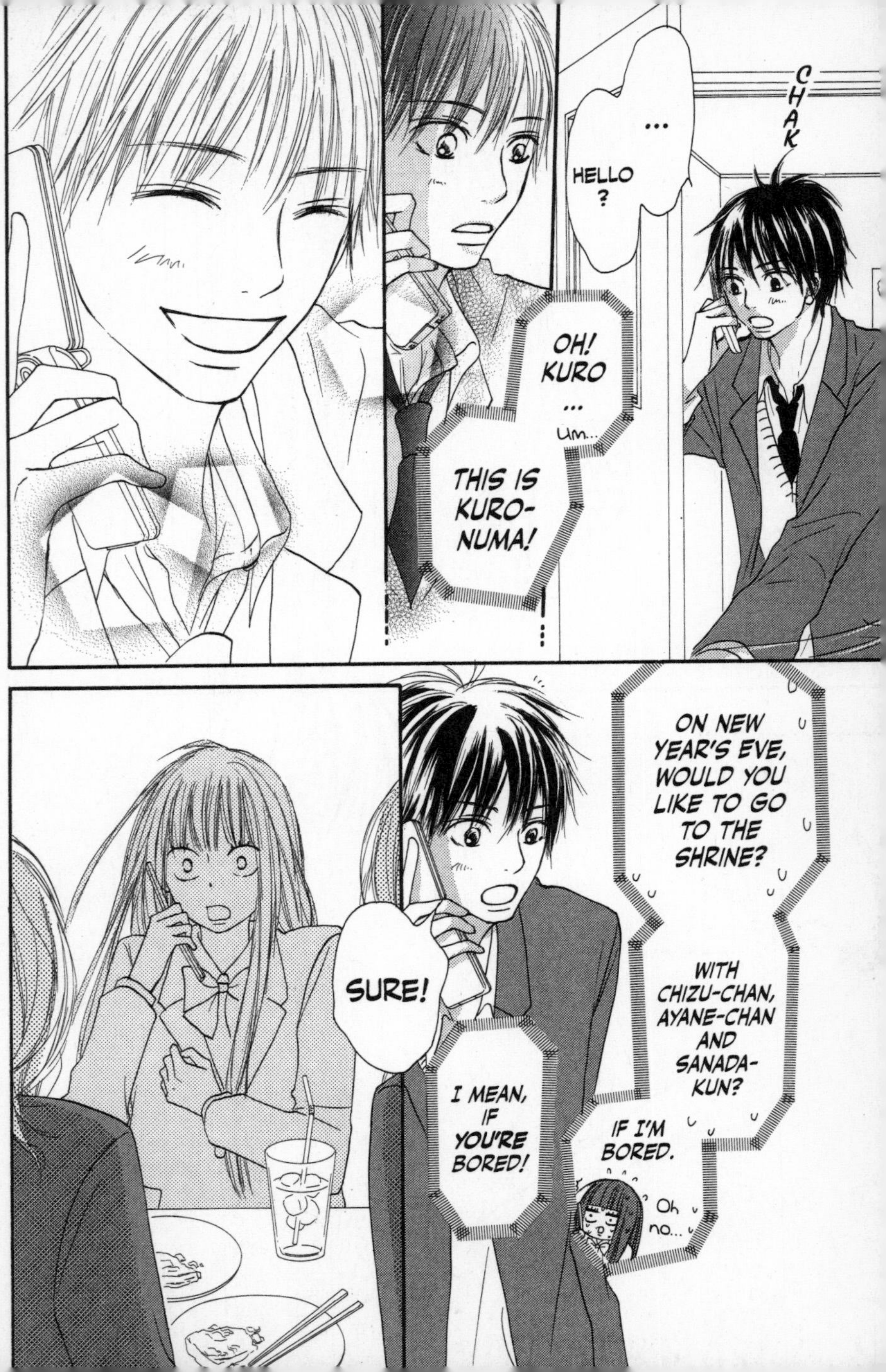
CHAK
... HELLO?
OH! KURO... Um...
THIS IS KURO-NUMA!
ON NEW YEAR'S EVE, WOULD YOU LIKE TO GO TO THE SHRINE?
WITH CHIZU-CHAN, AYANE-CHAN AND SANADA-KUN?
IF I'M BORED.
Oh no...
I MEAN, IF YOU'RE BORED!
SURE!

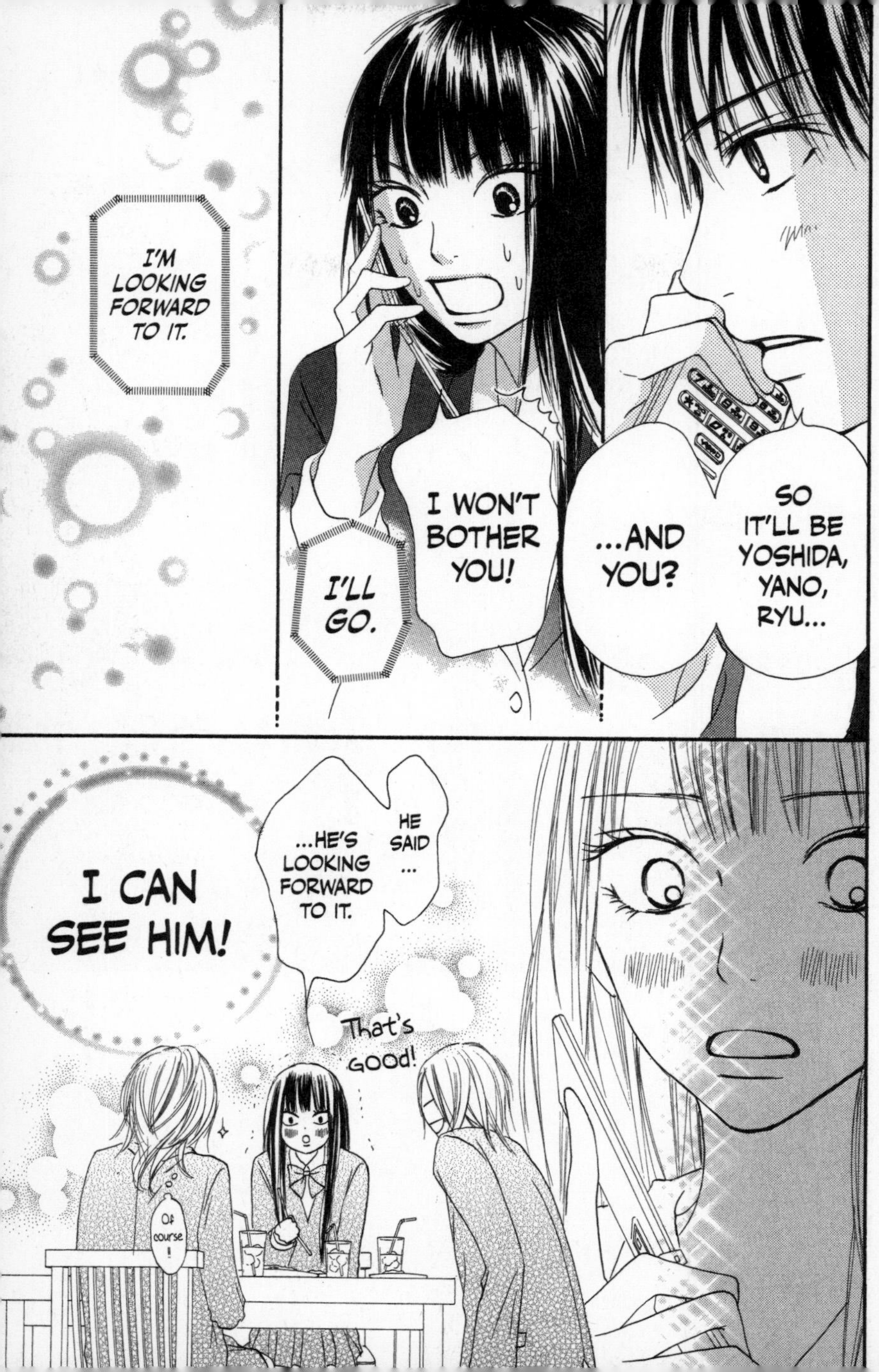
SO IT'LL BE YOSHIDA, YANO, RYU...
...AND YOU?
I WON'T BOTHER YOU!
I'LL GO.
I'M LOOKING FORWARD TO IT.
HE SAID...
...HE'S LOOKING FORWARD TO IT.
I CAN SEE HIM!
That's good!
Of course!

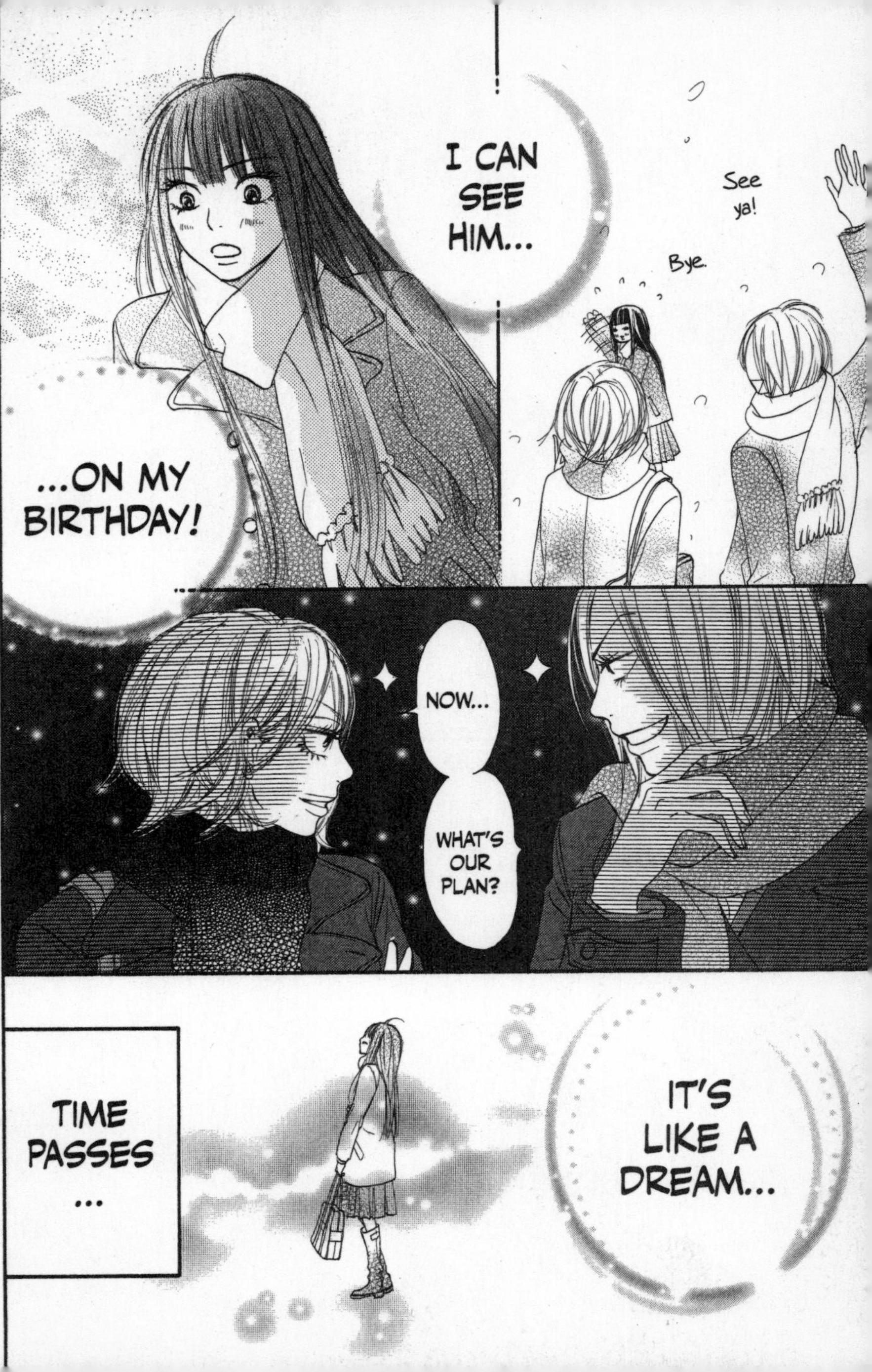
See ya!
Bye.
I CAN SEE HIM...
...ON MY BIRTHDAY!
NOW...
WHAT'S OUR PLAN?
IT'S LIKE A DREAM...
TIME PASSES ...

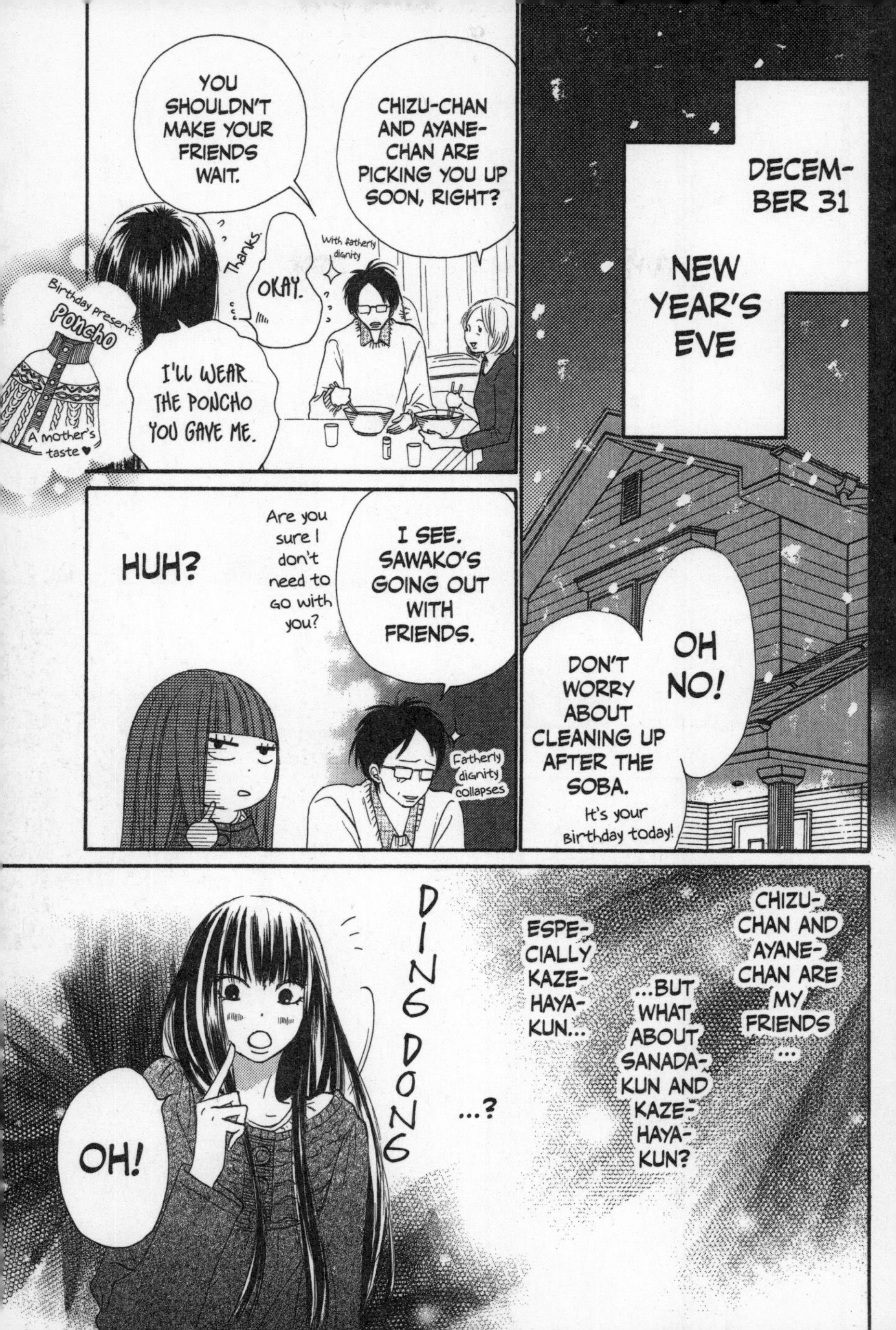
DECEMBER 31
NEW YEAR'S EVE
OH NO!
DON'T WORRY ABOUT CLEANING UP AFTER THE SOBA.
It's your birthday today!
CHIZU-CHAN AND AYANE-CHAN ARE PICKING YOU UP SOON, RIGHT?
With fatherly dignity
YOU SHOULDN'T MAKE YOUR FRIENDS WAIT.
Thanks.
OKAY.
I'LL WEAR THE PONCHO YOU GAVE ME.
Birthday present: Poncho
A mother's taste ♥
I SEE. SAWAKO'S GOING OUT WITH FRIENDS.
Are you sure I don't need to go with you?
HUH?
Fatherly dignity collapses
CHIZU-CHAN AND AYANE-CHAN ARE MY FRIENDS...
...BUT WHAT ABOUT SANADA-KUN AND KAZEHAYA-KUN?
ESPECIALLY KAZEHAYA-KUN...
...?
DING DONG
OH!

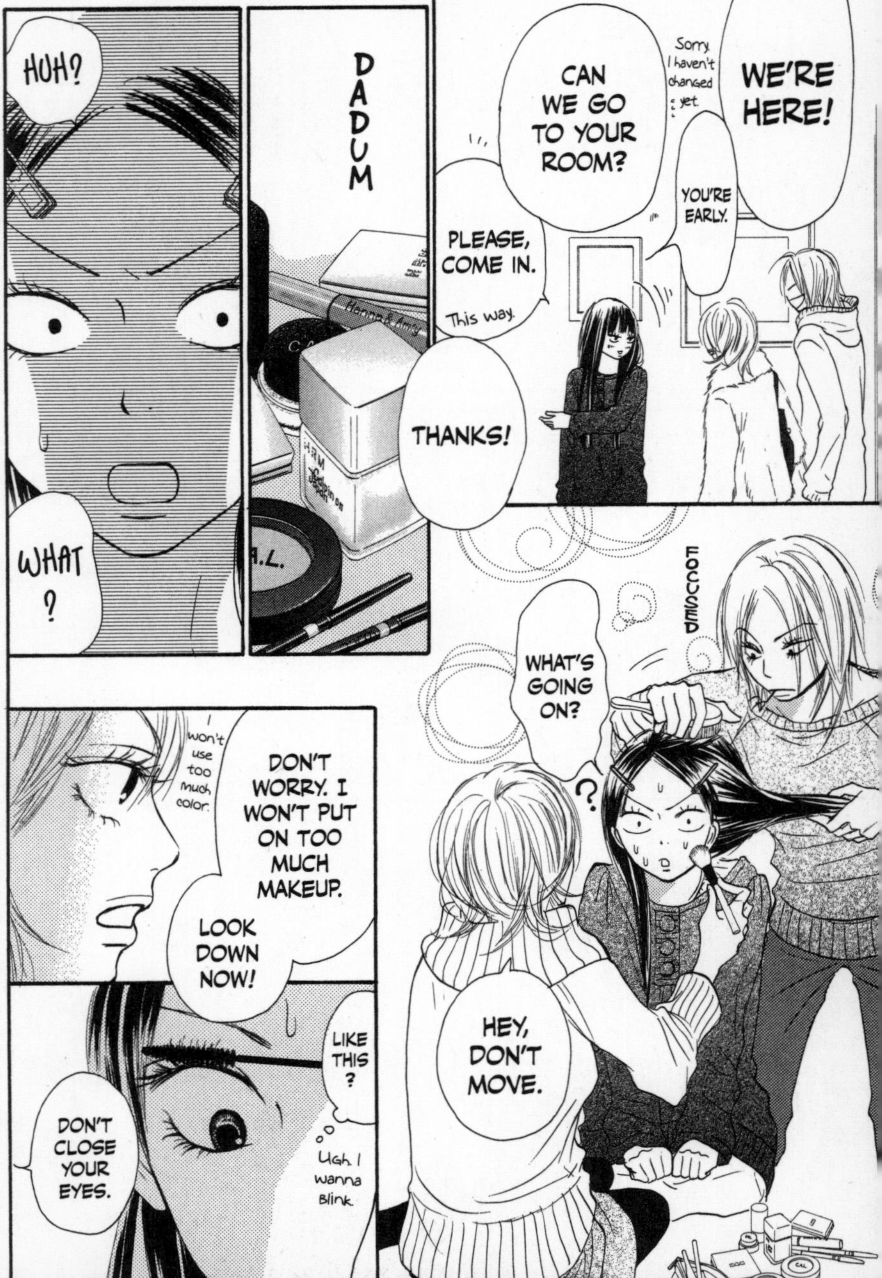
WE'RE HERE!
Sorry. I haven't changed yet.
YOU'RE EARLY.
CAN WE GO TO YOUR ROOM?
PLEASE, COME IN.
This way.
THANKS!
DADUM
HUH?
WHAT ?
FOCUSED
WHAT'S GOING ON?
?
HEY, DON'T MOVE.
DON'T WORRY. I WON'T PUT ON TOO MUCH MAKEUP.
I won't use too much color.
LOOK DOWN NOW!
LIKE THIS ?
Ugh. I wanna blink.
DON'T CLOSE YOUR EYES.

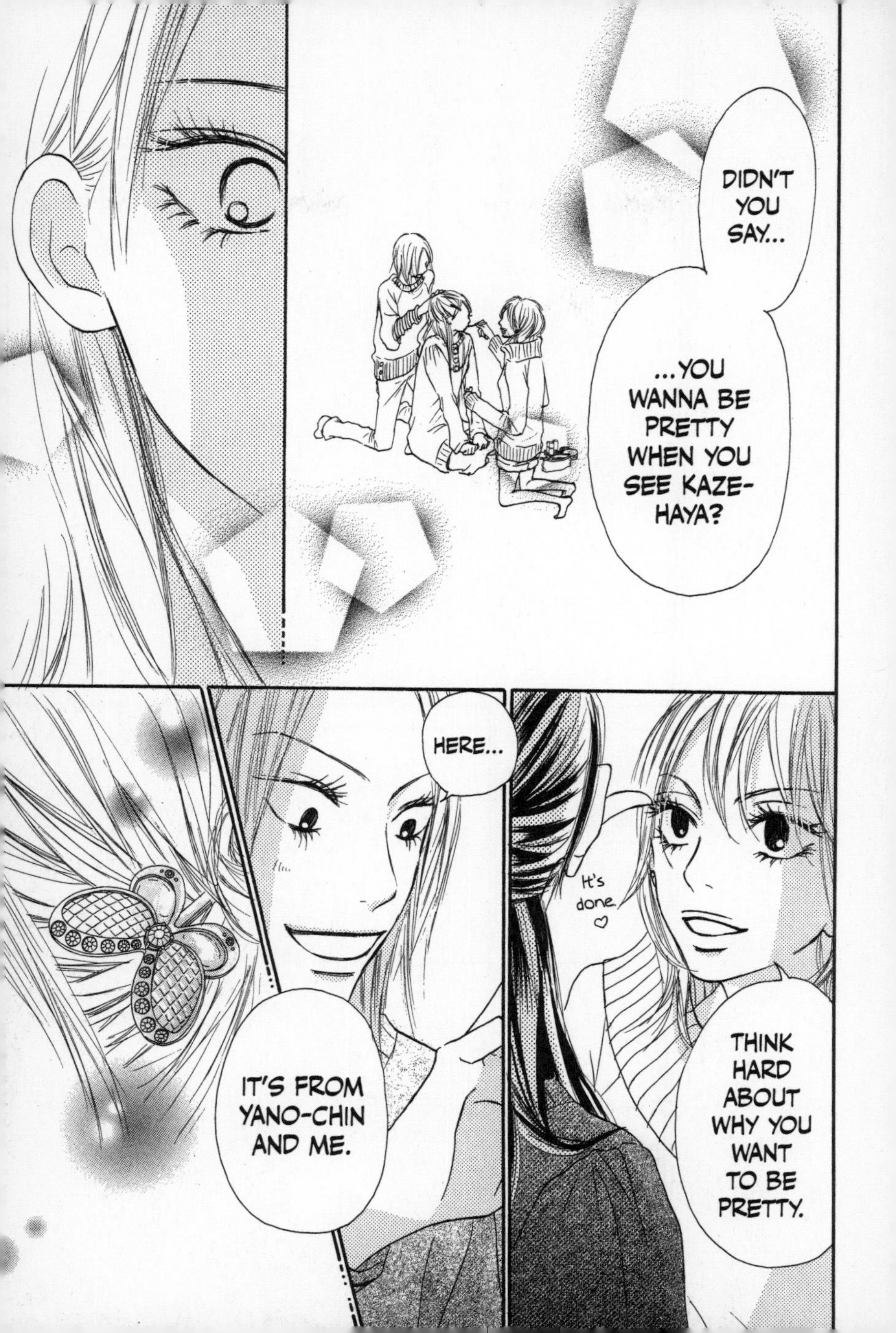
DIDN'T YOU SAY...
...YOU WANNA BE PRETTY WHEN YOU SEE KAZE-HAYA?
It's done. ♡
THINK HARD ABOUT WHY YOU WANT TO BE PRETTY.
HERE...
IT'S FROM YANO-CHIN AND ME.

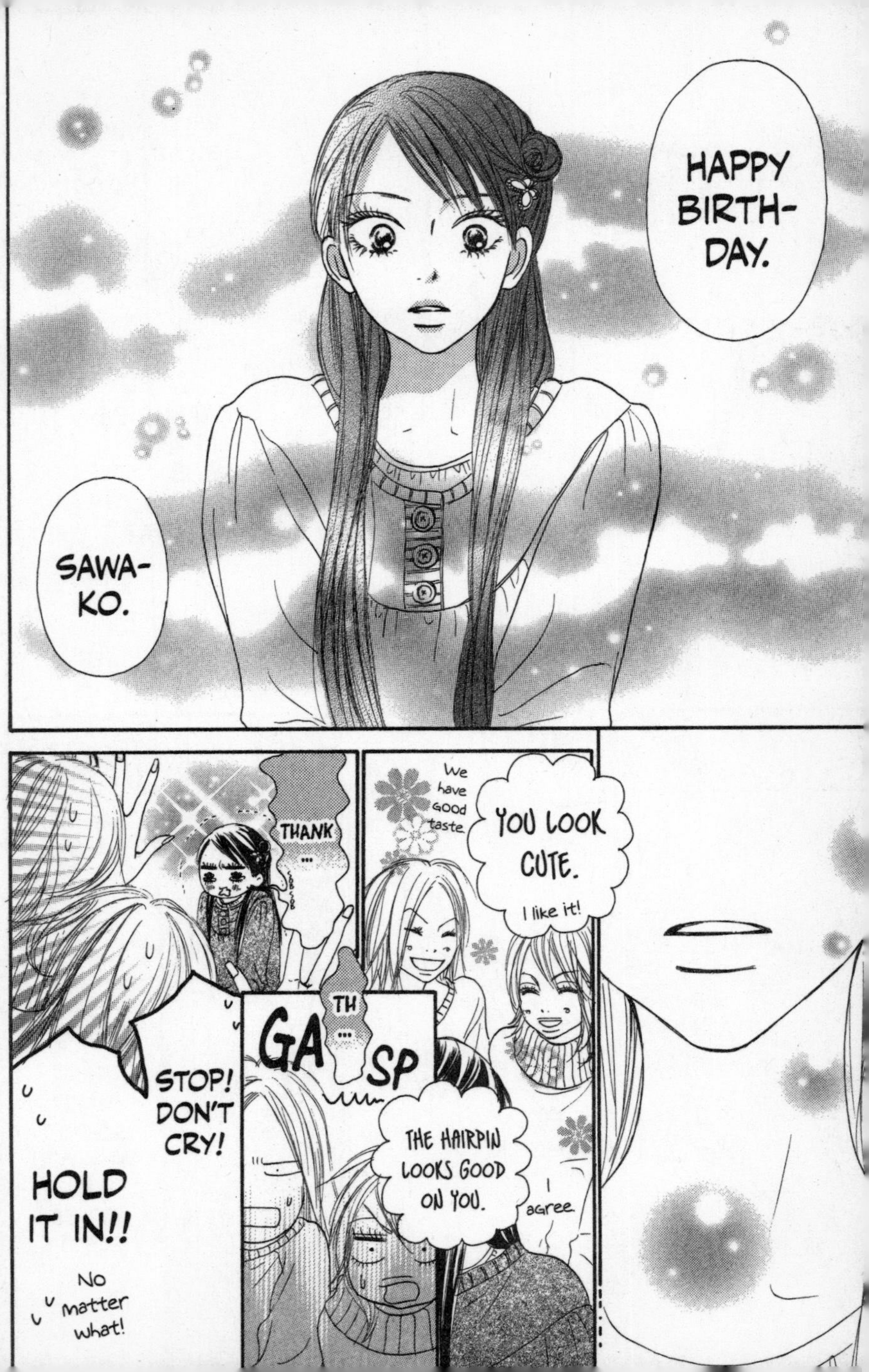
HAPPY BIRTH-DAY.
SAWA-KO.
We have good taste.
YOU LOOK CUTE.
I like it!
THE HAIRPIN LOOKS GOOD ON YOU.
I agree.
THANK...
SOB SOB
TH...
GASP
STOP! DON'T CRY!
HOLD IT IN!!
No matter what!

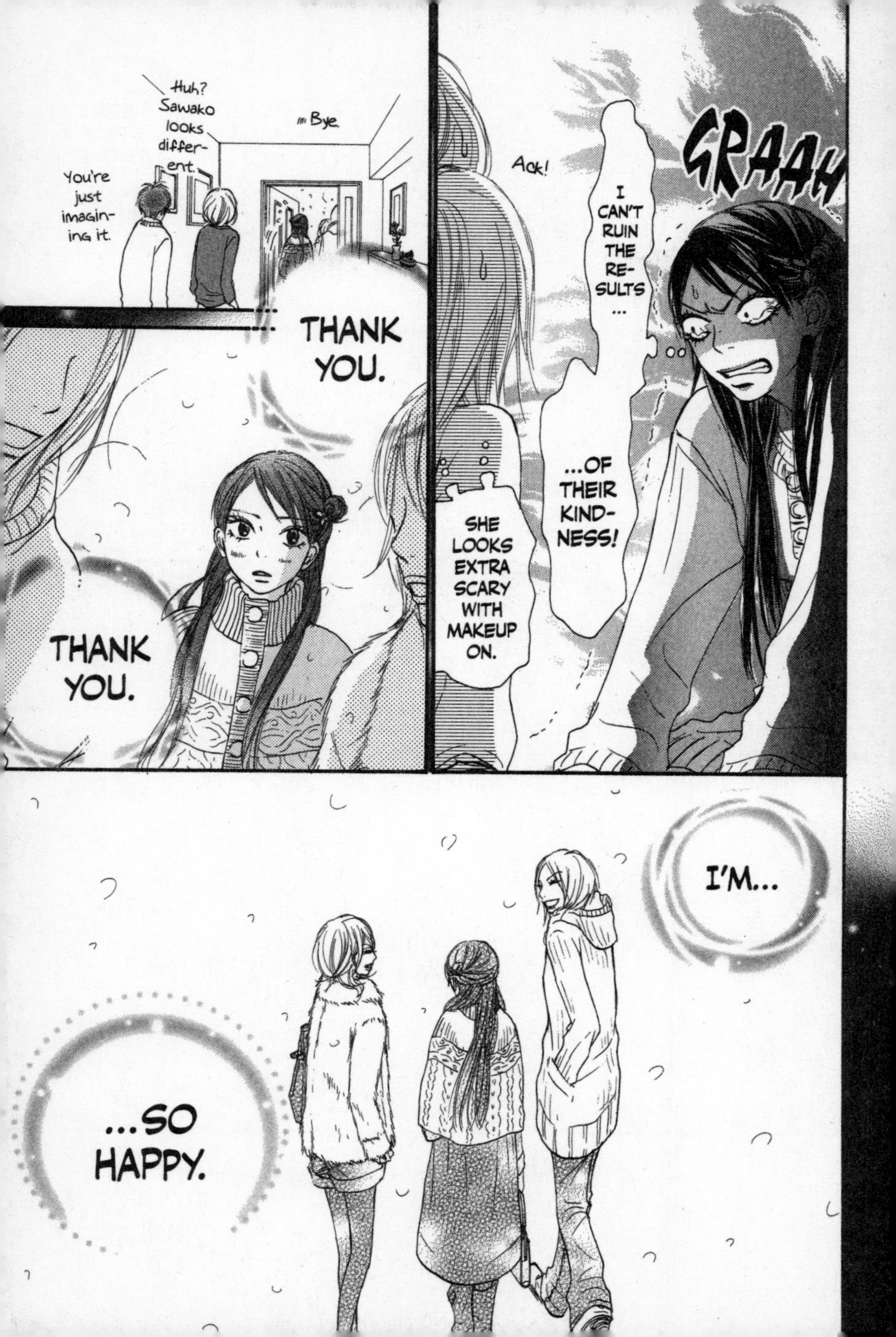
GRAAH
I CAN'T RUIN THE RE-SULTS...
Ack!
...OF THEIR KIND-NESS!
SHE LOOKS EXTRA SCARY WITH MAKEUP ON.
Bye.
Huh? Sawako looks differ-ent.
You're just imagin-ing it.
THANK YOU.
THANK YOU.
I'M...
...SO HAPPY.

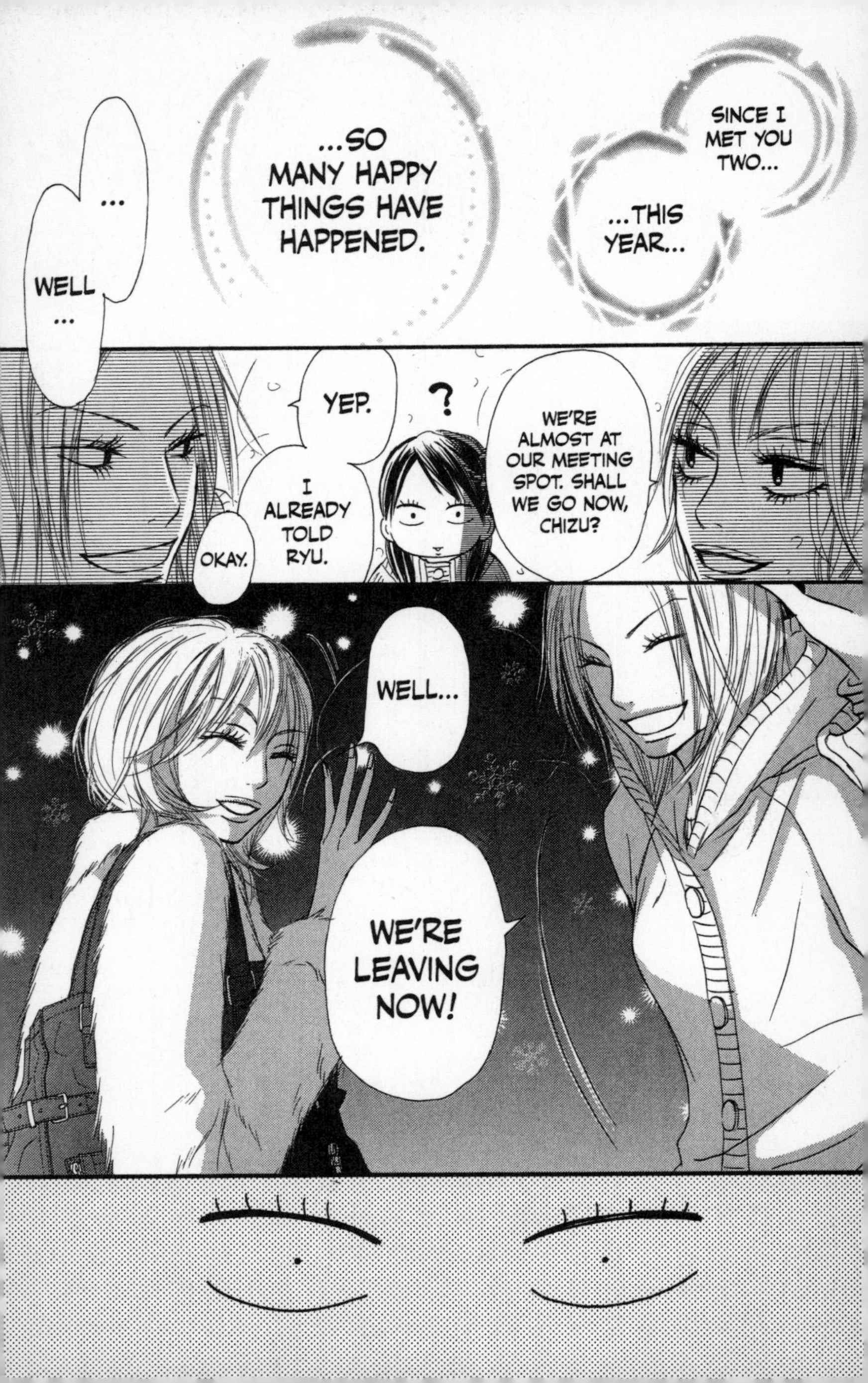
SINCE I MET YOU TWO...
...THIS YEAR...
...SO MANY HAPPY THINGS HAVE HAPPENED.
... WELL ...
WE'RE ALMOST AT OUR MEETING SPOT. SHALL WE GO NOW, CHIZU?
?
YEP.
I ALREADY TOLD RYU.
OKAY.
WELL...
WE'RE LEAVING NOW!

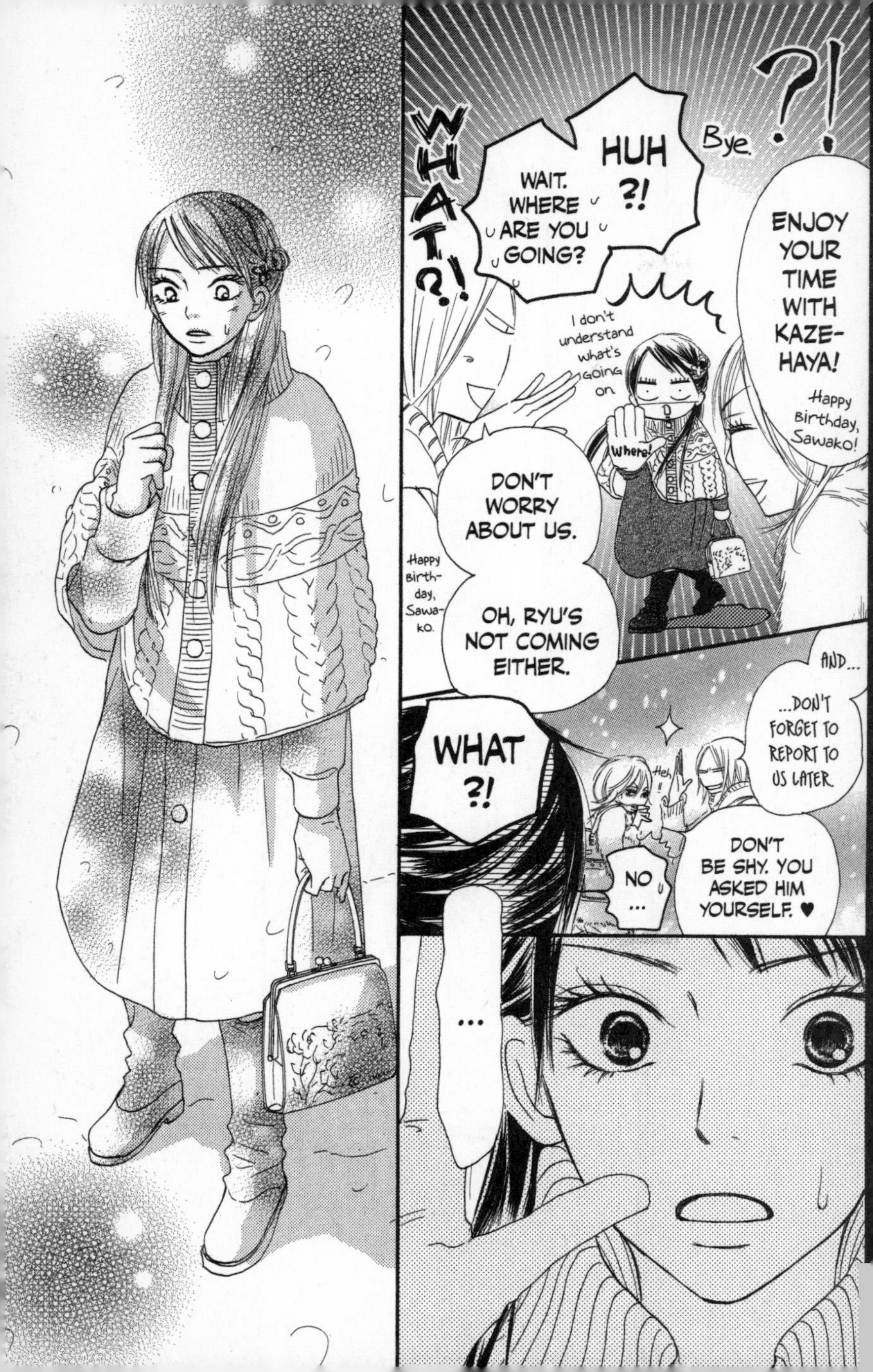
?!
Bye.
ENJOY YOUR TIME WITH KAZE-HAYA!
Happy Birthday, Sawako!
HUH ?!
WAIT. WHERE ARE YOU GOING?
WHAT?!
I don't understand what's going on.
Where!
DON'T WORRY ABOUT US.
OH, RYU'S NOT COMING EITHER.
Happy Birth-day, Sawa-ko.
AND...
...DON'T FORGET TO REPORT TO US LATER.
DON'T BE SHY. YOU ASKED HIM YOURSELF. ♥
Heh
NO ...
WHAT ?!
...

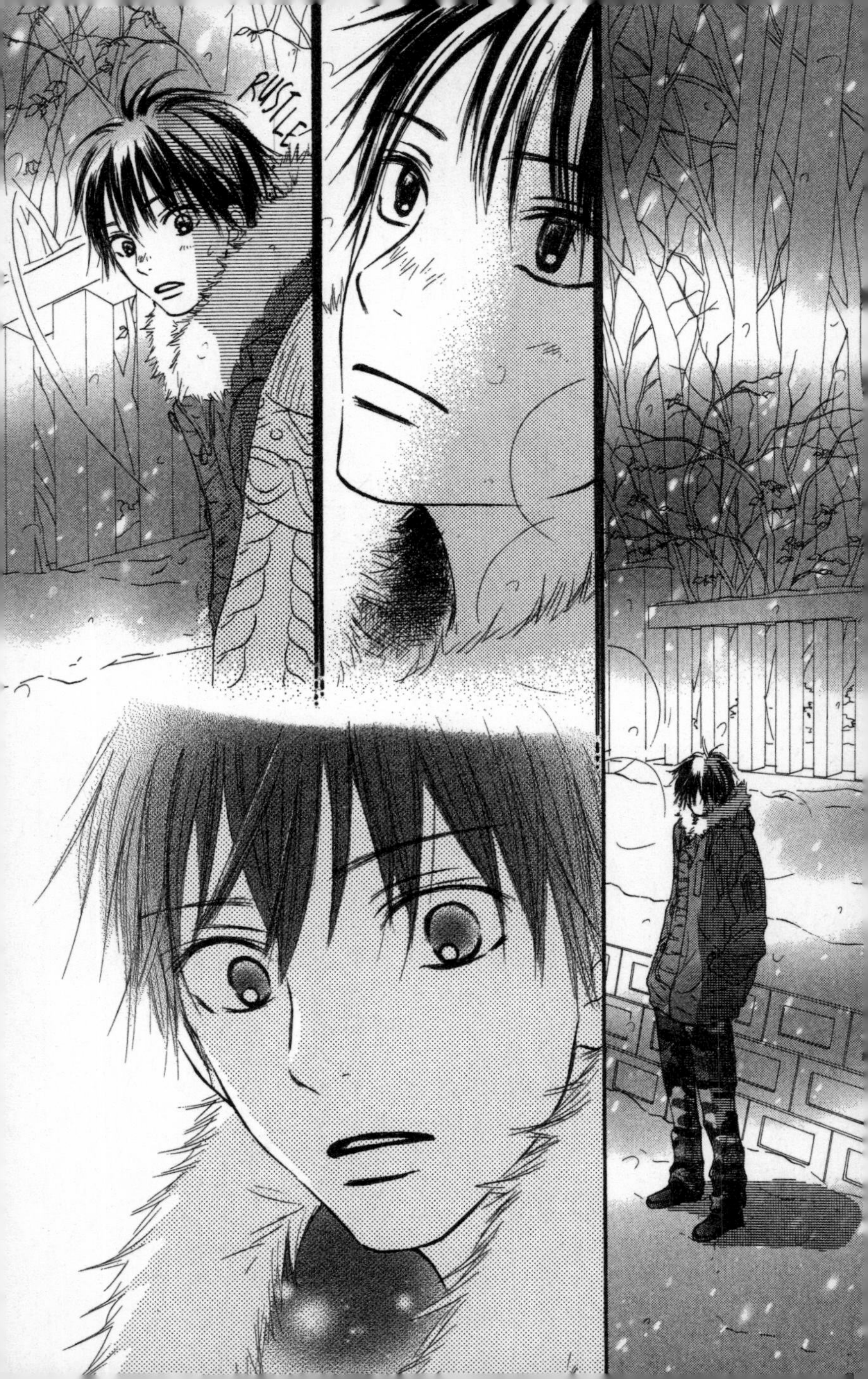
RUSTLE

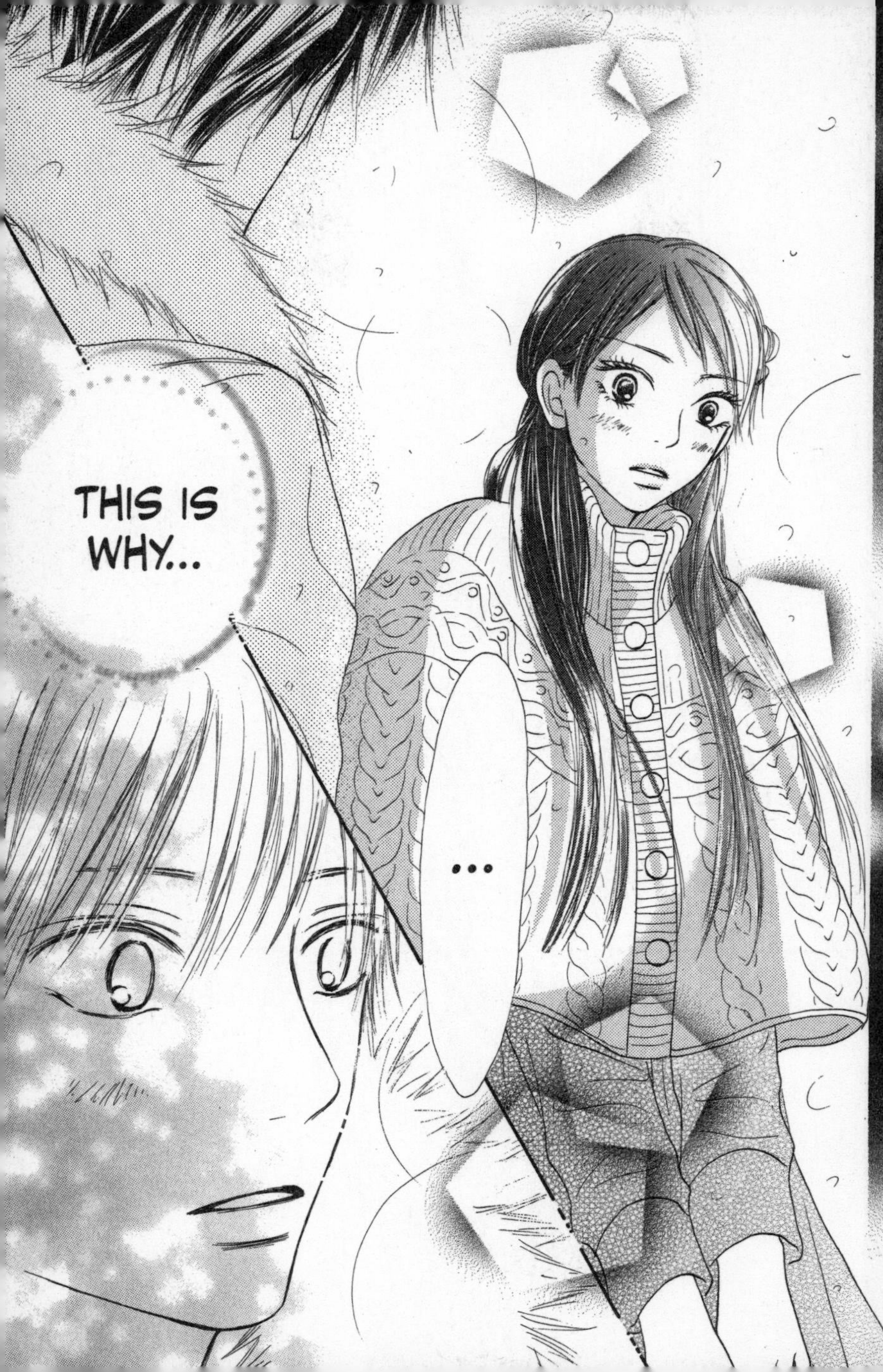
THIS IS WHY...
...

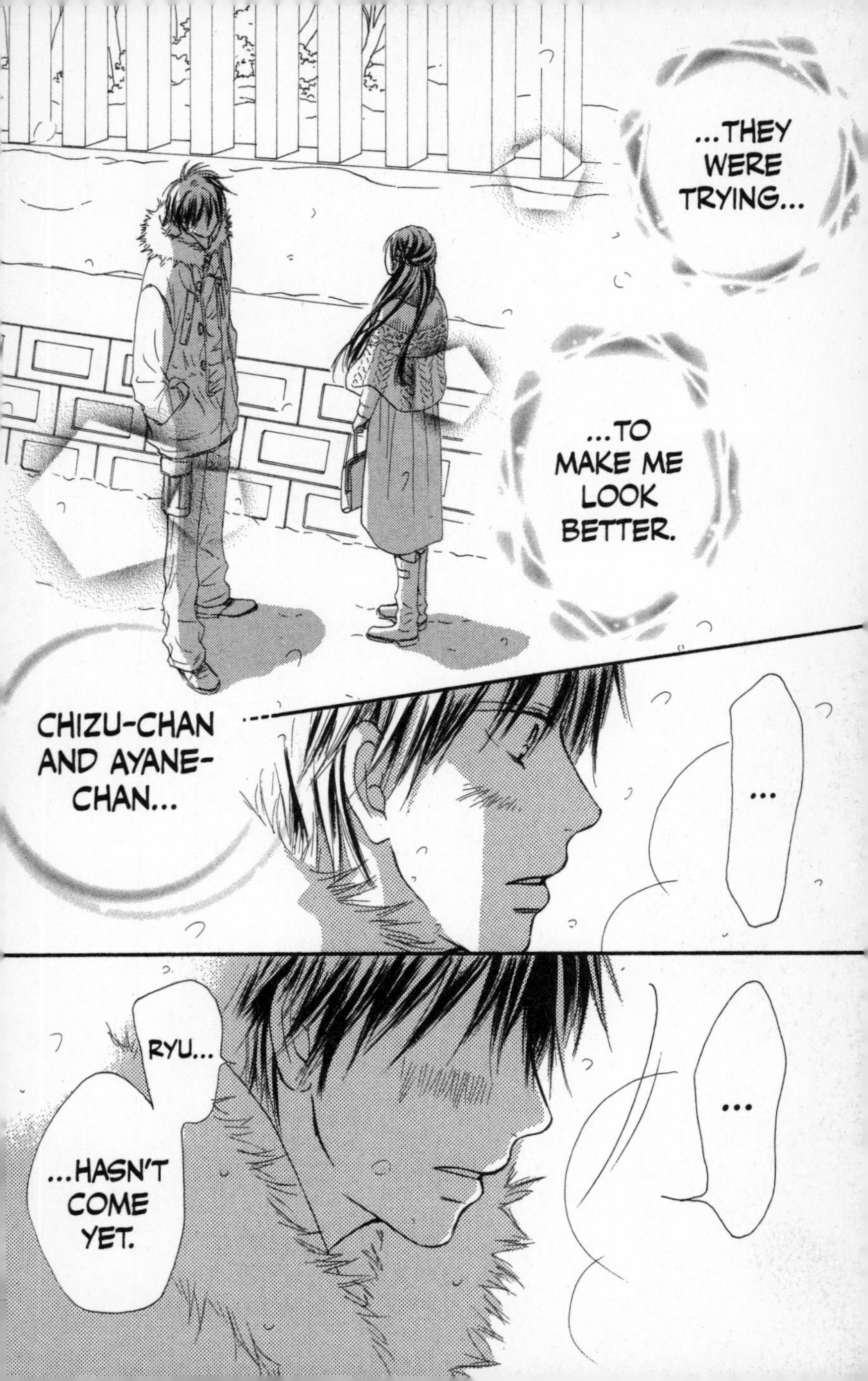
...THEY WERE TRYING...
...TO MAKE ME LOOK BETTER.
...
CHIZU-CHAN AND AYANE-CHAN...
...
RYU...
...HASN'T COME YET.

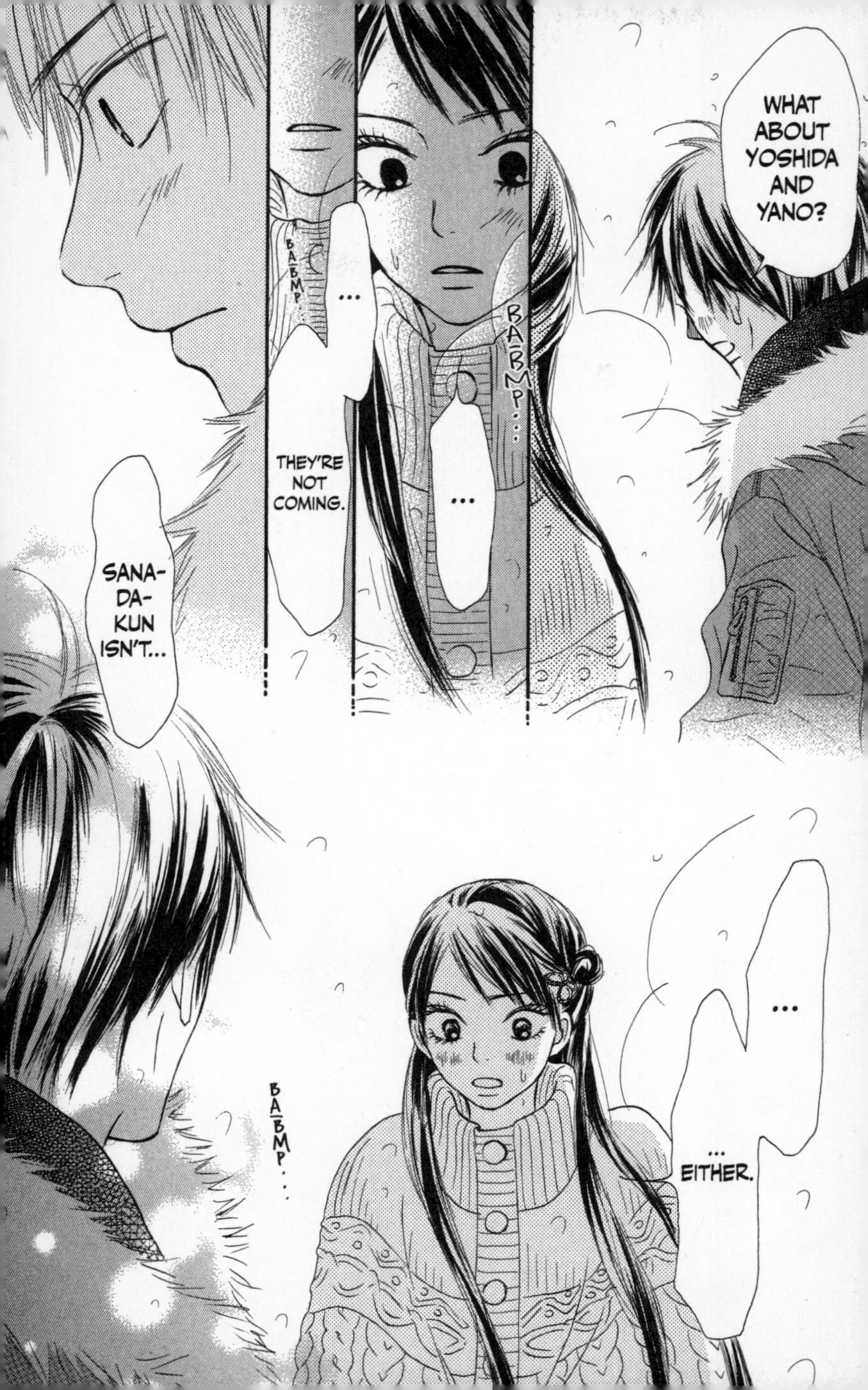
WHAT ABOUT YOSHIDA AND YANO?
BA-BMP...
...
...
THEY'RE NOT COMING.
BA-BMP
SANA-DA-KUN ISN'T...
...
... EITHER.
BA-BMP..

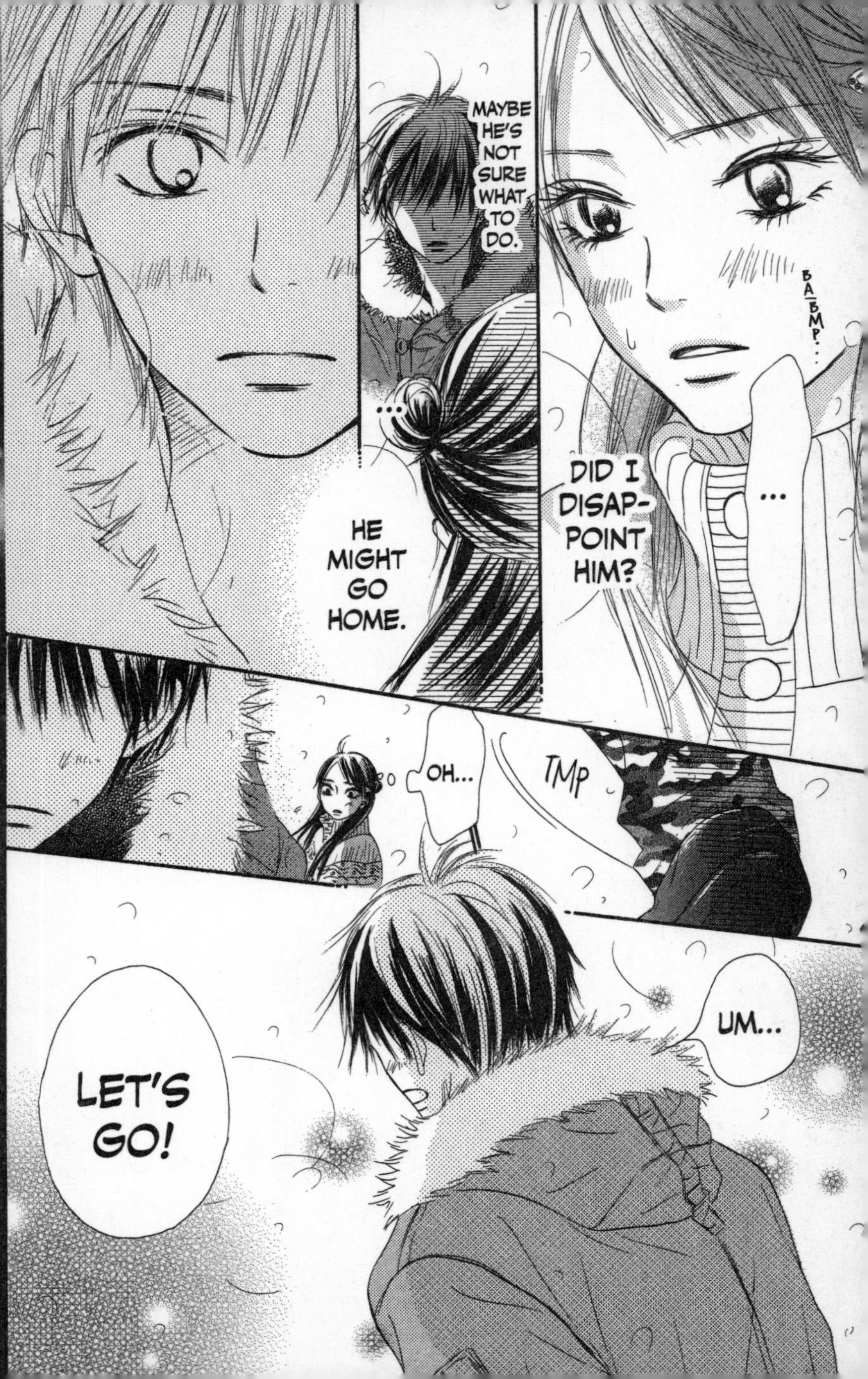
BA-BMP...
DID I DISAP-POINT HIM?
...
MAYBE HE'S NOT SURE WHAT TO DO.
...
HE MIGHT GO HOME.
TMP
OH...
UM...
LET'S GO!

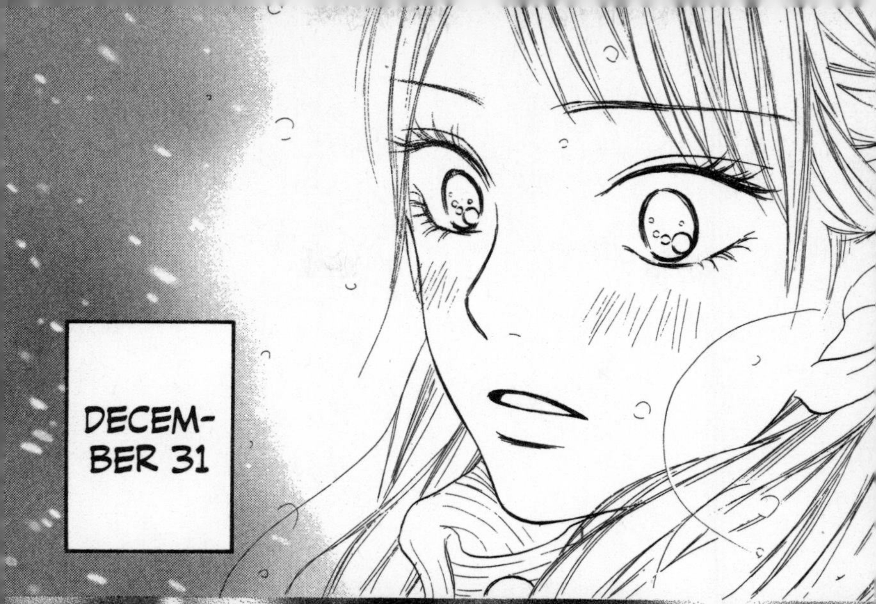
DECEMBER 31
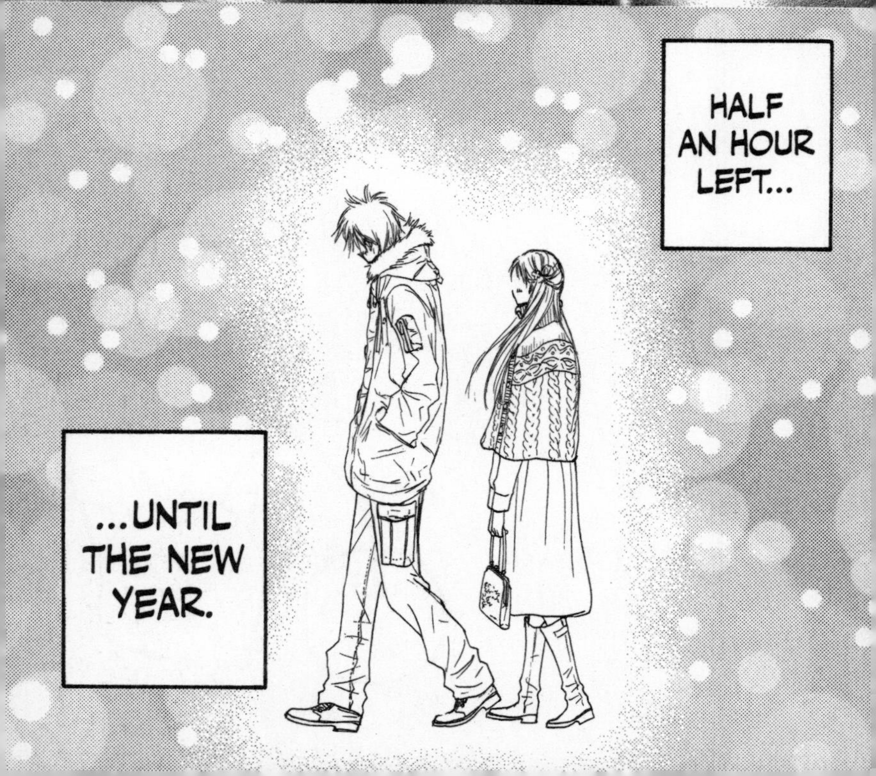
HALF AN HOUR LEFT...
...UNTIL THE NEW YEAR.

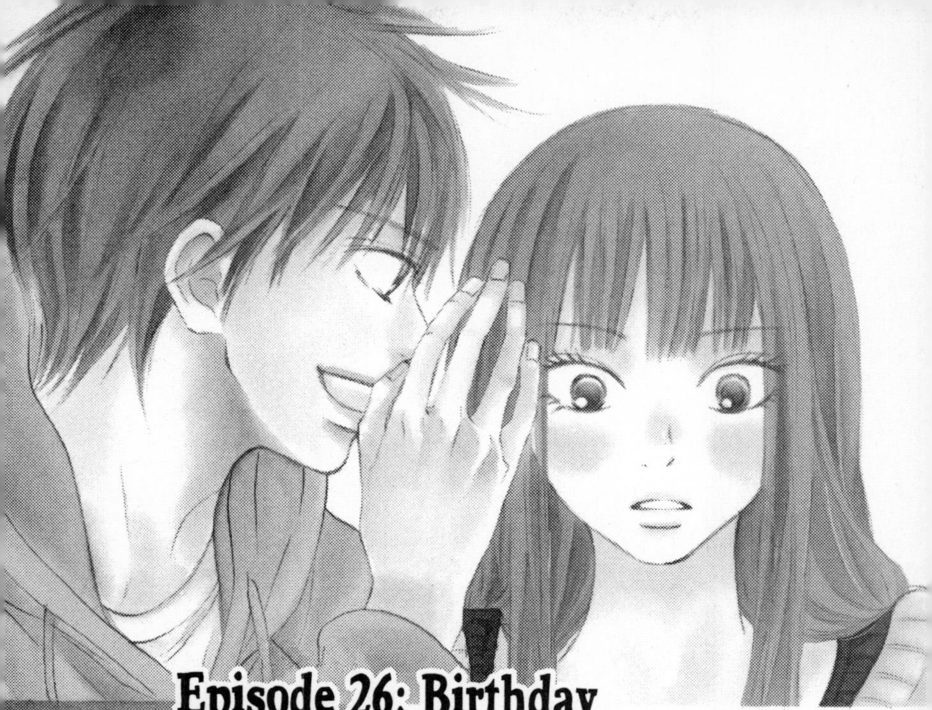

Episode 26: Birthday

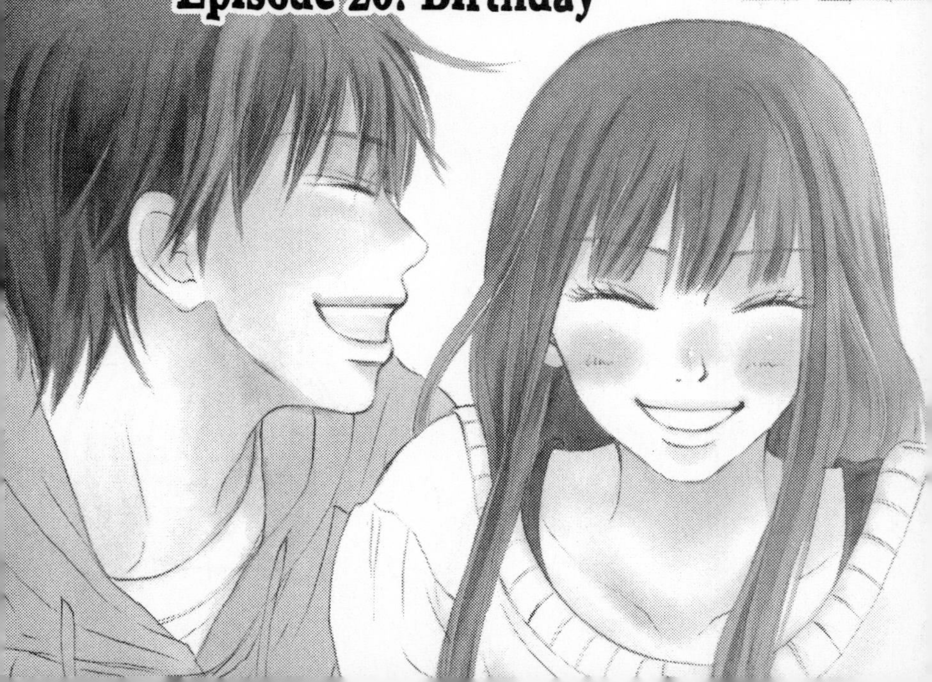

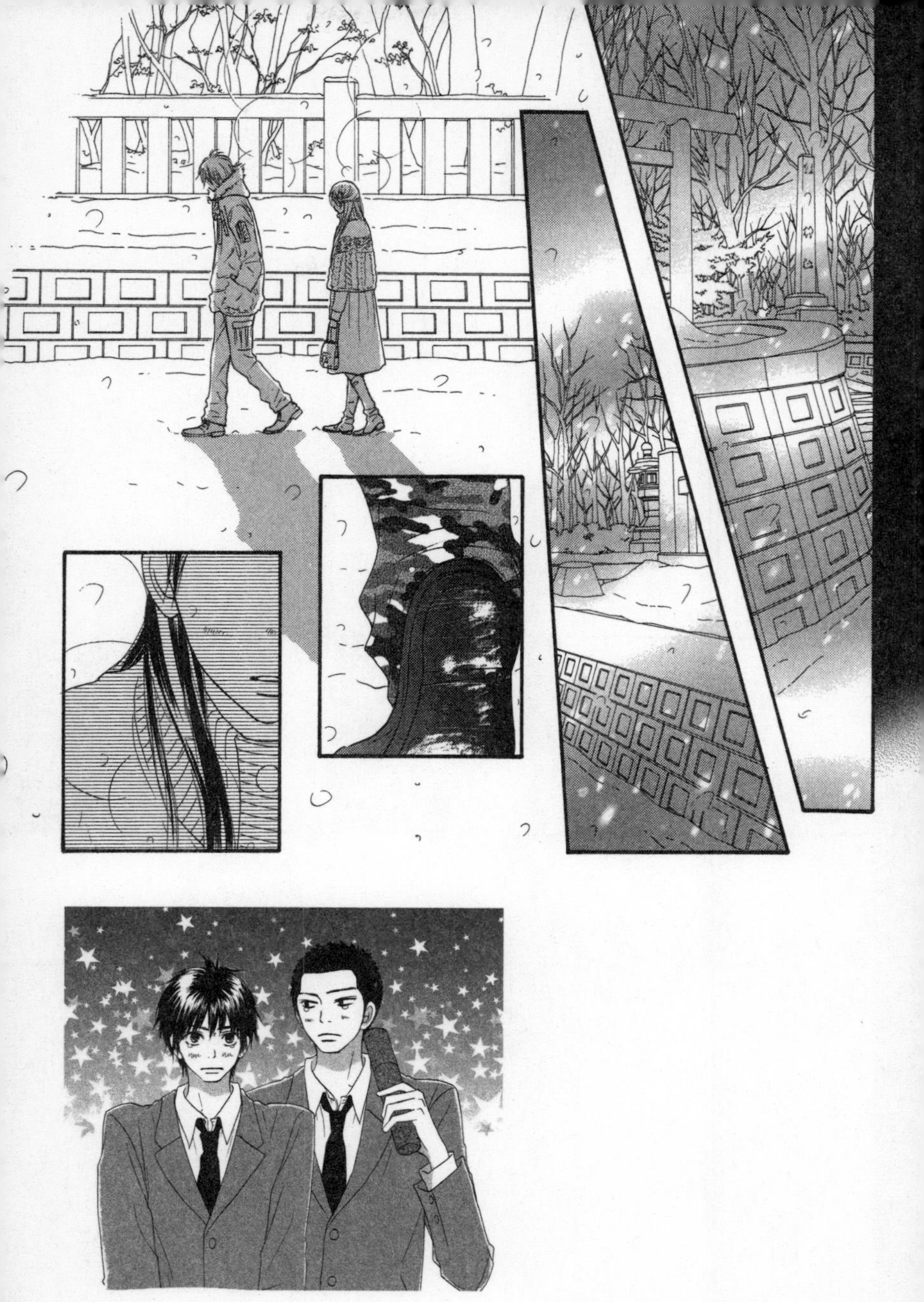

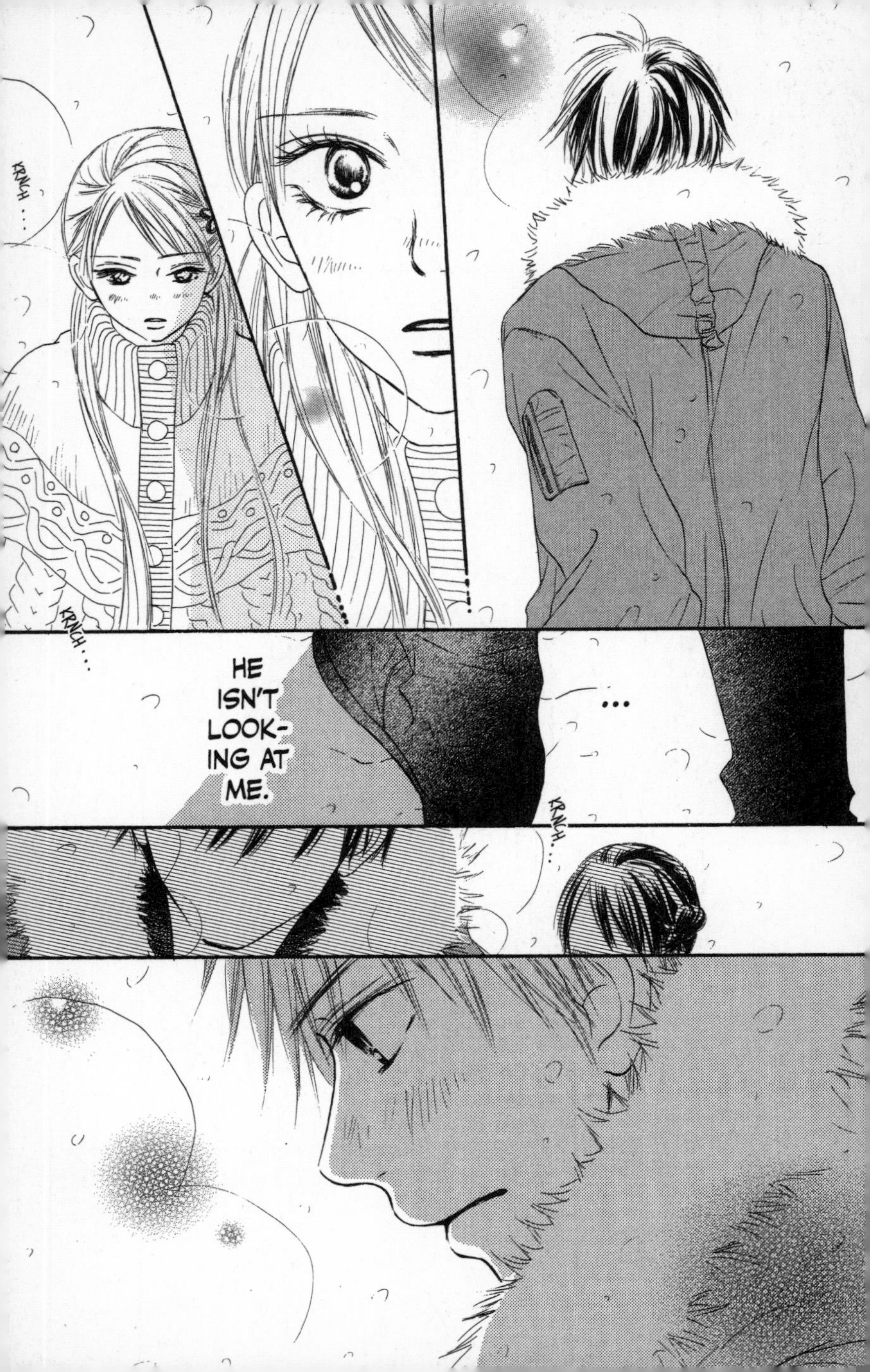
KRNCH ...
KRNCH ...
...
HE ISN'T LOOKING AT ME.
KRNCH ...

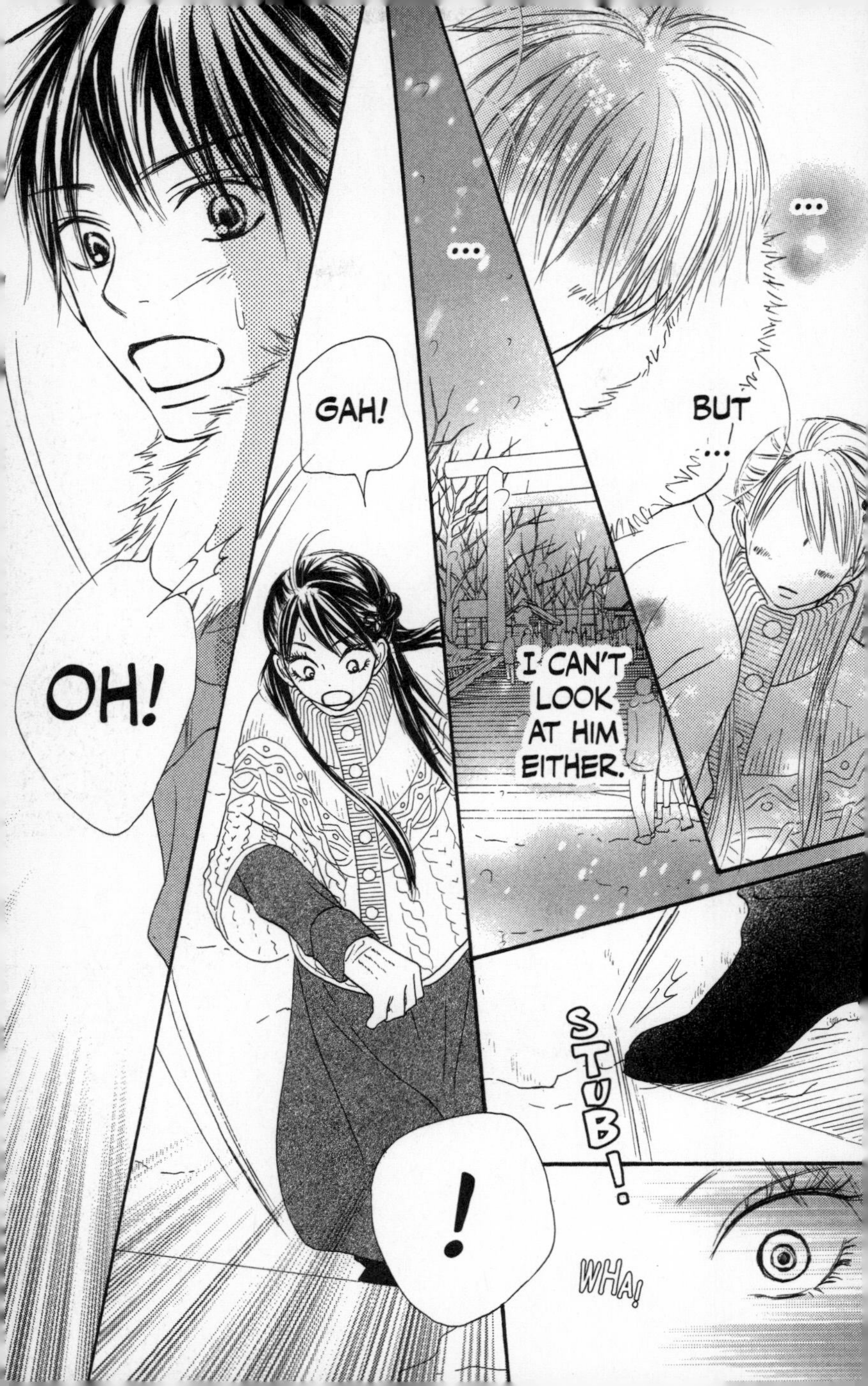
...
BUT ...
...
I CAN'T LOOK AT HIM EITHER.
GAH!
OH!
STUB!
!
WHA!

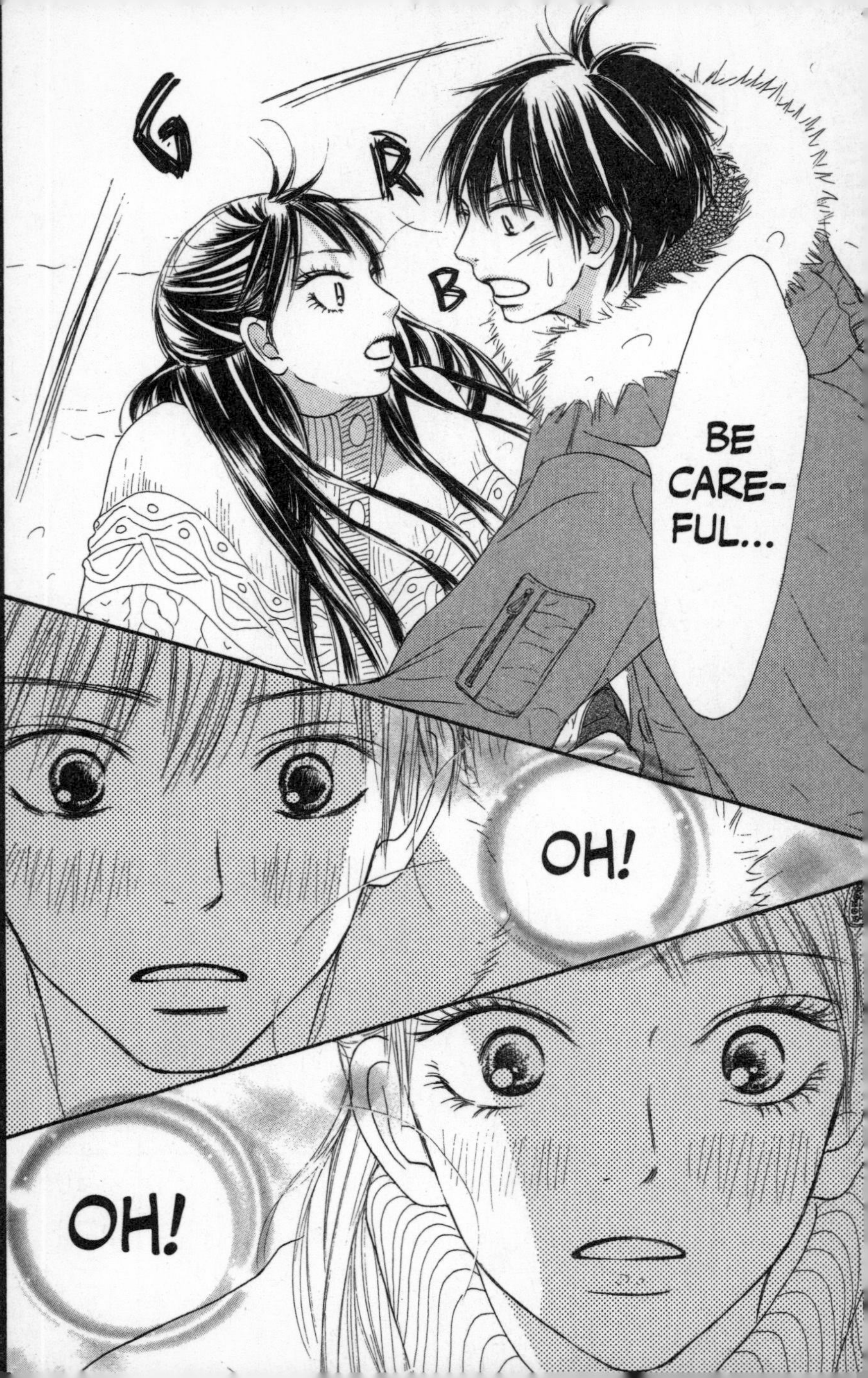
GRB
BE CARE-FUL...
OH!
OH!

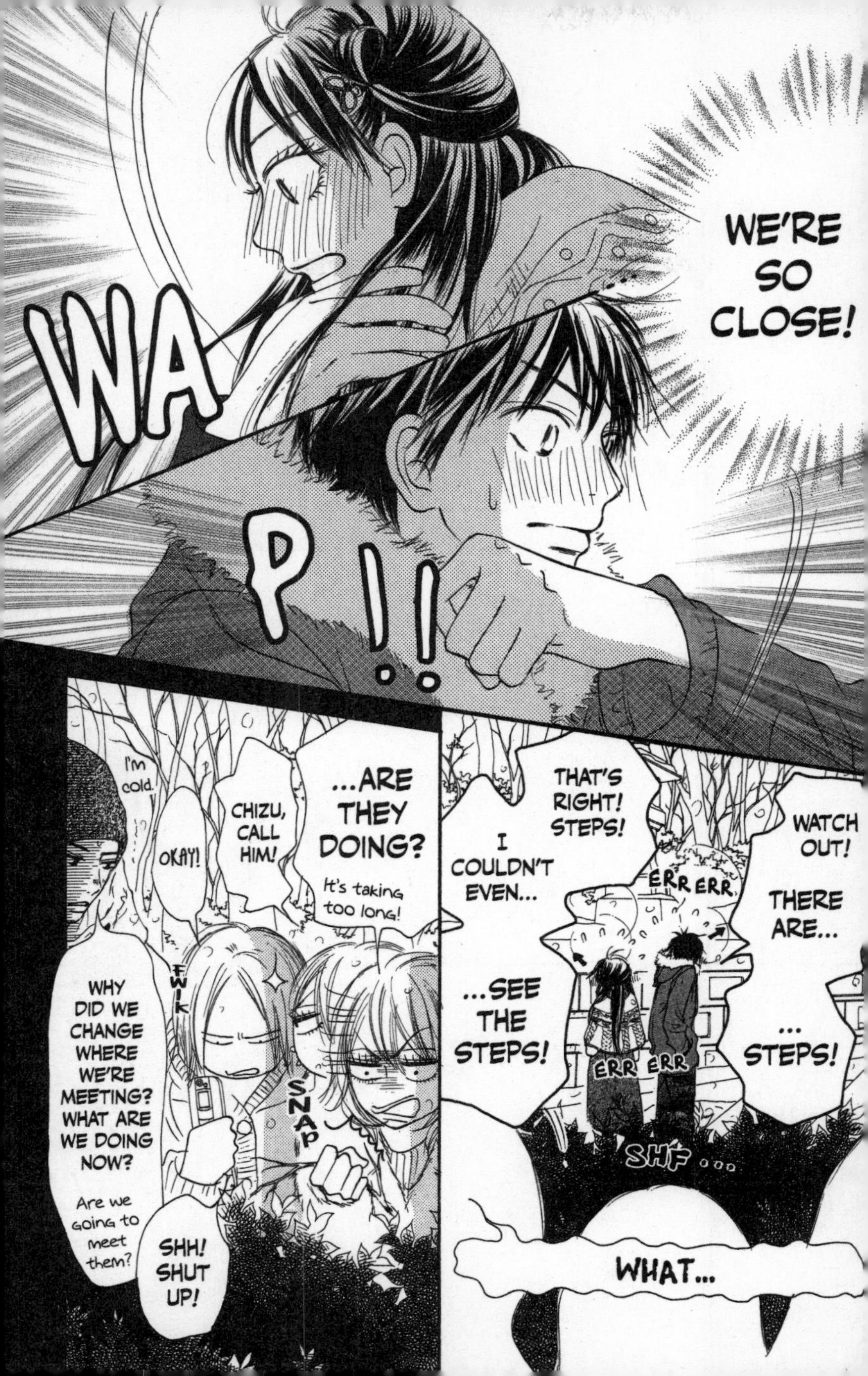
WE'RE SO CLOSE!
WAP!!
WATCH OUT! THERE ARE...
... STEPS!
ERR ERR
THAT'S RIGHT! STEPS!
I COULDN'T EVEN...
...SEE THE STEPS!
ERR ERR
SHF...
WHAT...
...ARE THEY DOING?
It's taking too long!
CHIZU, CALL HIM!
OKAY!
I'm cold.
WHY DID WE CHANGE WHERE WE'RE MEETING? WHAT ARE WE DOING NOW?
FWIK
SNAP
Are we going to meet them?
SHH! SHUT UP!

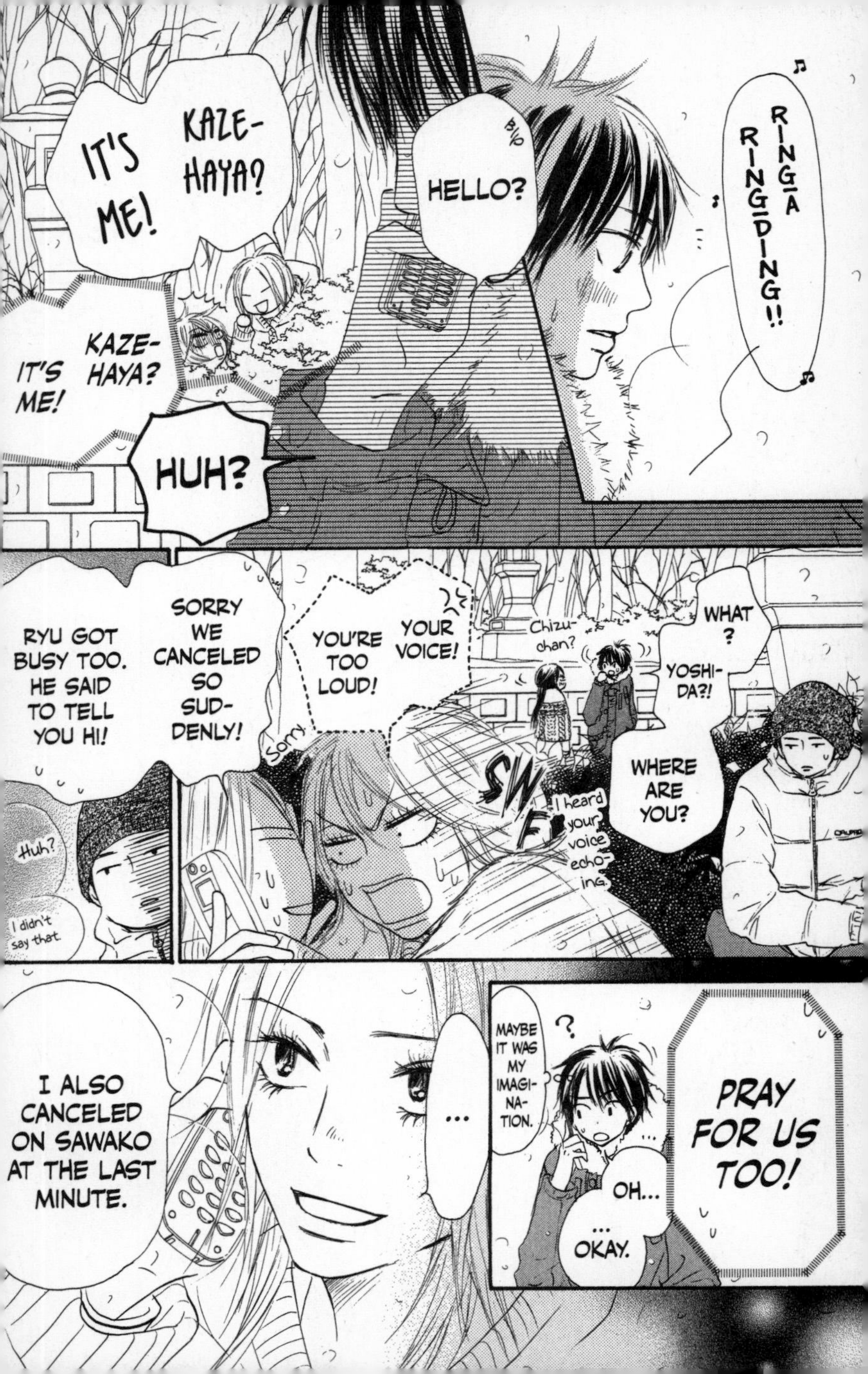
RING-A RING-DING!!
HELLO?
KAZE-HAYA? IT'S ME!
KAZE-HAYA? IT'S ME!
HUH?
WHAT? YOSHIDA?!
WHERE ARE YOU?
Chizu-chan?
I heard your voice echoing.
SWF
YOUR VOICE! YOU'RE TOO LOUD!
Sorry
SORRY WE CANCELED SO SUDDENLY!
RYU GOT BUSY TOO. HE SAID TO TELL YOU HI!
Huh?
I didn't say that.
PRAY FOR US TOO!
OH... ...OKAY.
...
MAYBE IT WAS MY IMAGINATION.
...
I ALSO CANCELED ON SAWAKO AT THE LAST MINUTE.

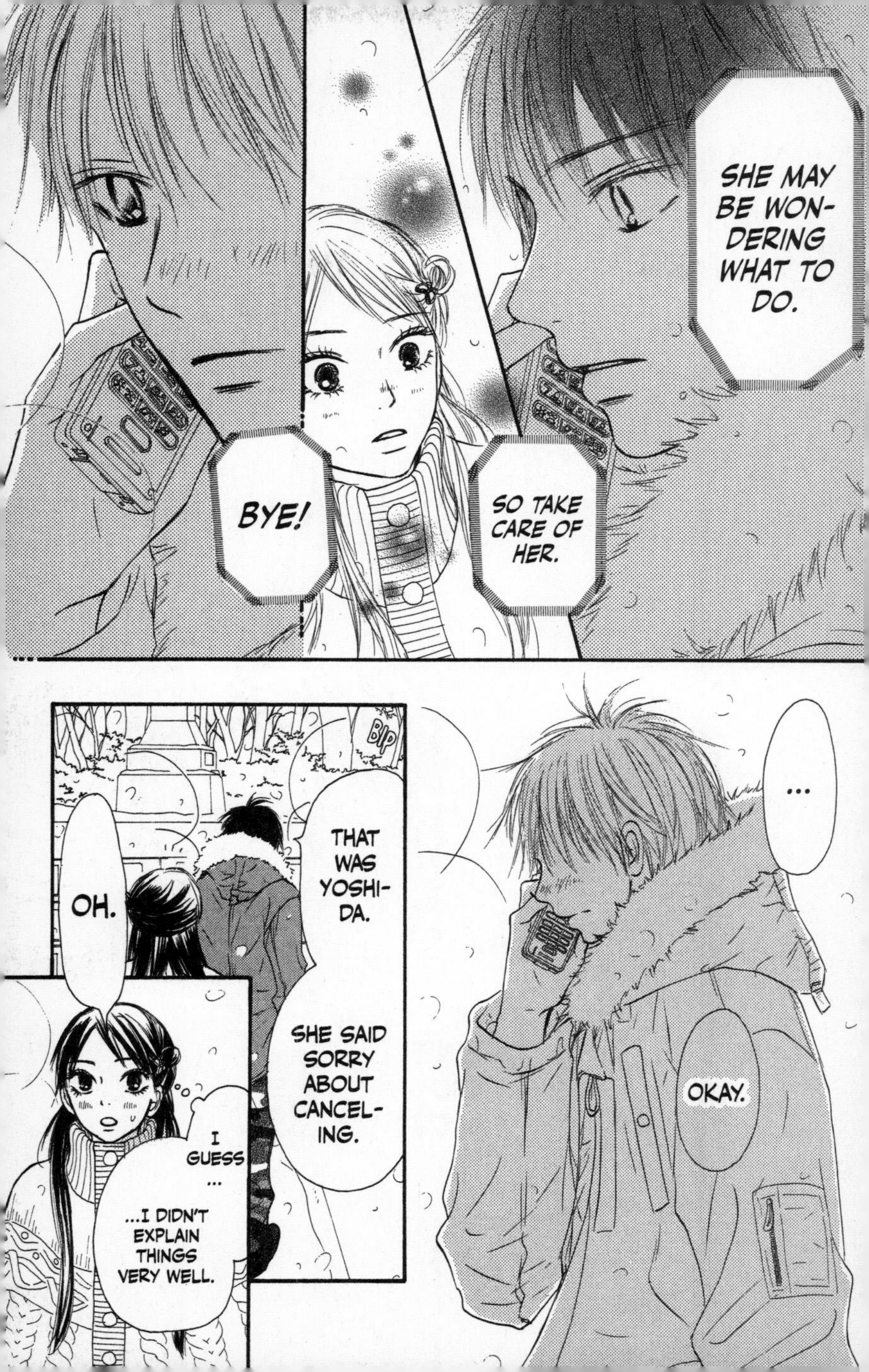
SHE MAY BE WONDERING WHAT TO DO.
SO TAKE CARE OF HER.
BYE!
...
OKAY.
BIP
THAT WAS YOSHIDA.
OH.
SHE SAID SORRY ABOUT CANCELING.
I GUESS...
...I DIDN'T EXPLAIN THINGS VERY WELL.

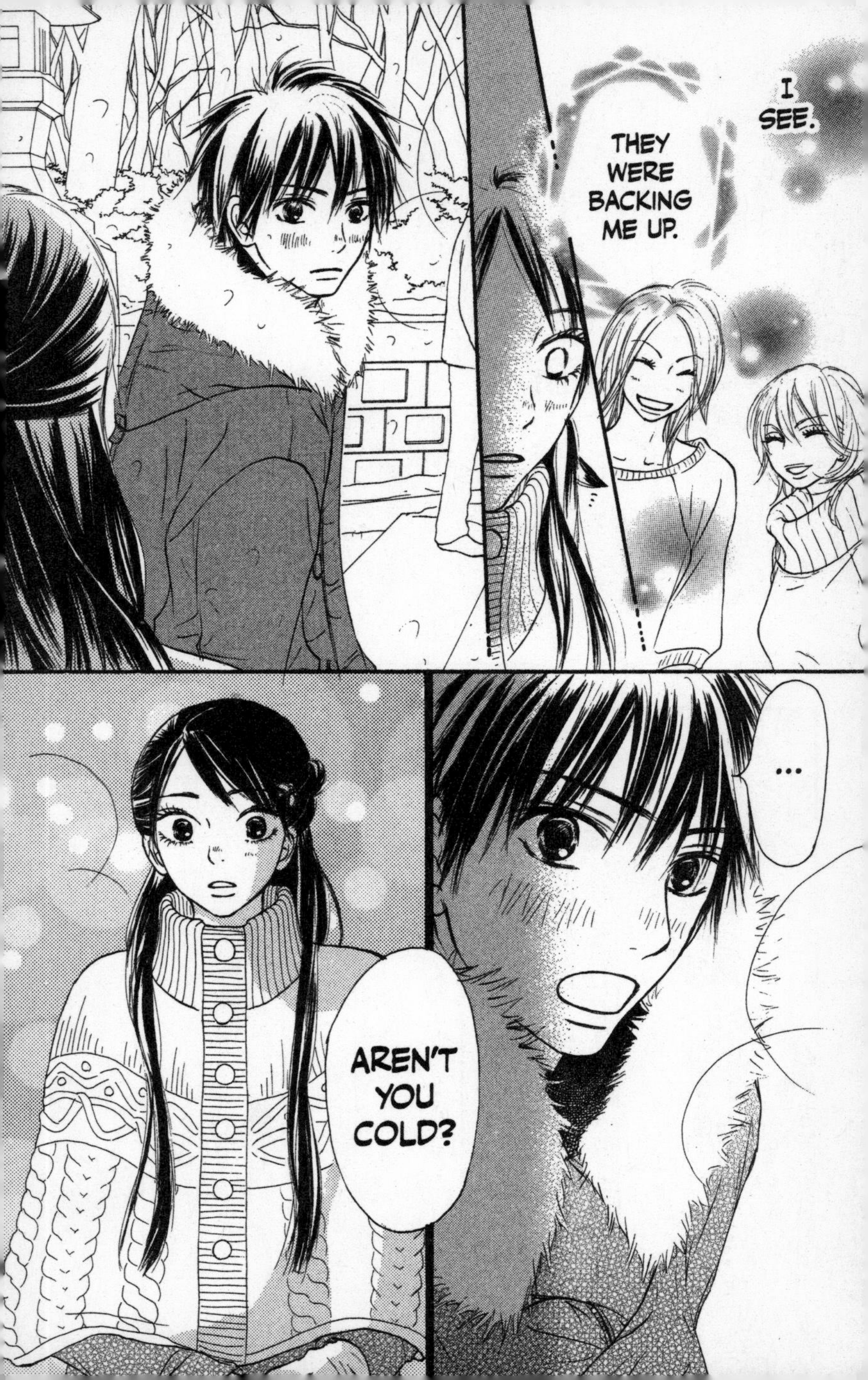
I SEE.
THEY WERE BACKING ME UP.
...
AREN'T YOU COLD?

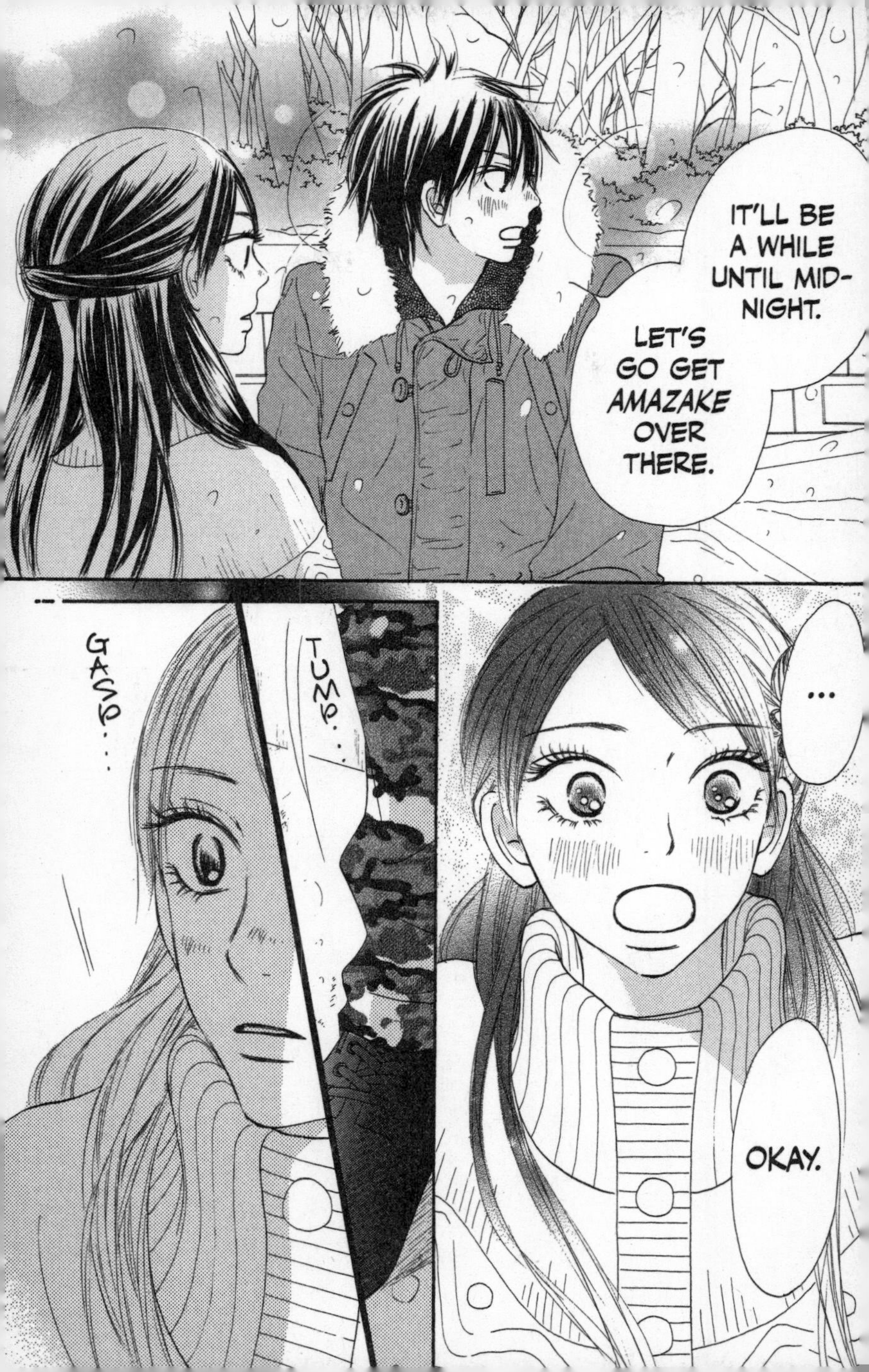
IT'LL BE A WHILE UNTIL MID-NIGHT.
LET'S GO GET AMAZAKE OVER THERE.
...
OKAY.
TUMP...
GASP...

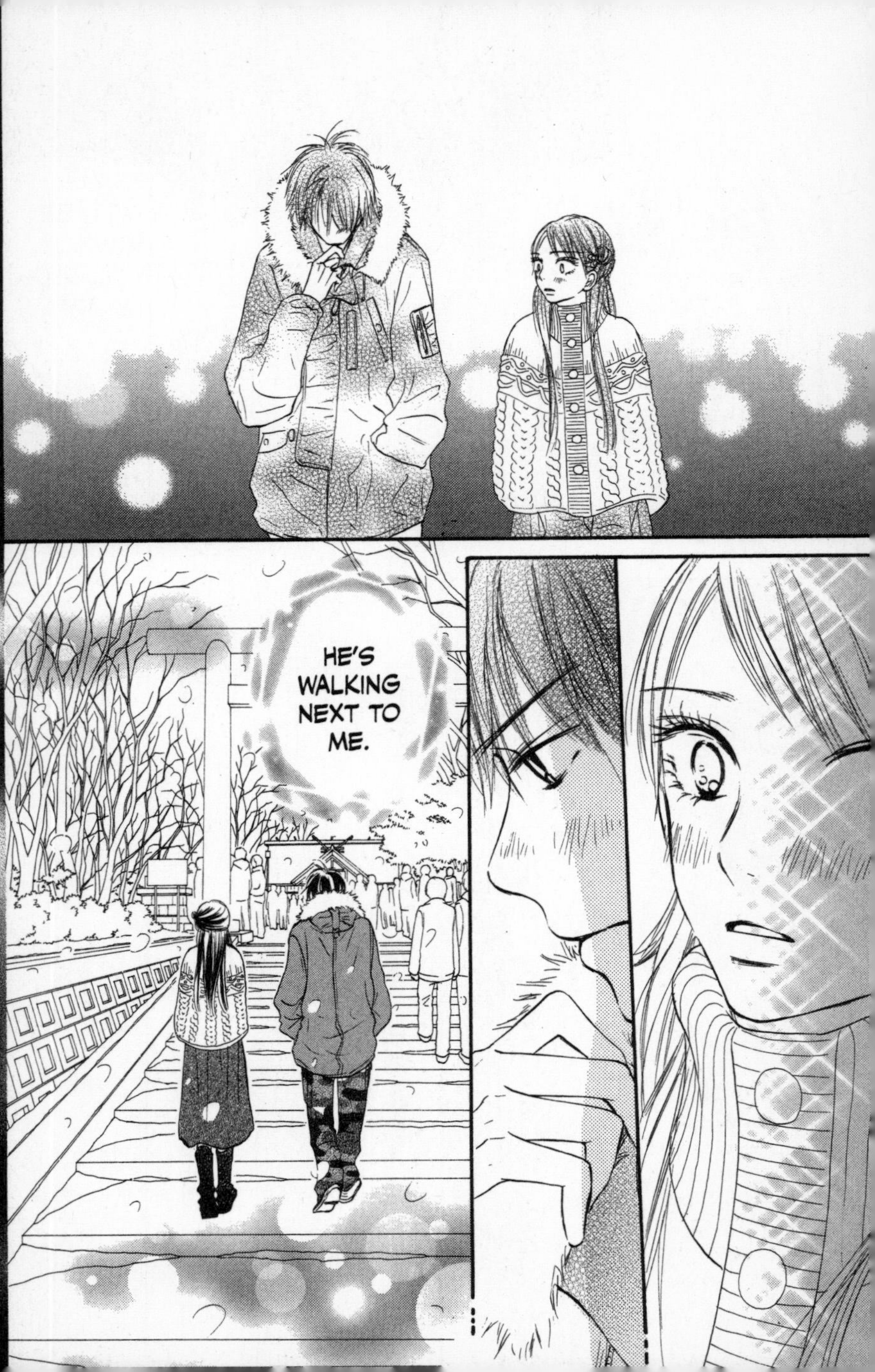
HE'S WALKING NEXT TO ME.

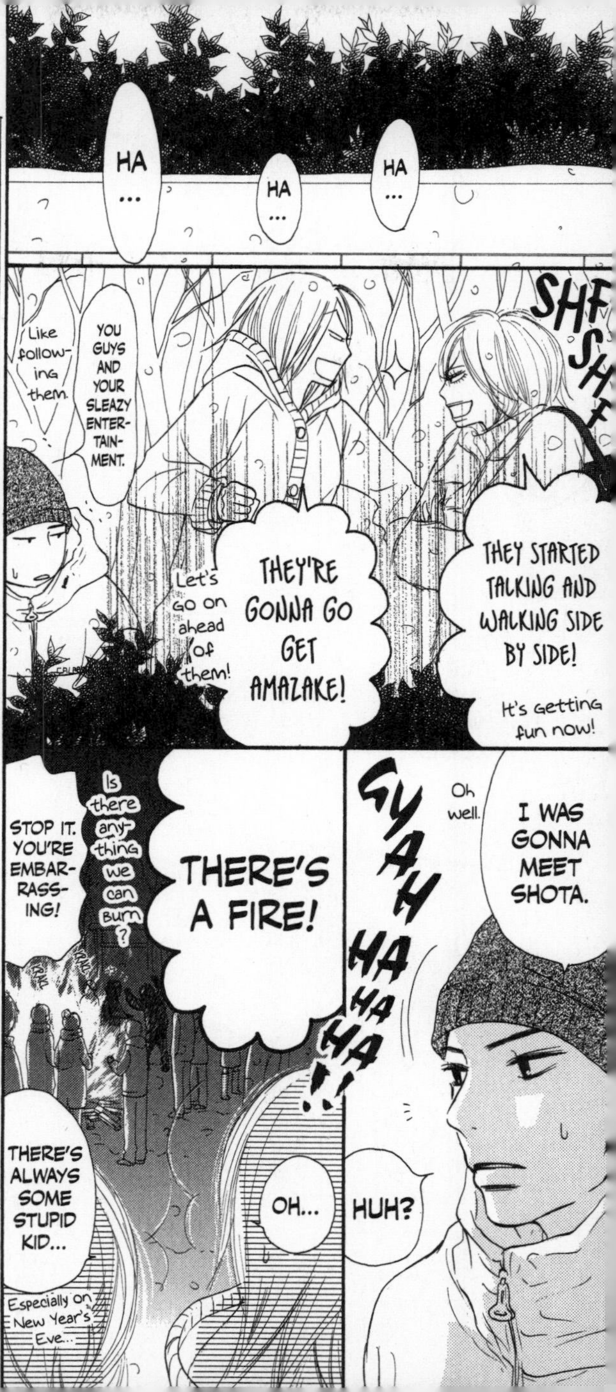
HA...
HA...
HA...
SHF SHF
THEY STARTED TALKING AND WALKING SIDE BY SIDE!
It's getting fun now!
THEY'RE GONNA GO GET AMAZAKE!
Let's go on ahead of them!
YOU GUYS AND YOUR SLEAZY ENTERTAINMENT.
Like following them.
I WAS GONNA MEET SHOTA.
Oh well.
GYAH HA HA HA!!
HUH?
OH...
THERE'S A FIRE!
Is there anything we can burn?
STOP IT. YOU'RE EMBARRASSING!
THERE'S ALWAYS SOME STUPID KID...
Especially on New Year's Eve...

KARUPIN on JAPAN 2

On the subject of novels... *Kimi ni Todoke* is being novelized by Kanae Shimokawa. Three volumes have been released.

In her novels, Ms. Shimokawa shows the characters' emotions in ways I couldn't show enough in the manga. So if you like to read, please read them.

Thank you, Ms. Shimokawa, for your wonderful writing, and please keep working together with me.

Please keep reading future volumes!

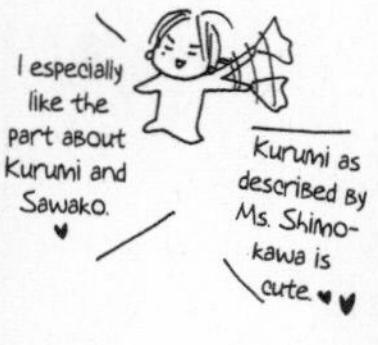
I especially like the part about Kurumi and Sawako. ♥
Kurumi as described by Ms. Shimokawa is cute. ♥♥

Ms. Shimokawa also novelized the film versions of *Nana* and *A Gentle Breeze in the Village*, as well as the manga *Yukan Club*. Please read them! ♡

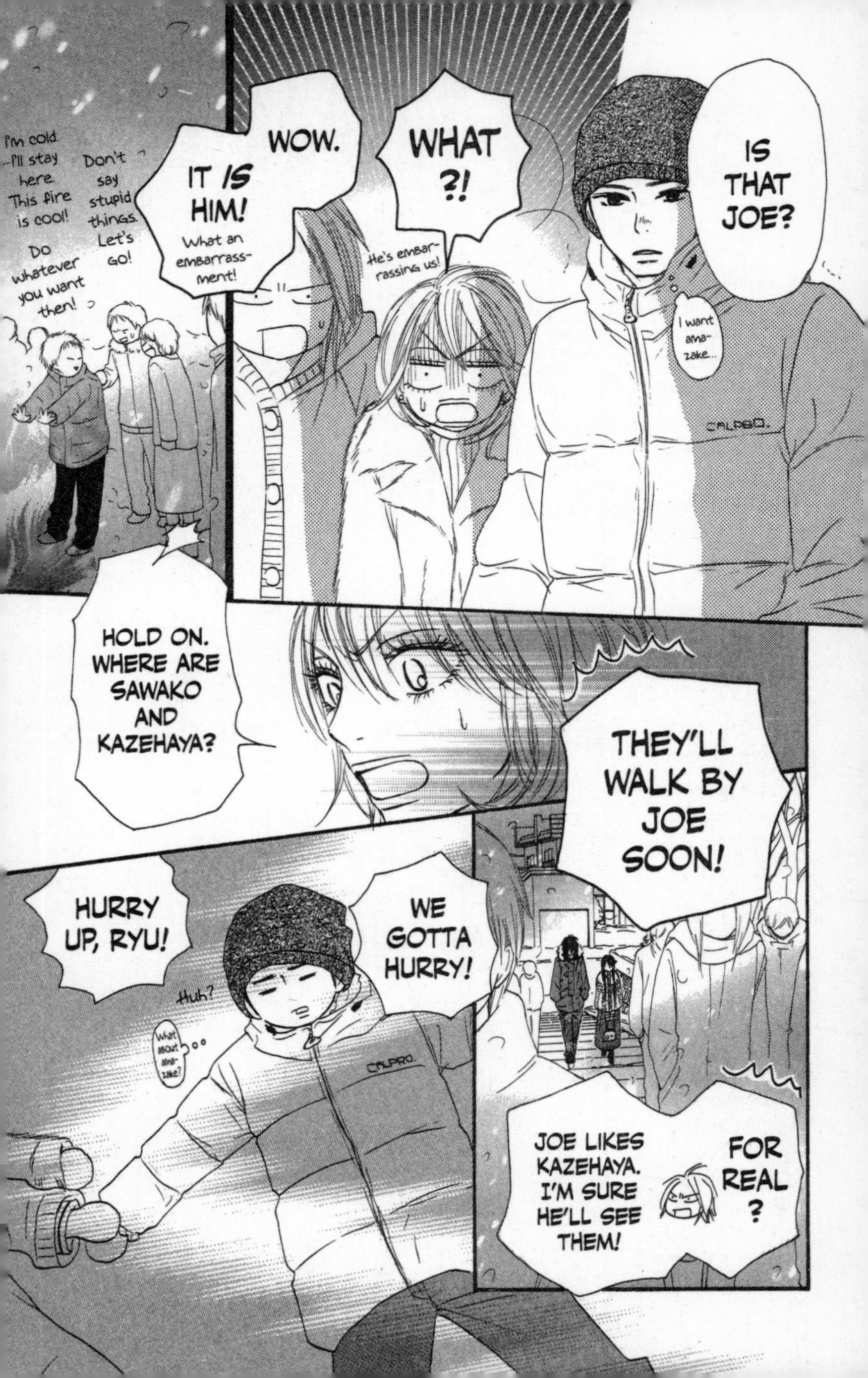
IS THAT JOE?
I want ama-zake...
WHAT?!
He's embarrassing us!
WOW.
IT IS HIM!
What an embarrassment!
I'm cold. I'll stay here. This fire is cool!
Don't say stupid things. Let's go!
Do whatever you want then!
HOLD ON. WHERE ARE SAWAKO AND KAZEHAYA?
THEY'LL WALK BY JOE SOON!
JOE LIKES KAZEHAYA. I'M SURE HE'LL SEE THEM!
FOR REAL?
WE GOTTA HURRY!
HURRY UP, RYU!
Huh?
What about ama-zake?

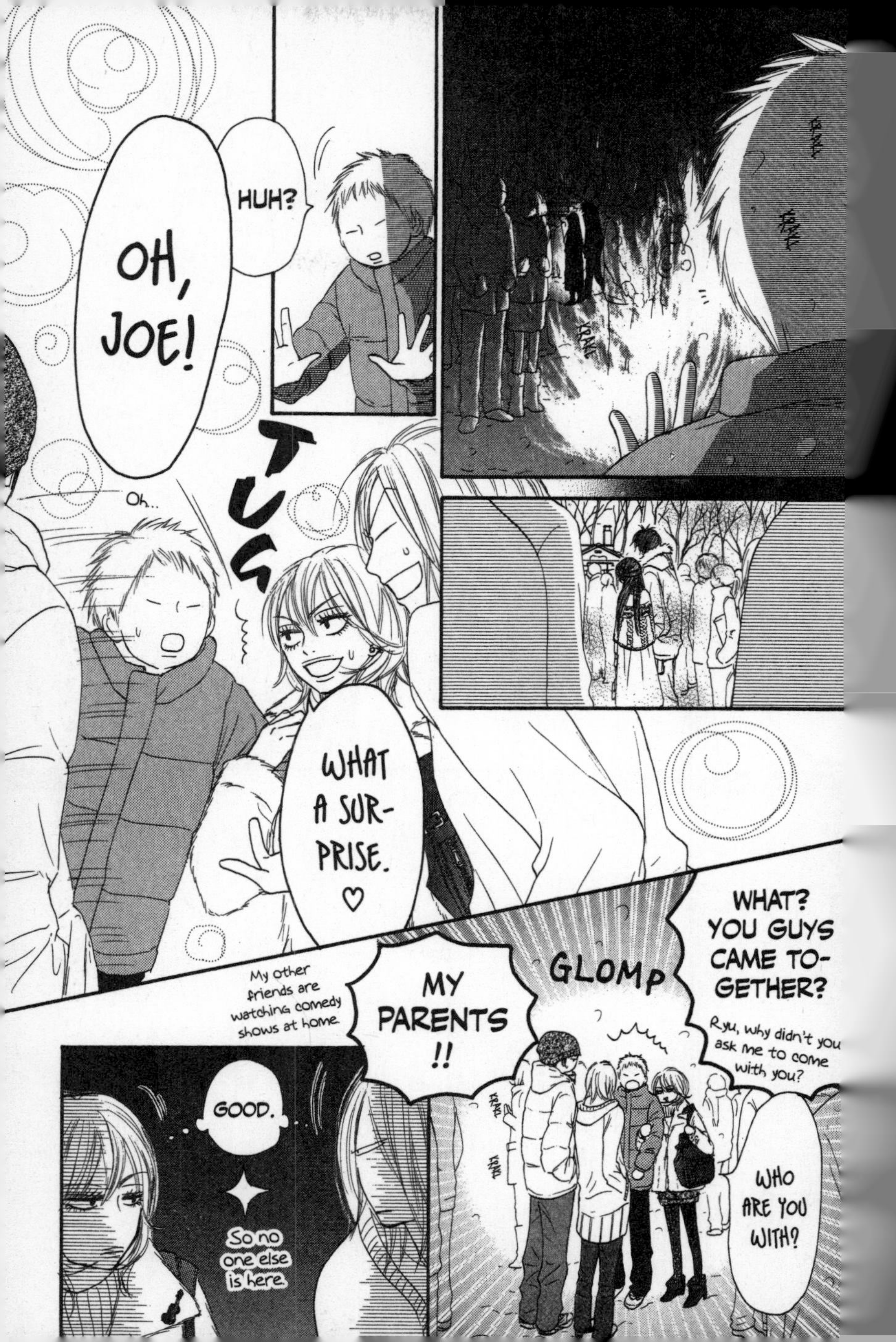
KRAK
KRAK
KRAK
HUH?
OH, JOE!
TUG
Oh..
WHAT A SUR-PRISE. ♡
WHAT? YOU GUYS CAME TO-GETHER?
GLOMP
Ryu, why didn't you ask me to come with you?
WHO ARE YOU WITH?
KRAK
KRAK
MY PARENTS!!
My other friends are watching comedy shows at home.
GOOD.
So no one else is here.

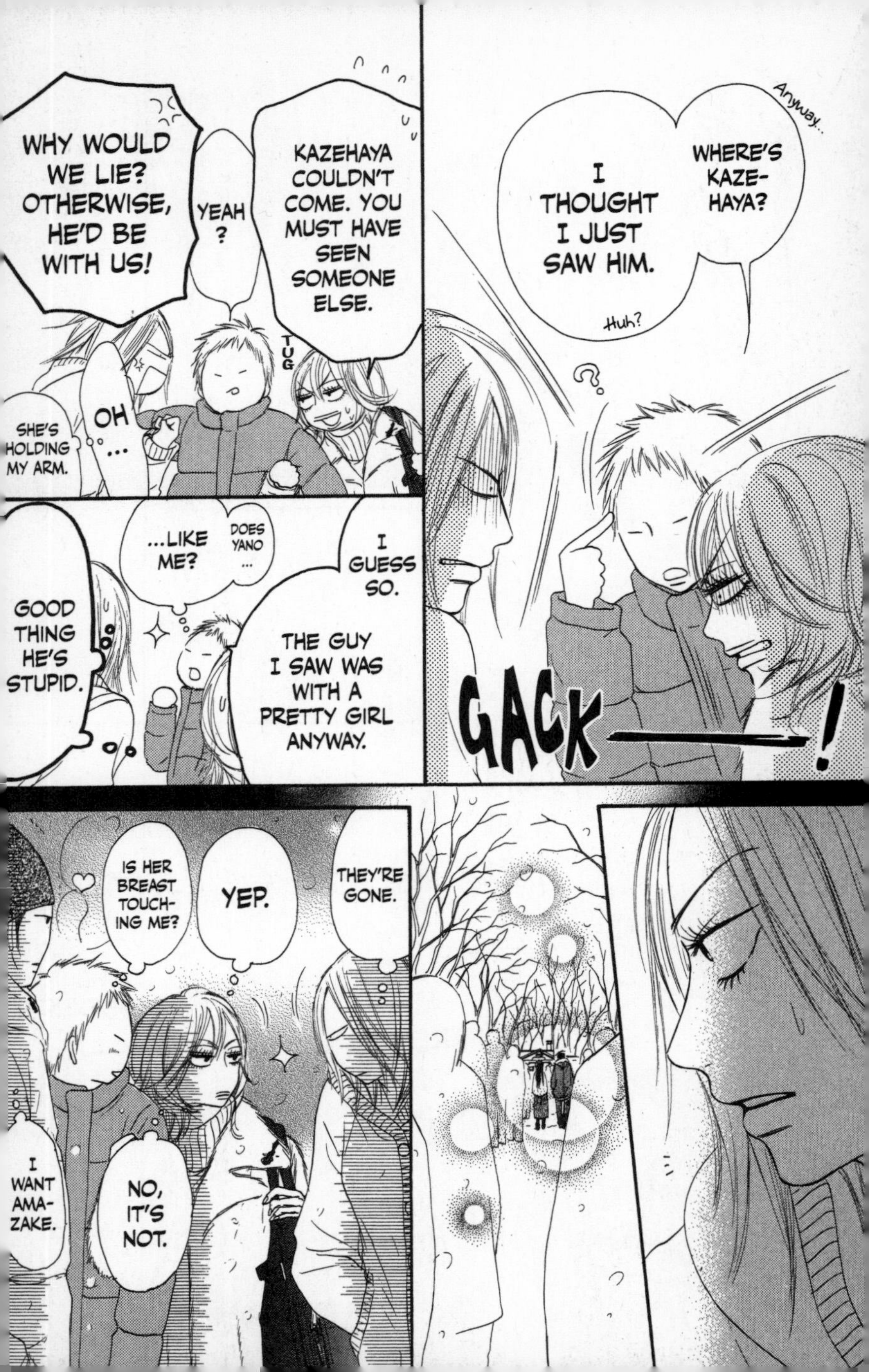
Anyway...
WHERE'S KAZE-HAYA?
I THOUGHT I JUST SAW HIM.
Huh?
GACK—!
KAZEHAYA COULDN'T COME. YOU MUST HAVE SEEN SOMEONE ELSE.
YEAH?
WHY WOULD WE LIE? OTHERWISE, HE'D BE WITH US!
TUG
OH...
SHE'S HOLDING MY ARM.
I GUESS SO.
DOES YANO...
...LIKE ME?
THE GUY I SAW WAS WITH A PRETTY GIRL ANYWAY.
GOOD THING HE'S STUPID.
THEY'RE GONE.
YEP.
IS HER BREAST TOUCHING ME?
NO, IT'S NOT.
I WANT AMA-ZAKE.

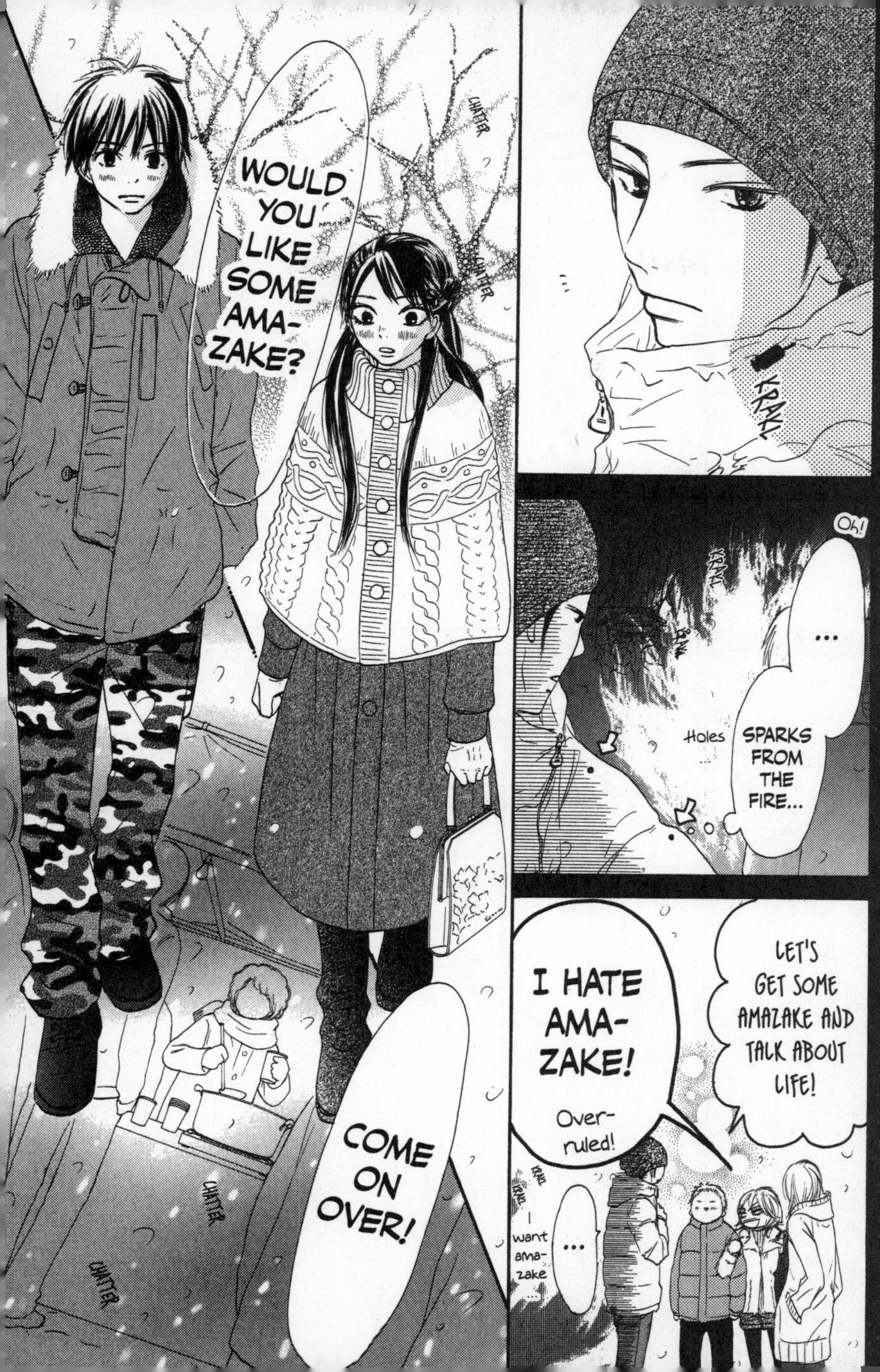
KRAKL
Oh!
KRAKL
...
SPARKS FROM THE FIRE...
Holes ...
LET'S GET SOME AMAZAKE AND TALK ABOUT LIFE!
I HATE AMA-ZAKE!
Over-ruled!
KRAKL
KRAKL
...
I want ama-zake ...
WOULD YOU LIKE SOME AMA-ZAKE?
CHATTER
CHATTER
COME ON OVER!
CHATTER
CHATTER

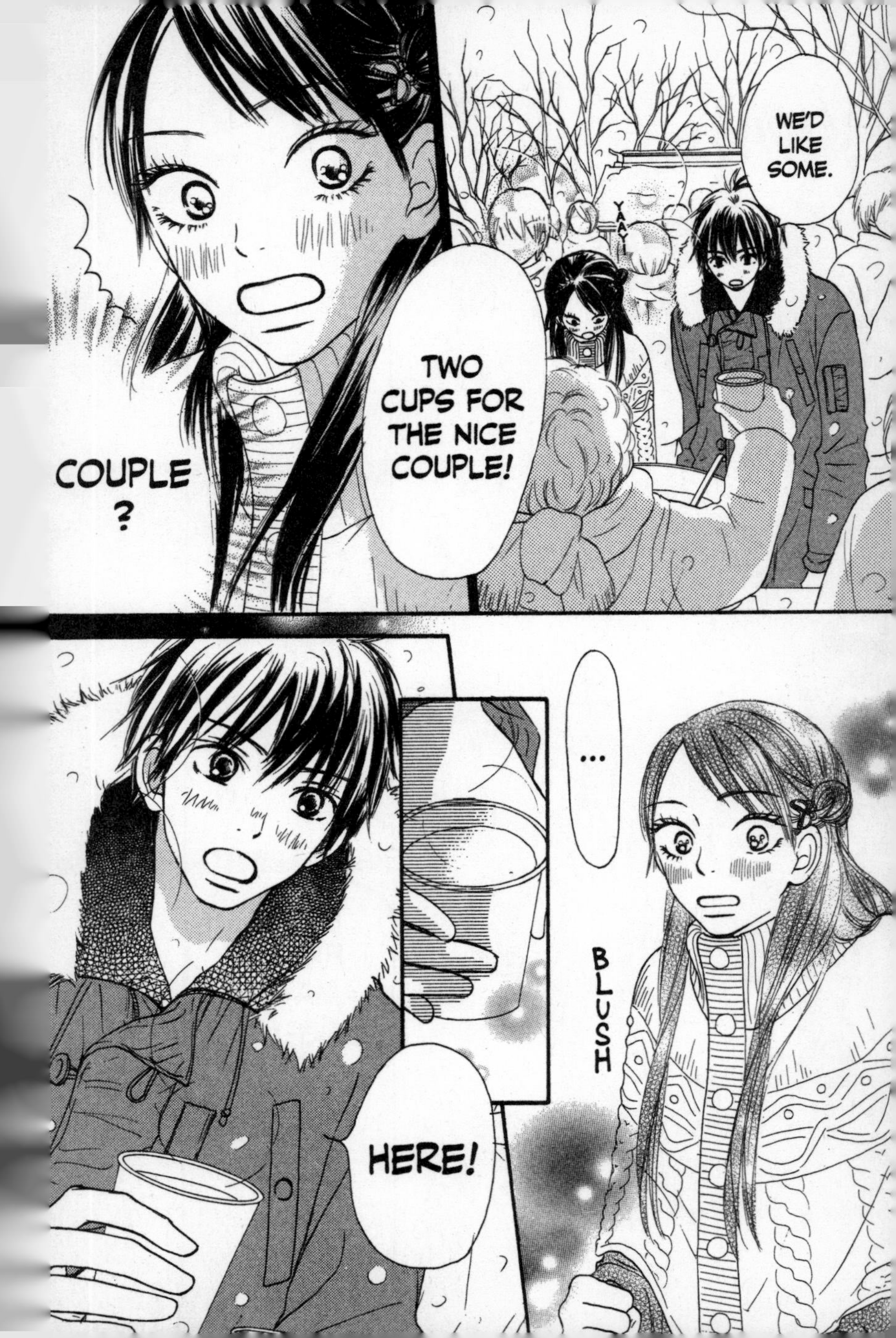
WE'D LIKE SOME.
YAAY
TWO CUPS FOR THE NICE COUPLE!
COUPLE ?
...
BLUSH
HERE!

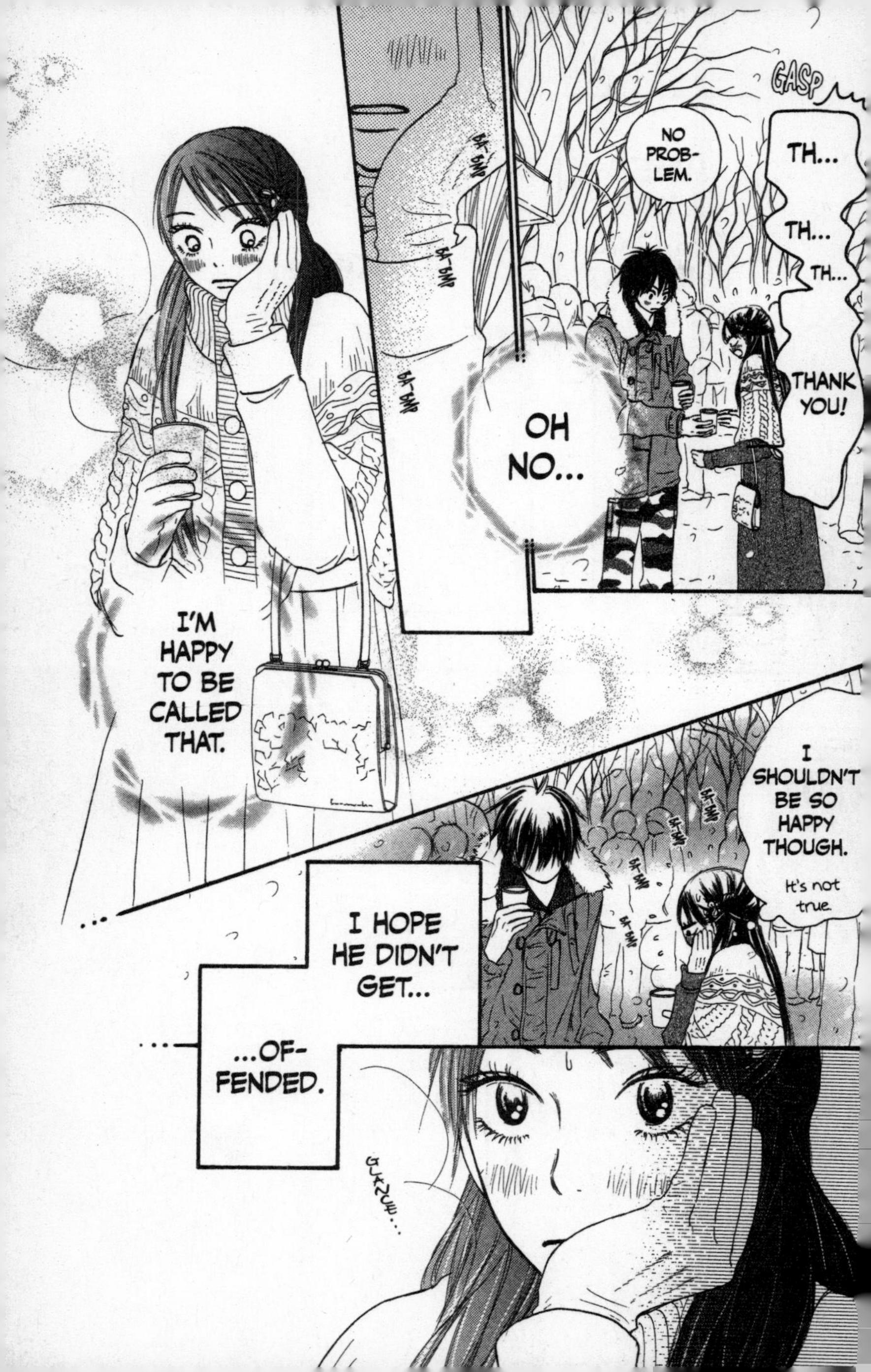
GASP
TH...
TH...
TH...
THANK YOU!
NO PROB-LEM.
OH NO...
BA-BMP
BA-BMP
BA-BMP
I'M HAPPY TO BE CALLED THAT.
I SHOULDN'T BE SO HAPPY THOUGH.
It's not true.
BA-BMP
BA-BMP
BA-BMP
BA-BMP
...
I HOPE HE DIDN'T GET...
...
...OF-FENDED.
GLANCE...

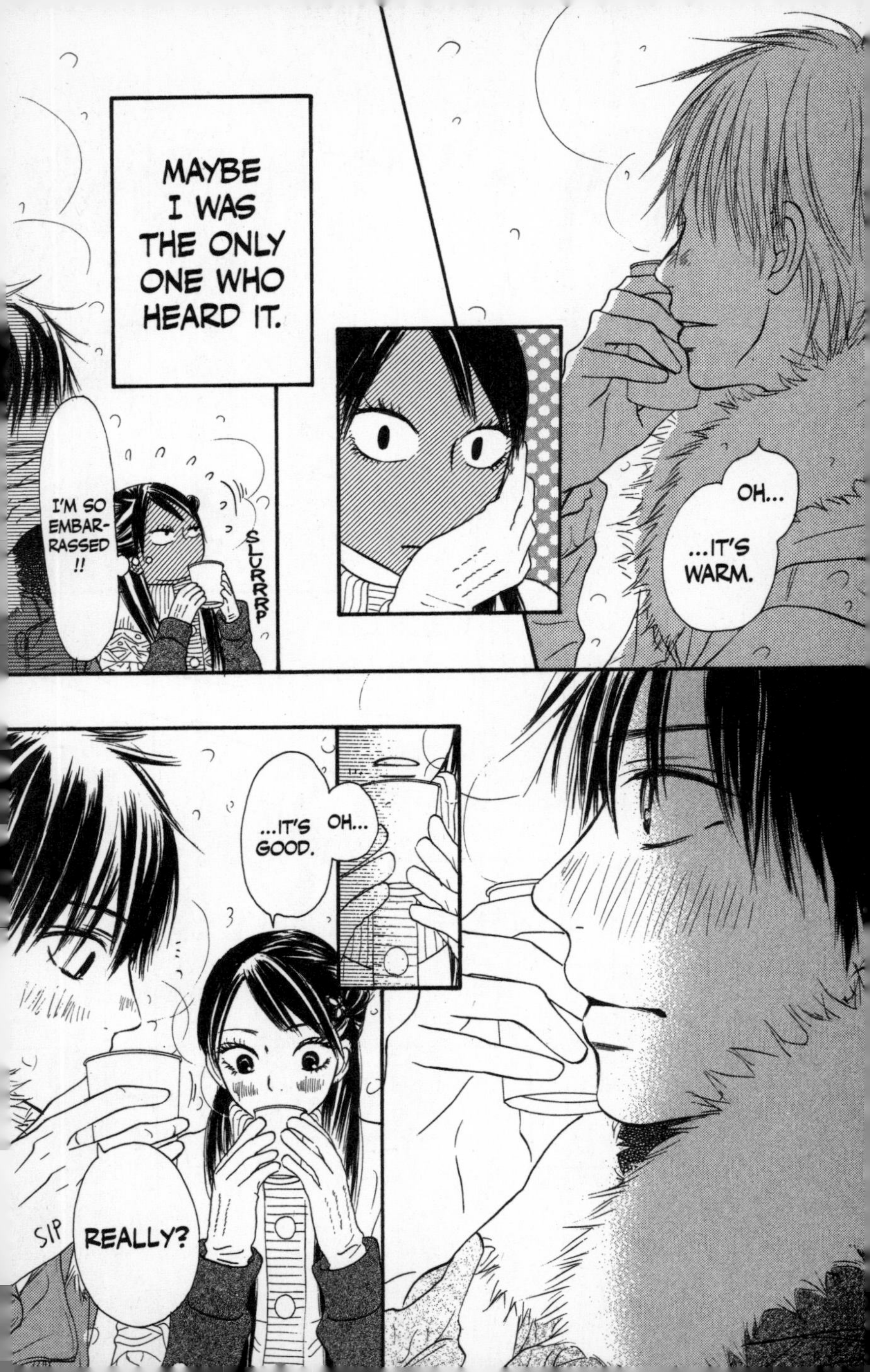
OH...
...IT'S WARM.
MAYBE I WAS THE ONLY ONE WHO HEARD IT.
SLURRRP
I'M SO EMBARRASSED!!
OH...
...IT'S GOOD.
REALLY?
SIP

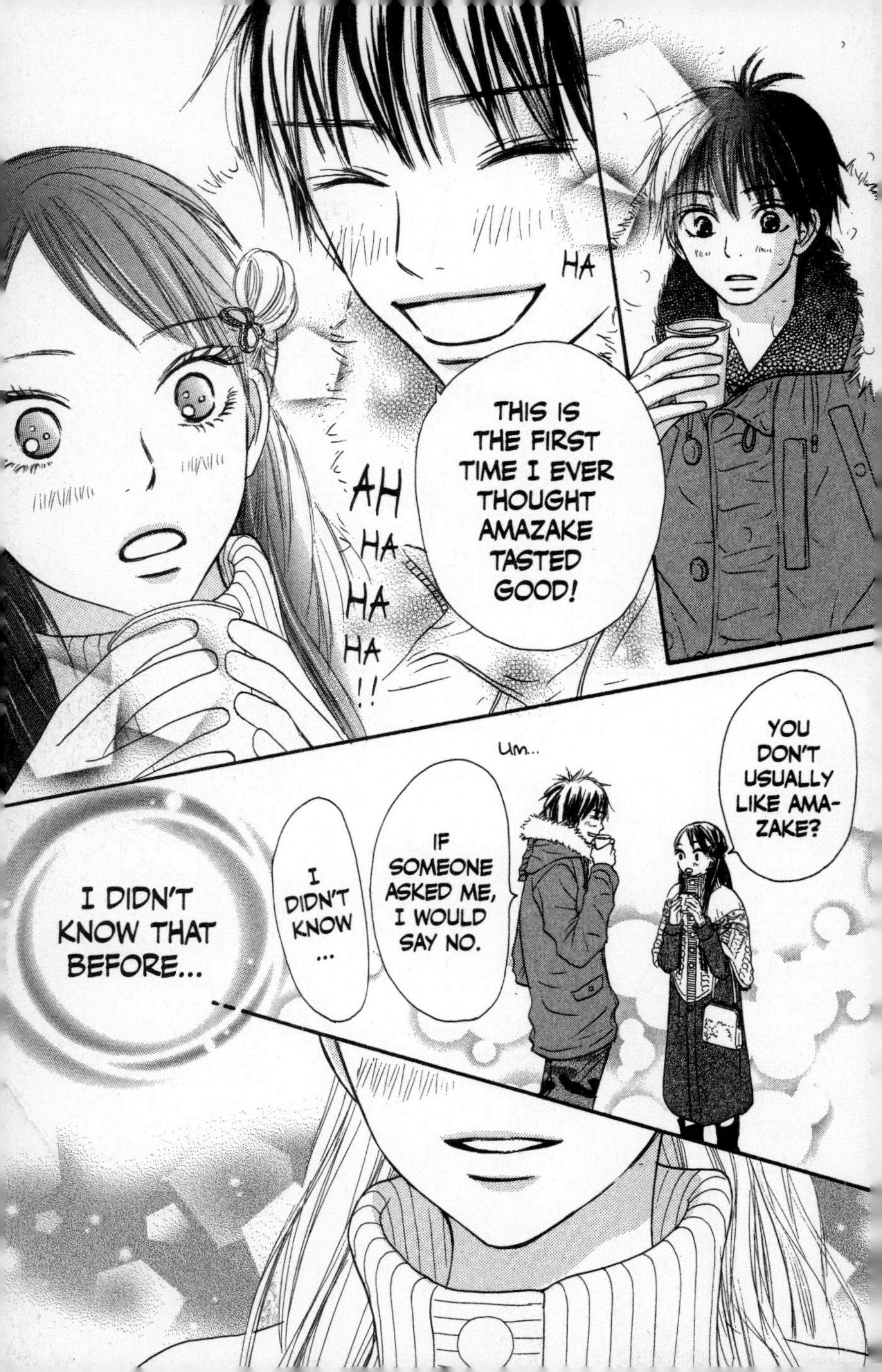
HA
THIS IS THE FIRST TIME I EVER THOUGHT AMAZAKE TASTED GOOD!
AH HA HA HA !!
YOU DON'T USUALLY LIKE AMA-ZAKE?
Um...
IF SOMEONE ASKED ME, I WOULD SAY NO.
I DIDN'T KNOW ...
I DIDN'T KNOW THAT BEFORE...

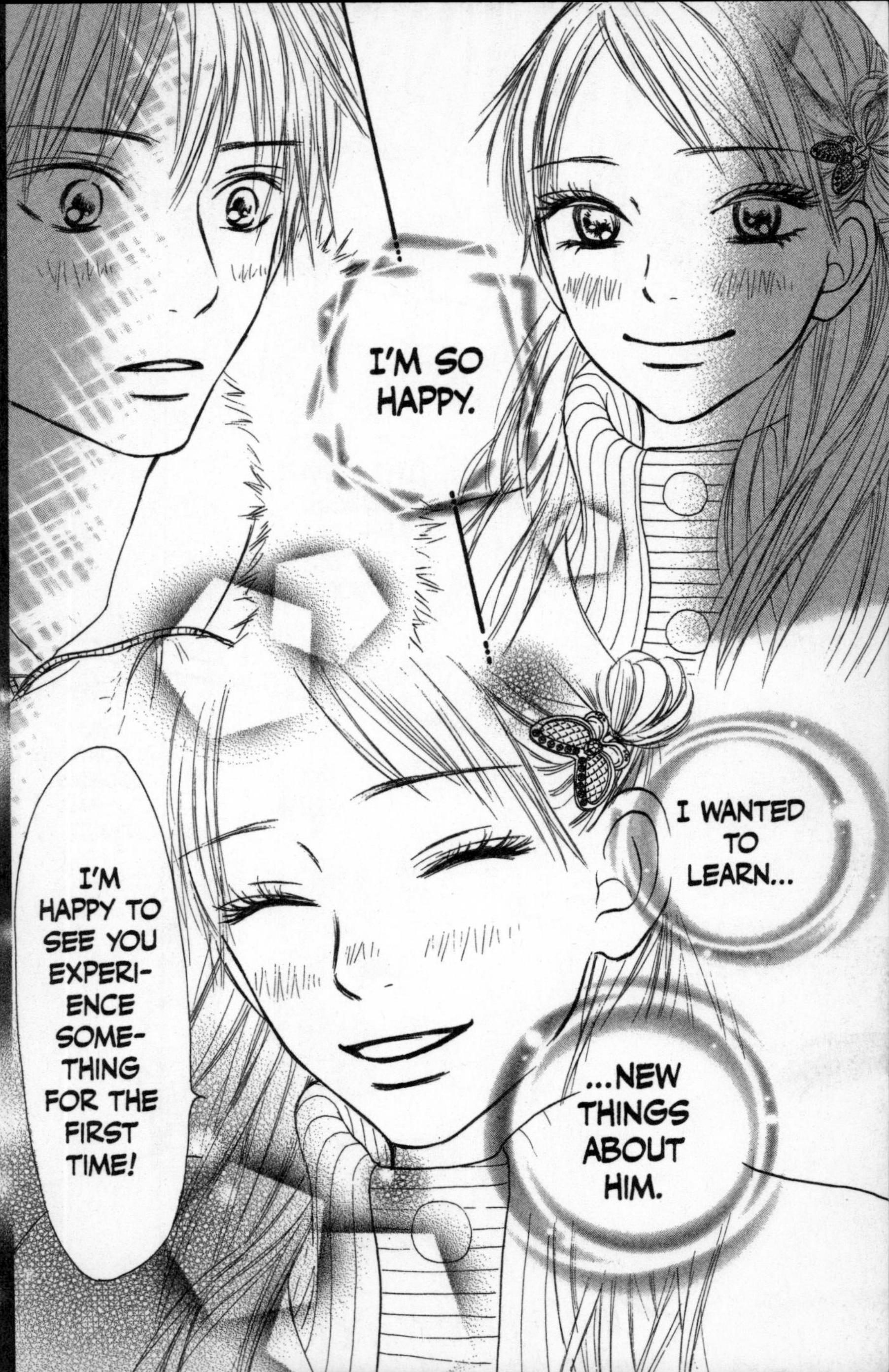
I'M SO HAPPY.
I WANTED TO LEARN...
...NEW THINGS ABOUT HIM.
I'M HAPPY TO SEE YOU EXPERIENCE SOMETHING FOR THE FIRST TIME!

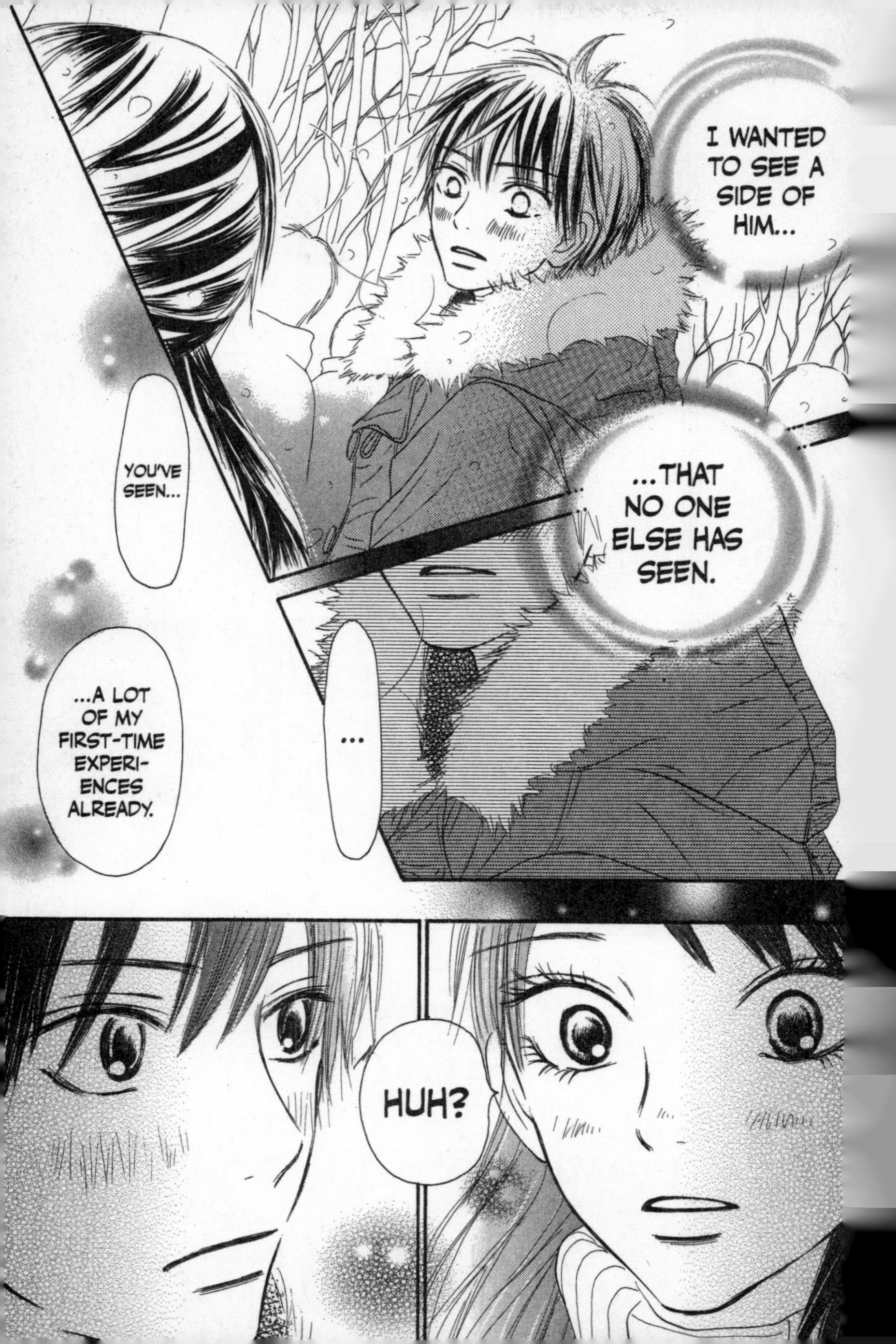
I WANTED TO SEE A SIDE OF HIM...
YOU'VE SEEN...
...THAT NO ONE ELSE HAS SEEN.
...
...A LOT OF MY FIRST-TIME EXPERI-ENCES ALREADY.
HUH?

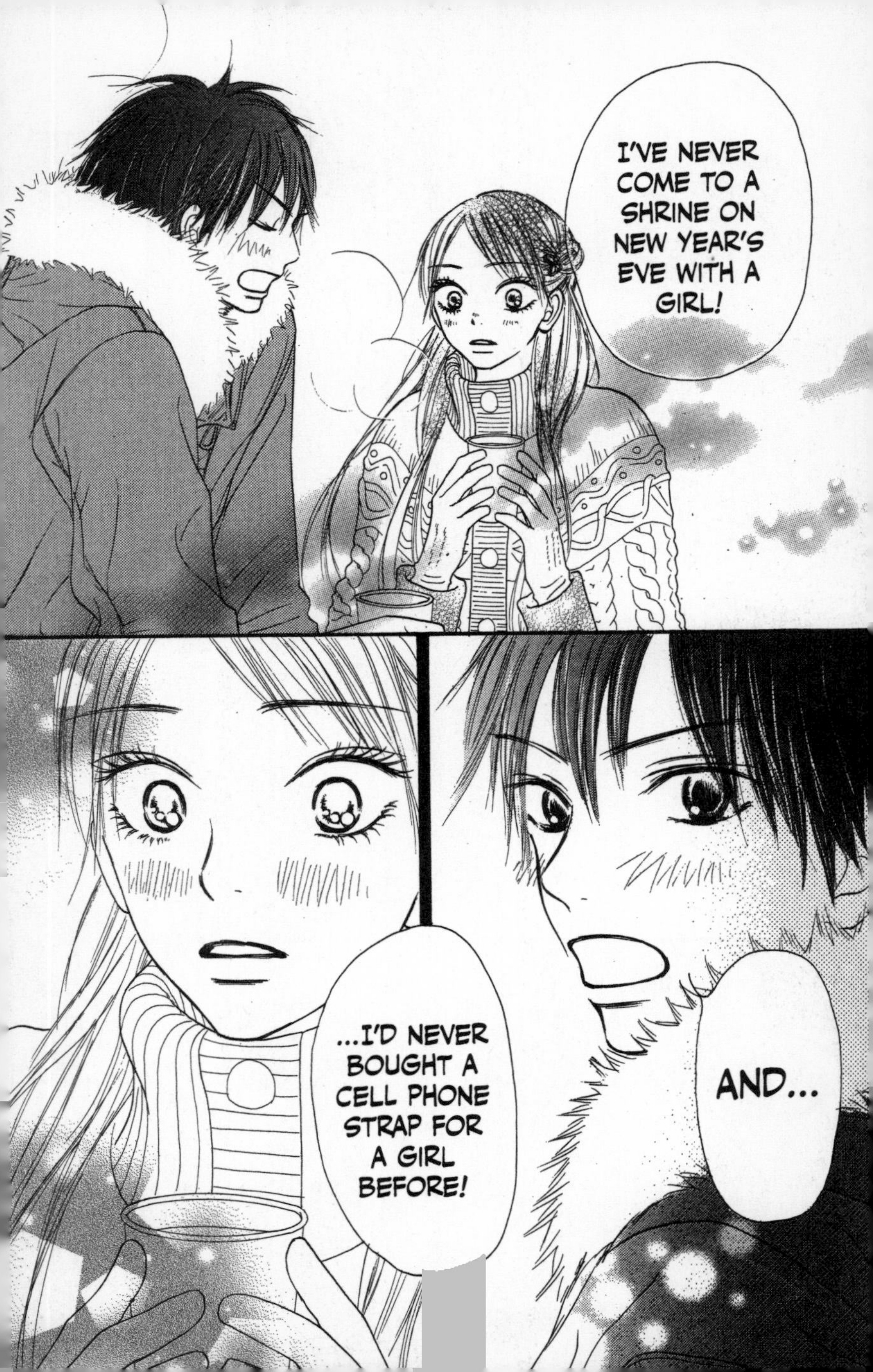
I'VE NEVER COME TO A SHRINE ON NEW YEAR'S EVE WITH A GIRL!
AND...
...I'D NEVER BOUGHT A CELL PHONE STRAP FOR A GIRL BEFORE!

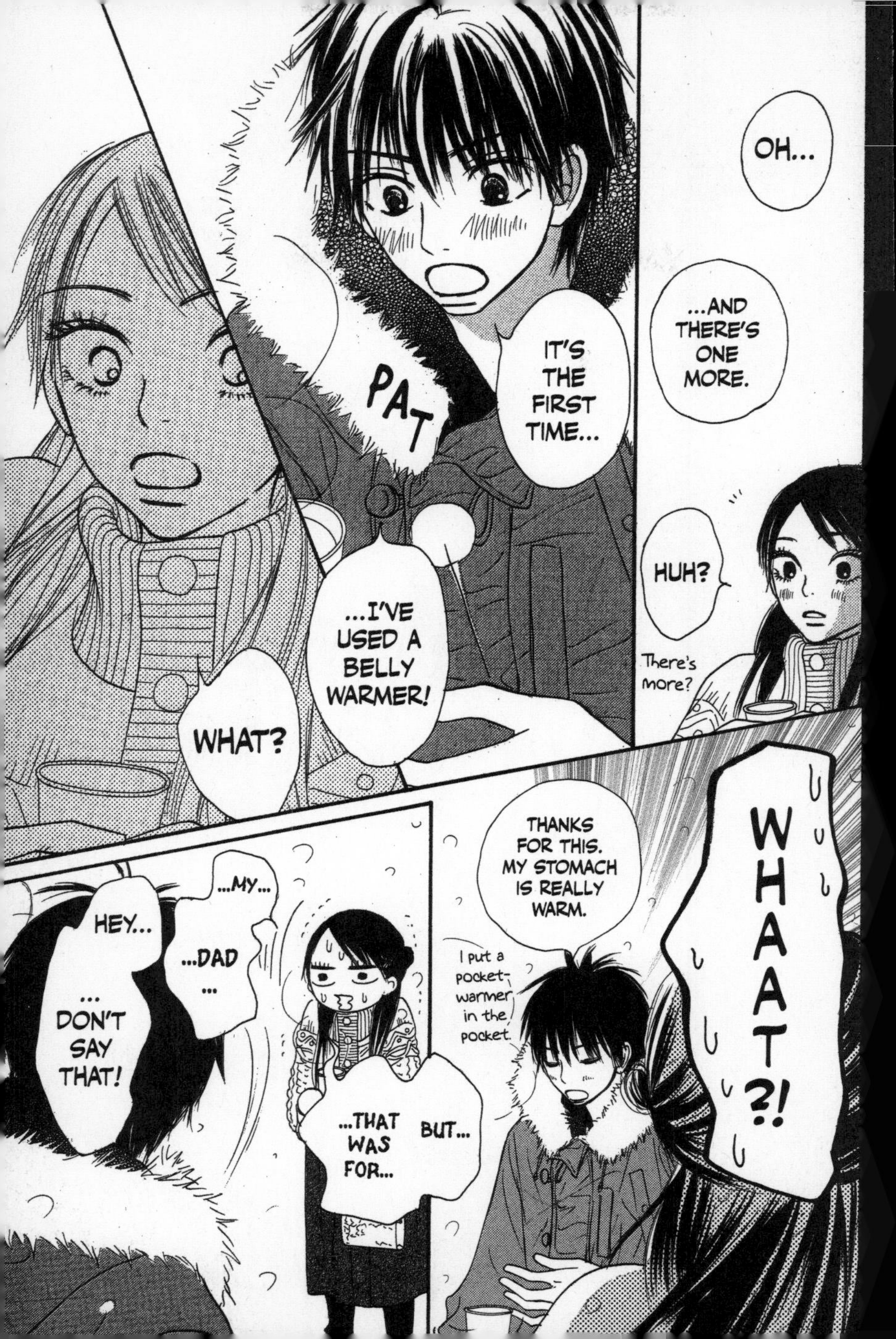
OH...
...AND THERE'S ONE MORE.
HUH?
There's more?
IT'S THE FIRST TIME...
PAT
...I'VE USED A BELLY WARMER!
WHAT?
WHAT?!
THANKS FOR THIS. MY STOMACH IS REALLY WARM.
I put a pocket-warmer in the pocket.
BUT...
...THAT WAS FOR...
...MY...
...DAD...
HEY...
...DON'T SAY THAT!

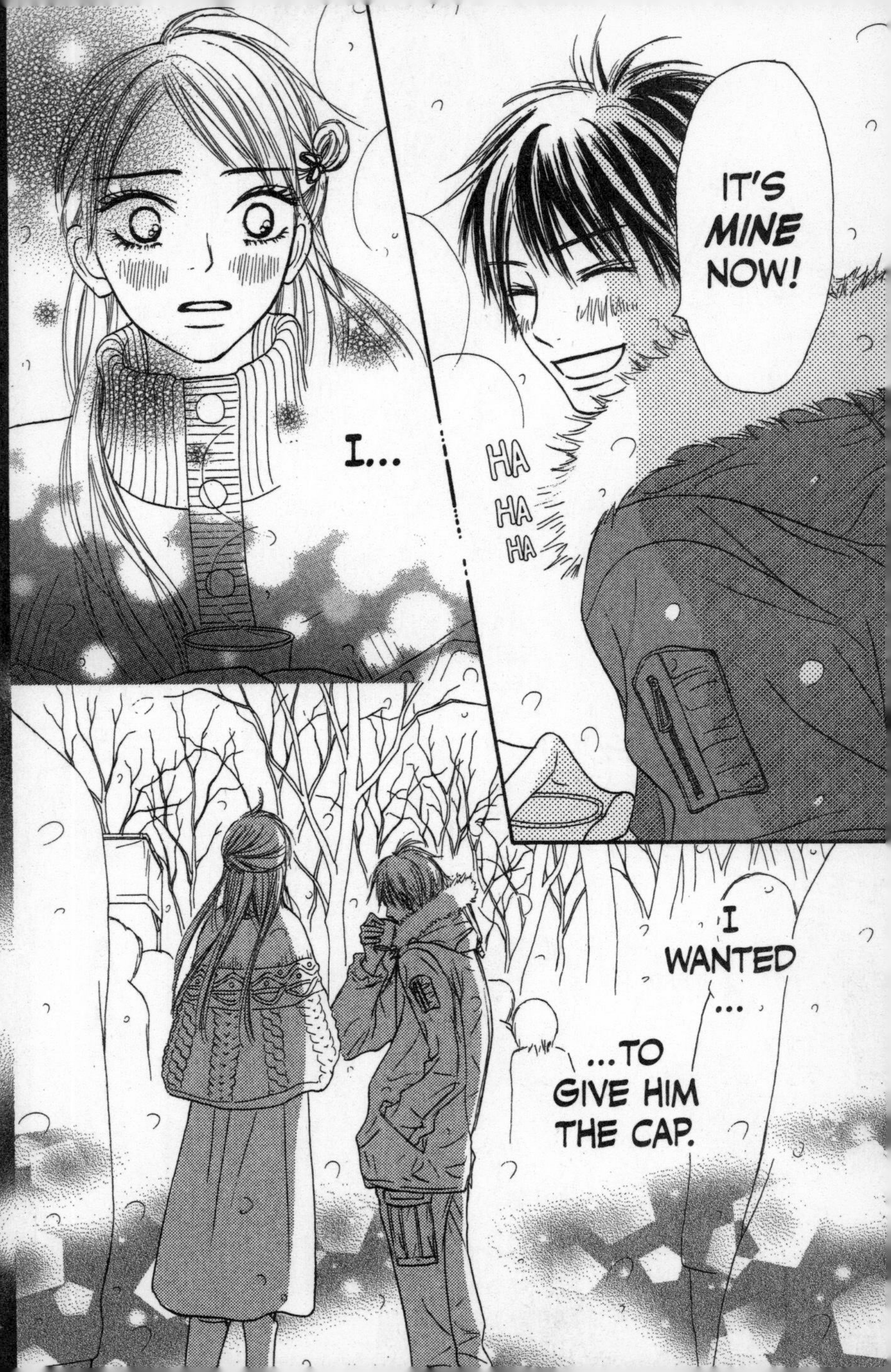
IT'S *MINE* NOW!
HA HA HA
I...
I WANTED ...
...TO GIVE HIM THE CAP.

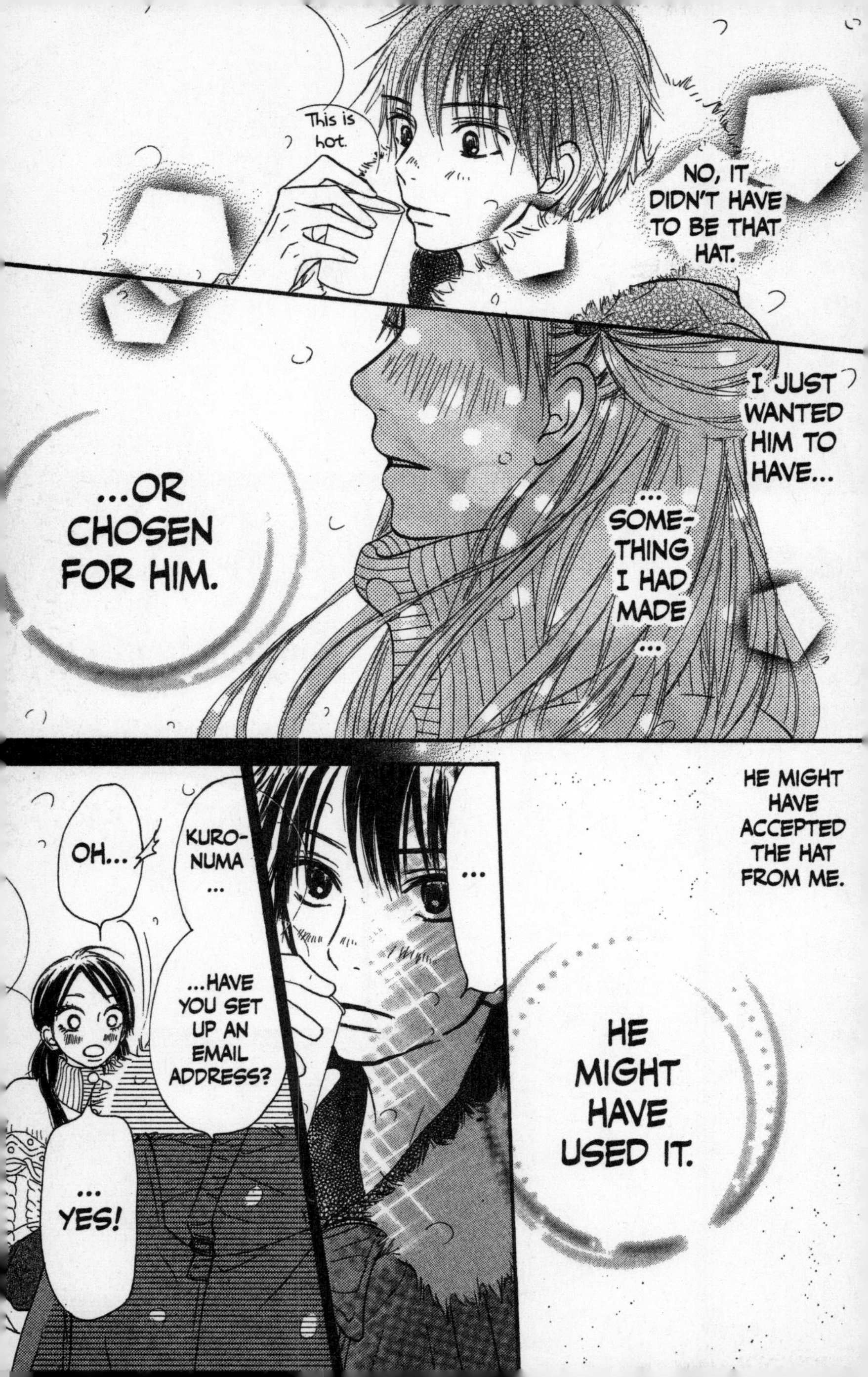
This is hot.
NO, IT DIDN'T HAVE TO BE THAT HAT.
I JUST WANTED HIM TO HAVE...
...SOMETHING I HAD MADE...
...OR CHOSEN FOR HIM.
HE MIGHT HAVE ACCEPTED THE HAT FROM ME.
...
HE MIGHT HAVE USED IT.
KURONUMA...
OH...
...HAVE YOU SET UP AN EMAIL ADDRESS?
...YES!

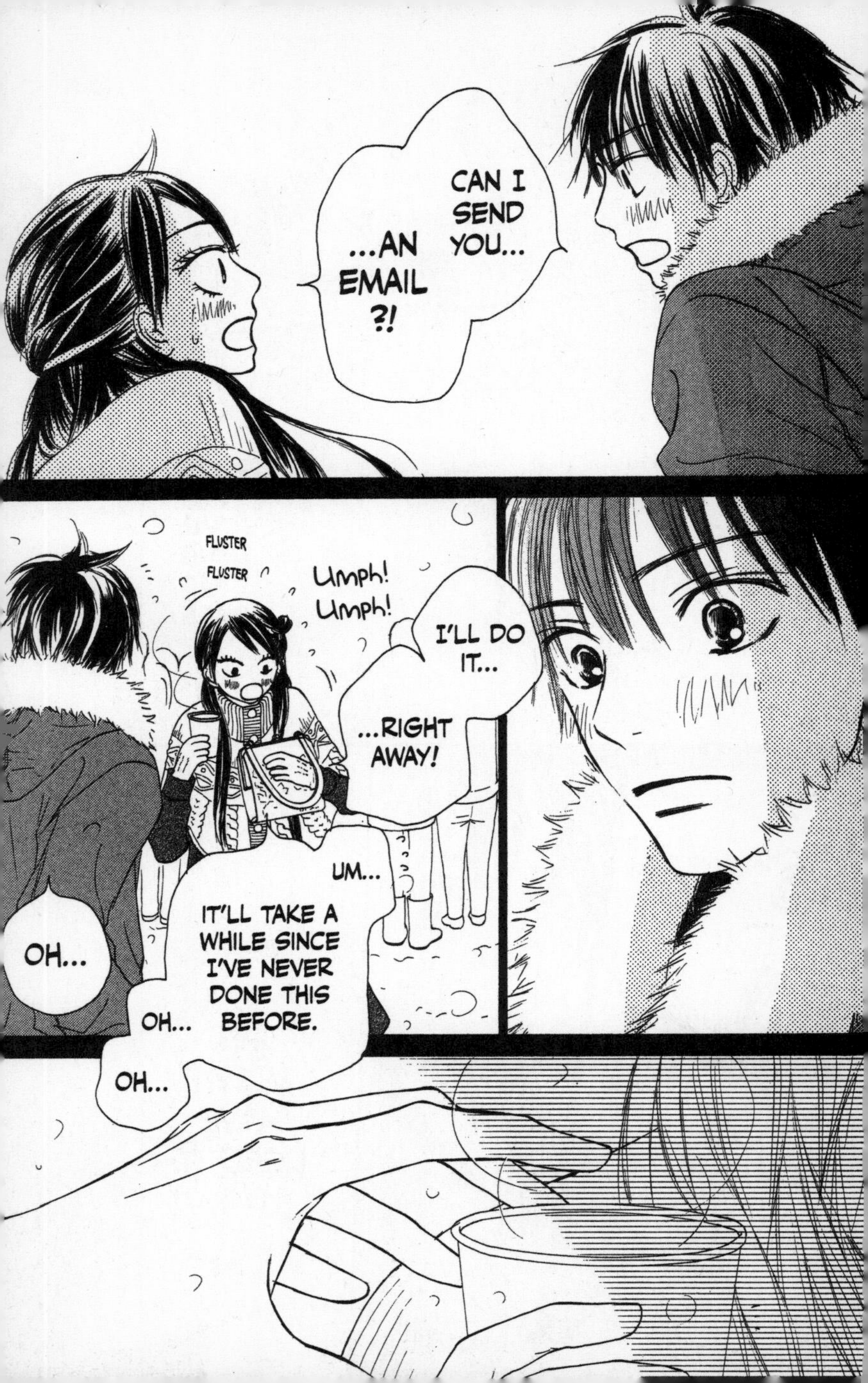
CAN I SEND YOU... ...AN EMAIL?!
I'LL DO IT... ...RIGHT AWAY!
Umph! Umph!
FLUSTER FLUSTER
UM... IT'LL TAKE A WHILE SINCE I'VE NEVER DONE THIS BEFORE.
OH...
OH...
OH...

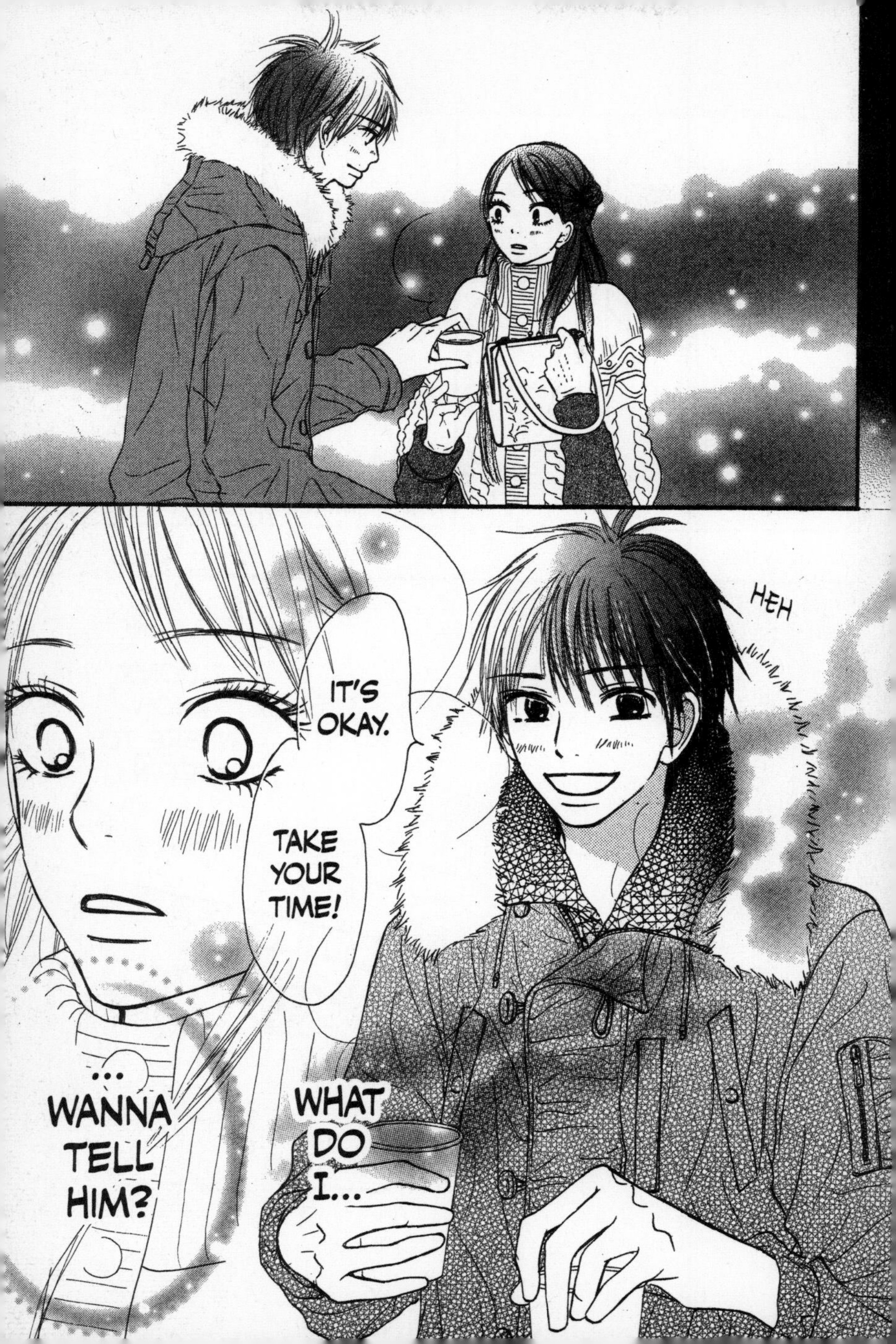
HEH
IT'S OKAY.
TAKE YOUR TIME!
WHAT DO I...
...WANNA TELL HIM?

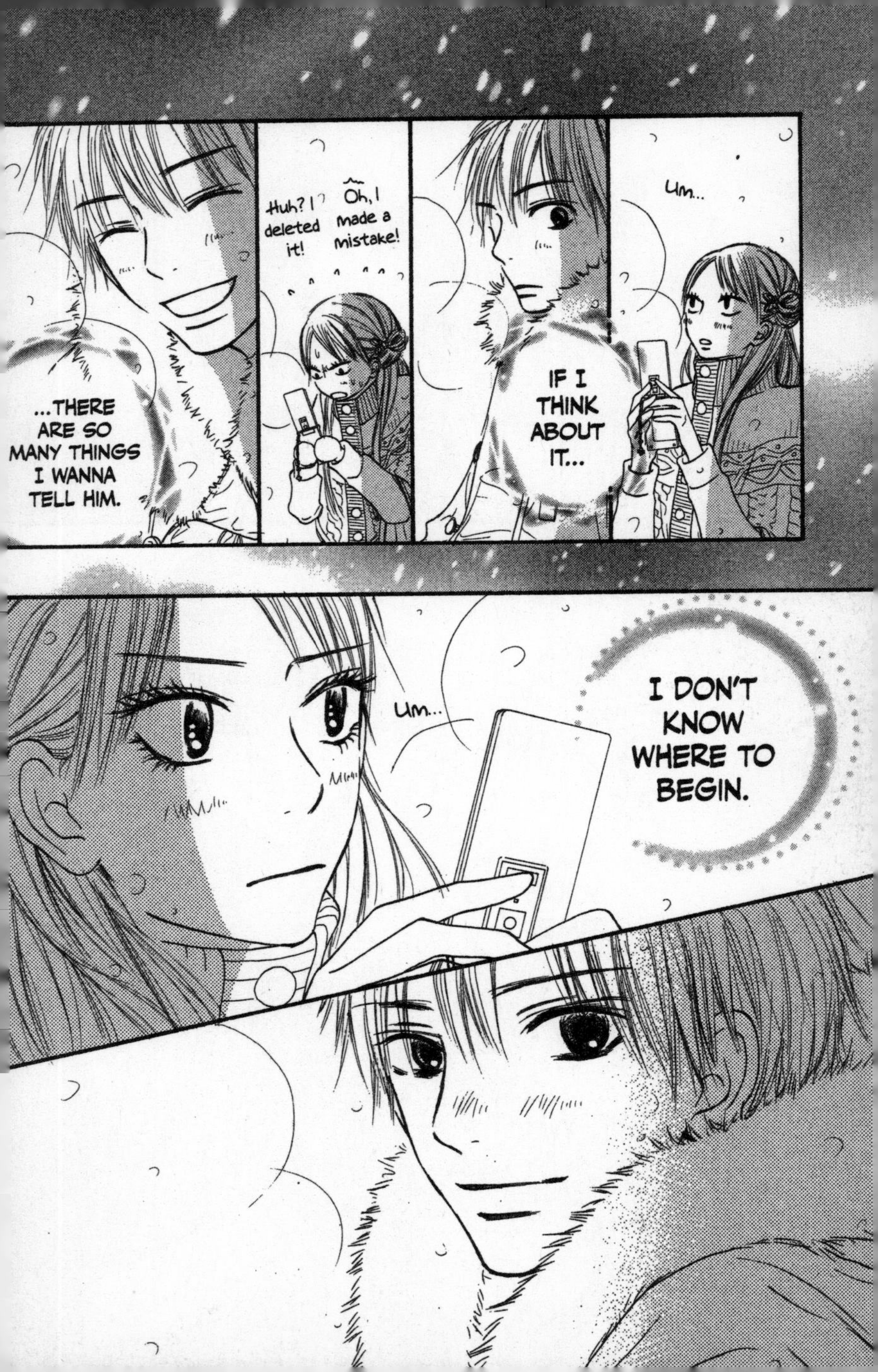
Um...
IF I THINK ABOUT IT...
Oh, I made a mistake!
Huh?! I deleted it!
...THERE ARE SO MANY THINGS I WANNA TELL HIM.
I DON'T KNOW WHERE TO BEGIN.
Um...

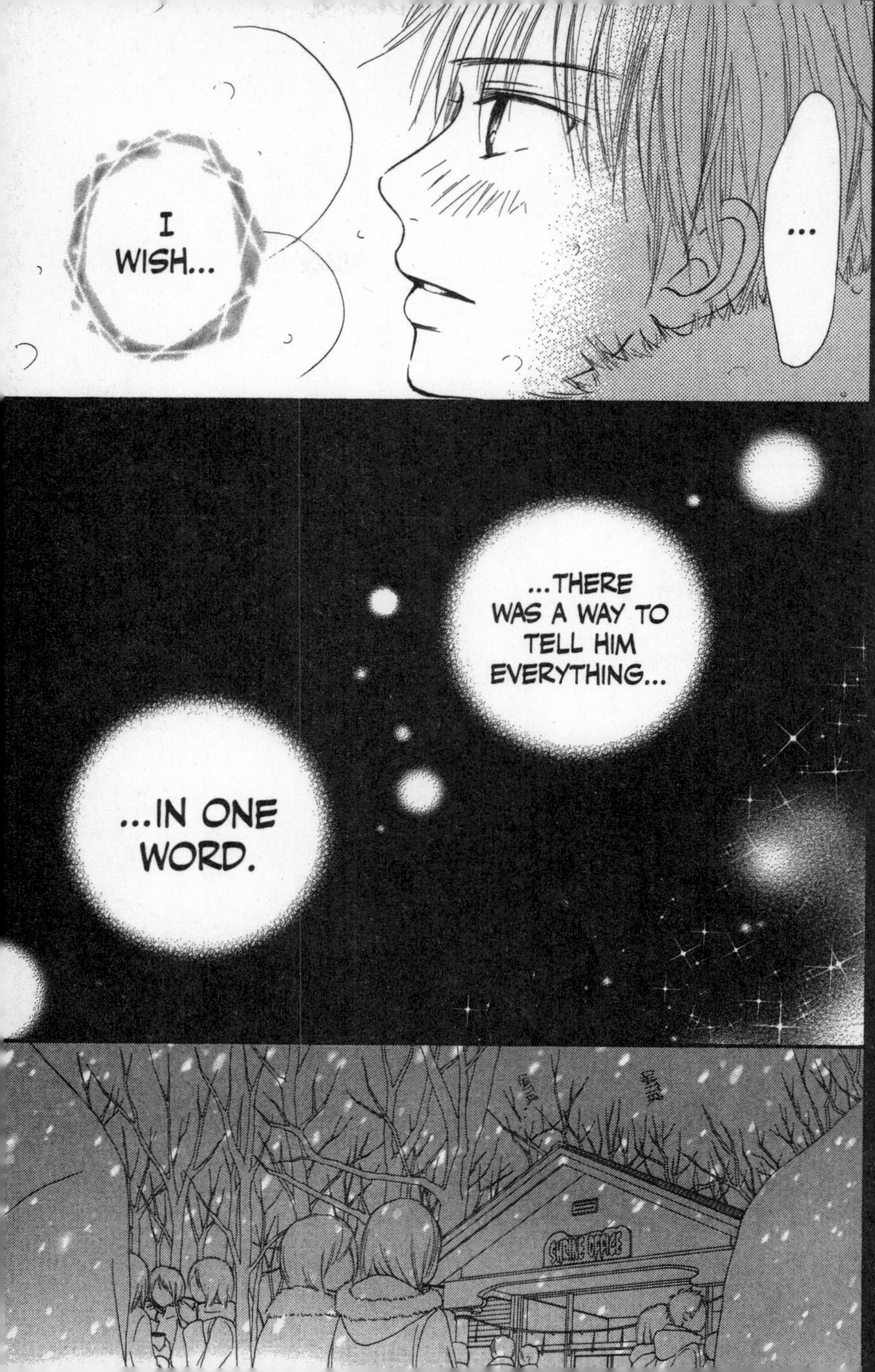
...
I WISH...
...THERE WAS A WAY TO TELL HIM EVERYTHING...
...IN ONE WORD.

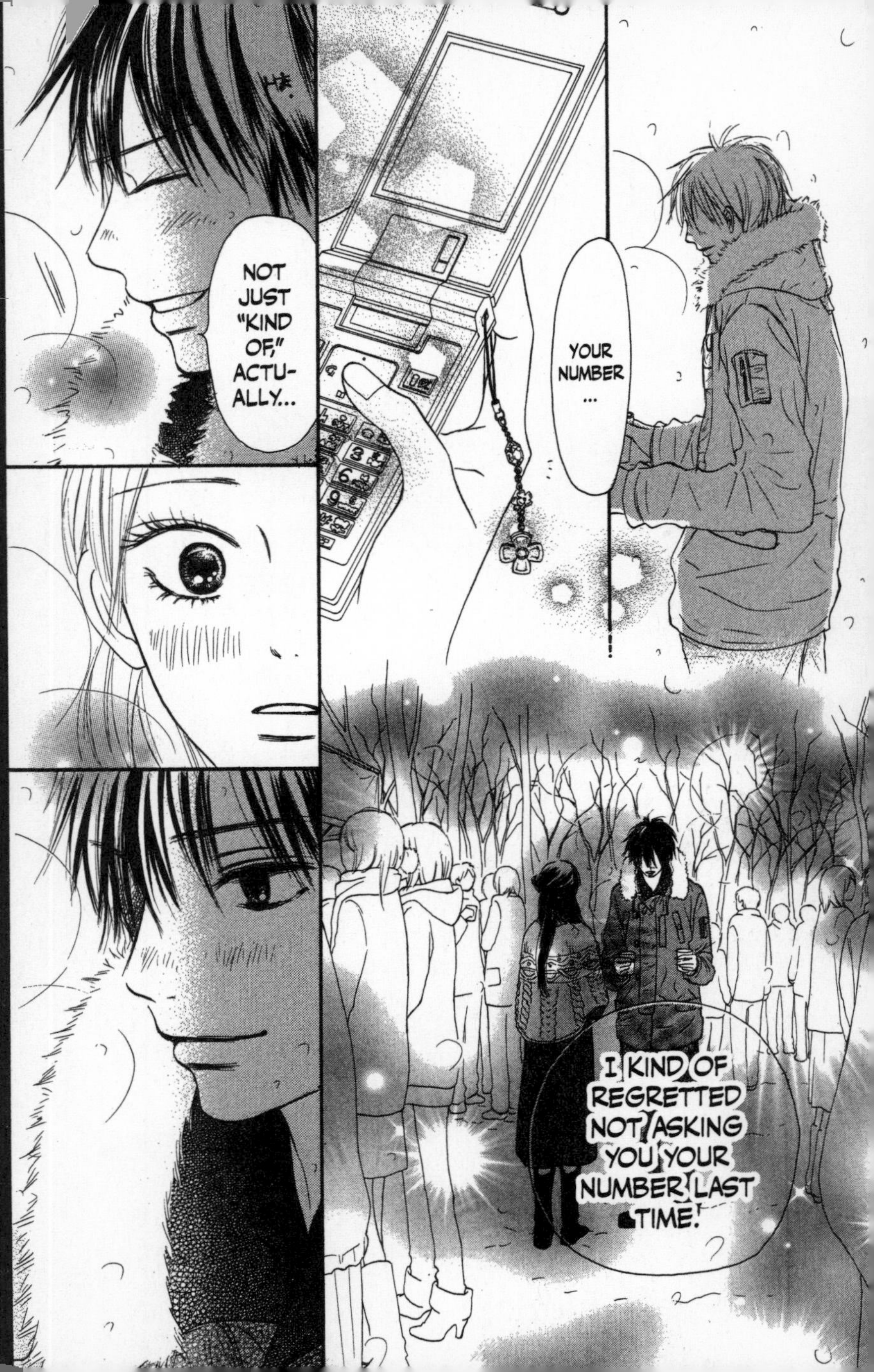
YOUR NUMBER ...
I KIND OF REGRETTED NOT ASKING YOU YOUR NUMBER LAST TIME.
NOT JUST "KIND OF," ACTU-ALLY...

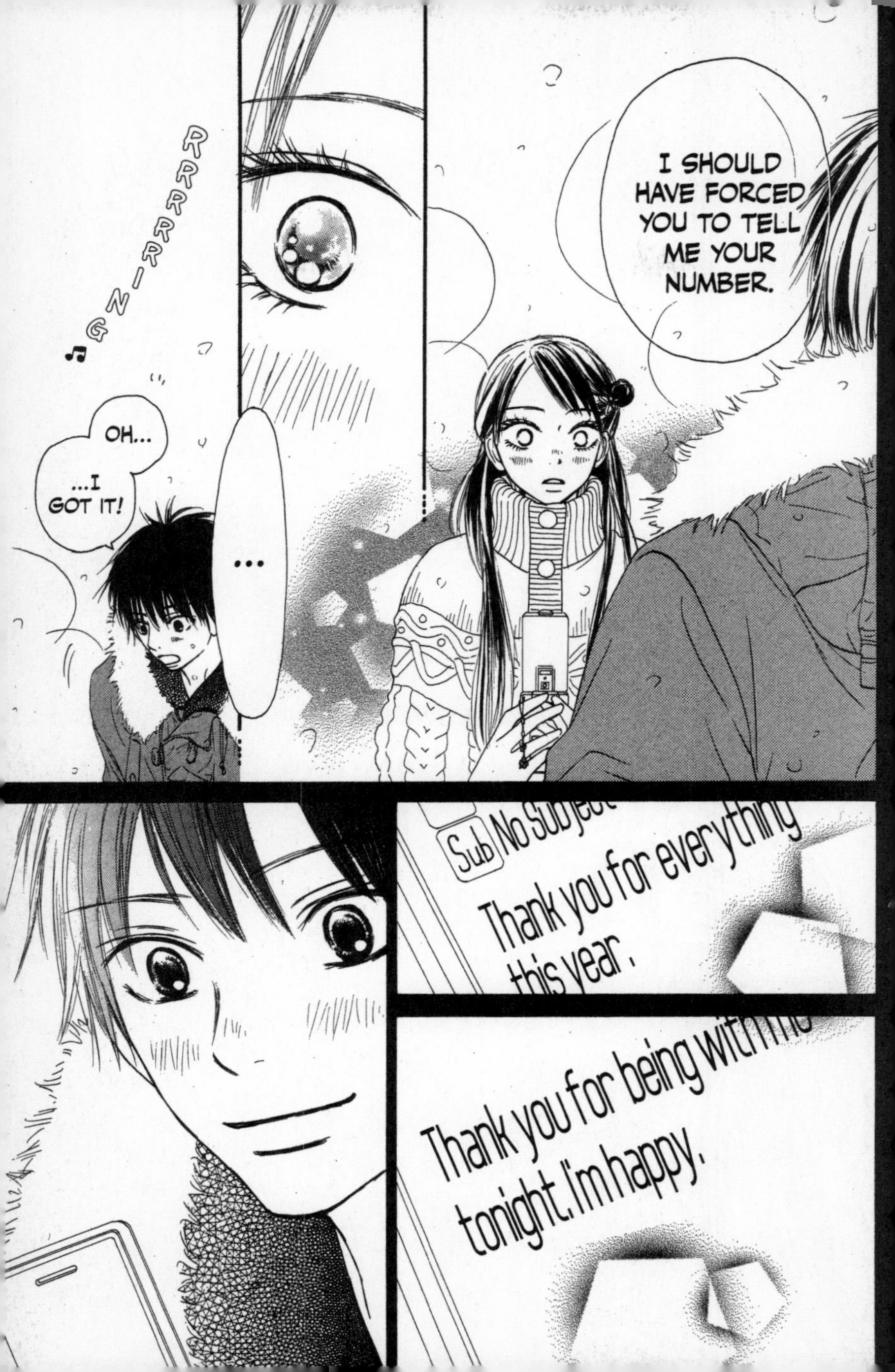
I SHOULD HAVE FORCED YOU TO TELL ME YOUR NUMBER.
...
RRRRRING ♫
OH...
...I GOT IT!
Sub No Subje
Thank you for everything this year.
Thank you for being with
tonight. I'm happy.

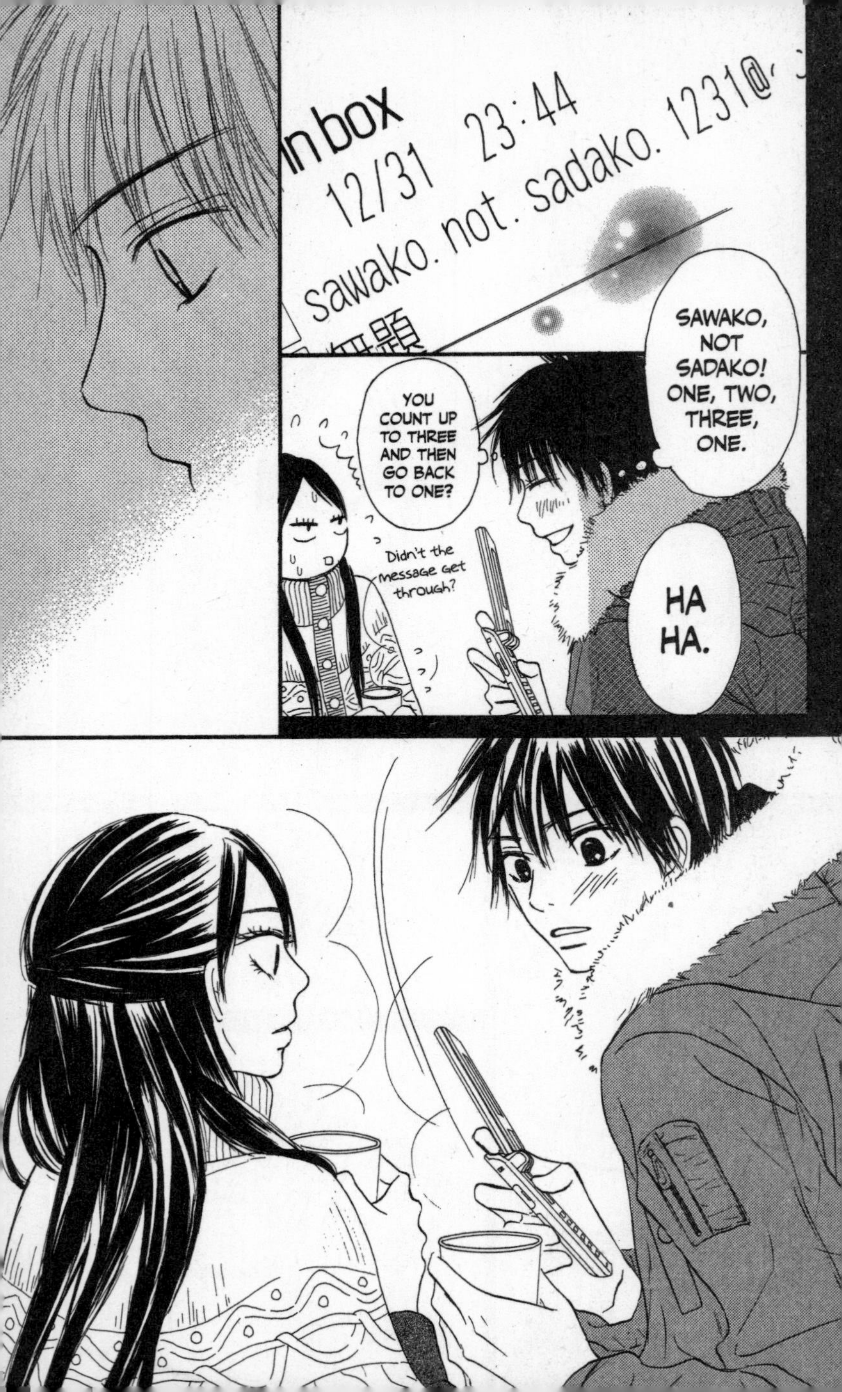
n box
12/31 23:44
sawako. not. sadako. 1231@
SAWAKO, NOT SADAKO! ONE, TWO, THREE, ONE.
HA HA.
YOU COUNT UP TO THREE AND THEN GO BACK TO ONE?
Didn't the message get through?

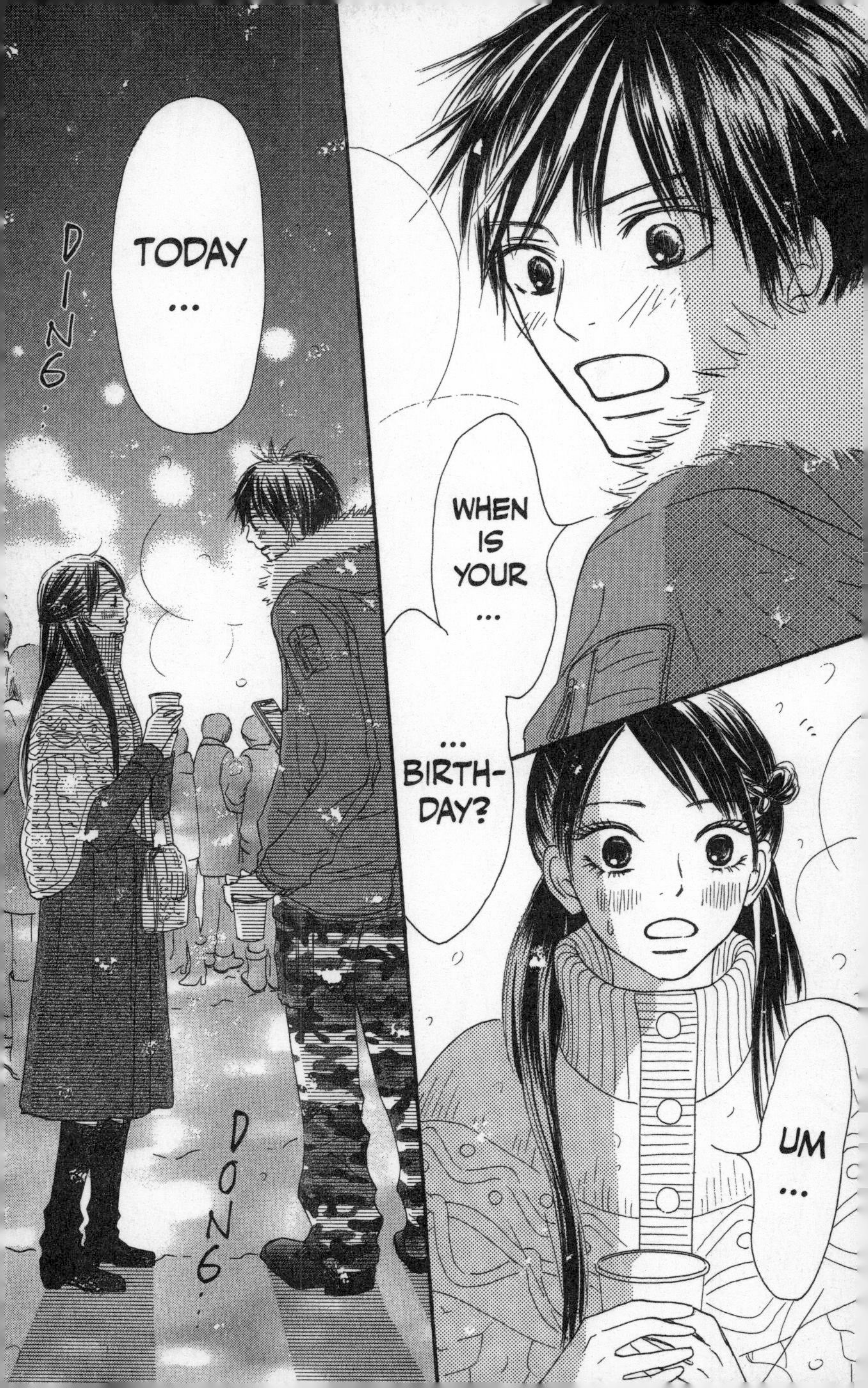
WHEN IS YOUR ...
... BIRTH-DAY?
UM ...
TODAY ...
DING...
DONG...

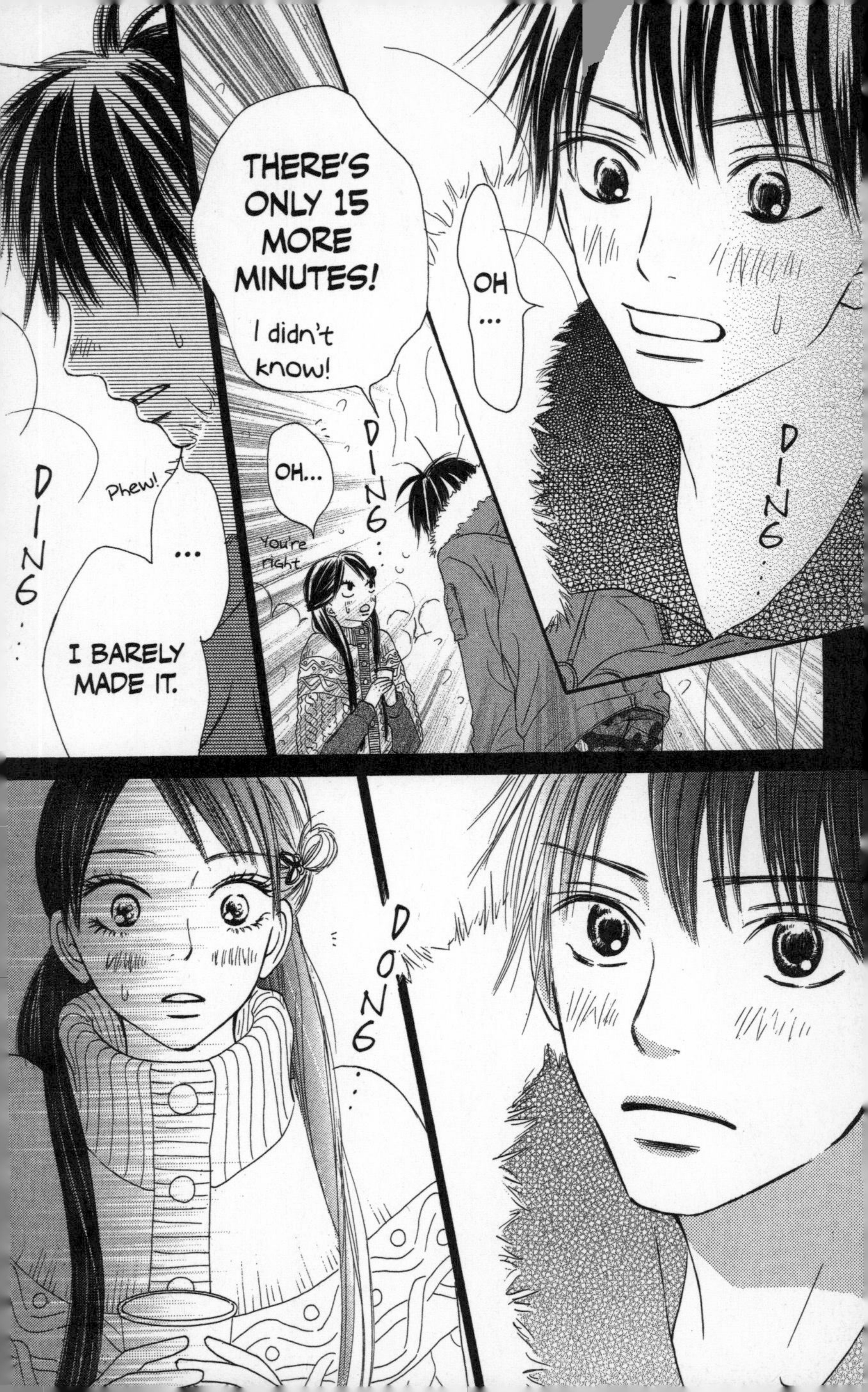
OH ...
DING...
THERE'S ONLY 15 MORE MINUTES!
I didn't know!
OH...
You're right
DING...
Phew!
...
I BARELY MADE IT.
DING...
DONG...

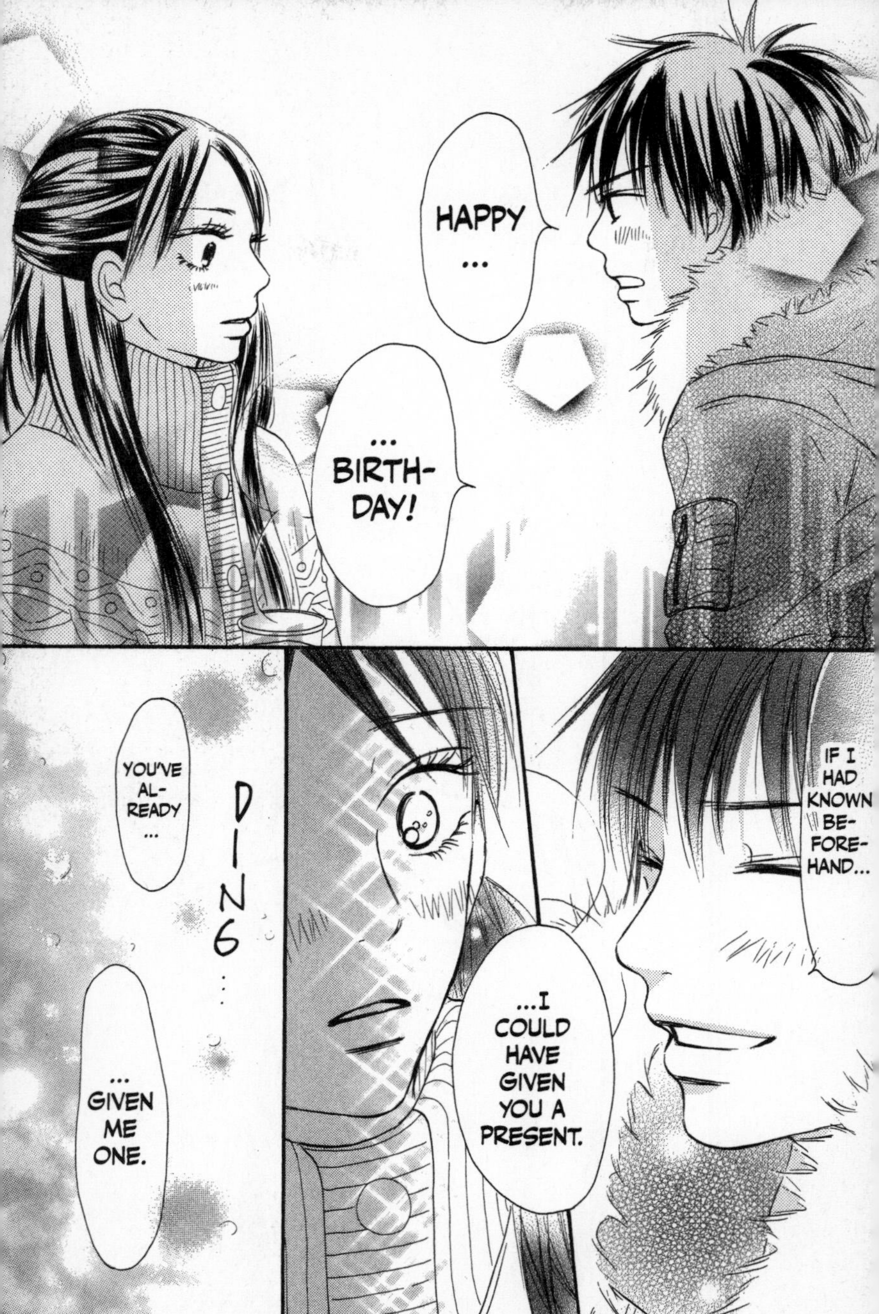
HAPPY ...
... BIRTH-DAY!
IF I HAD KNOWN BE-FORE-HAND...
...I COULD HAVE GIVEN YOU A PRESENT.
YOU'VE AL-READY ...
DING ...
... GIVEN ME ONE.

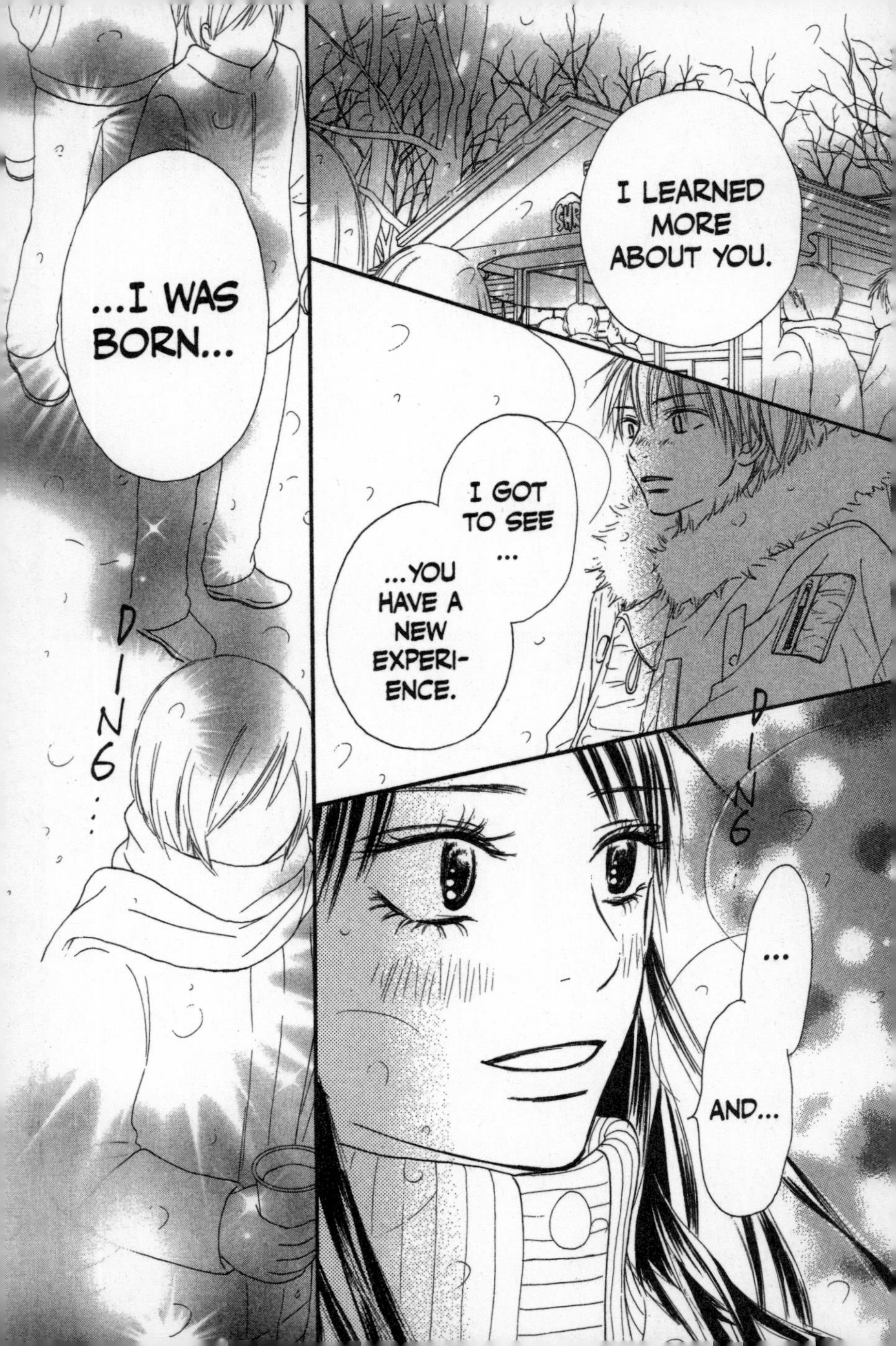
I LEARNED MORE ABOUT YOU.
I GOT TO SEE ...
...YOU HAVE A NEW EXPERI-ENCE.
DING...
...
AND...
...I WAS BORN...
DING...

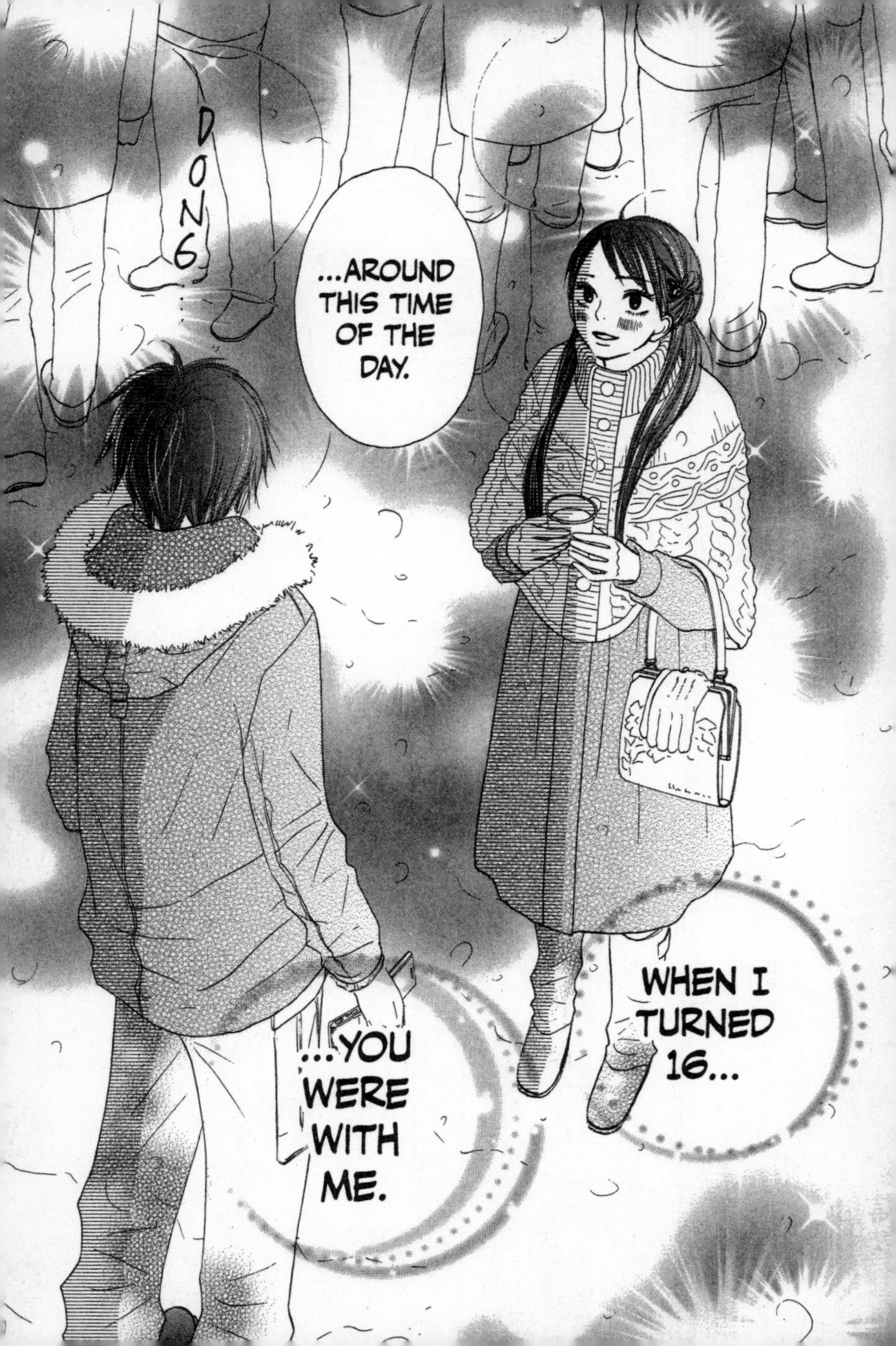
...AROUND THIS TIME OF THE DAY.
DONG
WHEN I TURNED 16...
...YOU WERE WITH ME.

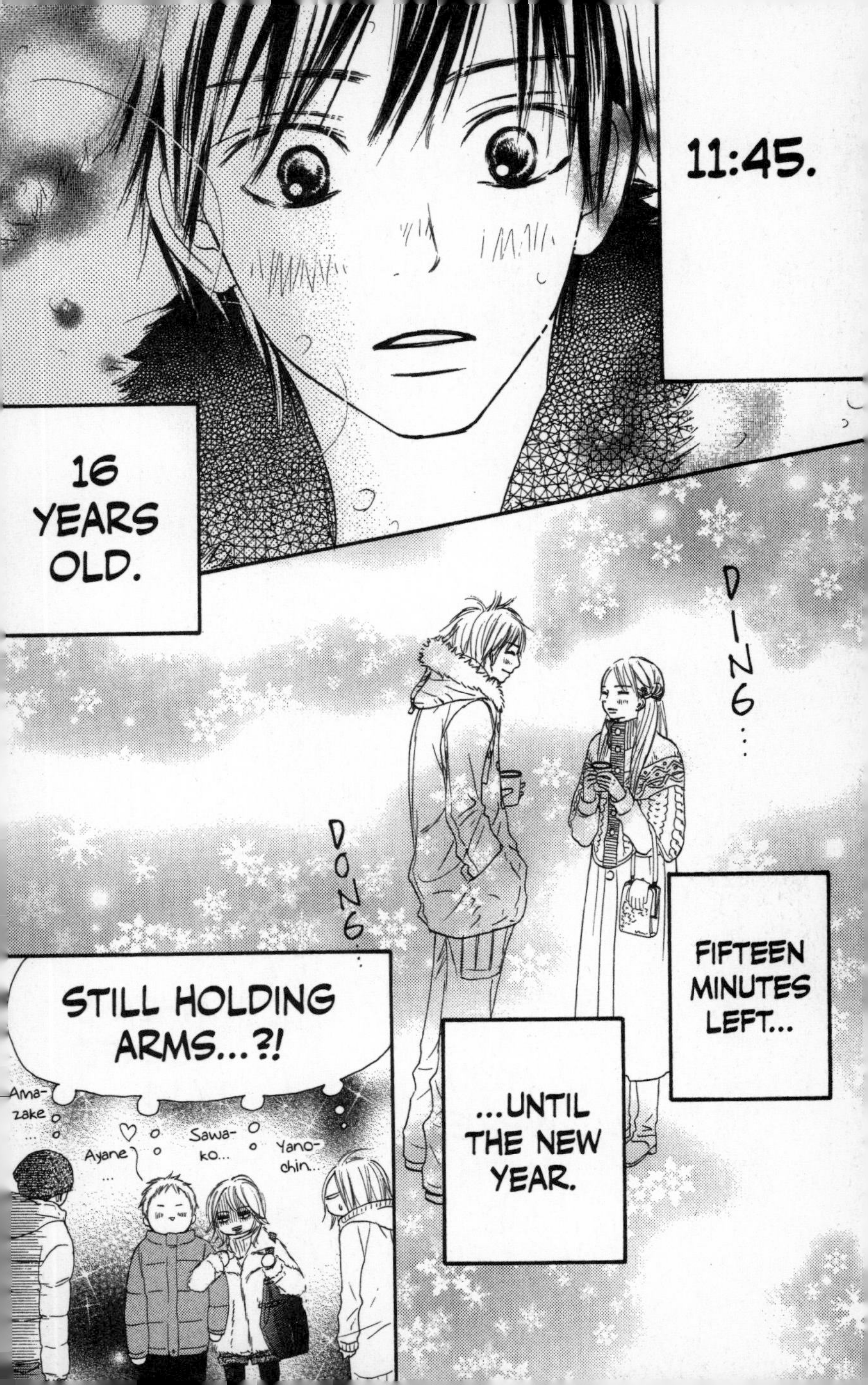
11:45.
16 YEARS OLD.
DING...
FIFTEEN MINUTES LEFT...
...UNTIL THE NEW YEAR.
DONG...
STILL HOLDING ARMS...?!
Yano-chin...
Sawa-ko...
Ayane ...
Ama-zake ...

Episode 27: New Year's

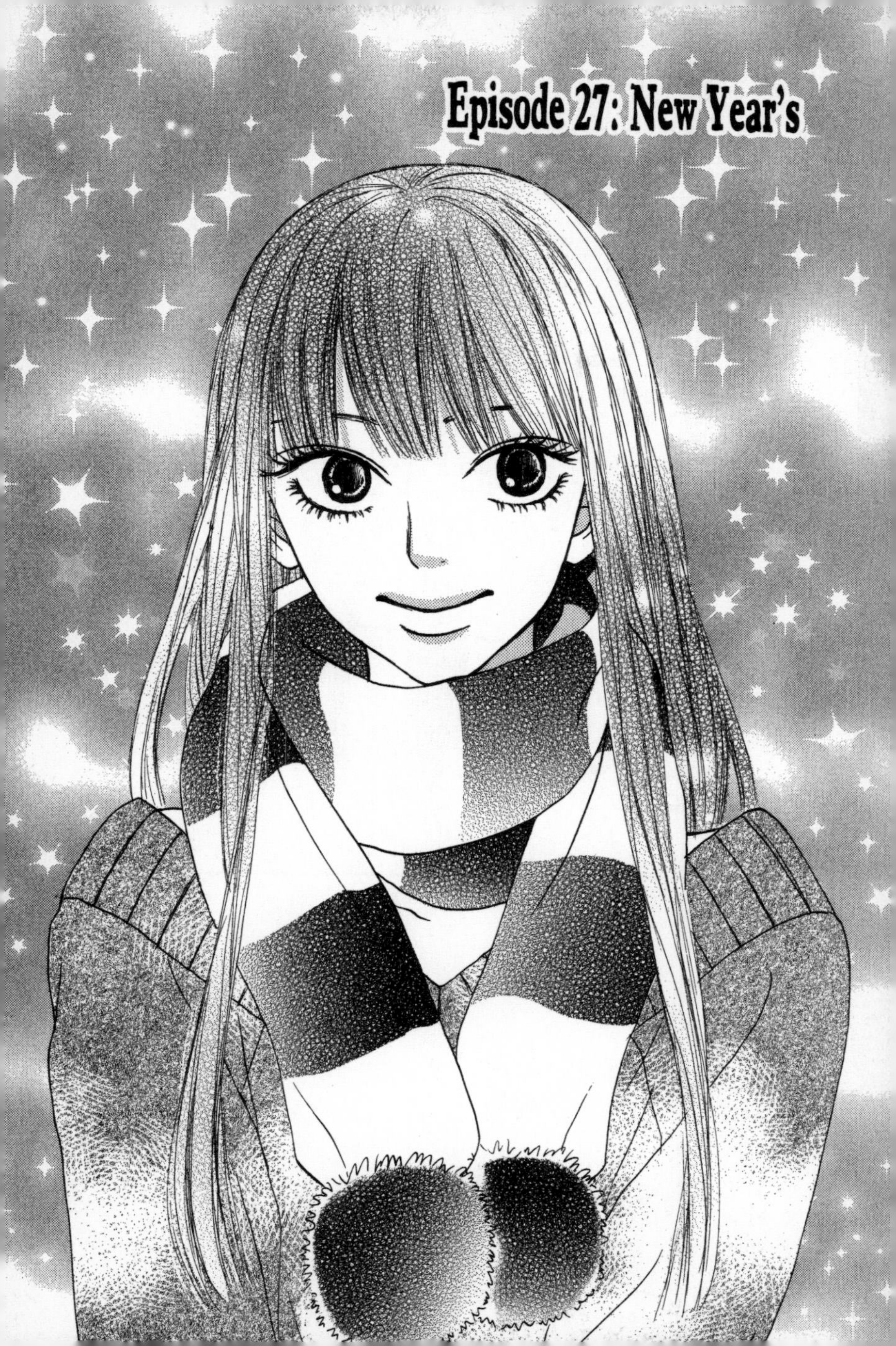

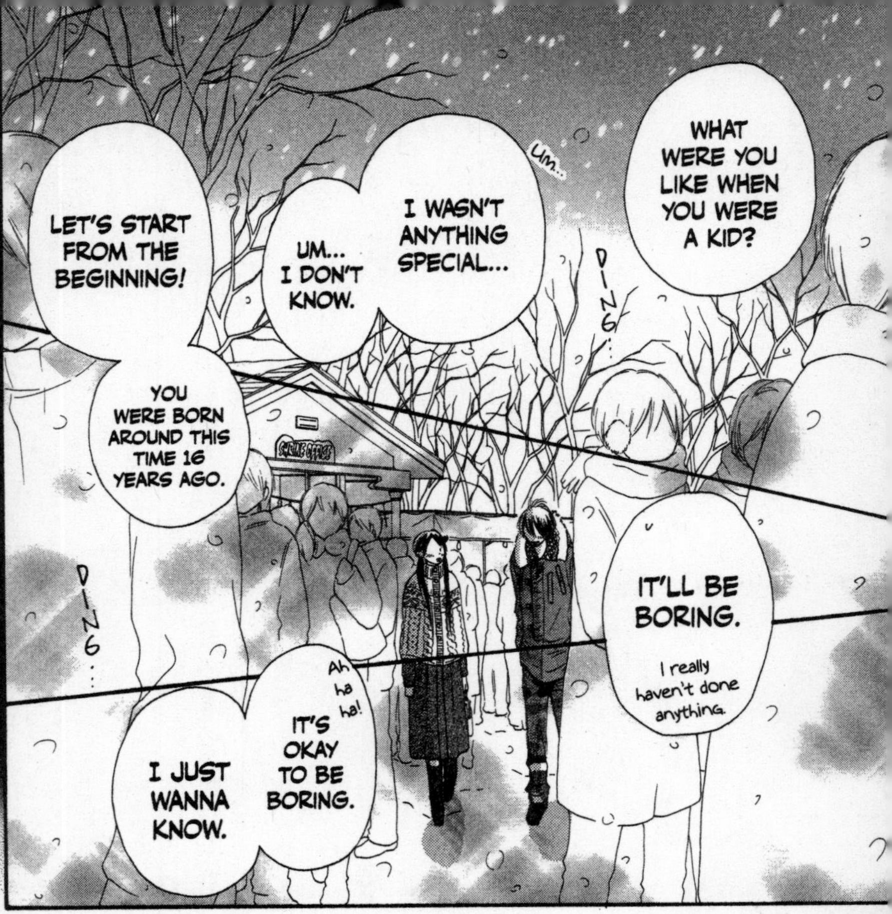
WHAT WERE YOU LIKE WHEN YOU WERE A KID?
Um...
DING...
I WASN'T ANYTHING SPECIAL...
UM... I DON'T KNOW.
LET'S START FROM THE BEGINNING!
SHRINE OFFICE
YOU WERE BORN AROUND THIS TIME 16 YEARS AGO.
IT'LL BE BORING.
I really haven't done anything.
Ah ha ha!
IT'S OKAY TO BE BORING.
I JUST WANNA KNOW.
DING...

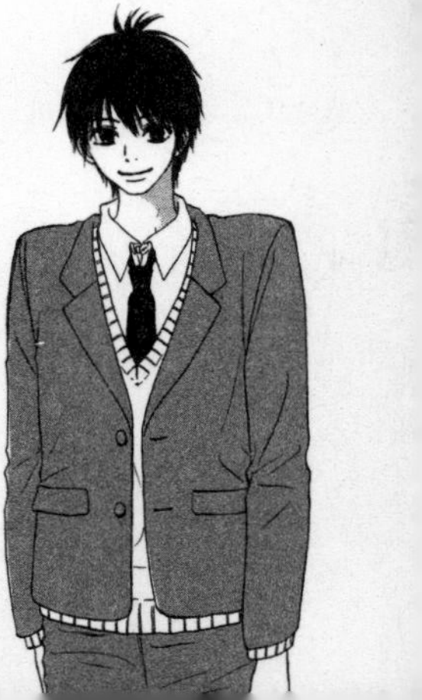

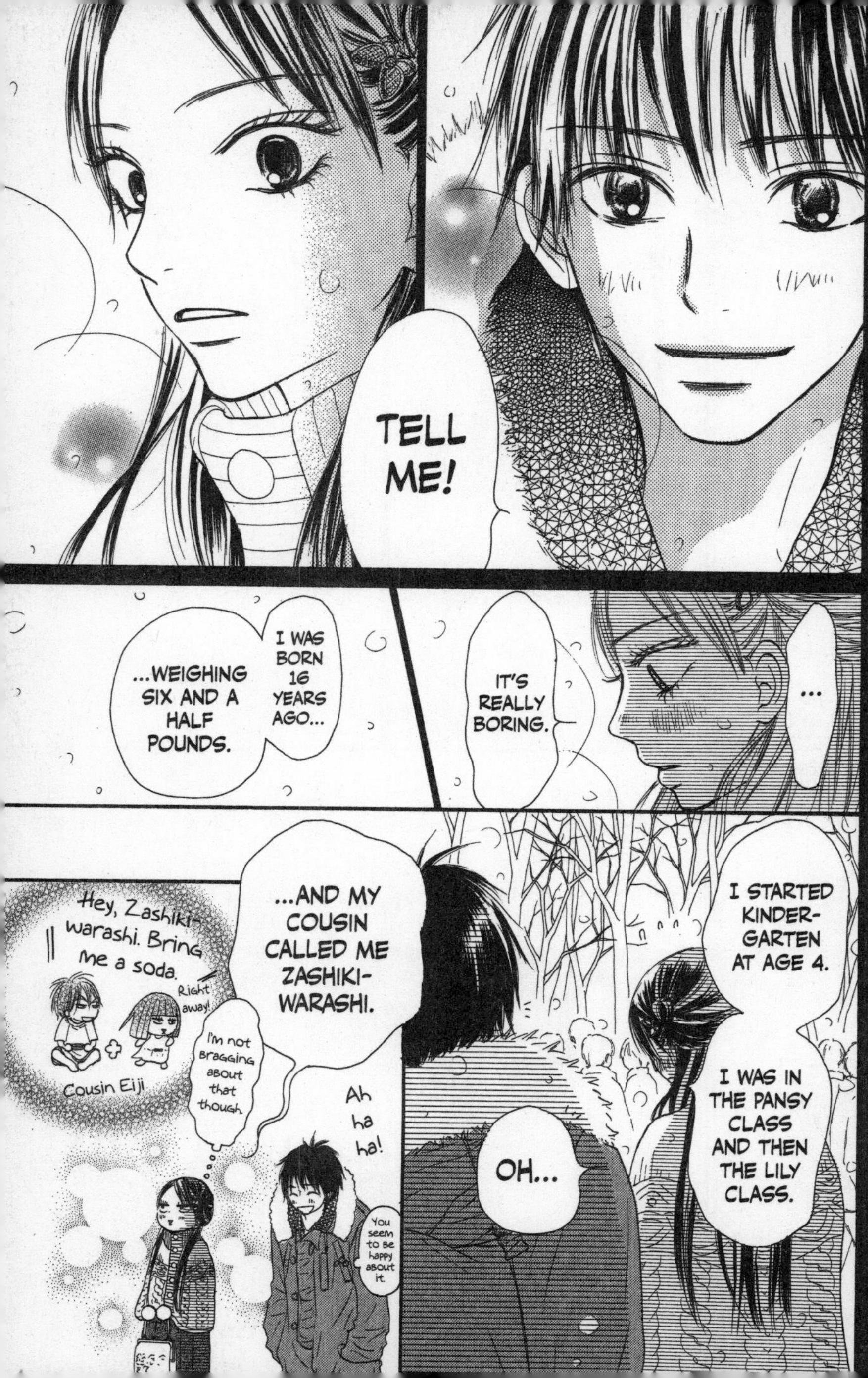
TELL ME!
...
IT'S REALLY BORING.
I WAS BORN 16 YEARS AGO...
...WEIGHING SIX AND A HALF POUNDS.
I STARTED KINDER-GARTEN AT AGE 4.
I WAS IN THE PANSY CLASS AND THEN THE LILY CLASS.
OH...
...AND MY COUSIN CALLED ME ZASHIKI-WARASHI.
Hey, Zashiki-warashi. Bring me a soda.
Right away!
Cousin Eiji
I'm not bragging about that though.
Ah ha ha!
You seem to be happy about it.

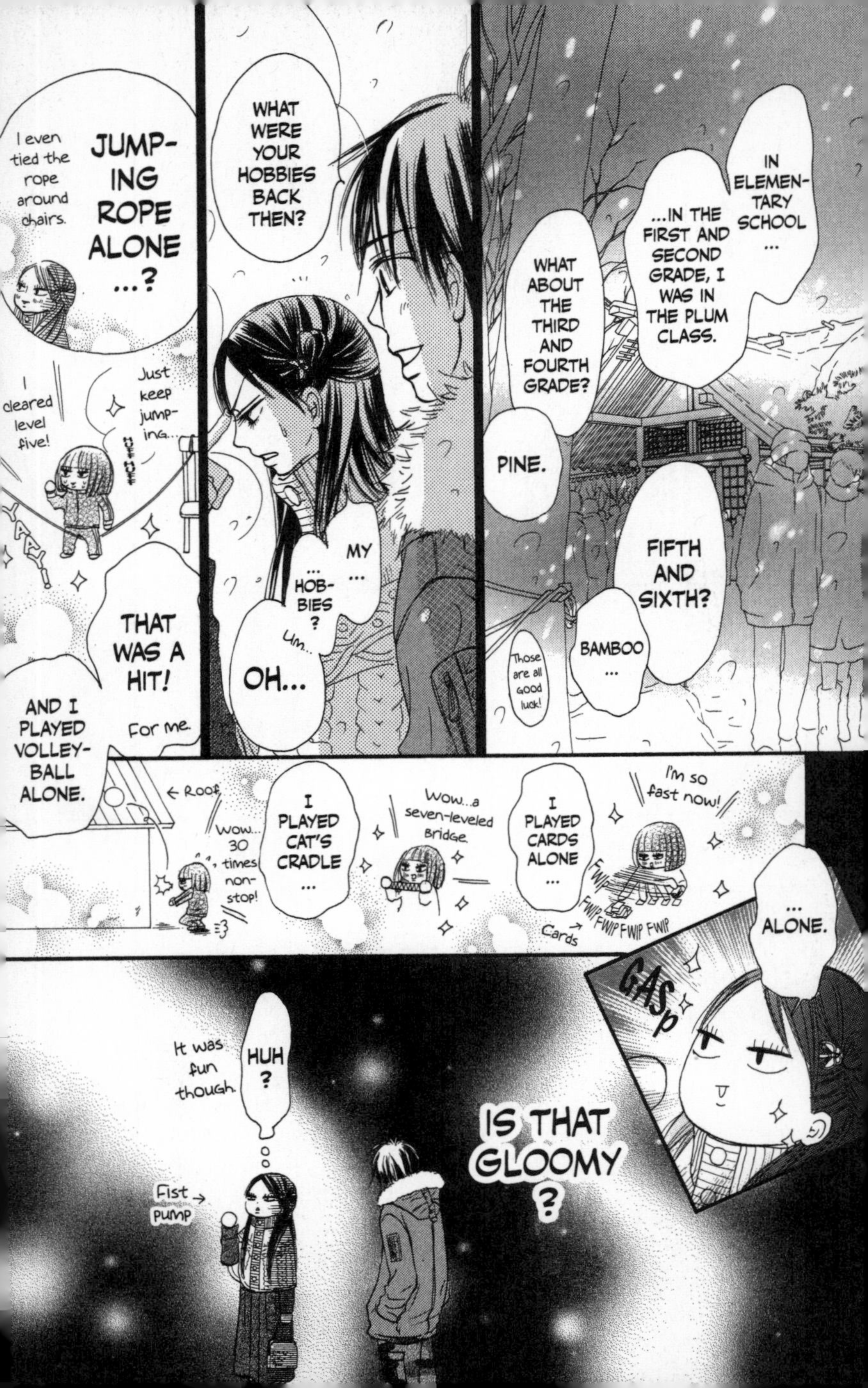
IN ELEMENTARY SCHOOL...
...IN THE FIRST AND SECOND GRADE, I WAS IN THE PLUM CLASS.
WHAT ABOUT THE THIRD AND FOURTH GRADE?
PINE.
FIFTH AND SIXTH?
BAMBOO...
Those are all good luck!
WHAT WERE YOUR HOBBIES BACK THEN?
MY...
...HOBBIES?
Um...
OH...
JUMPING ROPE ALONE...?
I even tied the rope around chairs.
Just keep jumping...
HUFF HUFF
I cleared level five!
YAAY!
THAT WAS A HIT!
For me.
AND I PLAYED VOLLEYBALL ALONE.
...ALONE.
I'm so fast now!
I PLAYED CARDS ALONE...
FWIP FWIP FWIP FWIP FWIP
Cards
Wow...a seven-leveled Bridge.
I PLAYED CAT'S CRADLE...
Wow... 30 times non-stop!
Roof
GASp
IS THAT GLOOMY?
HUH?
It was fun though.
Fist pump

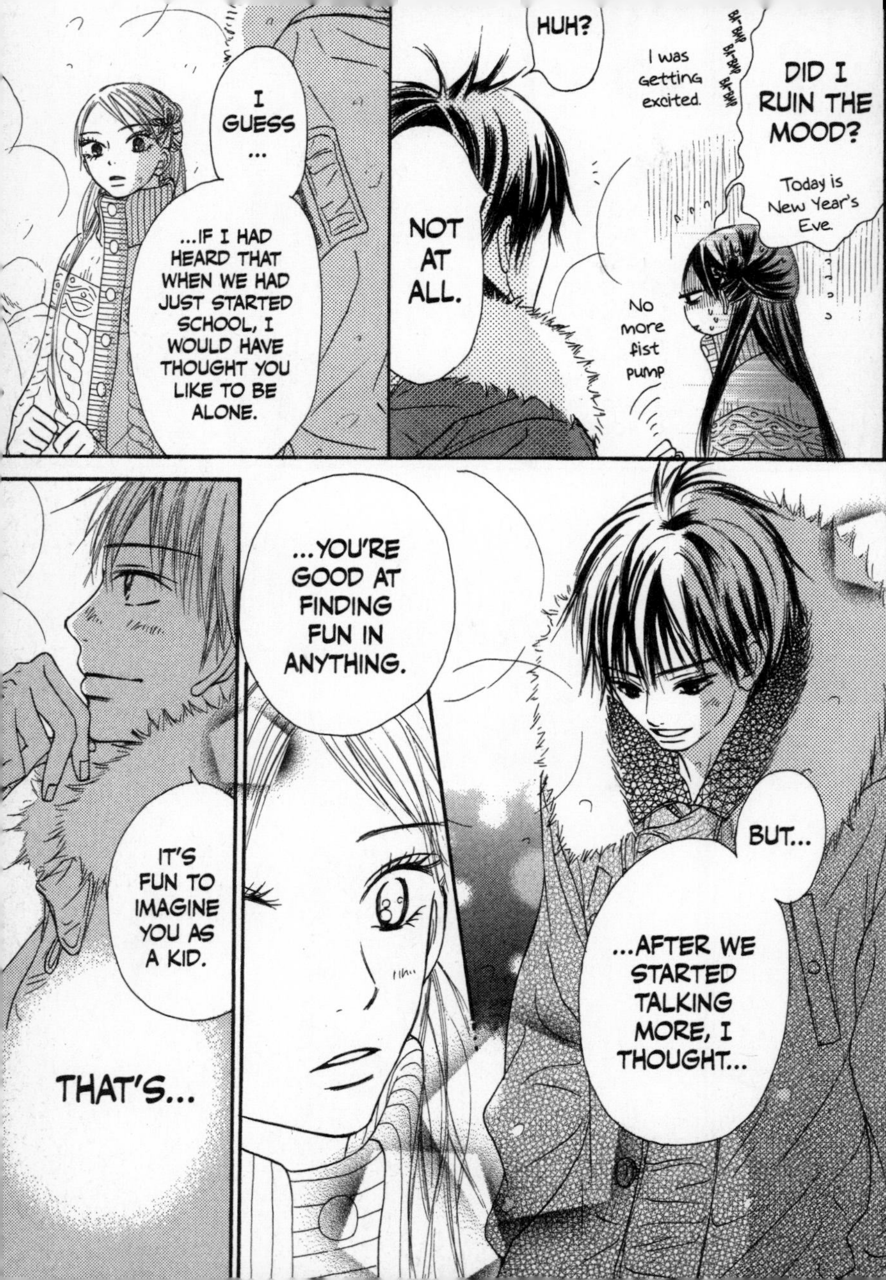
HUH?
DID I RUIN THE MOOD?
BA-BMP BA-BMP BA-BMP
I was getting excited.
Today is New Year's Eve.
No more fist pump
NOT AT ALL.
I GUESS ...
...IF I HAD HEARD THAT WHEN WE HAD JUST STARTED SCHOOL, I WOULD HAVE THOUGHT YOU LIKE TO BE ALONE.
BUT...
...AFTER WE STARTED TALKING MORE, I THOUGHT...
...YOU'RE GOOD AT FINDING FUN IN ANYTHING.
IT'S FUN TO IMAGINE YOU AS A KID.
THAT'S...

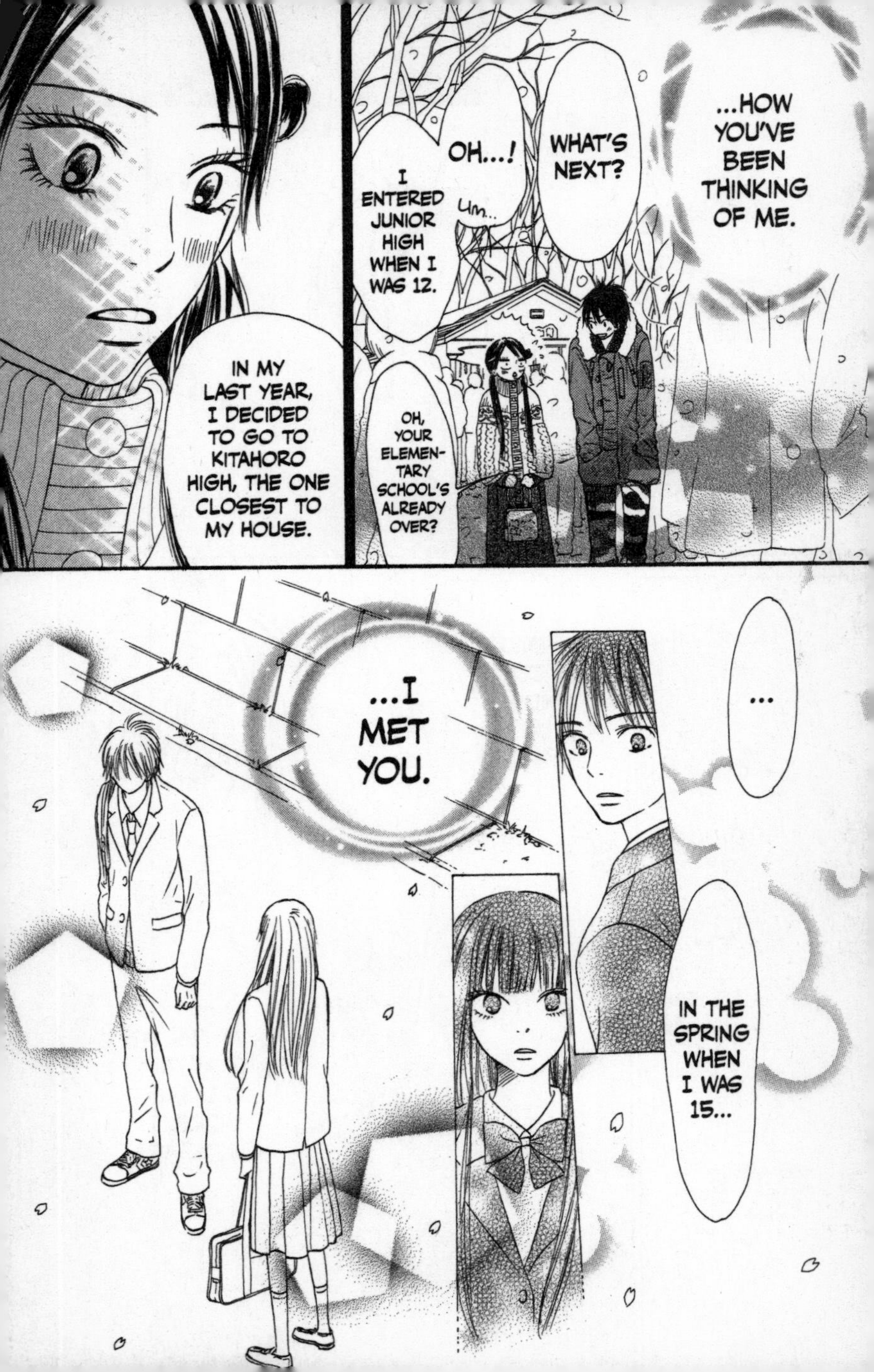
...HOW YOU'VE BEEN THINKING OF ME.
WHAT'S NEXT?
OH...!
Um...
I ENTERED JUNIOR HIGH WHEN I WAS 12.
OH, YOUR ELEMENTARY SCHOOL'S ALREADY OVER?
IN MY LAST YEAR, I DECIDED TO GO TO KITAHORO HIGH, THE ONE CLOSEST TO MY HOUSE.
...
IN THE SPRING WHEN I WAS 15...
...I MET YOU.

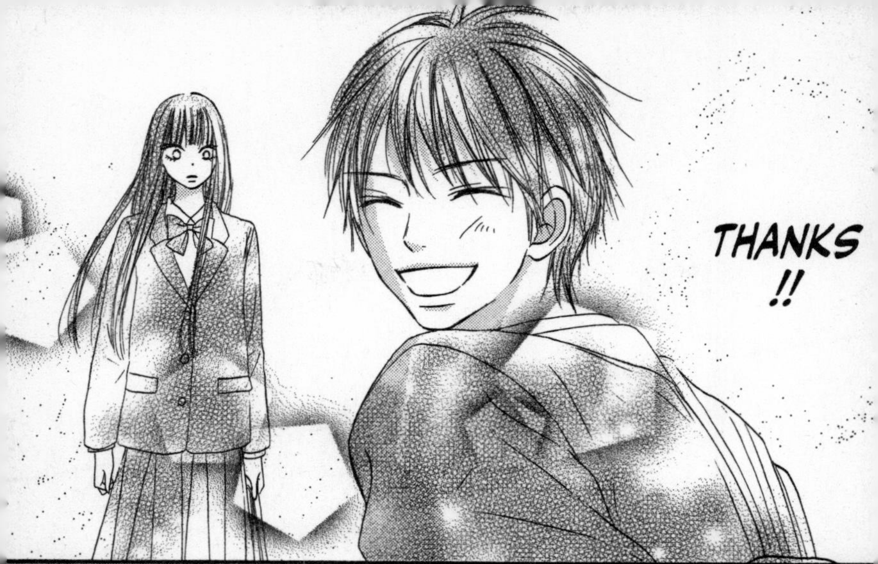
THANKS !!
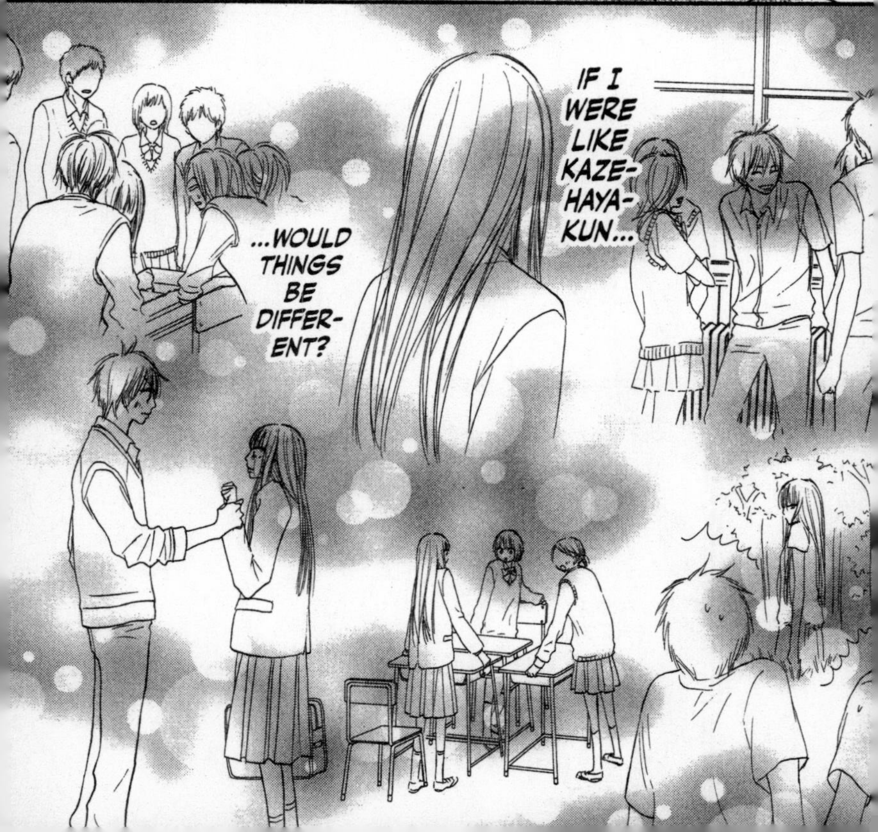
IF I WERE LIKE KAZE-HAYA-KUN...
...WOULD THINGS BE DIFFER-ENT?

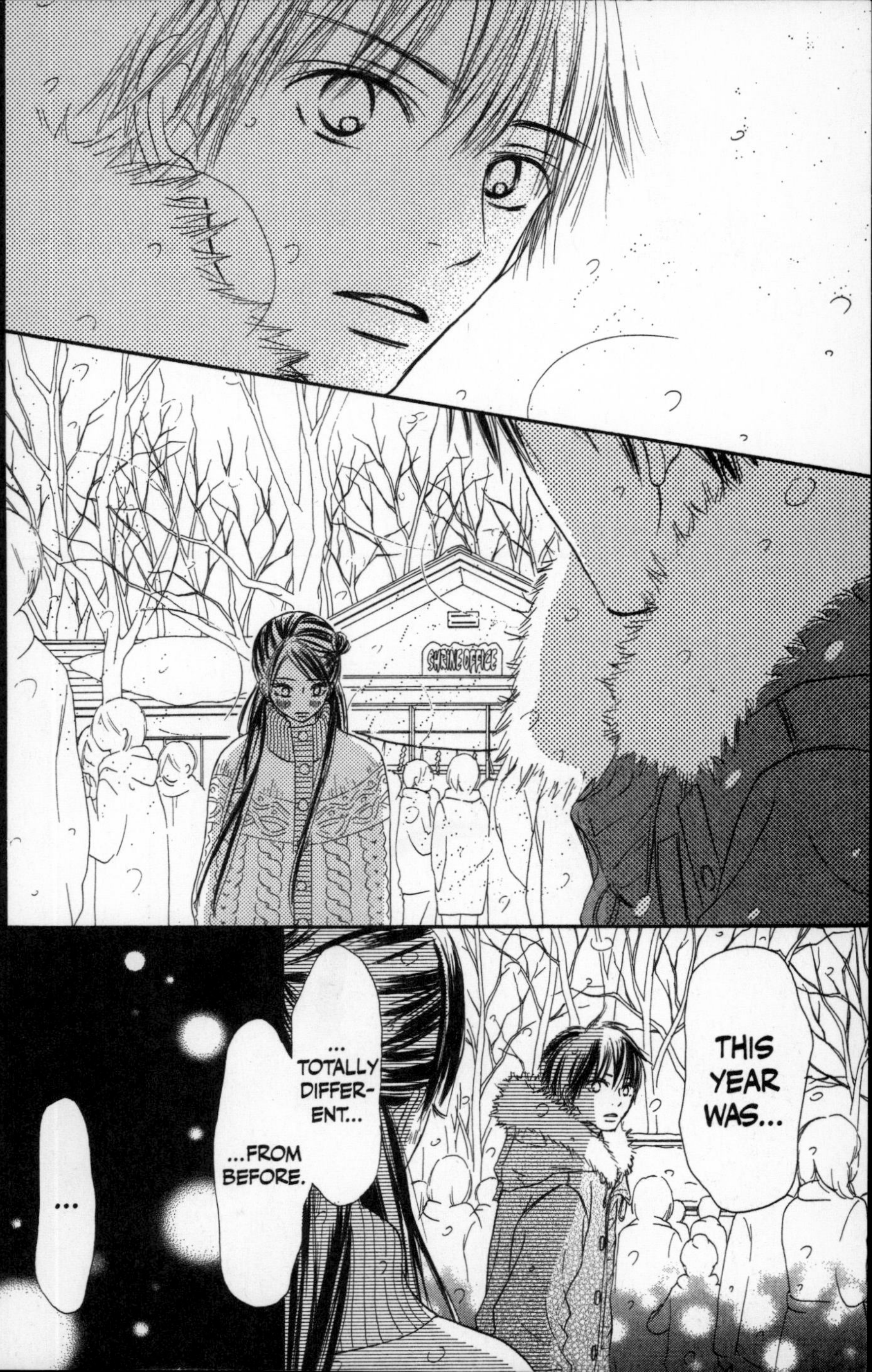
SHRINE OFFICE
THIS YEAR WAS...
...TOTALLY DIFFERENT...
...FROM BEFORE.
...

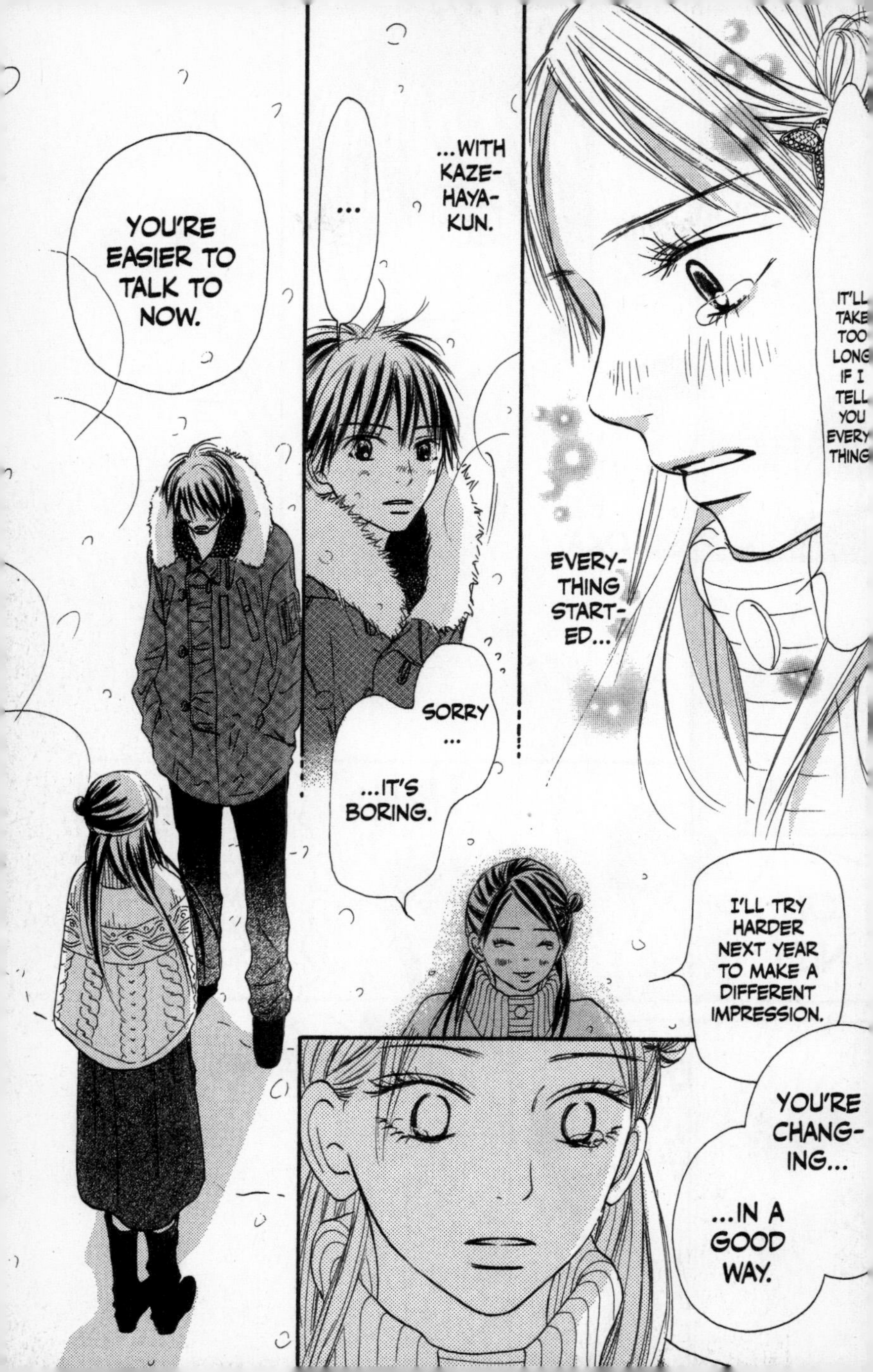
IT'LL TAKE TOO LONG IF I TELL YOU EVERYTHING
EVERY-THING START-ED...
...WITH KAZE-HAYA-KUN.
...
SORRY ... ...IT'S BORING.
I'LL TRY HARDER NEXT YEAR TO MAKE A DIFFERENT IMPRESSION.
YOU'RE CHANG-ING... ...IN A GOOD WAY.
YOU'RE EASIER TO TALK TO NOW.

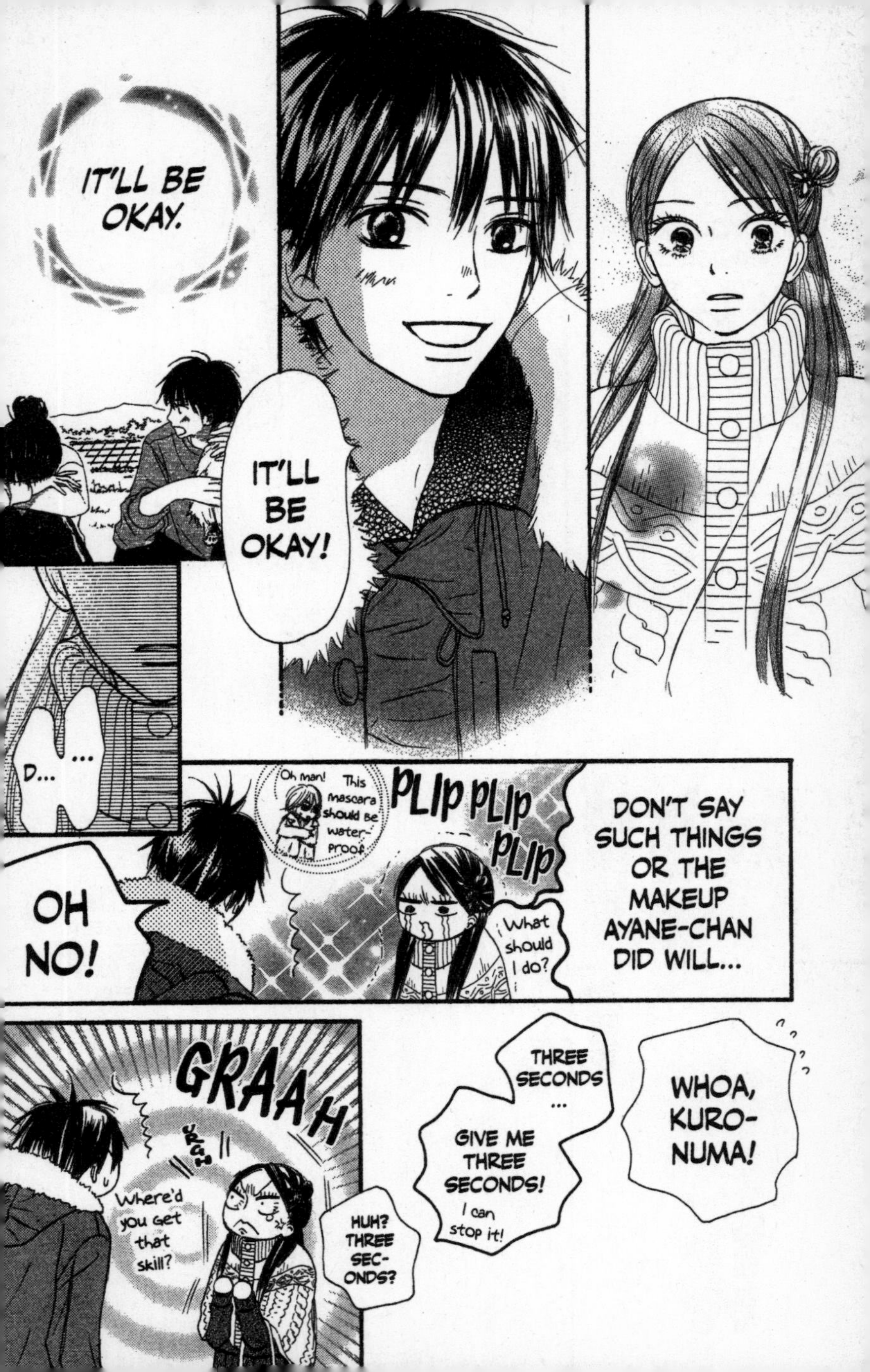
IT'LL BE OKAY!
IT'LL BE OKAY.
D...
...
DON'T SAY SUCH THINGS OR THE MAKEUP AYANE-CHAN DID WILL...
What should I do?
PLIP PLIP PLIP
Oh man! This mascara should be water-proof
OH NO!
WHOA, KURO-NUMA!
THREE SECONDS ...
GIVE ME THREE SECONDS!
I can stop it!
HUH? THREE SEC-ONDS?
GRAAH
URGH
Where'd you get that skill?

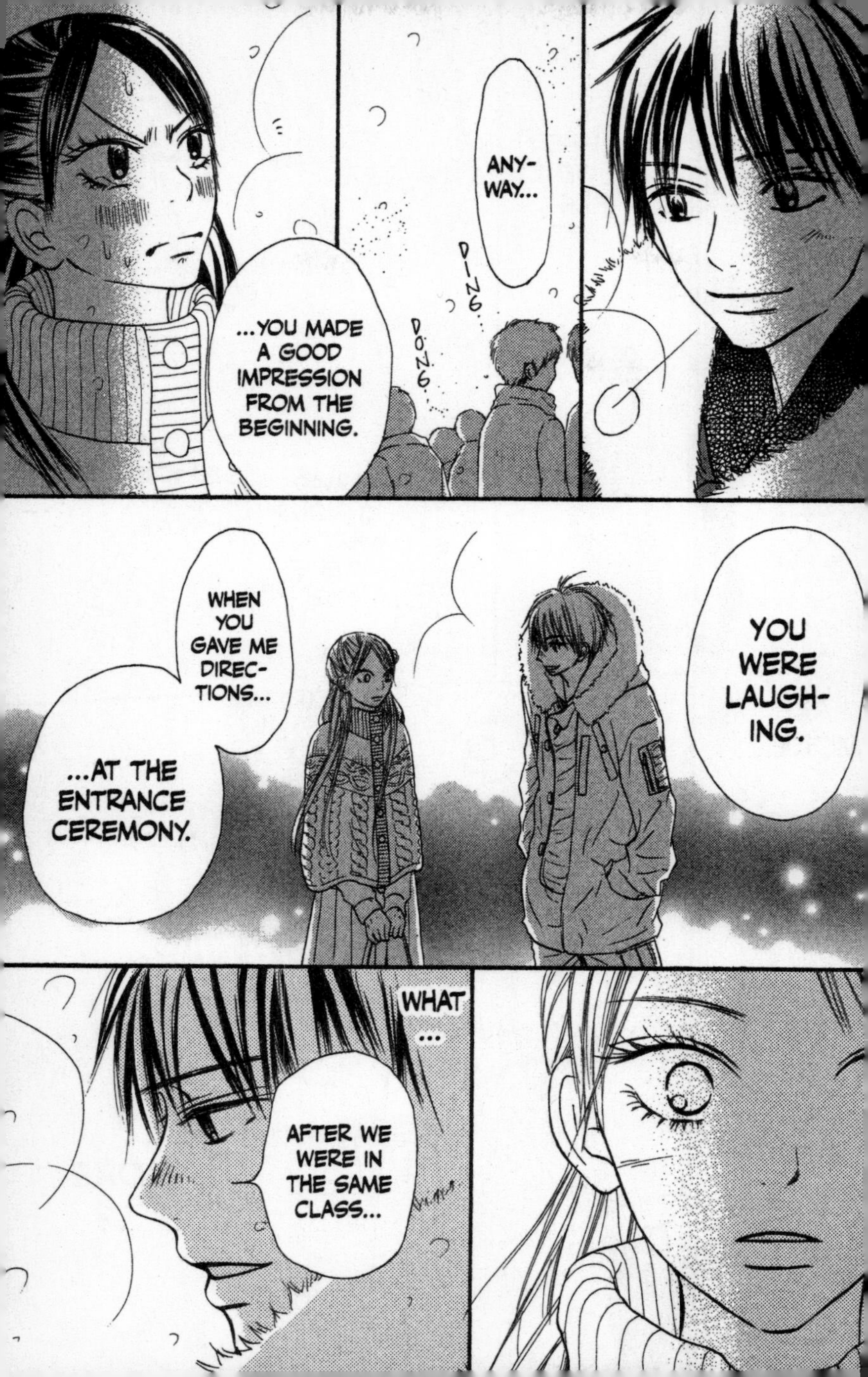
ANY-WAY...
DING...
DONG...
...YOU MADE A GOOD IMPRESSION FROM THE BEGINNING.
YOU WERE LAUGH-ING.
WHEN YOU GAVE ME DIREC-TIONS...
...AT THE ENTRANCE CEREMONY.
WHAT ...
AFTER WE WERE IN THE SAME CLASS...

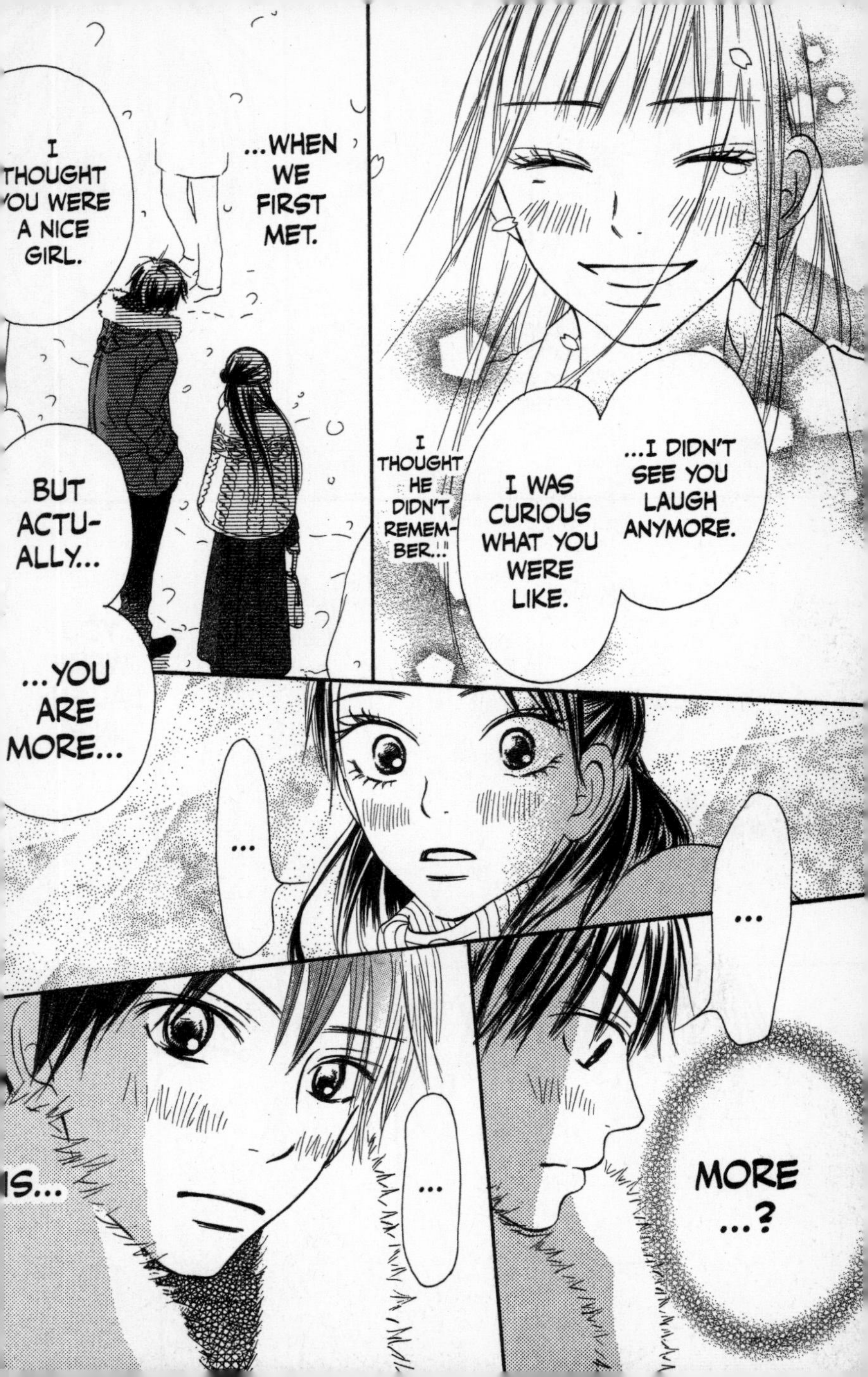
...I DIDN'T SEE YOU LAUGH ANYMORE.
I WAS CURIOUS WHAT YOU WERE LIKE.
I THOUGHT HE DIDN'T REMEMBER..!!
I THOUGHT YOU WERE A NICE GIRL.
...WHEN WE FIRST MET.
BUT ACTUALLY...
...YOU ARE MORE...
...
...
MORE ...?
...
IS...

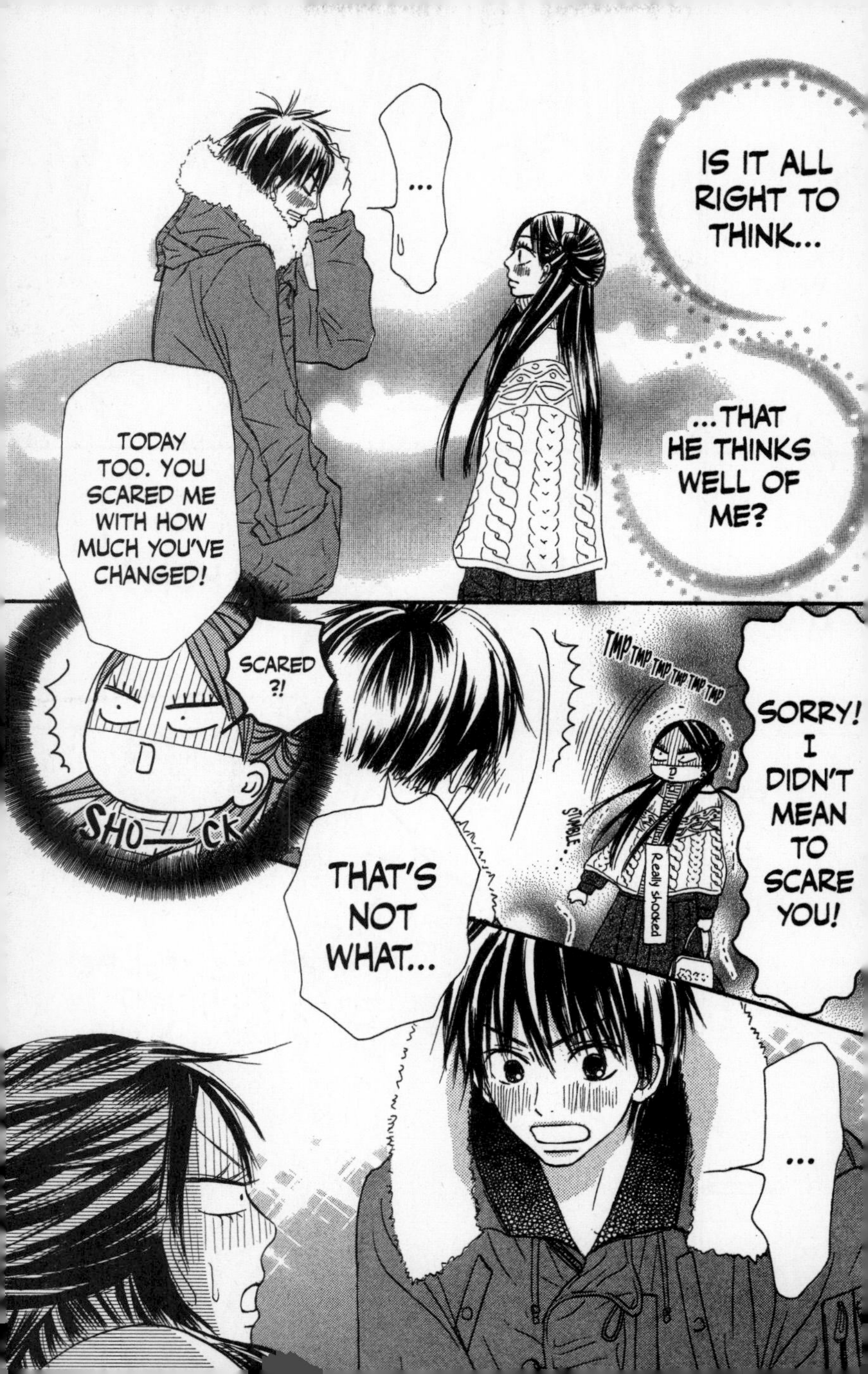
IS IT ALL RIGHT TO THINK...
...THAT HE THINKS WELL OF ME?
...
TODAY TOO. YOU SCARED ME WITH HOW MUCH YOU'VE CHANGED!
SORRY! I DIDN'T MEAN TO SCARE YOU!
TMP TMP TMP TMP TMP TMP
STUMBLE...
Really shocked
SCARED ?!
SHO—CK
THAT'S NOT WHAT...
...

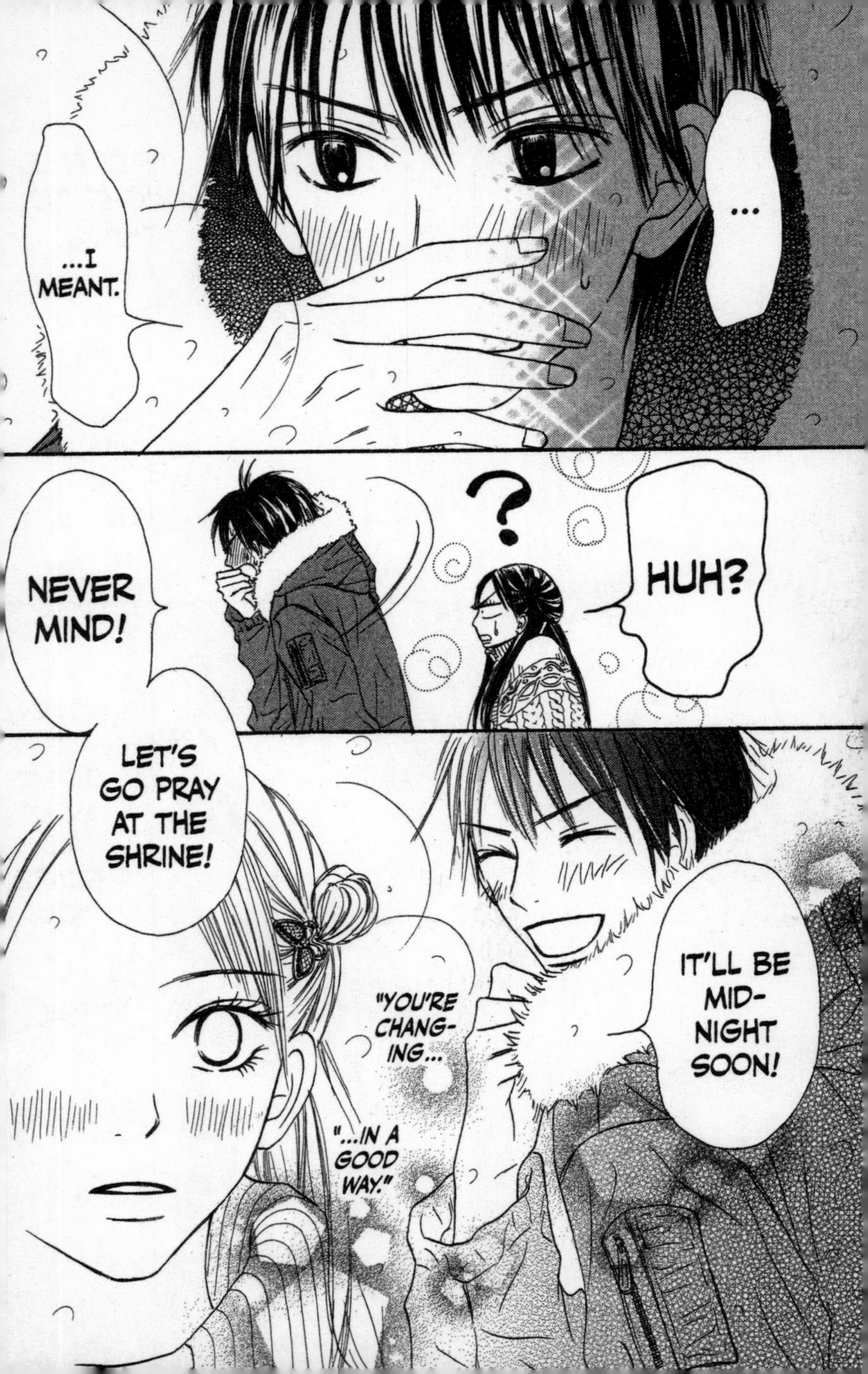
...
...I MEANT.
HUH?
NEVER MIND!
IT'LL BE MID-NIGHT SOON!
LET'S GO PRAY AT THE SHRINE!
"YOU'RE CHANG-ING...
"...IN A GOOD WAY."

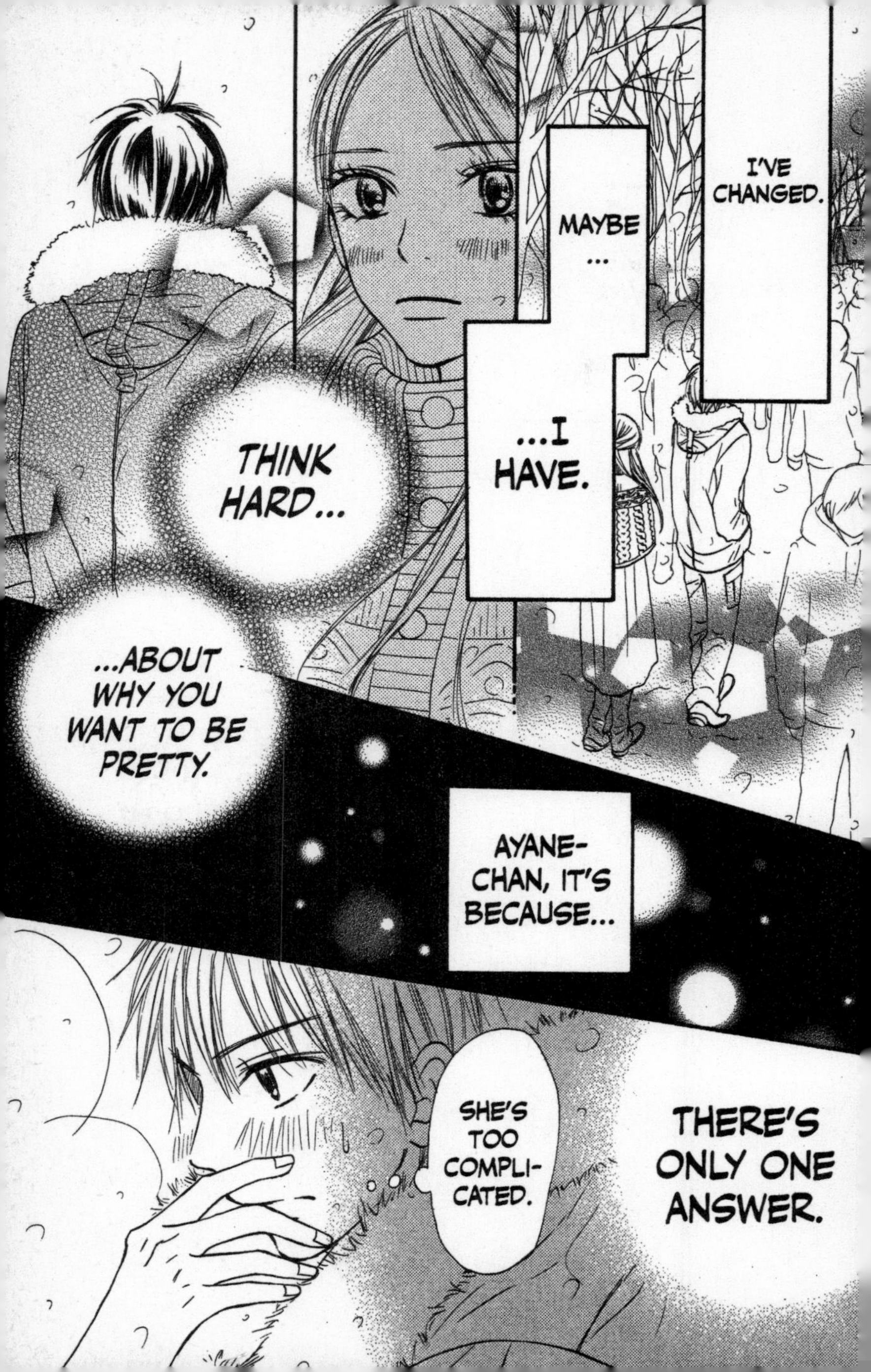
I'VE CHANGED.
MAYBE ...
...I HAVE.
THINK HARD...
...ABOUT WHY YOU WANT TO BE PRETTY.
AYANE-CHAN, IT'S BECAUSE...
THERE'S ONLY ONE ANSWER.
SHE'S TOO COMPLI-CATED.

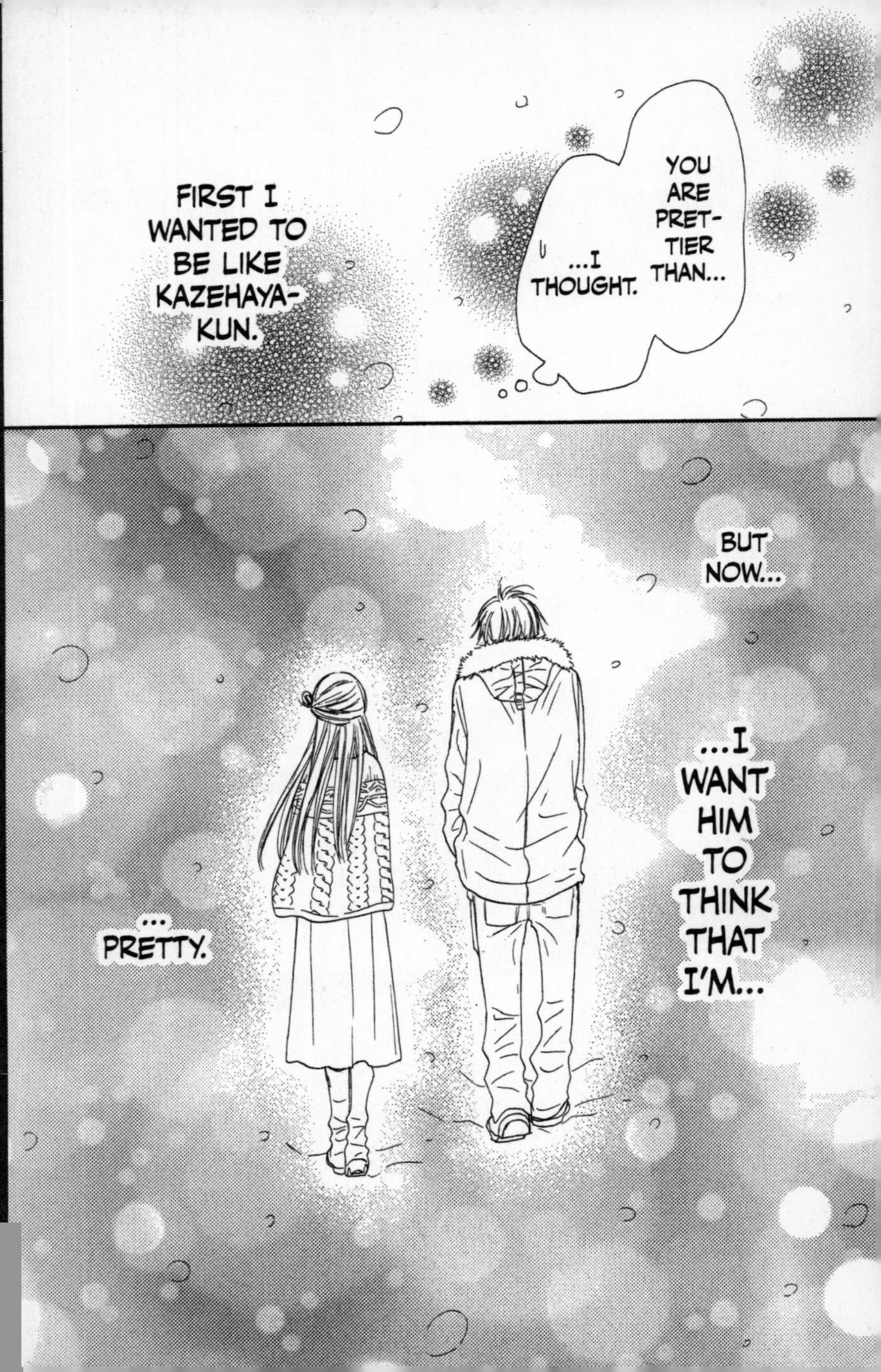
YOU ARE PRETTIER THAN...
...I THOUGHT.
FIRST I WANTED TO BE LIKE KAZEHAYA-KUN.
BUT NOW...
...I WANT HIM TO THINK THAT I'M...
...PRETTY.

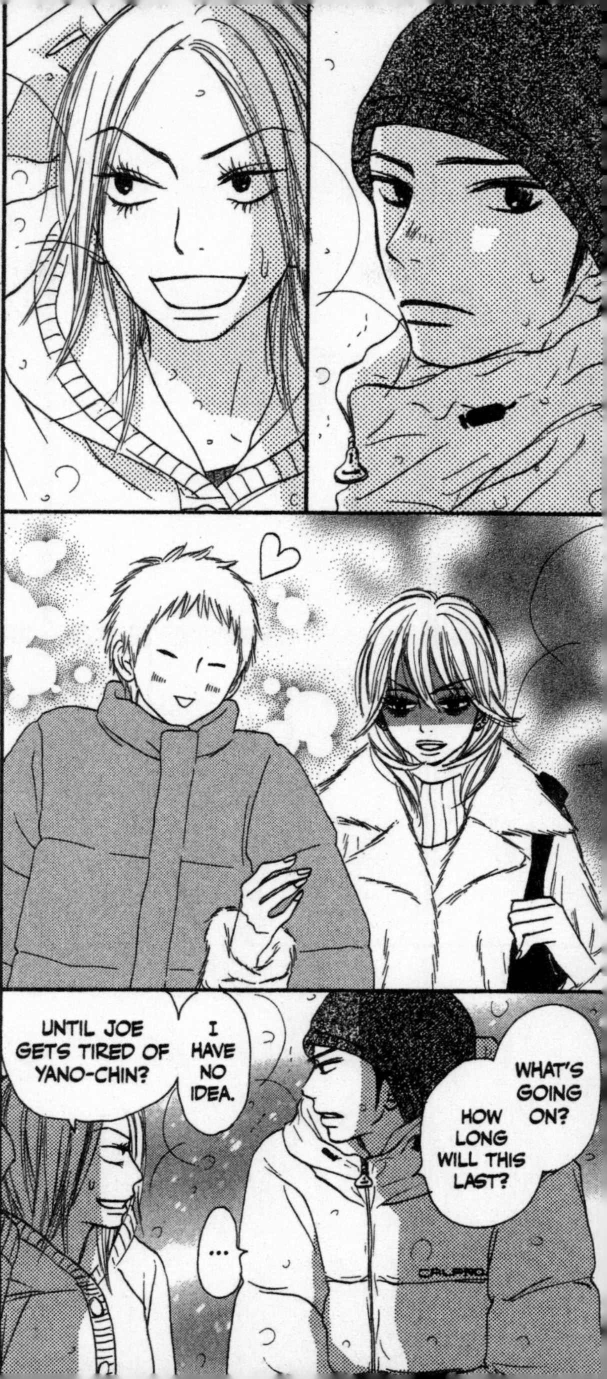
WHAT'S GOING ON? HOW LONG WILL THIS LAST?
I HAVE NO IDEA.
UNTIL JOE GETS TIRED OF YANO-CHIN?
...

KARUPIN on JAPAN 3

I'm writing this in May 2008. The last couple months I have been so into this one thing.

And it is...

Shiroi Kyoto...!

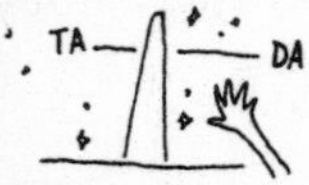
TA
DA

Five years after it was originally broadcast. I don't watch TV dramas (since I can't remember when they're on—I mean, I never even know what the date is...), but I caught afternoon reruns.

When I saw it, it was already almost the end of season one.

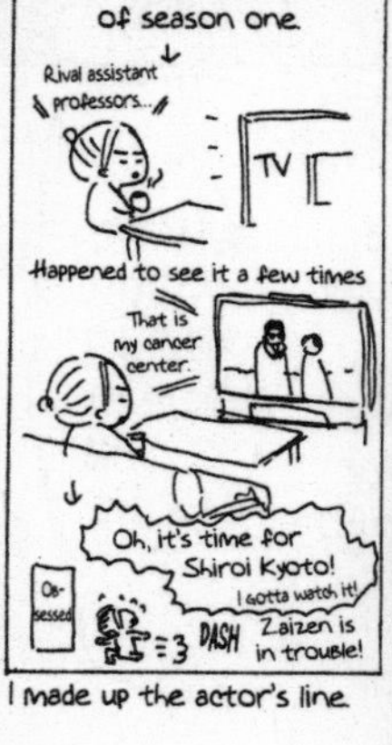
Rival assistant professors...
TV
Happened to see it a few times
That is my cancer center.
Oh, it's time for Shiroi Kyoto!
I gotta watch it!
Zaizen is in trouble!
Ob-sessed
DASH

I made up the actor's line.

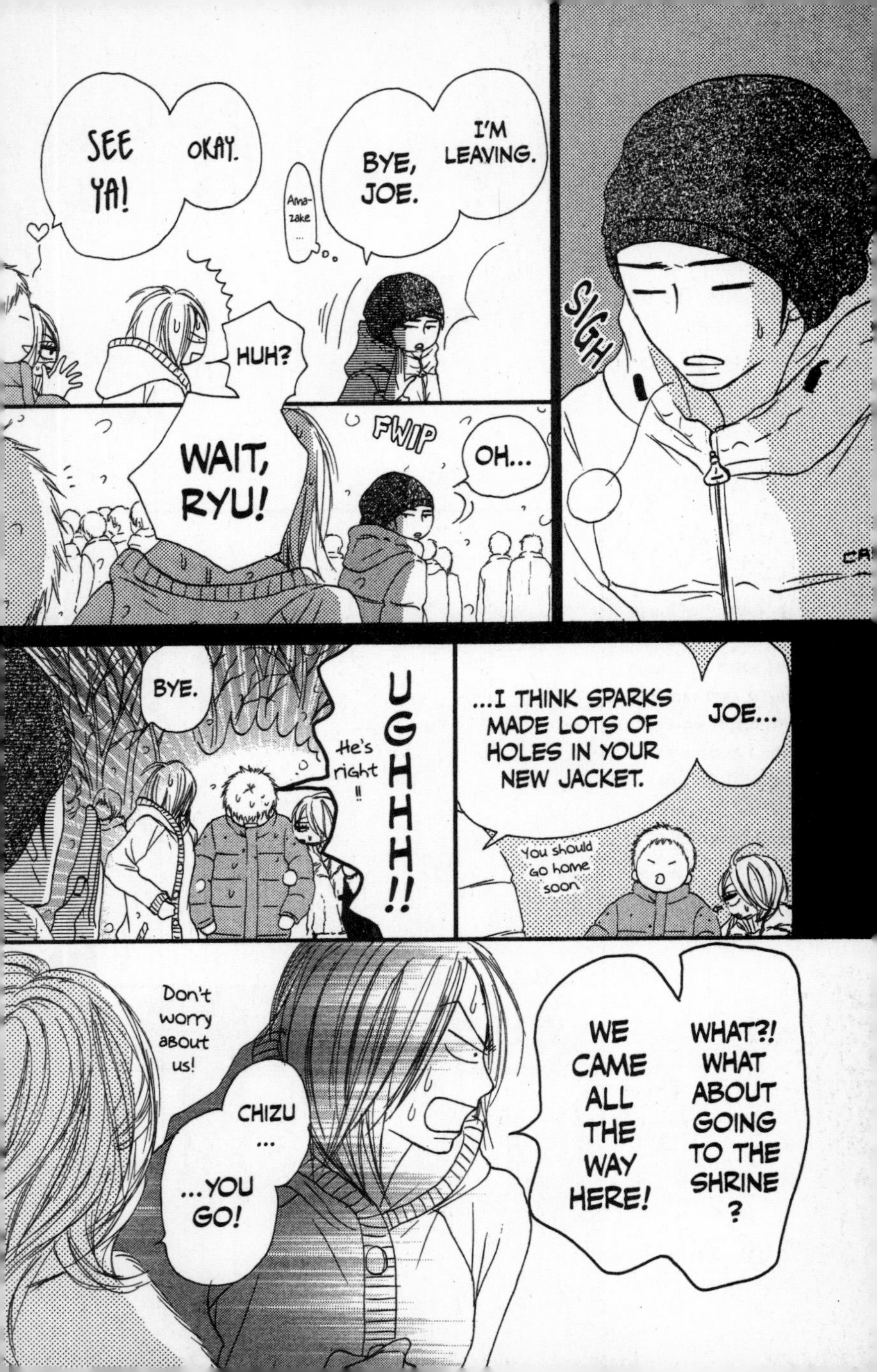
SIGH
CRA
I'M LEAVING.
BYE, JOE.
Ama-zake...
OKAY.
SEE YA!
HUH?
OH...
FWIP
WAIT, RYU!
JOE...
...I THINK SPARKS MADE LOTS OF HOLES IN YOUR NEW JACKET.
You should go home soon
UGHHH!!
He's right!!
BYE.
WHAT?! WHAT ABOUT GOING TO THE SHRINE?
WE CAME ALL THE WAY HERE!
CHIZU...
...YOU GO!
Don't worry about us!

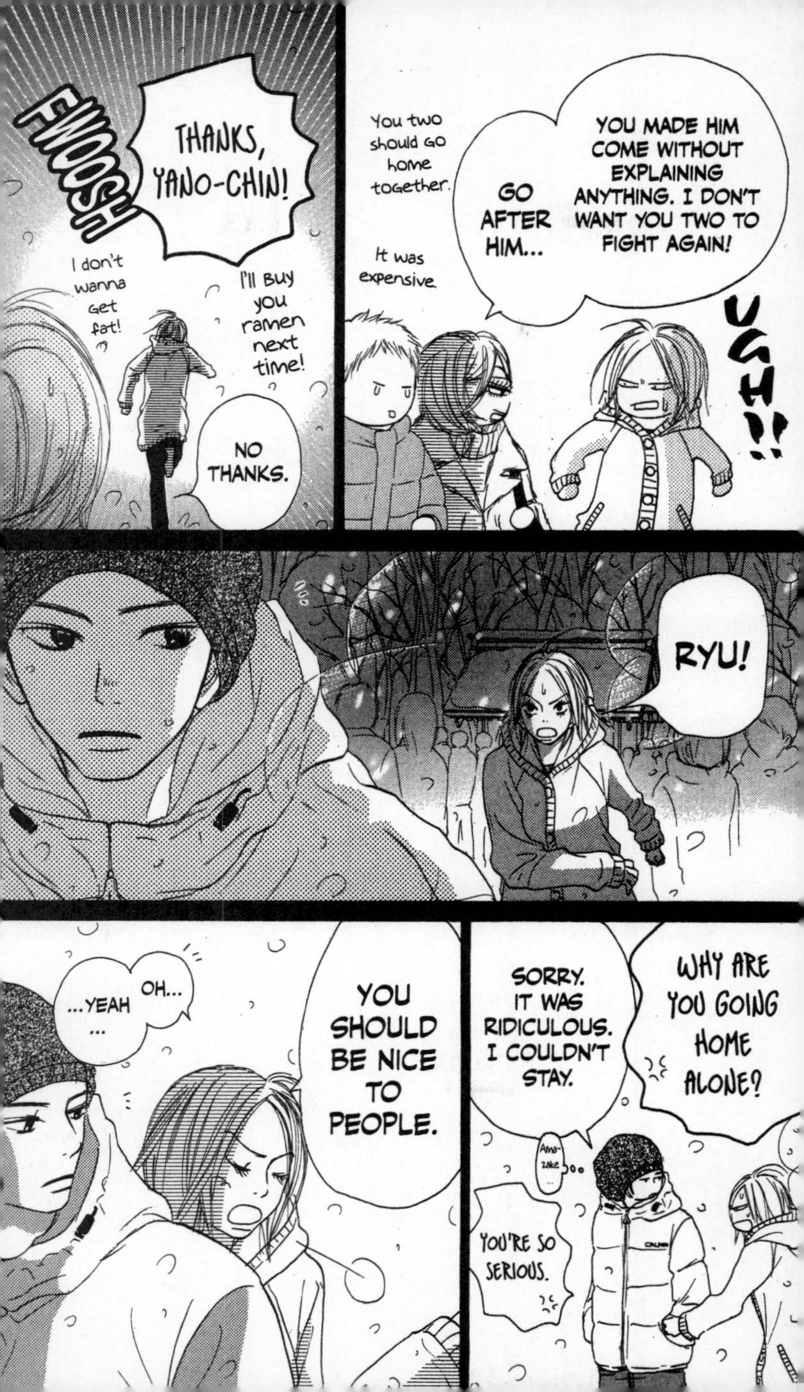
YOU MADE HIM COME WITHOUT EXPLAINING ANYTHING. I DON'T WANT YOU TWO TO FIGHT AGAIN!
GO AFTER HIM...
UGH!!
You two should go home together.
It was expensive.
THANKS, YANO-CHIN!
FWOOSH
I'll buy you ramen next time!
NO THANKS.
I don't wanna get fat!
RYU!
WHY ARE YOU GOING HOME ALONE?
SORRY. IT WAS RIDICULOUS. I COULDN'T STAY.
Ama-zake...
YOU'RE SO SERIOUS.
YOU SHOULD BE NICE TO PEOPLE.
OH...
...YEAH ...

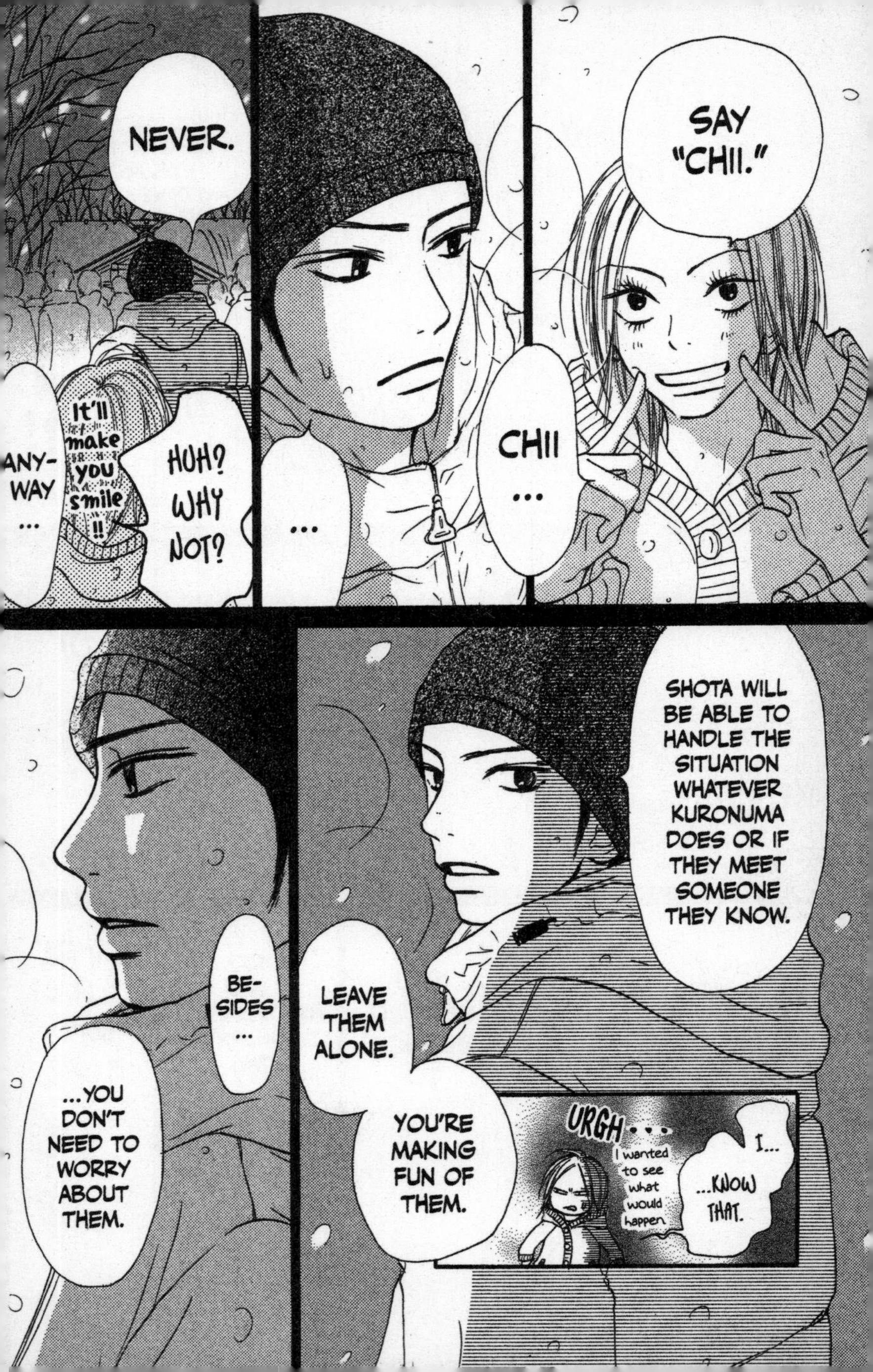
SAY "CHII."
CHII ...
...
NEVER.
HUH? WHY NOT?
It'll make you smile!!
ANY-WAY ...
SHOTA WILL BE ABLE TO HANDLE THE SITUATION WHATEVER KURONUMA DOES OR IF THEY MEET SOMEONE THEY KNOW.
LEAVE THEM ALONE.
YOU'RE MAKING FUN OF THEM.
I... ...KNOW THAT.
URGH...
I wanted to see what would happen.
BE-SIDES ...
...YOU DON'T NEED TO WORRY ABOUT THEM.

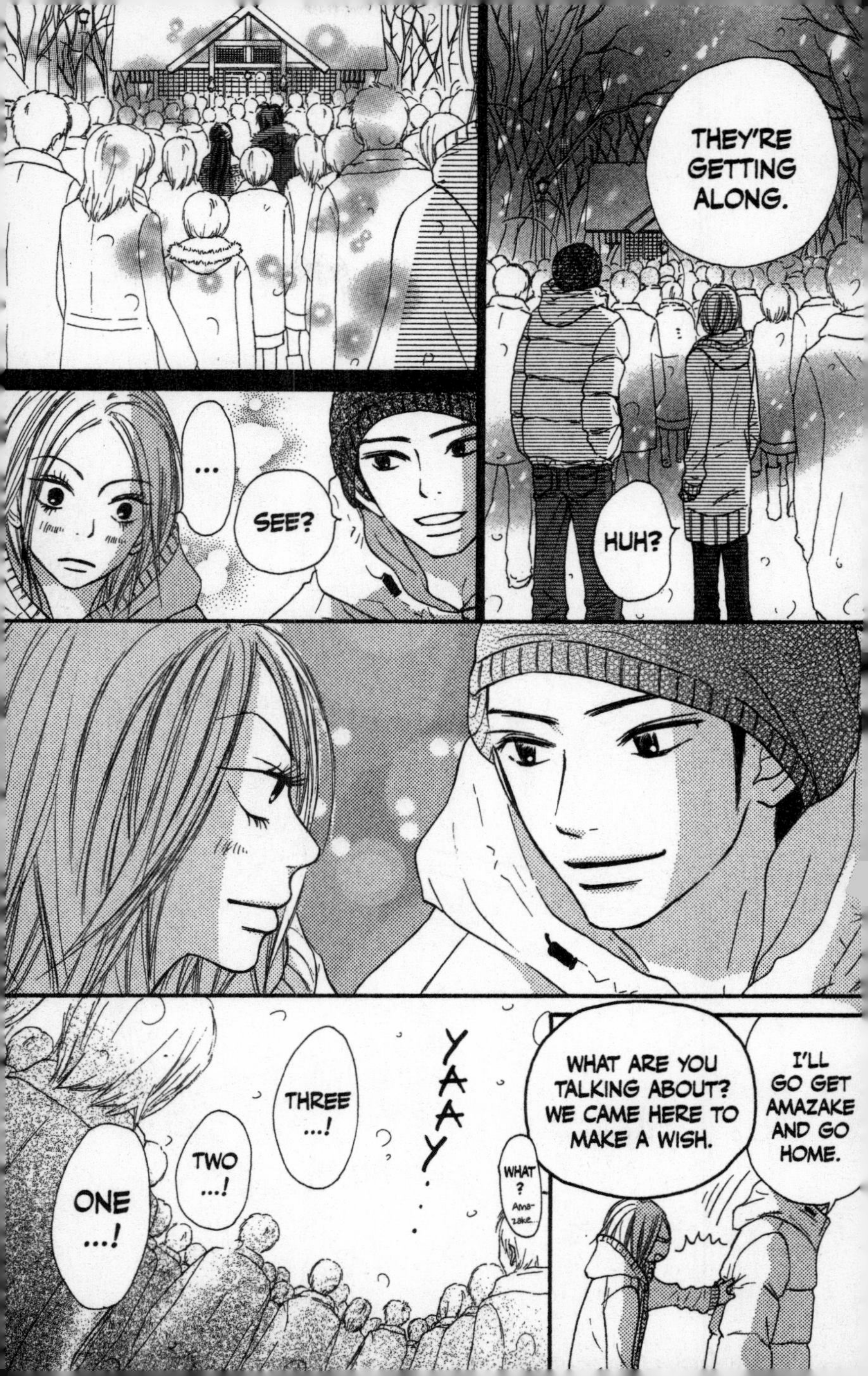
THEY'RE GETTING ALONG.
HUH?
SEE?
...
I'LL GO GET AMAZAKE AND GO HOME.
WHAT ARE YOU TALKING ABOUT? WE CAME HERE TO MAKE A WISH.
WHAT? Ama-zake...
YAAAY...
THREE ...!
TWO ...!
ONE ...!

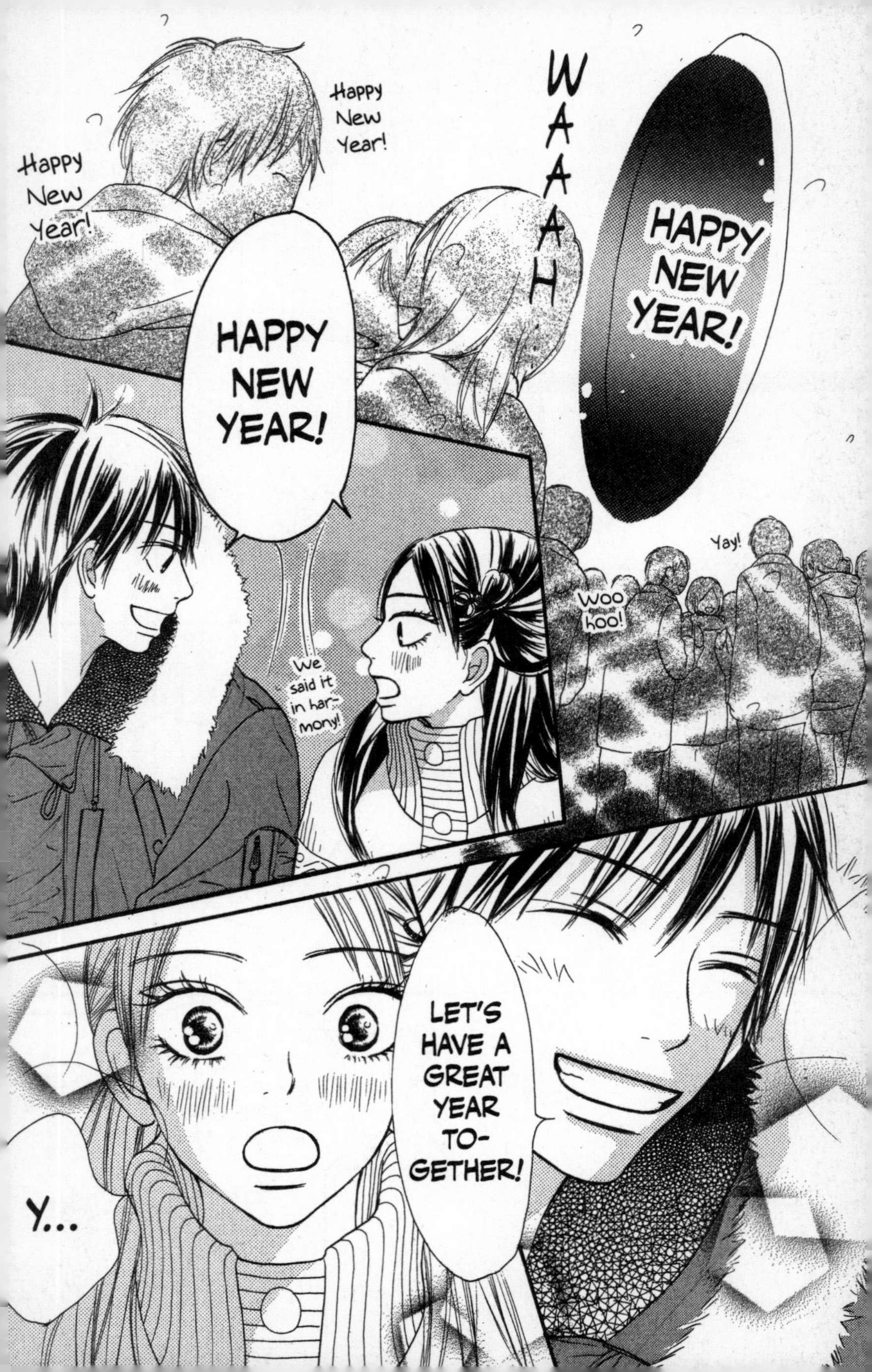
WAAAAH
HAPPY NEW YEAR!
Happy New Year!
Happy New Year!
Yay!
Woo hoo!
HAPPY NEW YEAR!
We said it in harmony!
LET'S HAVE A GREAT YEAR TOGETHER!
Y...

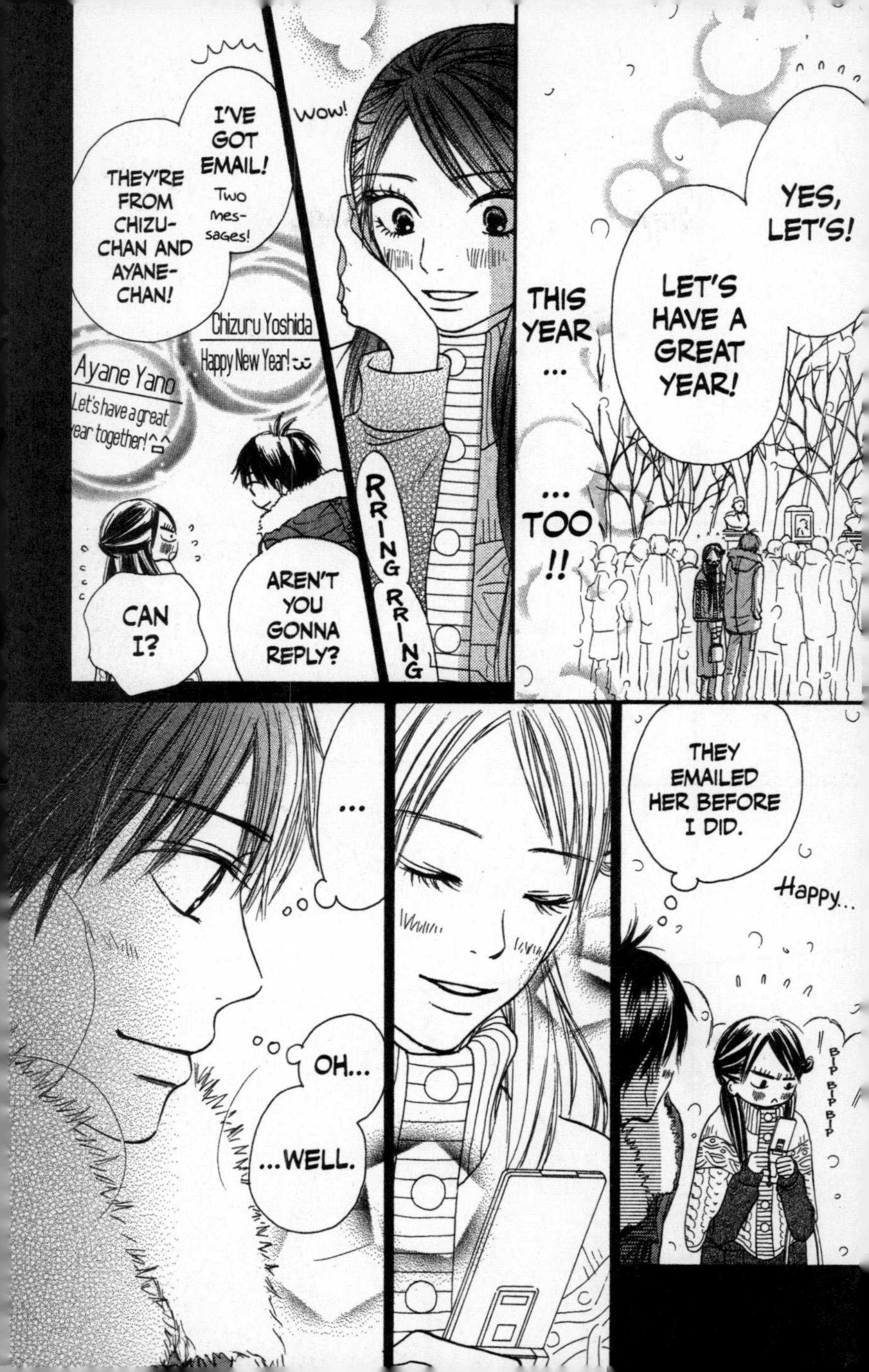
YES, LET'S!
LET'S HAVE A GREAT YEAR!
THIS YEAR ...
... TOO !!
WOW!
RRING RRING
I'VE GOT EMAIL!
Two mes-sages!
THEY'RE FROM CHIZU-CHAN AND AYANE-CHAN!
Chizuru Yoshida
Happy New Year!
Ayane Yano
Let's have a great year together! ^_^
AREN'T YOU GONNA REPLY?
CAN I?
THEY EMAILED HER BEFORE I DID.
Happy...
BIP BIP BIP
...
OH...
...WELL.

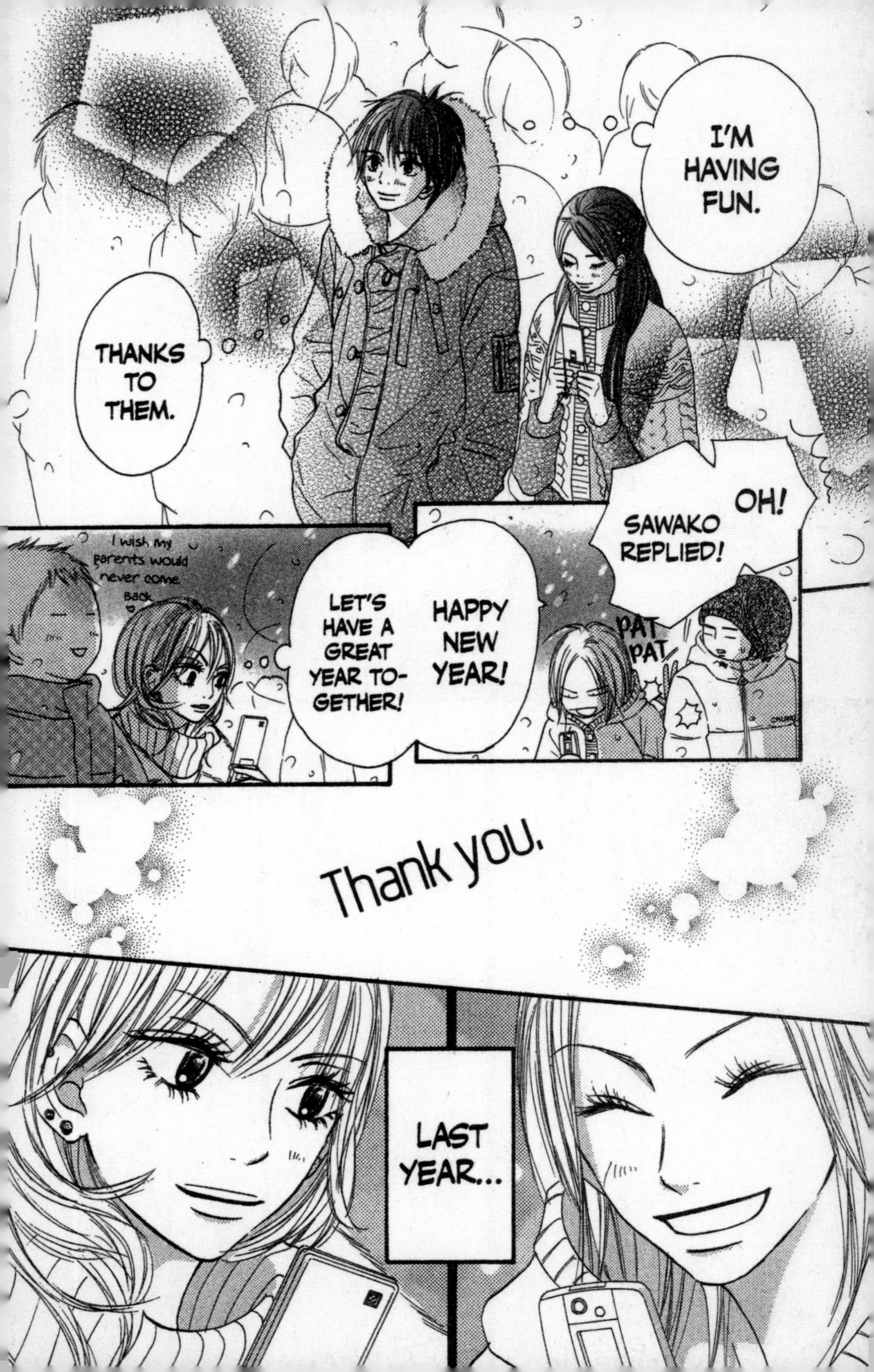
I'M HAVING FUN.
THANKS TO THEM.
OH!
SAWAKO REPLIED!
PAT PAT
HAPPY NEW YEAR!
LET'S HAVE A GREAT YEAR TO-GETHER!
I wish my parents would never come back.
Thank you.
LAST YEAR...

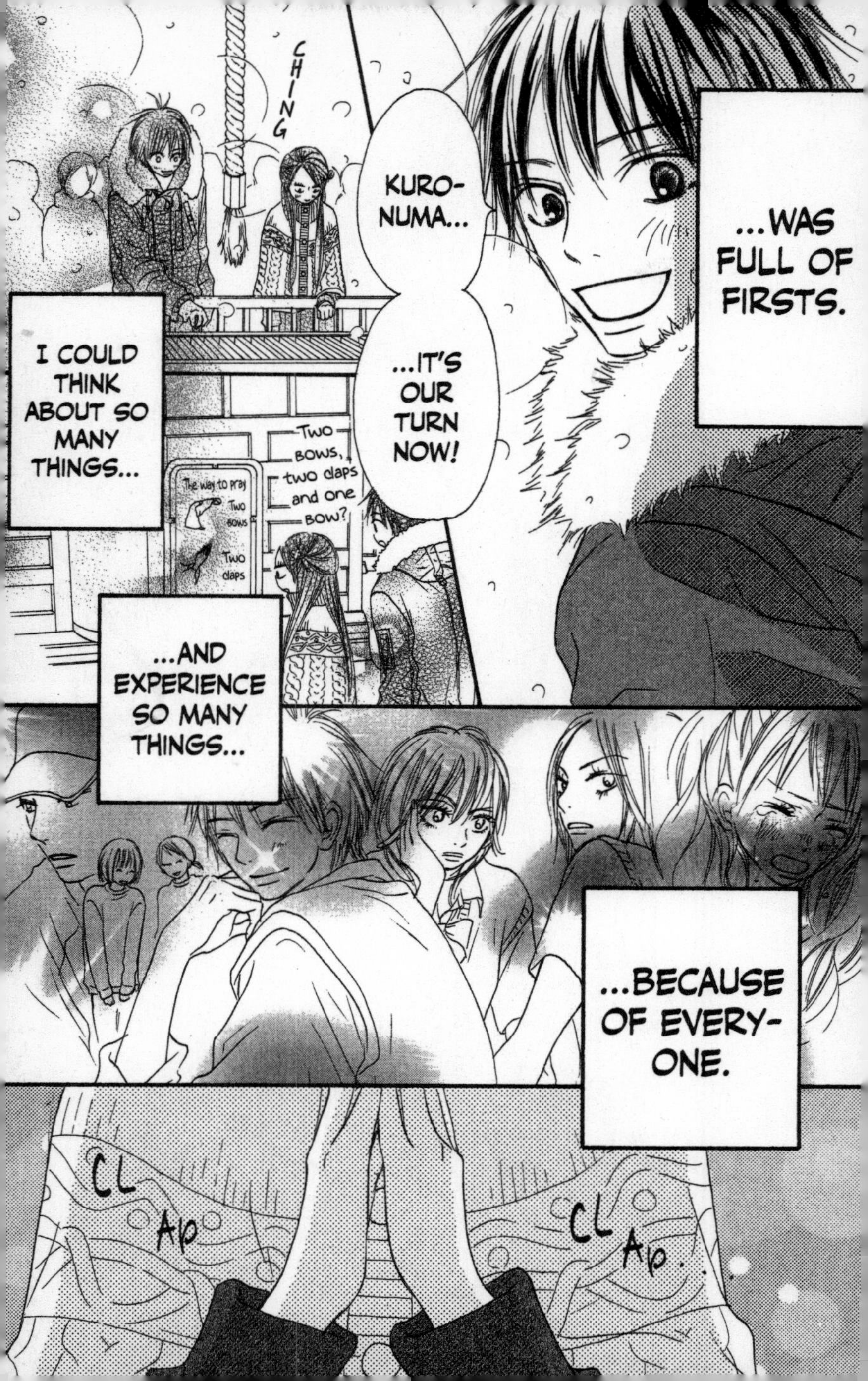
...WAS FULL OF FIRSTS.
KURO-NUMA...
...IT'S OUR TURN NOW!
CHING
I COULD THINK ABOUT SO MANY THINGS...
The way to pray
Two bows
Two claps
Two bows, two claps and one bow?
...AND EXPERIENCE SO MANY THINGS...
...BECAUSE OF EVERY-ONE.
CLAp
CLAp.

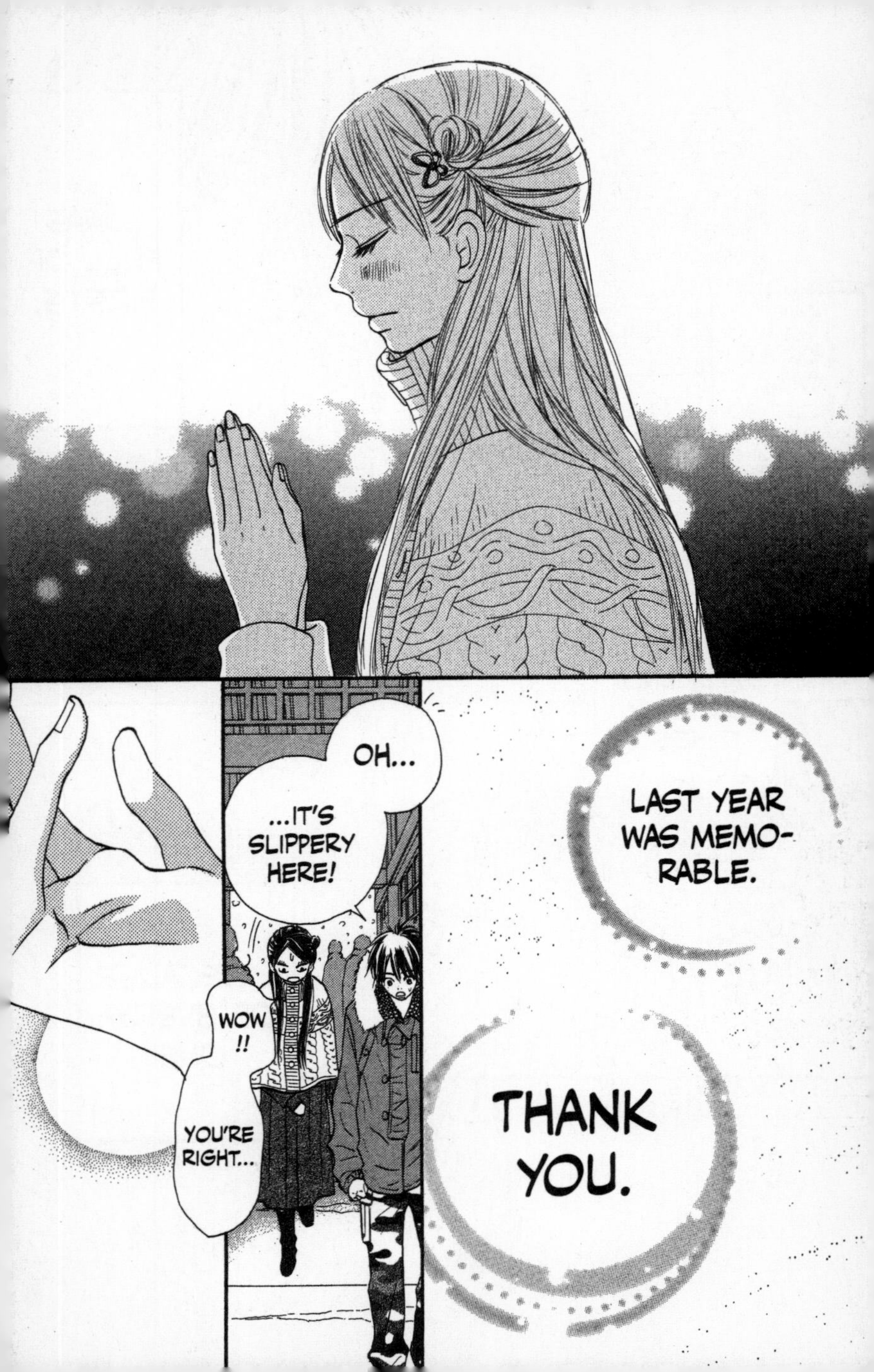
LAST YEAR WAS MEMO-RABLE.
THANK YOU.
OH...
...IT'S SLIPPERY HERE!
WOW!!
YOU'RE RIGHT...

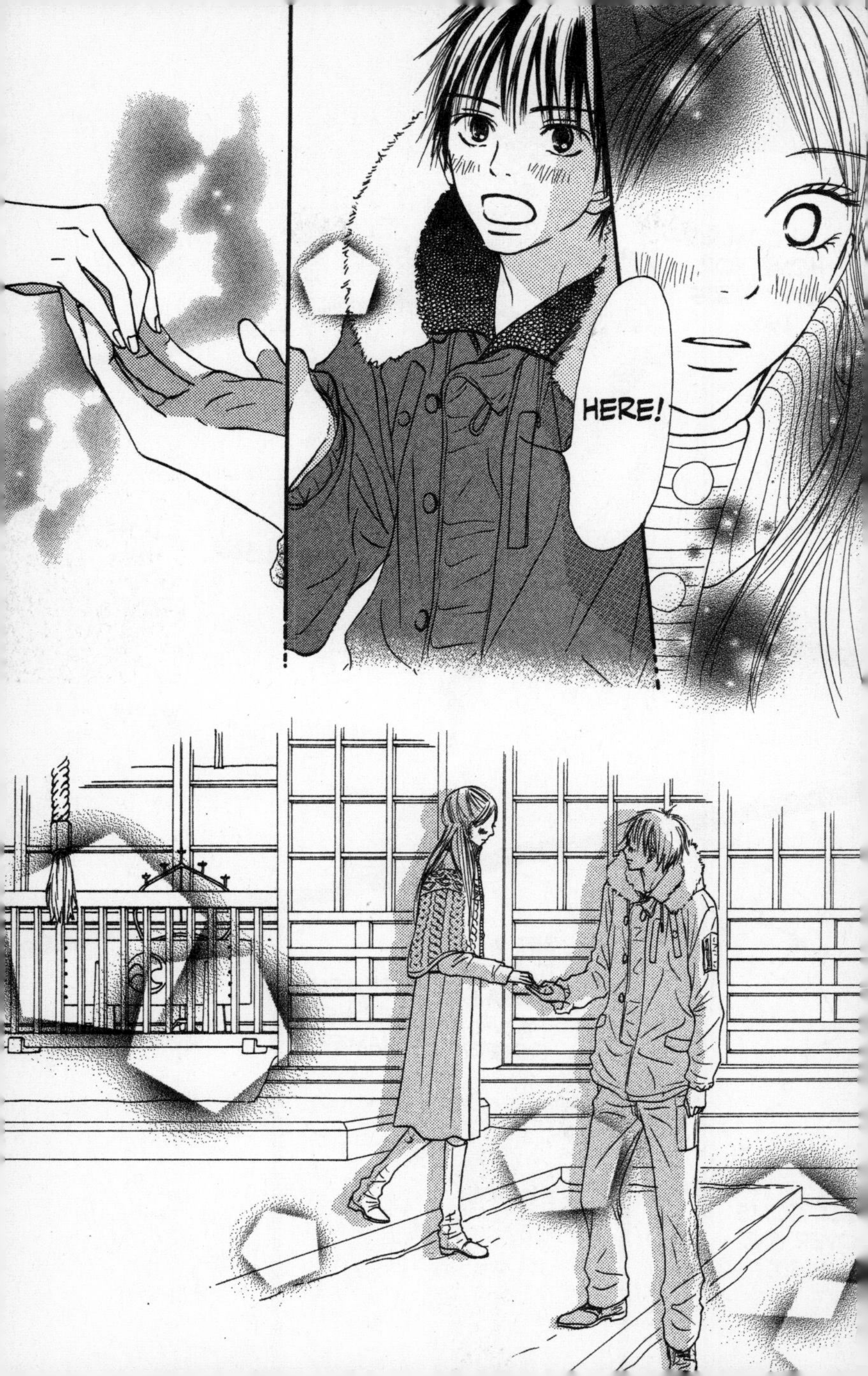
HERE!

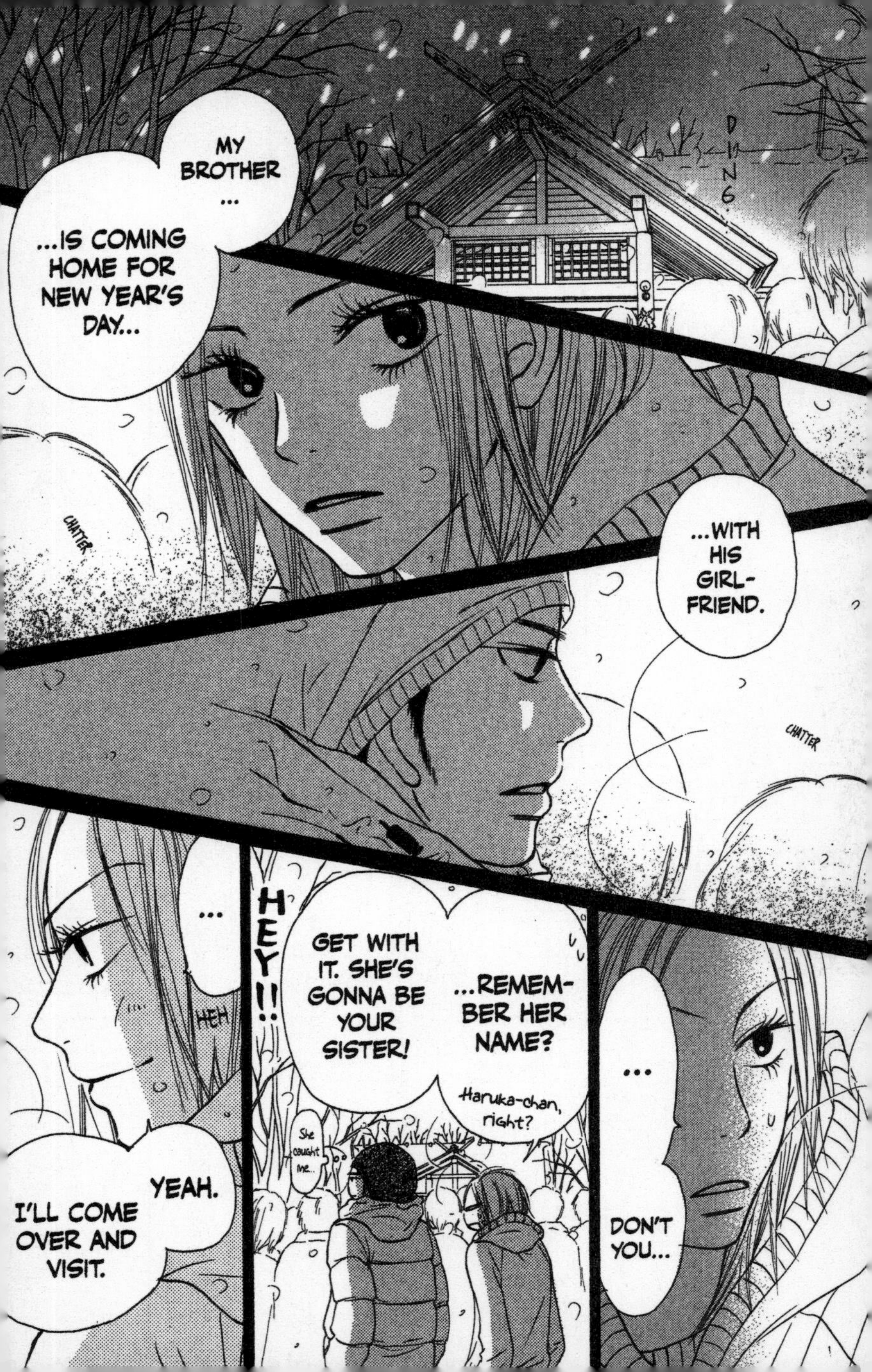
DING
DONG
MY BROTHER ...
...IS COMING HOME FOR NEW YEAR'S DAY...
CHATTER
...WITH HIS GIRL-FRIEND.
CHATTER
...
DON'T YOU...
HEY!!
...REMEM-BER HER NAME?
Haruka-chan, right?
GET WITH IT. SHE'S GONNA BE YOUR SISTER!
She caught me..
...
HEH
YEAH.
I'LL COME OVER AND VISIT.

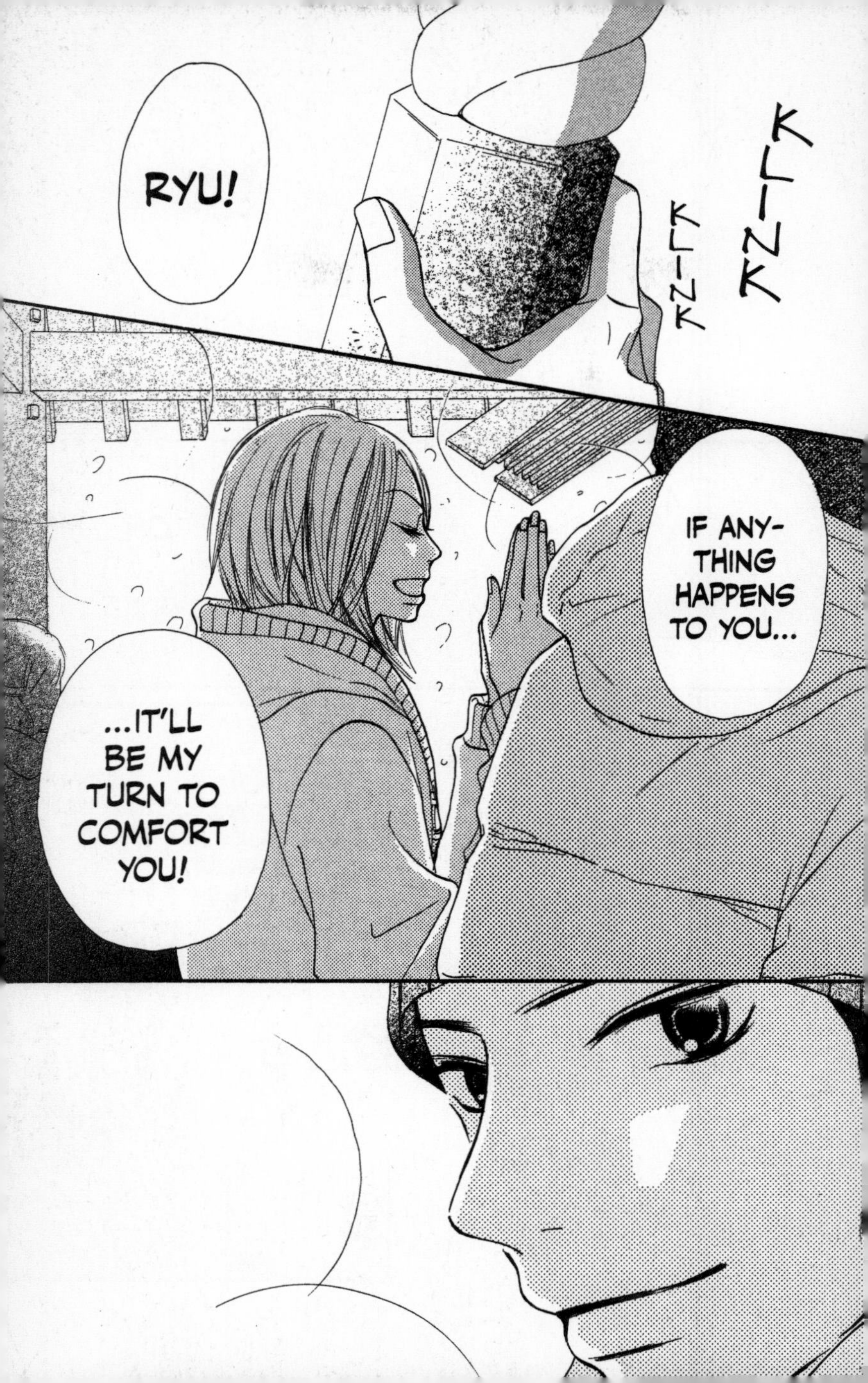
KLINK
KLINK
RYU!
IF ANY-THING HAPPENS TO YOU...
...IT'LL BE MY TURN TO COMFORT YOU!

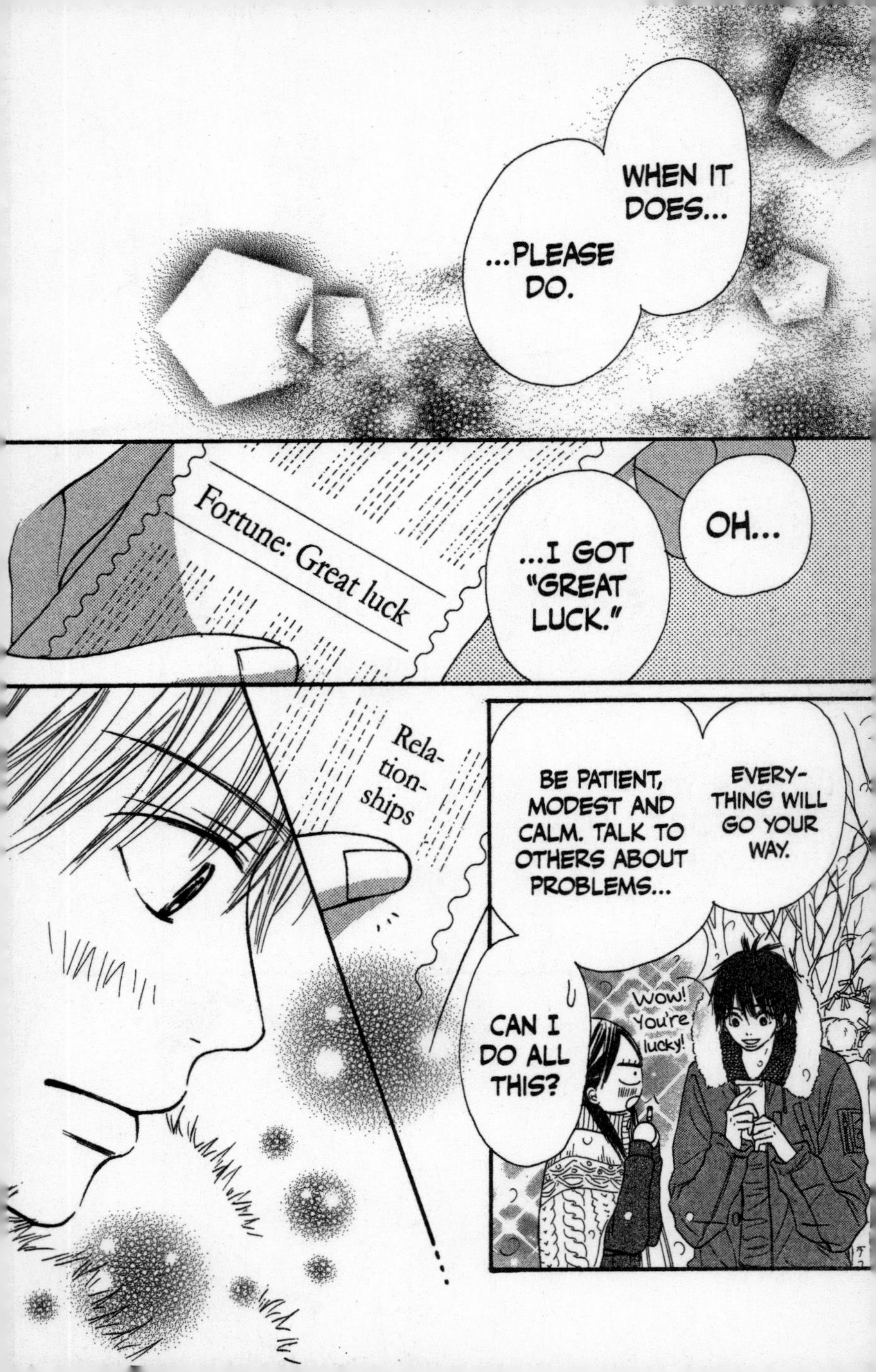
WHEN IT DOES...
...PLEASE DO.
OH...
...I GOT "GREAT LUCK."
Fortune: Great luck
EVERY-THING WILL GO YOUR WAY.
BE PATIENT, MODEST AND CALM. TALK TO OTHERS ABOUT PROBLEMS...
Wow! You're lucky!
CAN I DO ALL THIS?
Rela-tion-ships

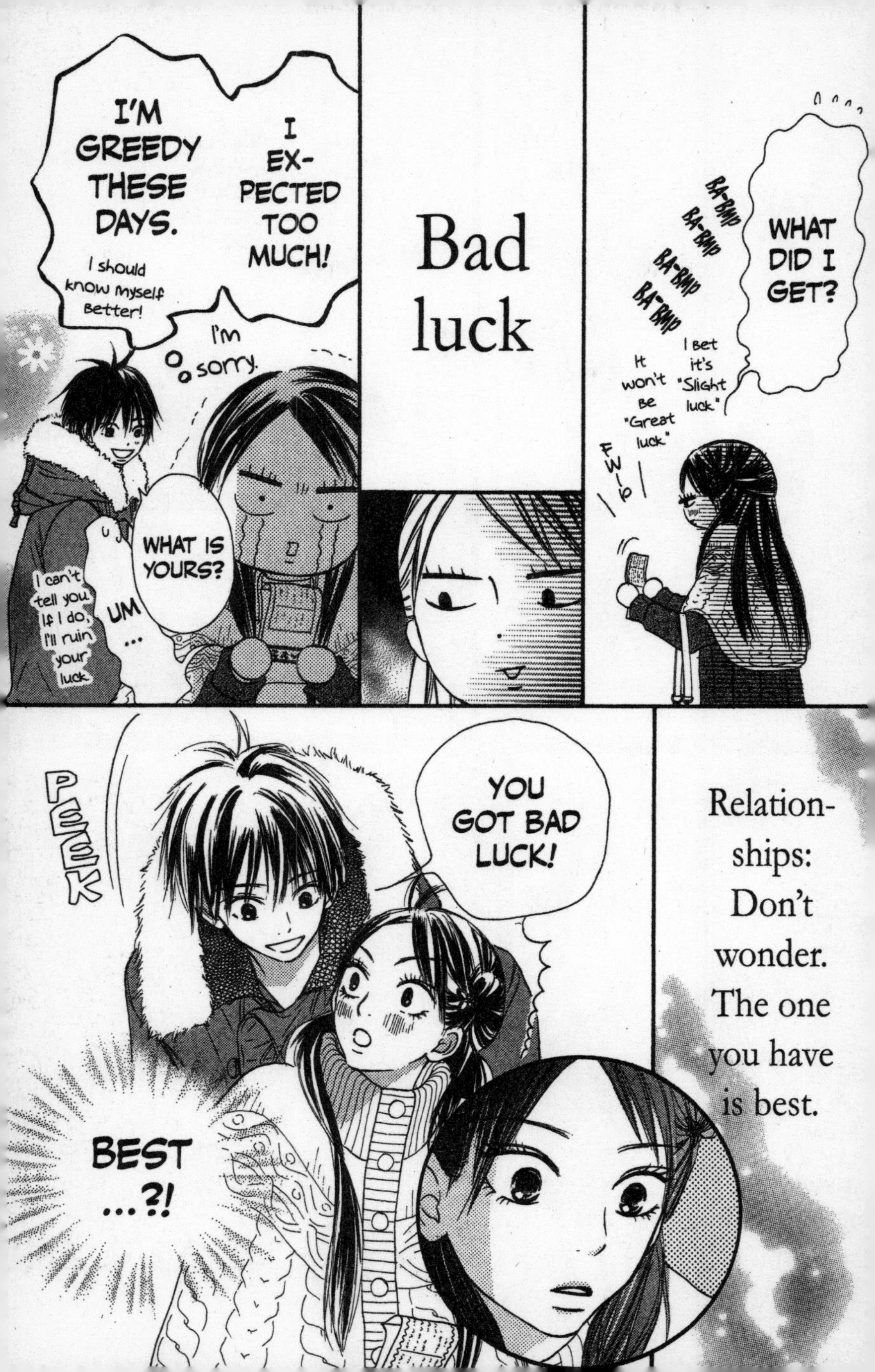
WHAT DID I GET?
BA-BMP BA-BMP BA-BMP BA-BMP
I bet it's "Slight luck"
It won't be "Great luck"
FWIP
Bad luck
I'M GREEDY THESE DAYS. I EX-PECTED TOO MUCH!
I should know myself better!
I'm sorry.
WHAT IS YOURS?
UM ...
I can't tell you. If I do, I'll ruin your luck.
Relation-ships: Don't wonder. The one you have is best.
PEEK
YOU GOT BAD LUCK!
BEST ...?!

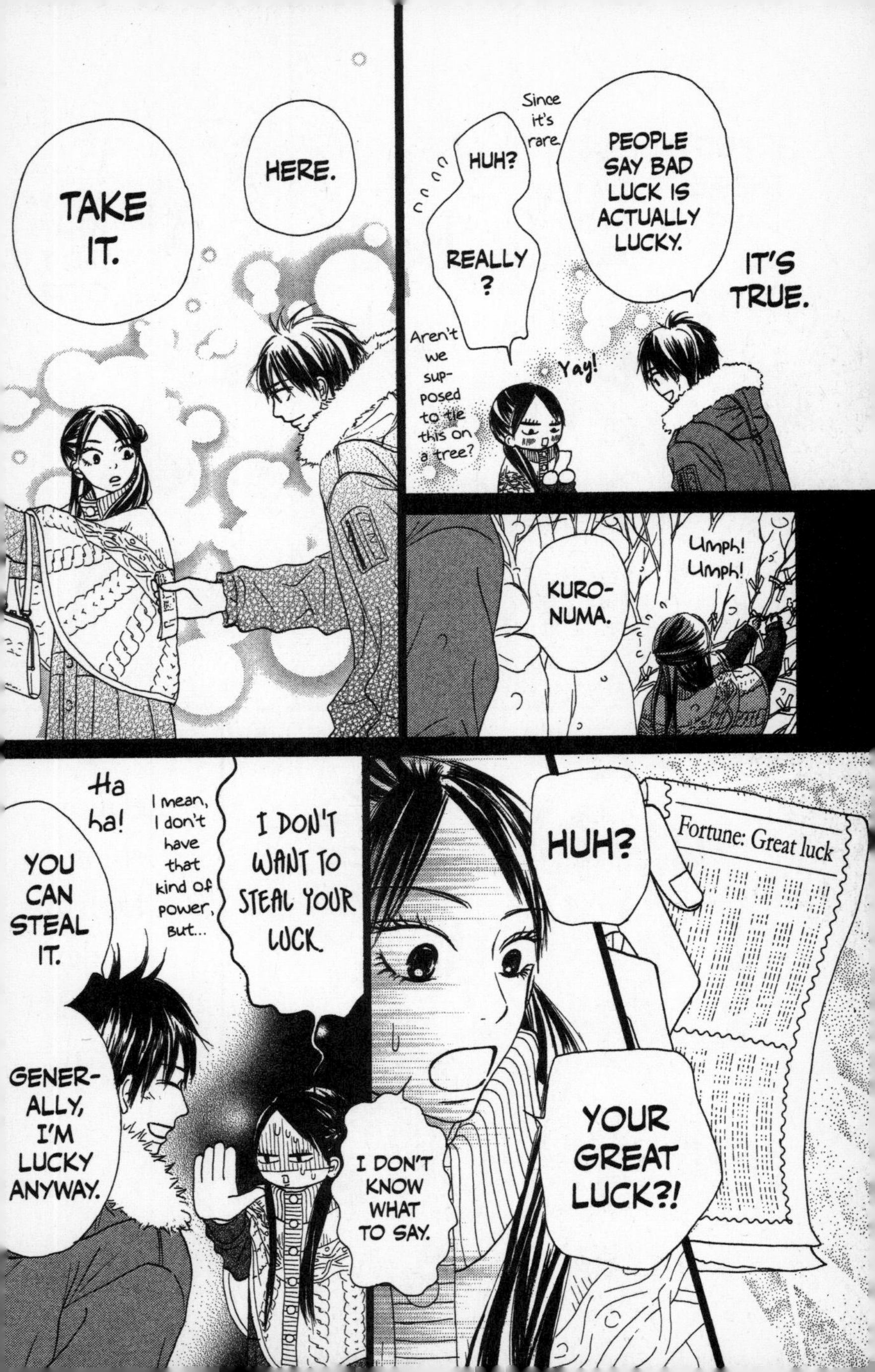
PEOPLE SAY BAD LUCK IS ACTUALLY LUCKY.
Since it's rare.
HUH?
REALLY?
IT'S TRUE.
Yay!
Aren't we supposed to tie this on a tree?
Umph! Umph!
KURO-NUMA.
HERE.
TAKE IT.
HUH?
Fortune: Great luck
YOUR GREAT LUCK?!
I DON'T WANT TO STEAL YOUR LUCK.
I mean, I don't have that kind of power, but...
Ha ha!
YOU CAN STEAL IT.
GENER-ALLY, I'M LUCKY ANYWAY.
I DON'T KNOW WHAT TO SAY.

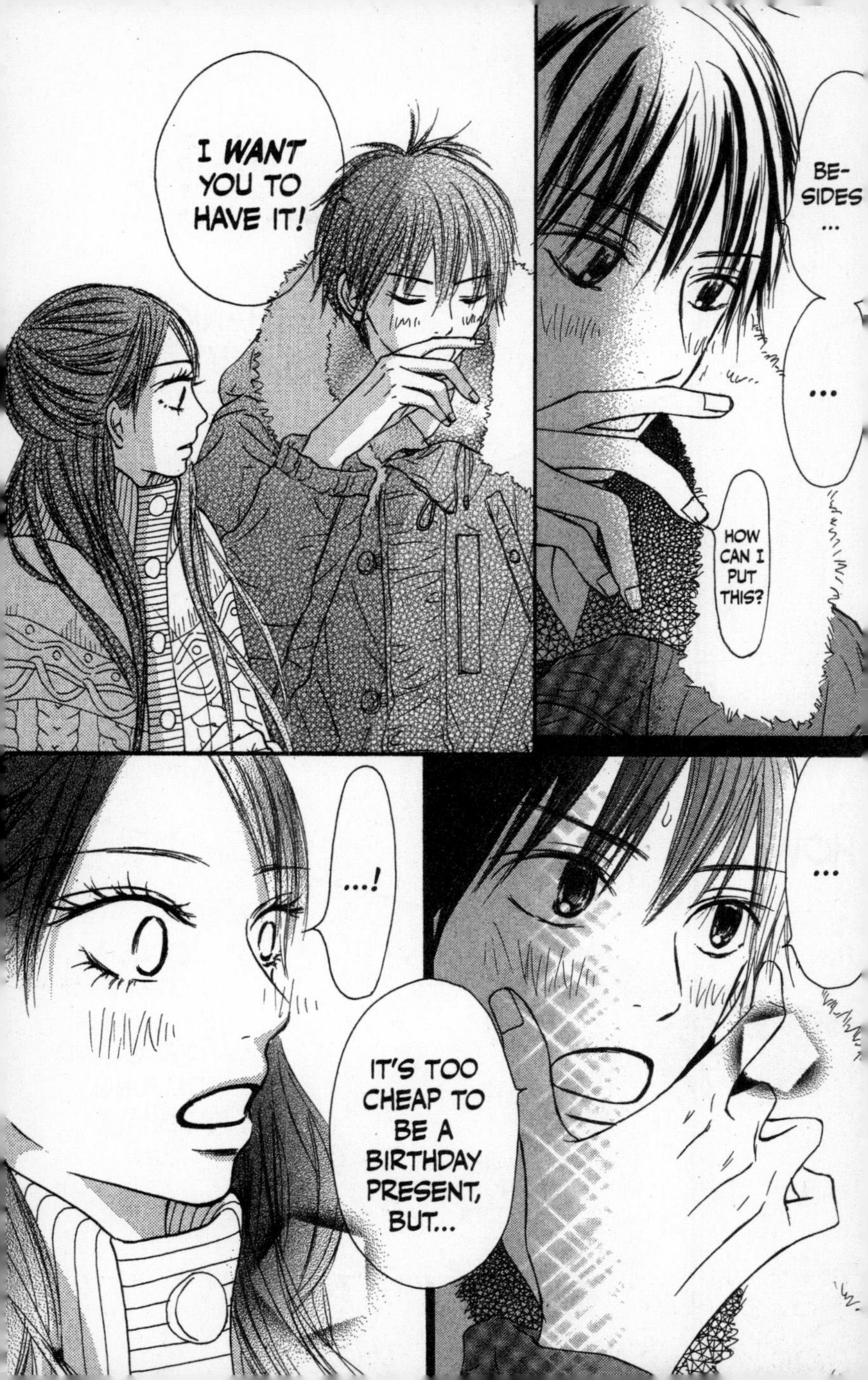
BE-SIDES ...
...
HOW CAN I PUT THIS?
I WANT YOU TO HAVE IT!
...
IT'S TOO CHEAP TO BE A BIRTHDAY PRESENT, BUT...
...!

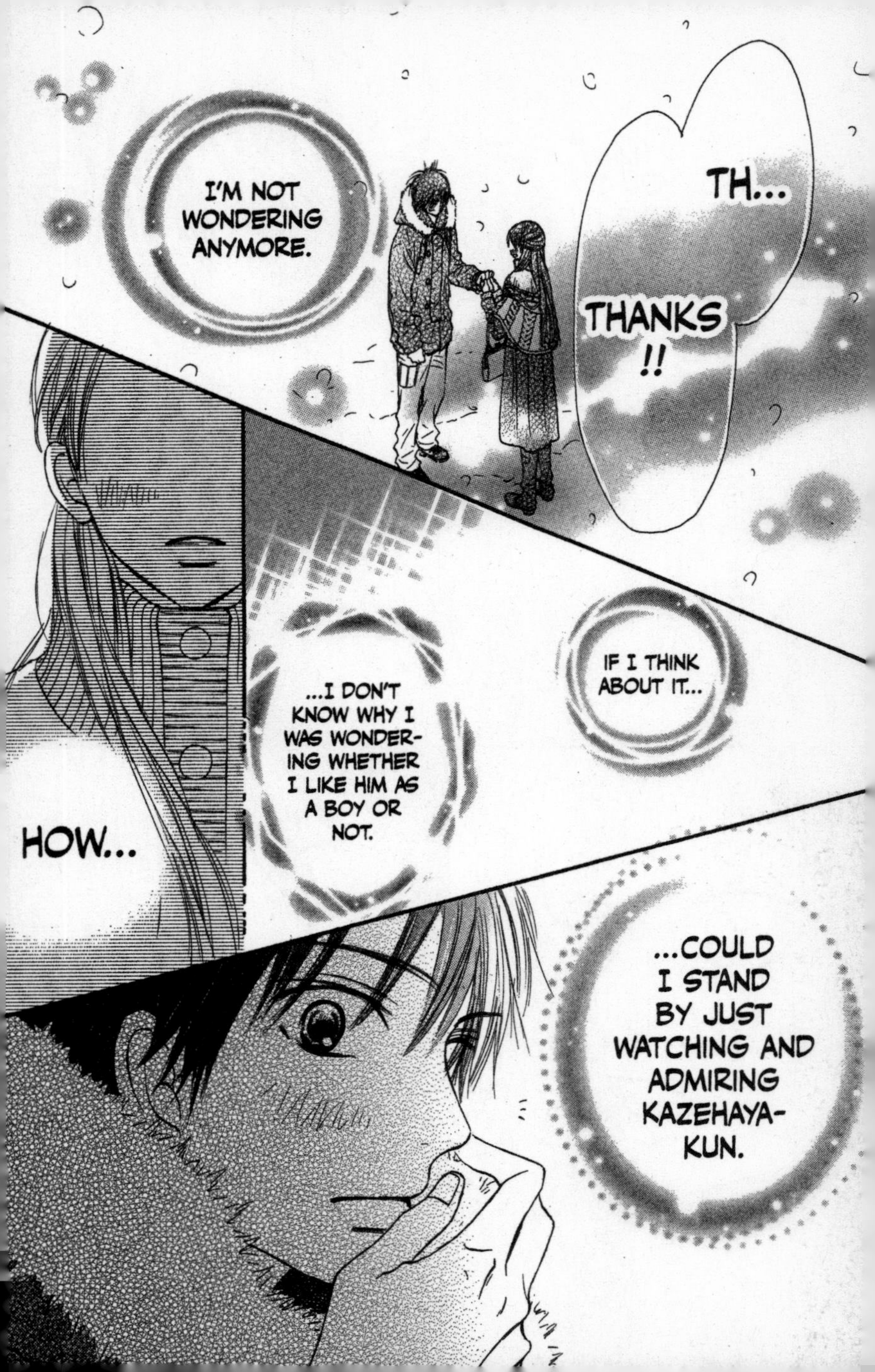
TH...
THANKS!!
I'M NOT WONDERING ANYMORE.
IF I THINK ABOUT IT...
...I DON'T KNOW WHY I WAS WONDERING WHETHER I LIKE HIM AS A BOY OR NOT.
HOW...
...COULD I STAND BY JUST WATCHING AND ADMIRING KAZEHAYA-KUN.

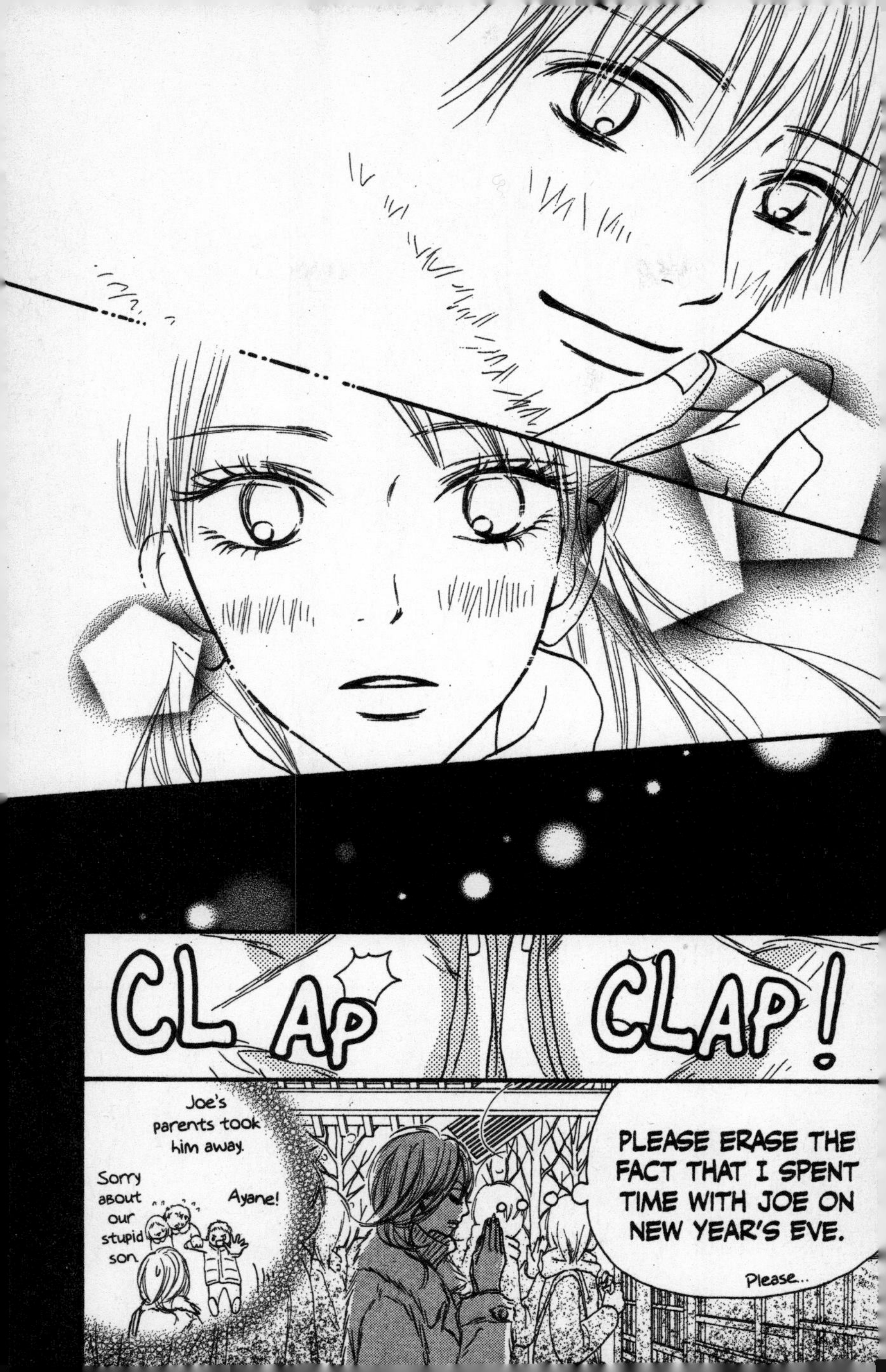
CLAP CLAP!
PLEASE ERASE THE FACT THAT I SPENT TIME WITH JOE ON NEW YEAR'S EVE.
Please...
Joe's parents took him away.
Ayane!
Sorry about our stupid son.

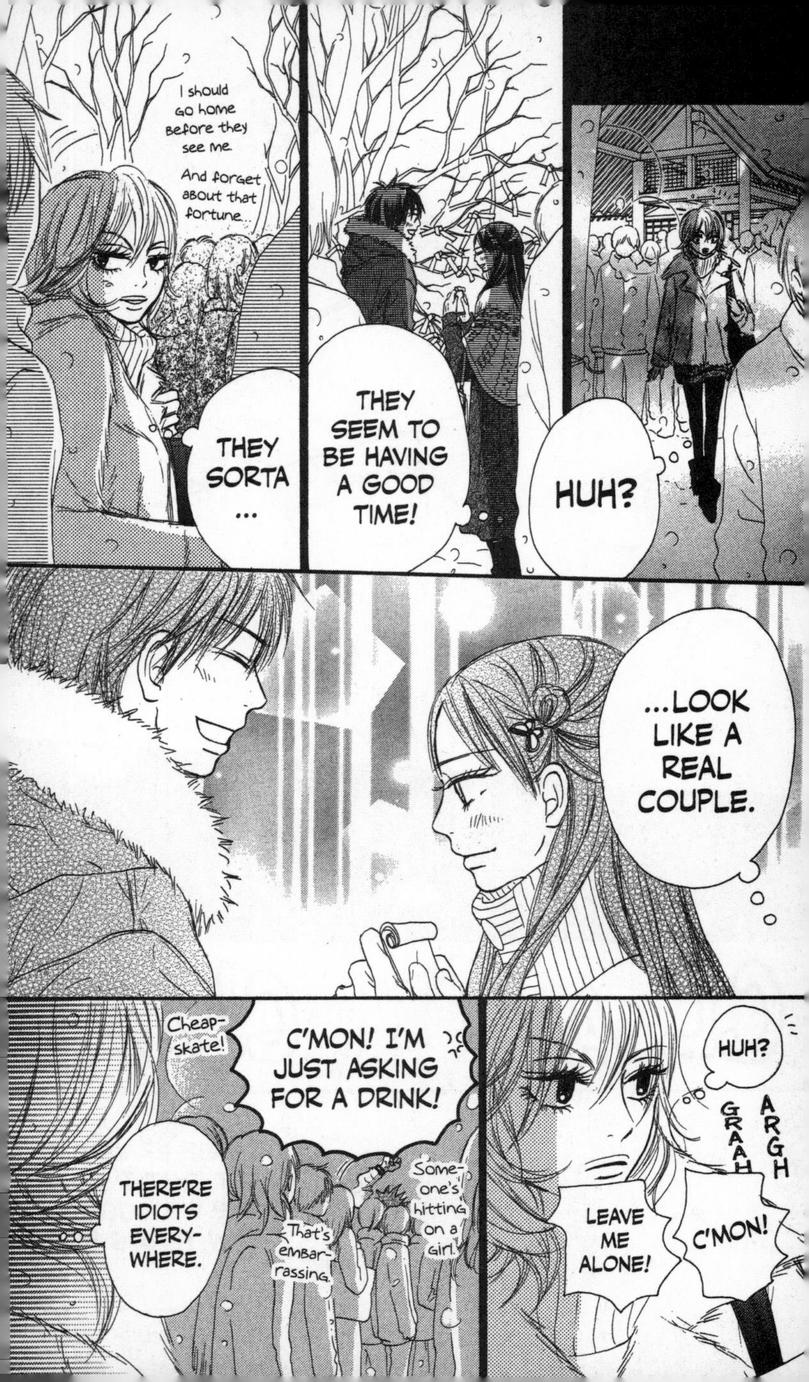
HUH?
THEY SEEM TO BE HAVING A GOOD TIME!
I should go home before they see me.
And forget about that fortune...
THEY SORTA ...
...LOOK LIKE A REAL COUPLE.
HUH?
ARGH
GRAAAH
C'MON!
LEAVE ME ALONE!
C'MON! I'M JUST ASKING FOR A DRINK!
Cheap-skate!
Some-one's hitting on a girl.
That's embar-rassing.
THERE'RE IDIOTS EVERY-WHERE.

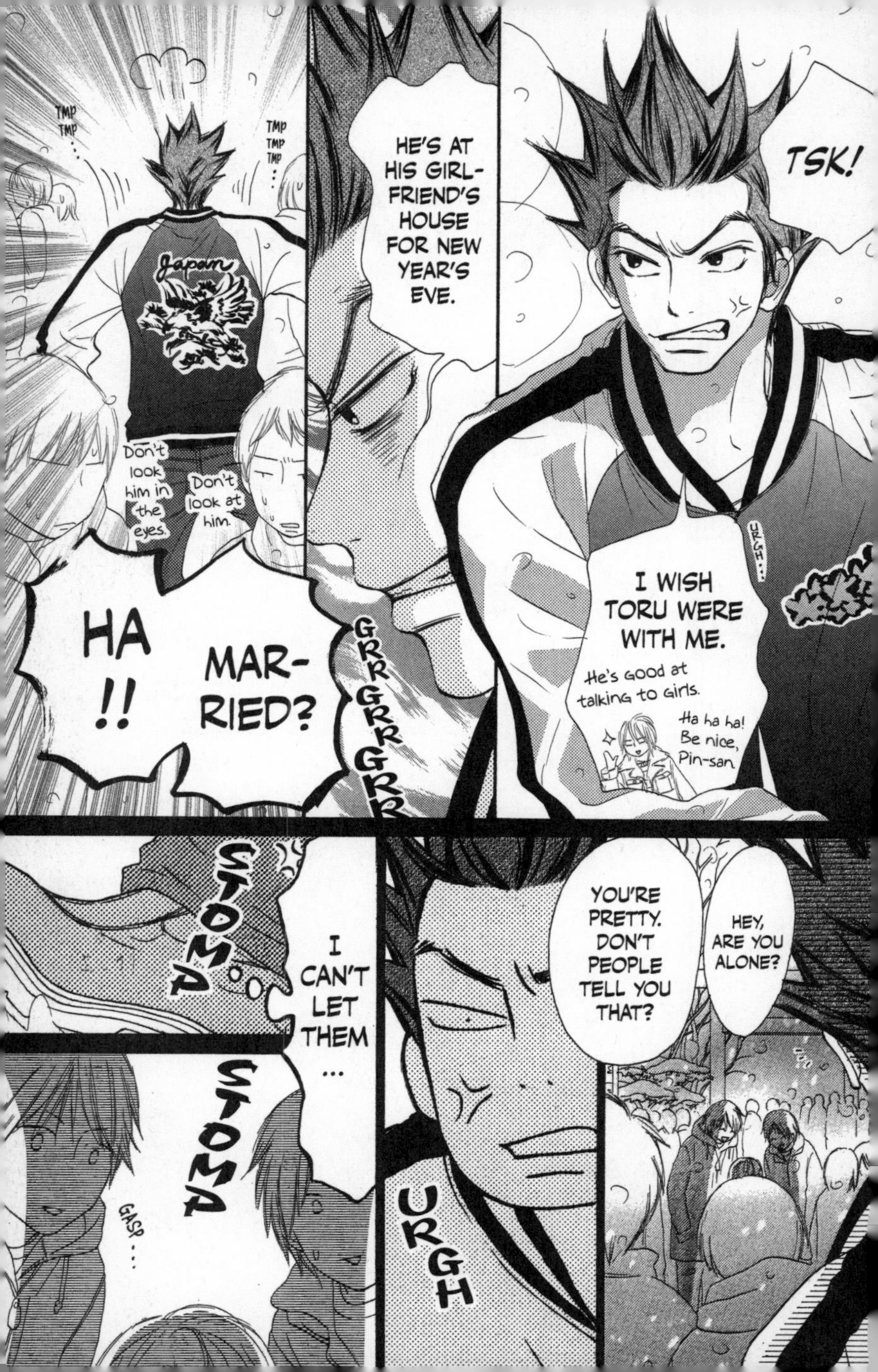
TSK!
I WISH TORU WERE WITH ME.
He's good at talking to girls.
Ha ha ha! Be nice, Pin-san.
URGH...
HE'S AT HIS GIRL-FRIEND'S HOUSE FOR NEW YEAR'S EVE.
GRR GRR GRR
TMP TMP TMP...
TMP TMP...
Don't look at him.
Don't look him in the eyes.
HA!! MAR-RIED?
HEY, ARE YOU ALONE?
YOU'RE PRETTY. DON'T PEOPLE TELL YOU THAT?
URGH
STOMP
I CAN'T LET THEM...
STOMP
GASP...

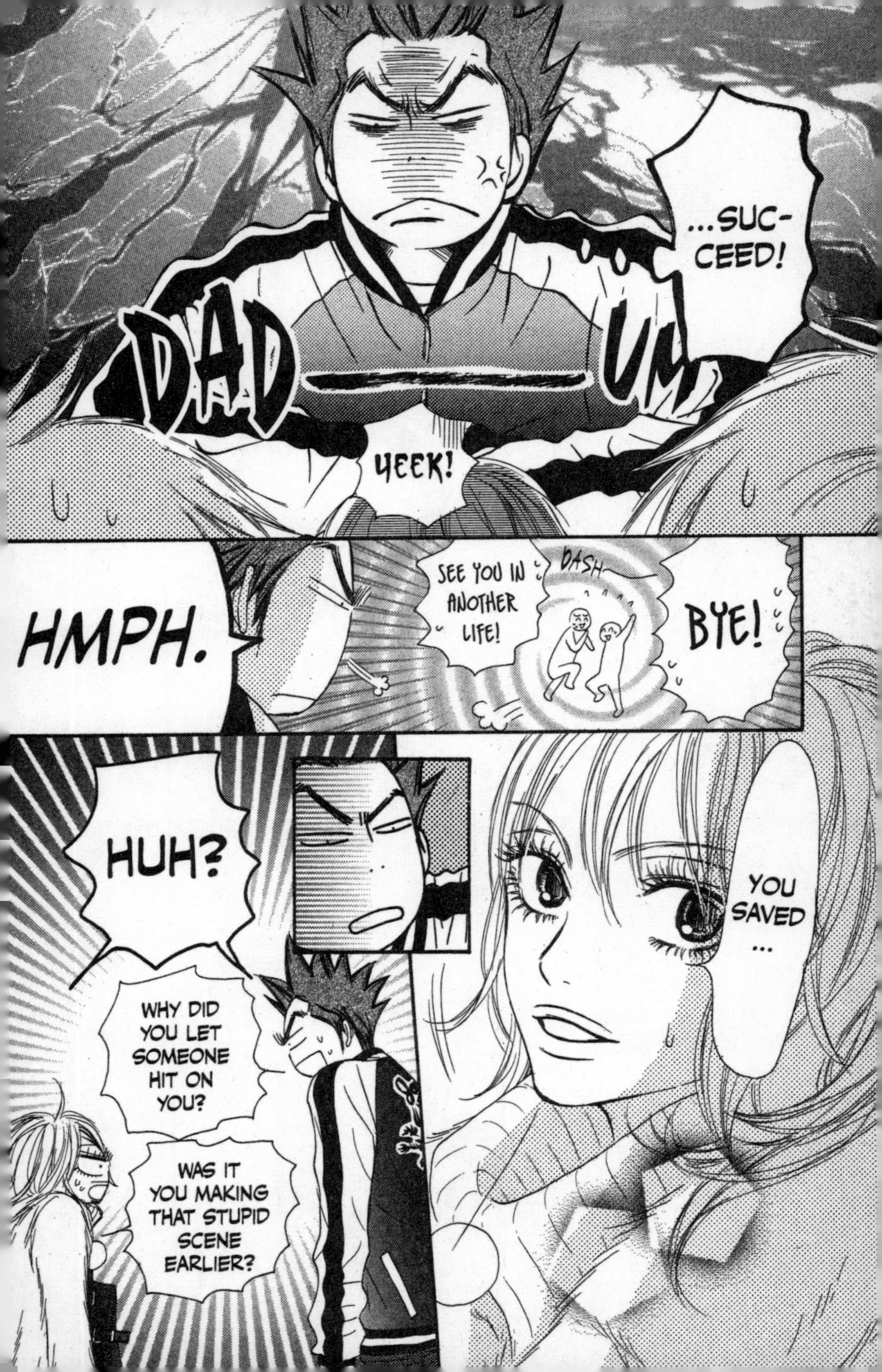
...SUC-CEED!
DAD—UM
YEEK!
BYE!
DASH
SEE YOU IN ANOTHER LIFE!
HMPH.
YOU SAVED ...
HUH?
WHY DID YOU LET SOMEONE HIT ON YOU?
WAS IT YOU MAKING THAT STUPID SCENE EARLIER?

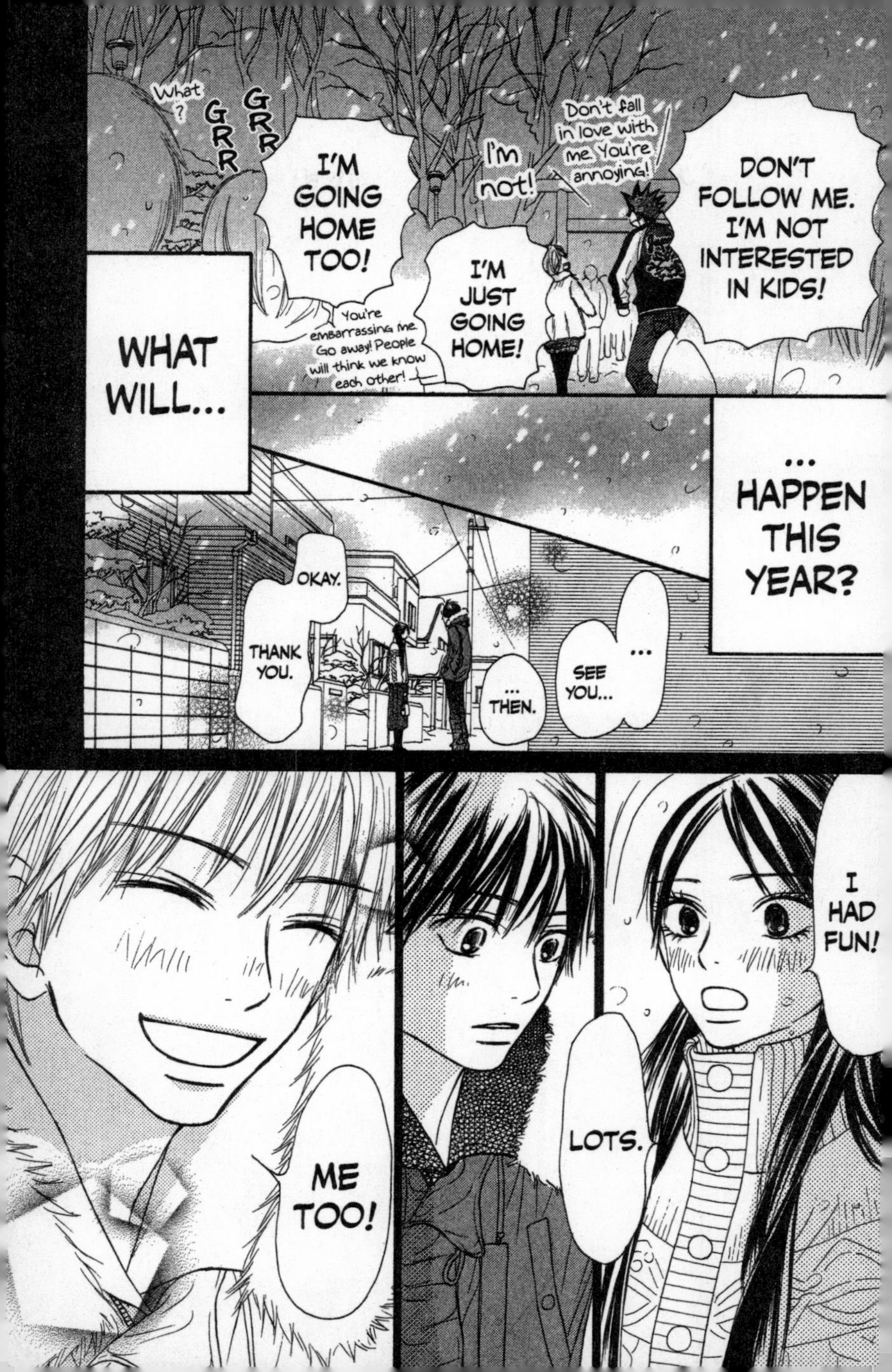
DON'T FOLLOW ME. I'M NOT INTERESTED IN KIDS!
Don't fall in love with me. You're annoying!
I'm not!
I'M JUST GOING HOME!
You're embarrassing me. Go away! People will think we know each other!
I'M GOING HOME TOO!
GRR
GRR
What?
WHAT WILL...
... HAPPEN THIS YEAR?
...
SEE YOU...
... THEN.
OKAY.
THANK YOU.
I HAD FUN!
LOTS.
ME TOO!

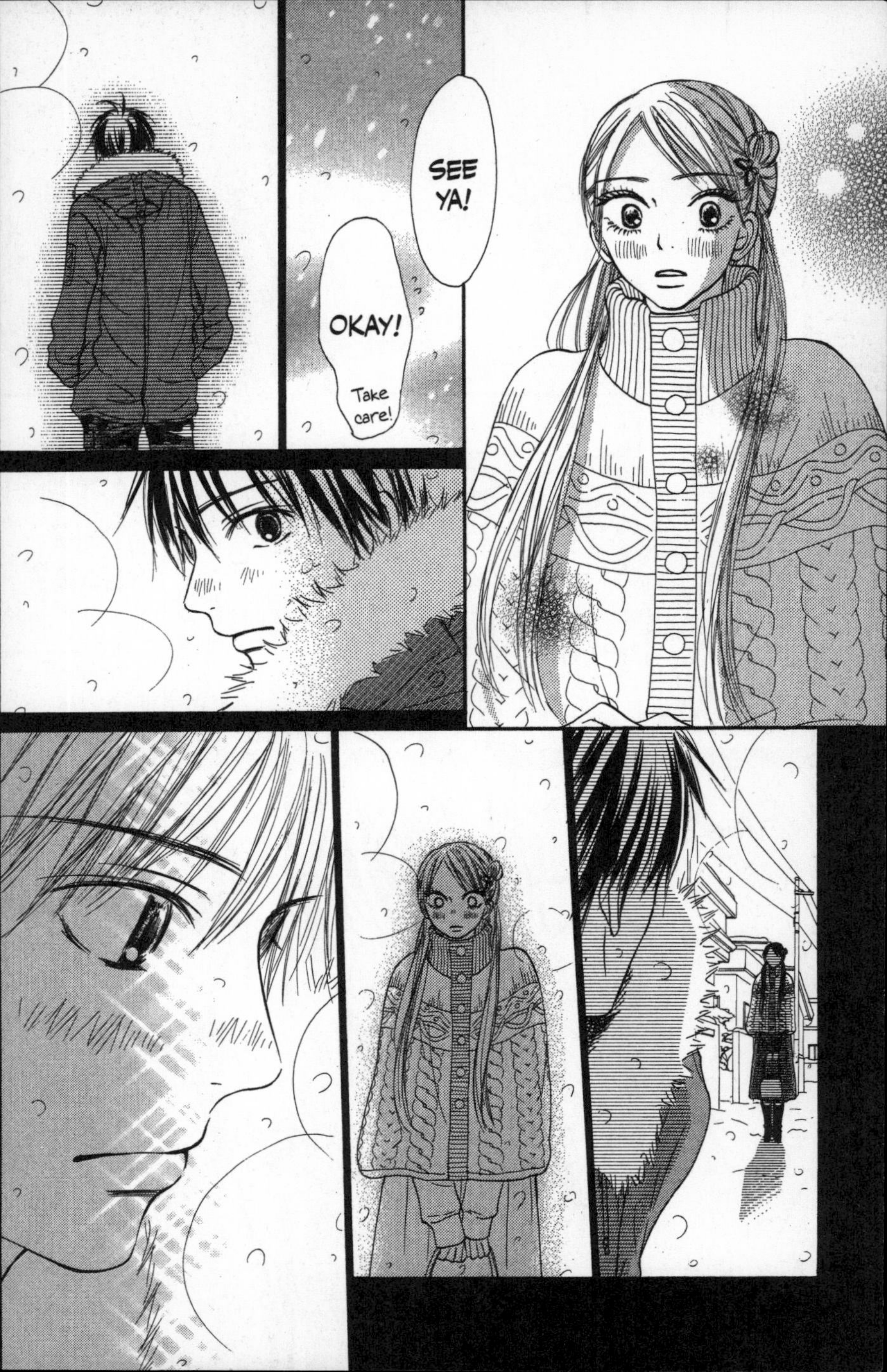
SEE YA!
OKAY!
Take care!

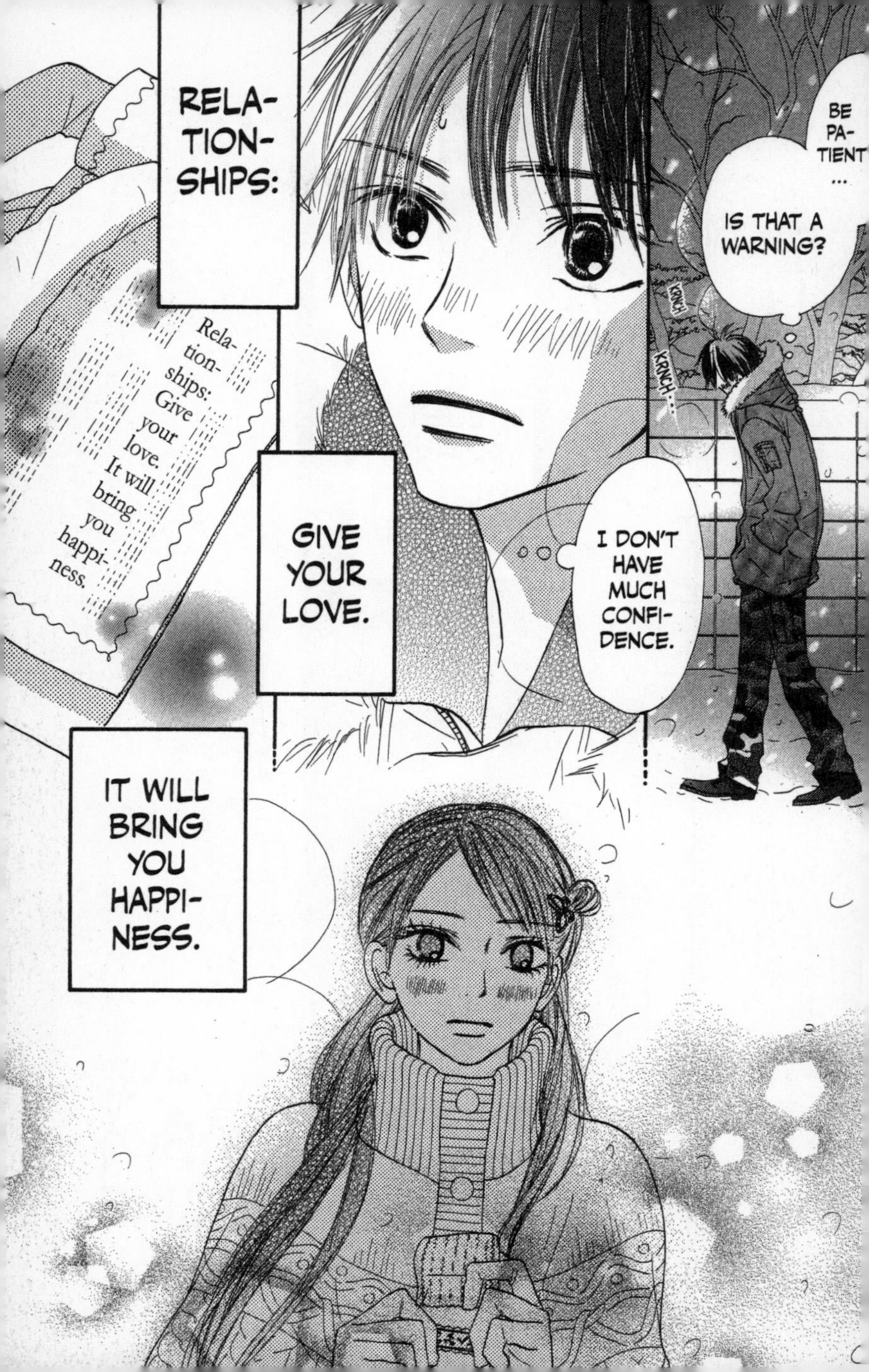
BE PATIENT...
IS THAT A WARNING?
KRNCH
KRNCH...
I DON'T HAVE MUCH CONFIDENCE.
RELATIONSHIPS:
Relationships: Give your love. It will bring you happiness.
GIVE YOUR LOVE.
IT WILL BRING YOU HAPPINESS.

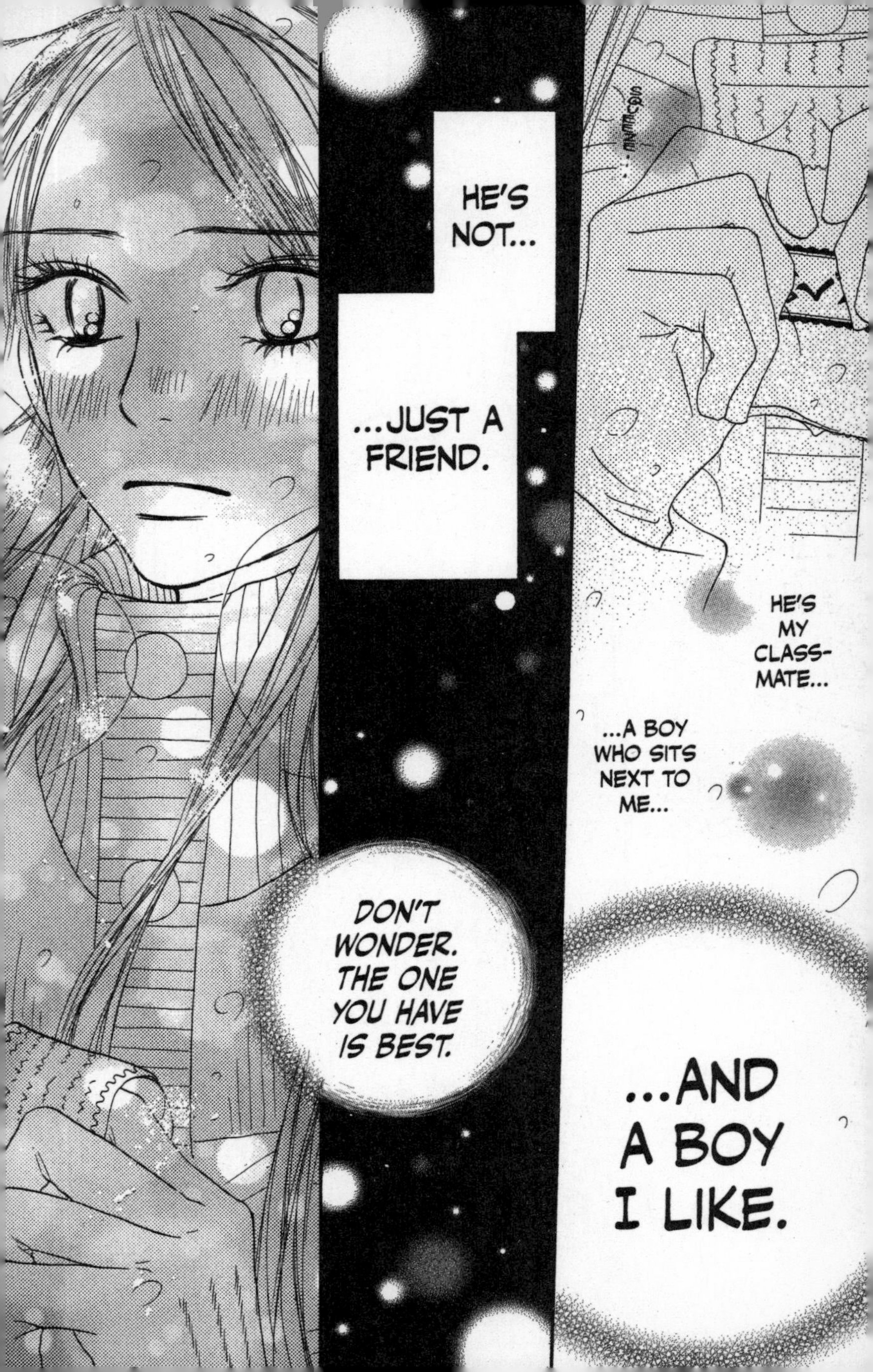
HE'S MY CLASS-MATE...
...A BOY WHO SITS NEXT TO ME...
...AND A BOY I LIKE.
HE'S NOT...
...JUST A FRIEND.
DON'T WONDER. THE ONE YOU HAVE IS BEST.

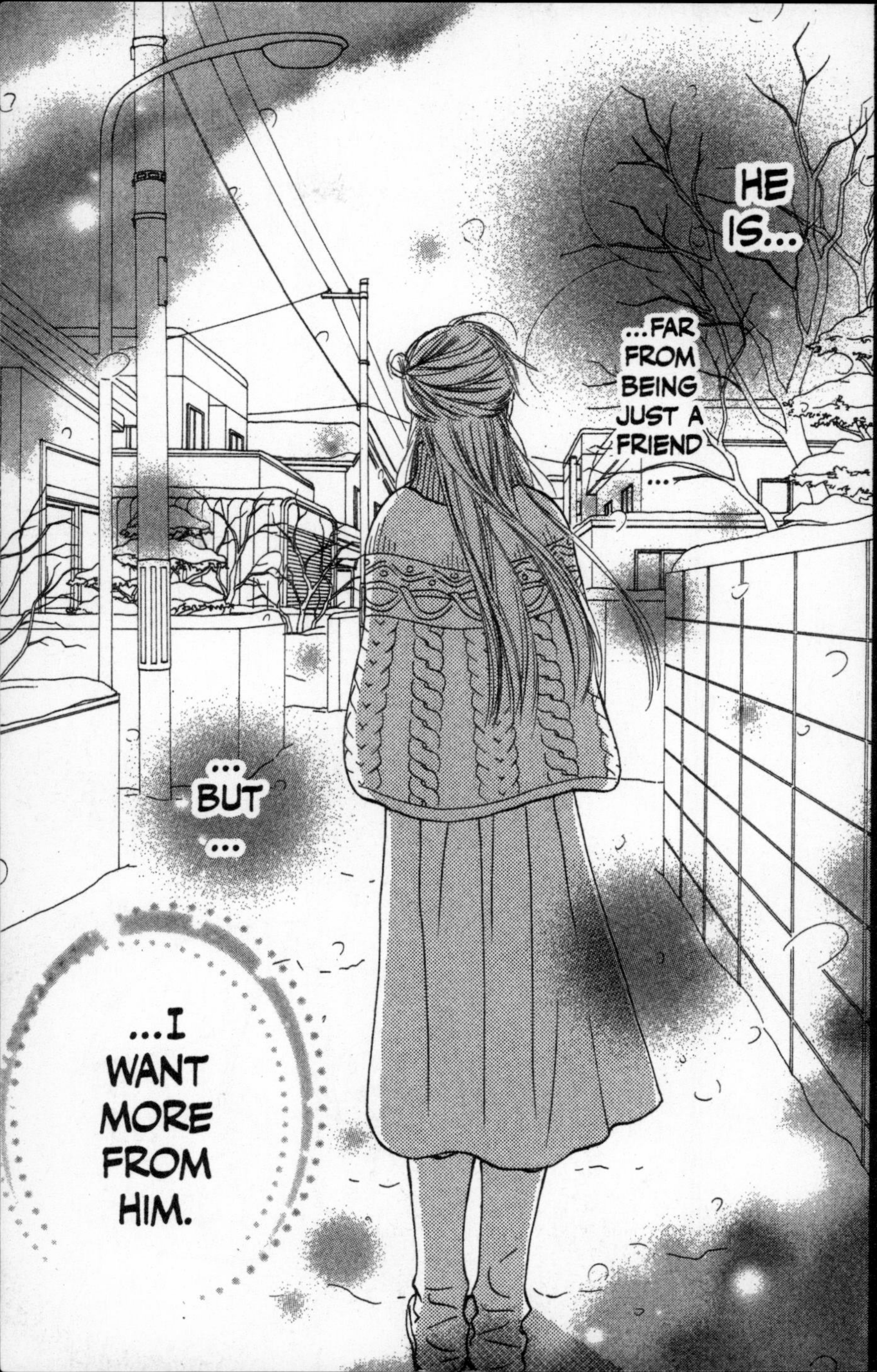
HE IS...
...FAR FROM BEING JUST A FRIEND...
...BUT...
...I WANT MORE FROM HIM.

Episode 28: Valentine's Day

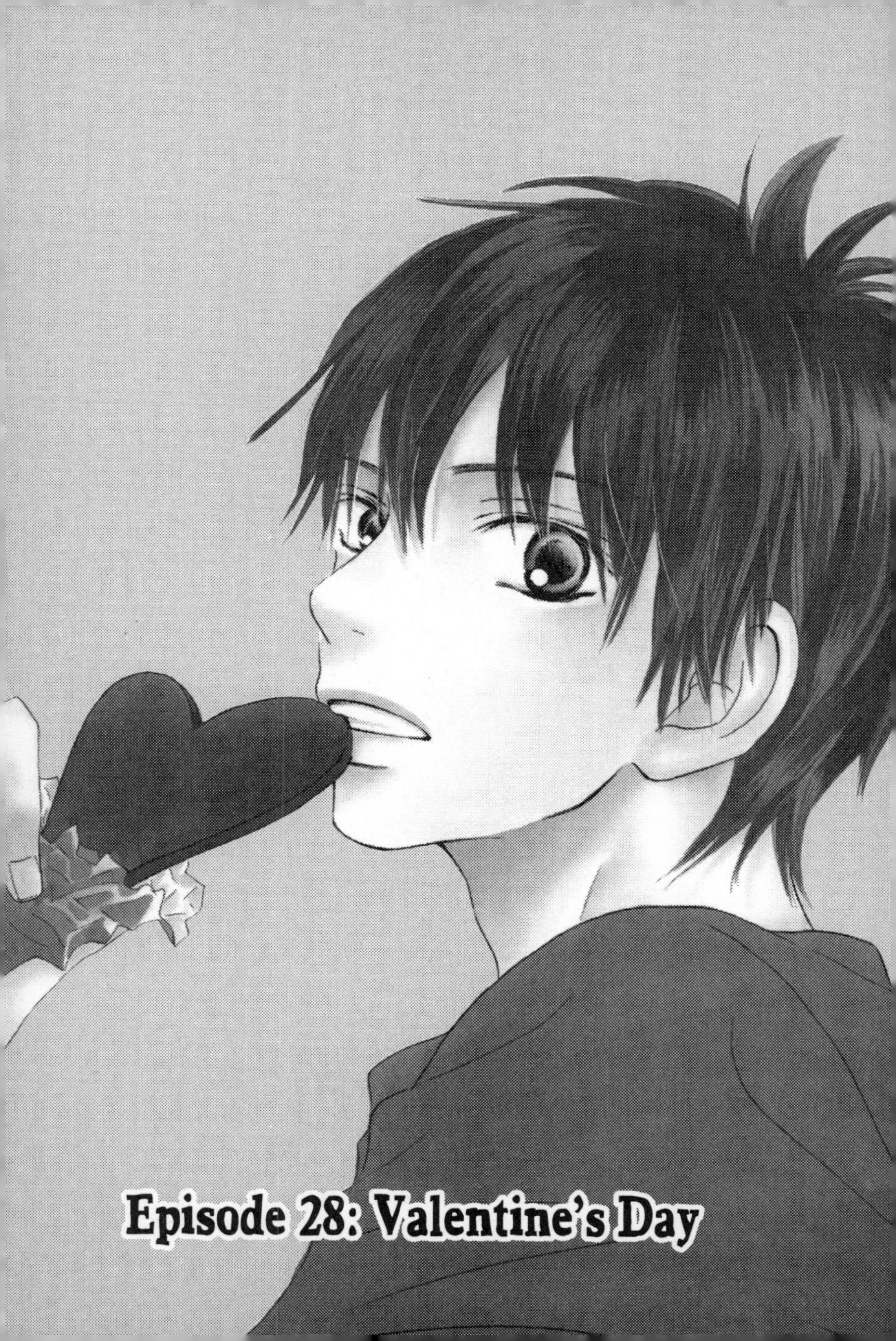

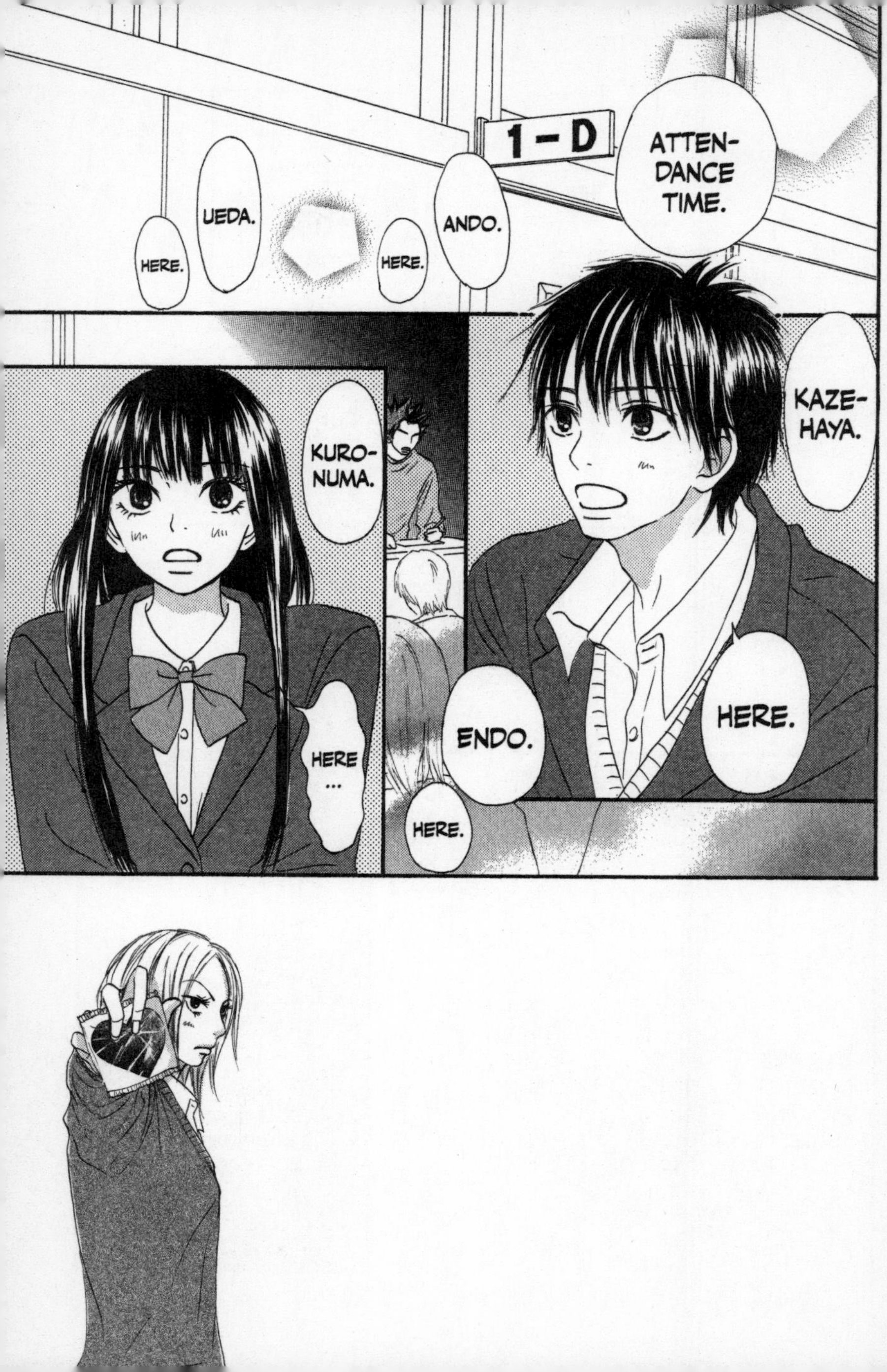
1 – D
ATTEN-DANCE TIME.
ANDO.
HERE.
UEDA.
HERE.
ENDO.
HERE.
KAZE-HAYA.
HERE.
KURO-NUMA.
HERE ...

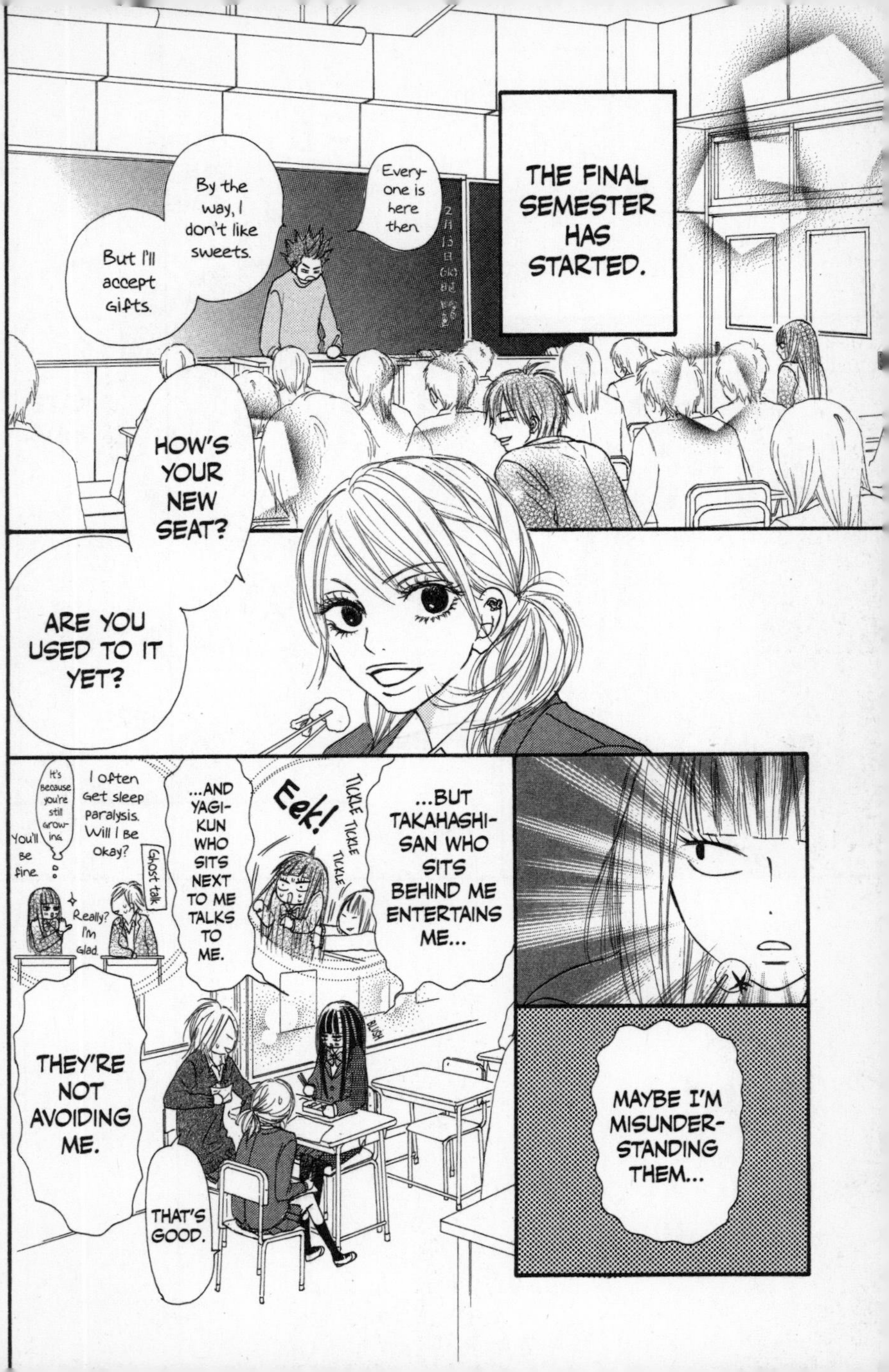
THE FINAL SEMESTER HAS STARTED.
Every-one is here then.
By the way, I don't like sweets.
But I'll accept gifts.
HOW'S YOUR NEW SEAT?
ARE YOU USED TO IT YET?
...BUT TAKAHASHI-SAN WHO SITS BEHIND ME ENTERTAINS ME...
Eek!
TICKLE TICKLE
TICKLE
...AND YAGI-KUN WHO SITS NEXT TO ME TALKS TO ME.
Ghost talk
I often get sleep paralysis. Will I be okay?
It's because you're still grow-ing.
You'll be fine.
Really? I'm glad.
MAYBE I'M MISUNDER-STANDING THEM...
THEY'RE NOT AVOIDING ME.
BLUSH
THAT'S GOOD.

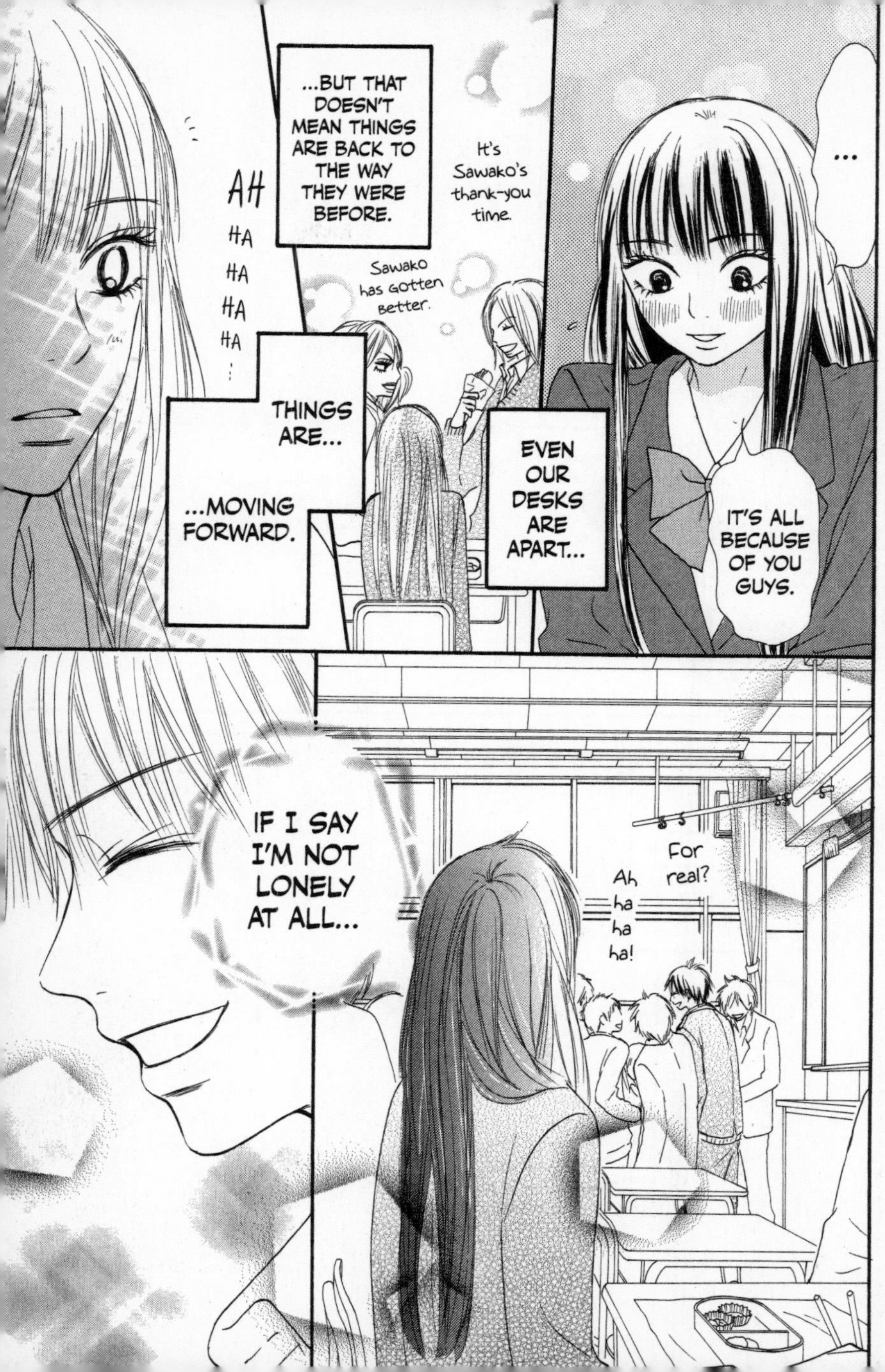
...
IT'S ALL BECAUSE OF YOU GUYS.
EVEN OUR DESKS ARE APART...
It's Sawako's thank-you time.
Sawako has gotten better.
...BUT THAT DOESN'T MEAN THINGS ARE BACK TO THE WAY THEY WERE BEFORE.
THINGS ARE...
...MOVING FORWARD.
AH HA HA HA HA
For real?
Ah ha ha ha!
IF I SAY I'M NOT LONELY AT ALL...

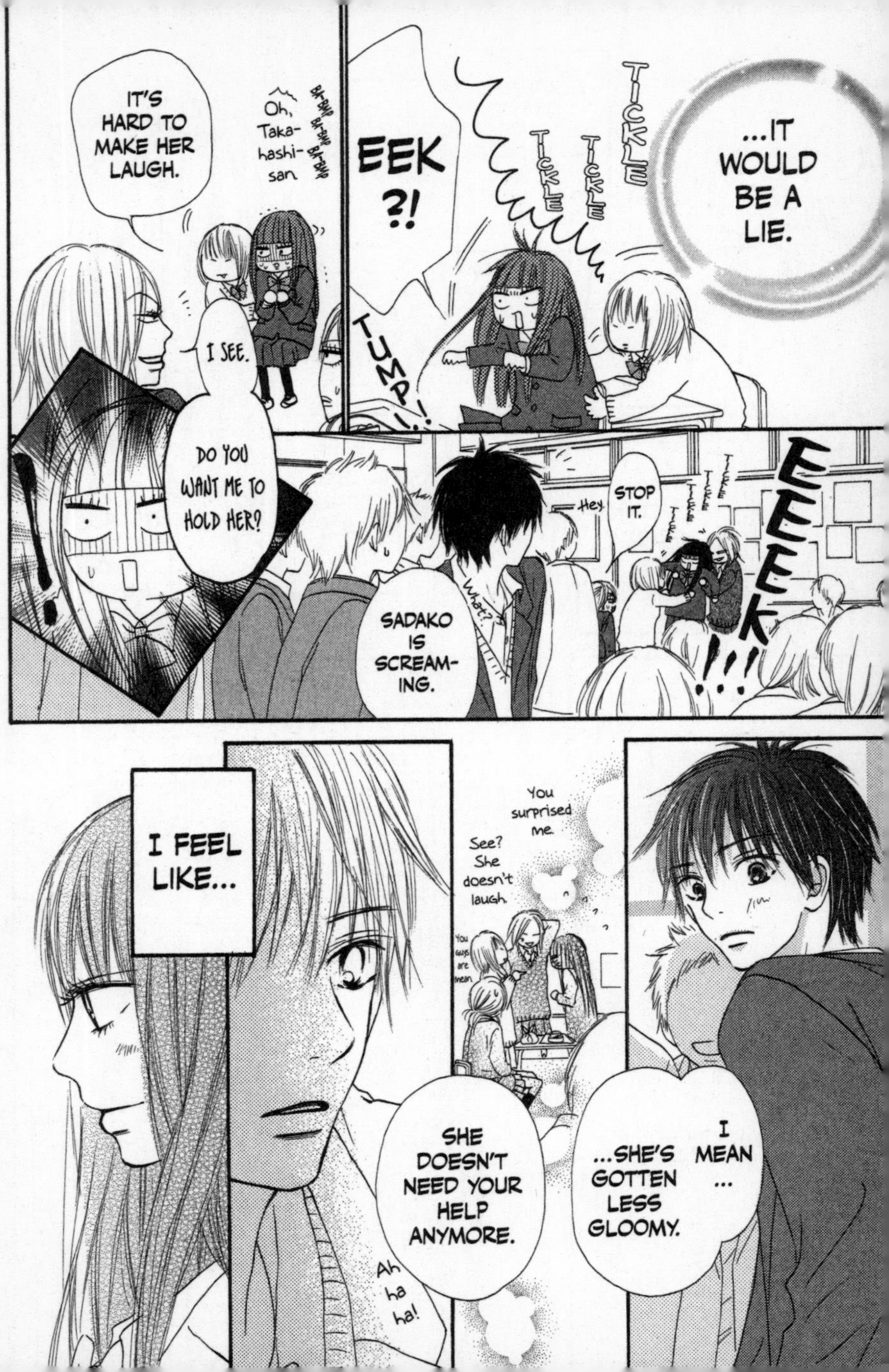
...IT WOULD BE A LIE.
TICKLE
TICKLE
TICKLE
EEK ?!
TUMP!!
IT'S HARD TO MAKE HER LAUGH.
Oh, Taka-hashi-san.
BA-BUMP BA-BUMP BA-BUMP
I SEE.
EEEEK!!!
TICKLE TICKLE TICKLE TICKLE
STOP IT.
Hey.
What?
SADAKO IS SCREAM-ING.
DO YOU WANT ME TO HOLD HER?
!
I MEAN ...
...SHE'S GOTTEN LESS GLOOMY.
You surprised me.
See? She doesn't laugh.
You guys are mean
SHE DOESN'T NEED YOUR HELP ANYMORE.
Ah ha ha!
I FEEL LIKE...

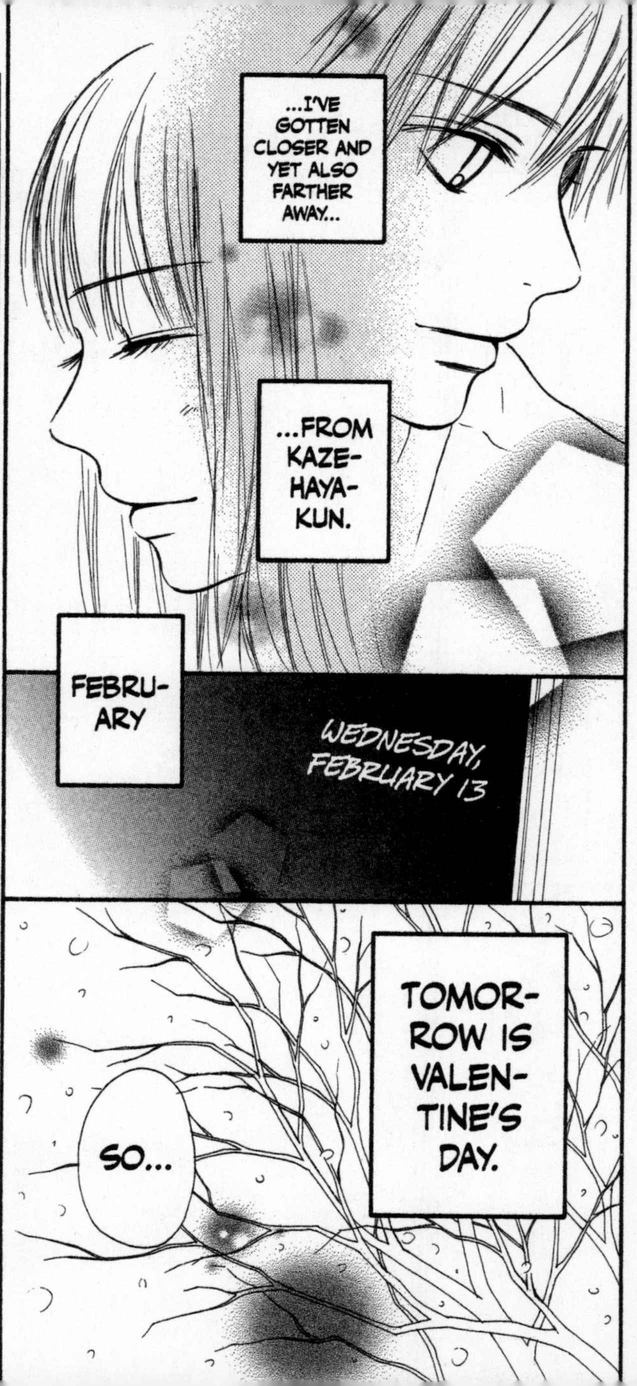
...I'VE GOTTEN CLOSER AND YET ALSO FARTHER AWAY...
...FROM KAZE-HAYA-KUN.
FEBRU-ARY
WEDNESDAY, FEBRUARY 13
TOMOR-ROW IS VALEN-TINE'S DAY.
SO...

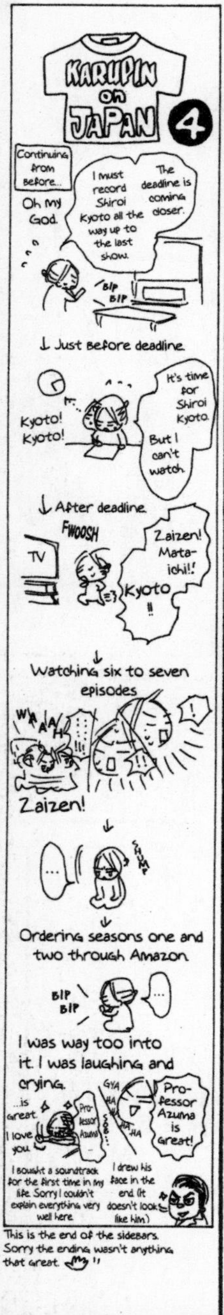
KARUPIN on JAPAN 4
Continuing from before...
Oh my God.
I must record Shiroi Kyoto all the way up to the last show.
The deadline is coming closer.
BIP BIP
↓ Just before deadline.
Kyoto! Kyoto!
It's time for Shiroi Kyoto.
But I can't watch.
↓ After deadline.
TV
FWOOSH
Zaizen! Mata-ichi!! Kyoto!!
↓ Watching six to seven episodes
WAAAH
Zaizen!
SHUMP
...
↓ Ordering seasons one and two through Amazon
BIP BIP
...
I was way too into it. I was laughing and crying.
...is Great.
I love you.
Pro-fessor Azuma
GYA HA HA HA
Pro-fessor Azuma is Great!
I bought a soundtrack for the first time in my life. Sorry I couldn't explain everything very well here.
I drew his face in the end. (It doesn't look like him.)
This is the end of the sidebars. Sorry the ending wasn't anything that great.

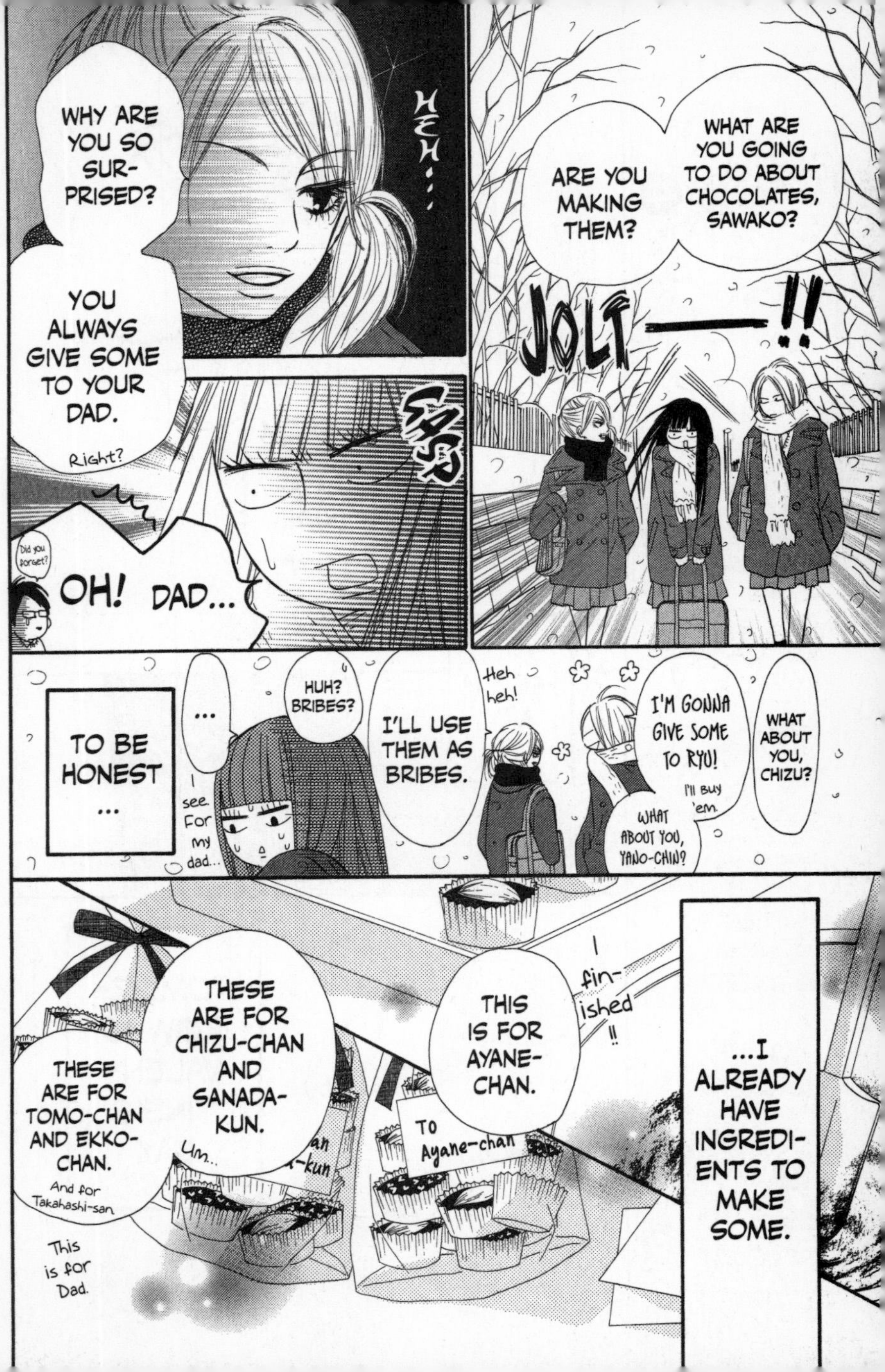
WHAT ARE YOU GOING TO DO ABOUT CHOCOLATES, SAWAKO?
ARE YOU MAKING THEM?
JOLT——!!
HEH...
WHY ARE YOU SO SURPRISED?
YOU ALWAYS GIVE SOME TO YOUR DAD.
Right?
GASP
OH! DAD...
Did you forget?
WHAT ABOUT YOU, CHIZU?
I'M GONNA GIVE SOME TO RYU!
I'll buy 'em.
WHAT ABOUT YOU, YANO-CHIN?
Heh heh!
I'LL USE THEM AS BRIBES.
HUH? BRIBES?
...
I see. For my dad...
TO BE HONEST ...
...I ALREADY HAVE INGREDIENTS TO MAKE SOME.
I finished!!
THIS IS FOR AYANE-CHAN.
To Ayane-chan
THESE ARE FOR CHIZU-CHAN AND SANADA-KUN.
THESE ARE FOR TOMO-CHAN AND EKKO-CHAN.
Um...
And for Takahashi-san.
This is for Dad.

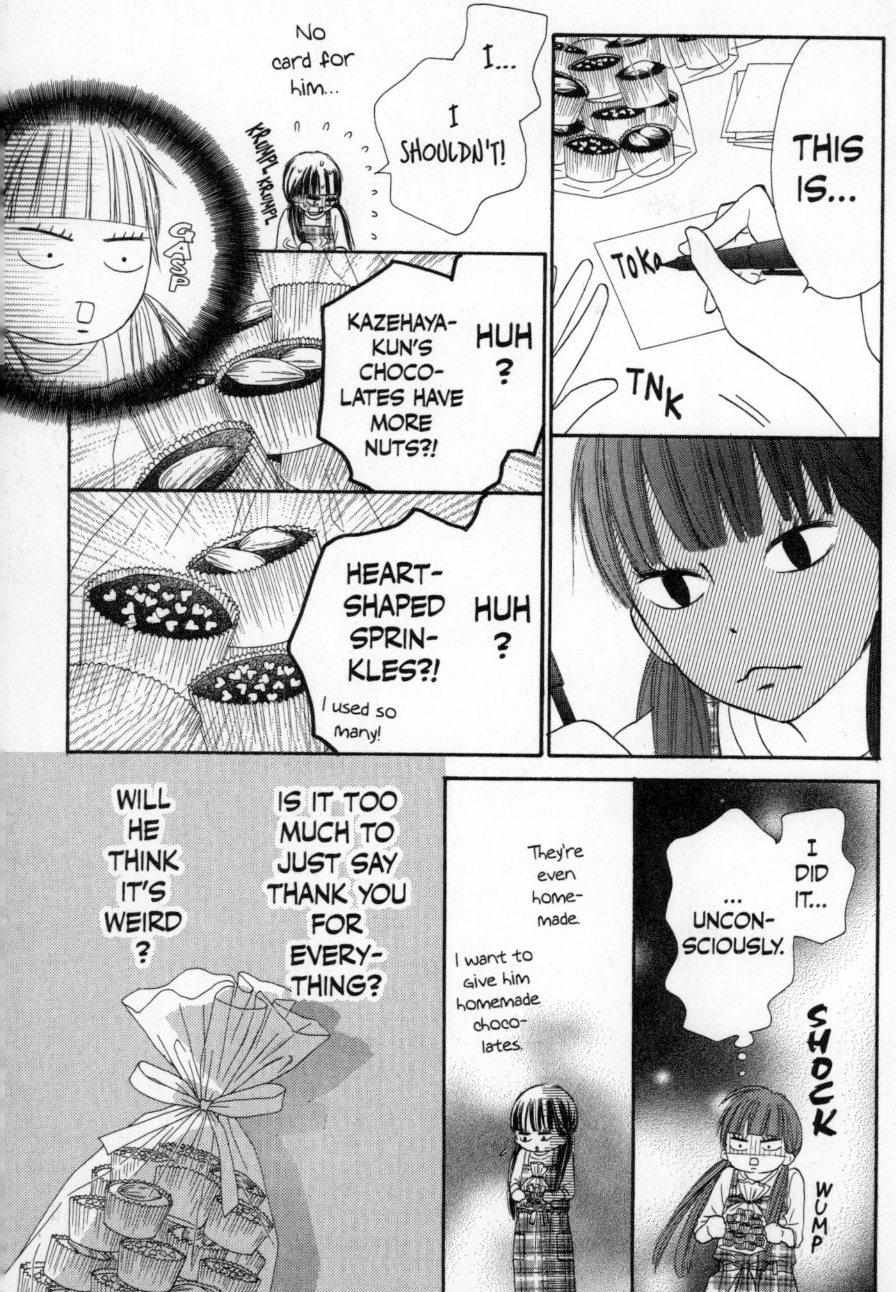
THIS IS...
TOKA
TNK
I... I SHOULDN'T!
No card for him...
KRUMPL KRUMPL
GASP
HUH?
KAZEHAYA-KUN'S CHOCOLATES HAVE MORE NUTS?!
HUH?
HEART-SHAPED SPRINKLES?!
I used so many!
I DID IT... ...UNCONSCIOUSLY.
SHOCK
WUMP
They're even homemade.
I want to give him homemade chocolates.
IS IT TOO MUCH TO JUST SAY THANK YOU FOR EVERYTHING?
WILL HE THINK IT'S WEIRD?

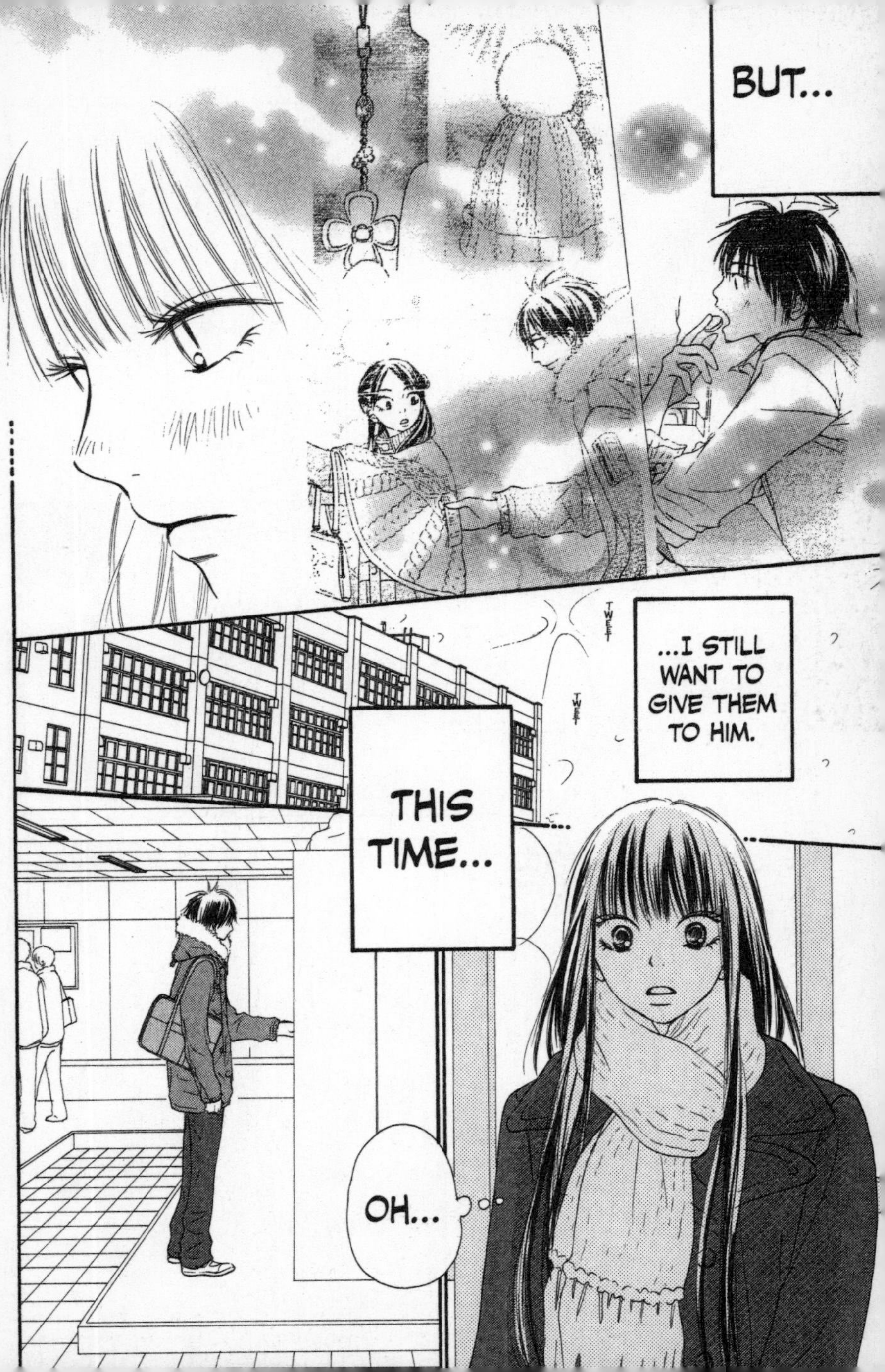
BUT...
TWEET
TWEET
...I STILL WANT TO GIVE THEM TO HIM.
THIS TIME...
OH...

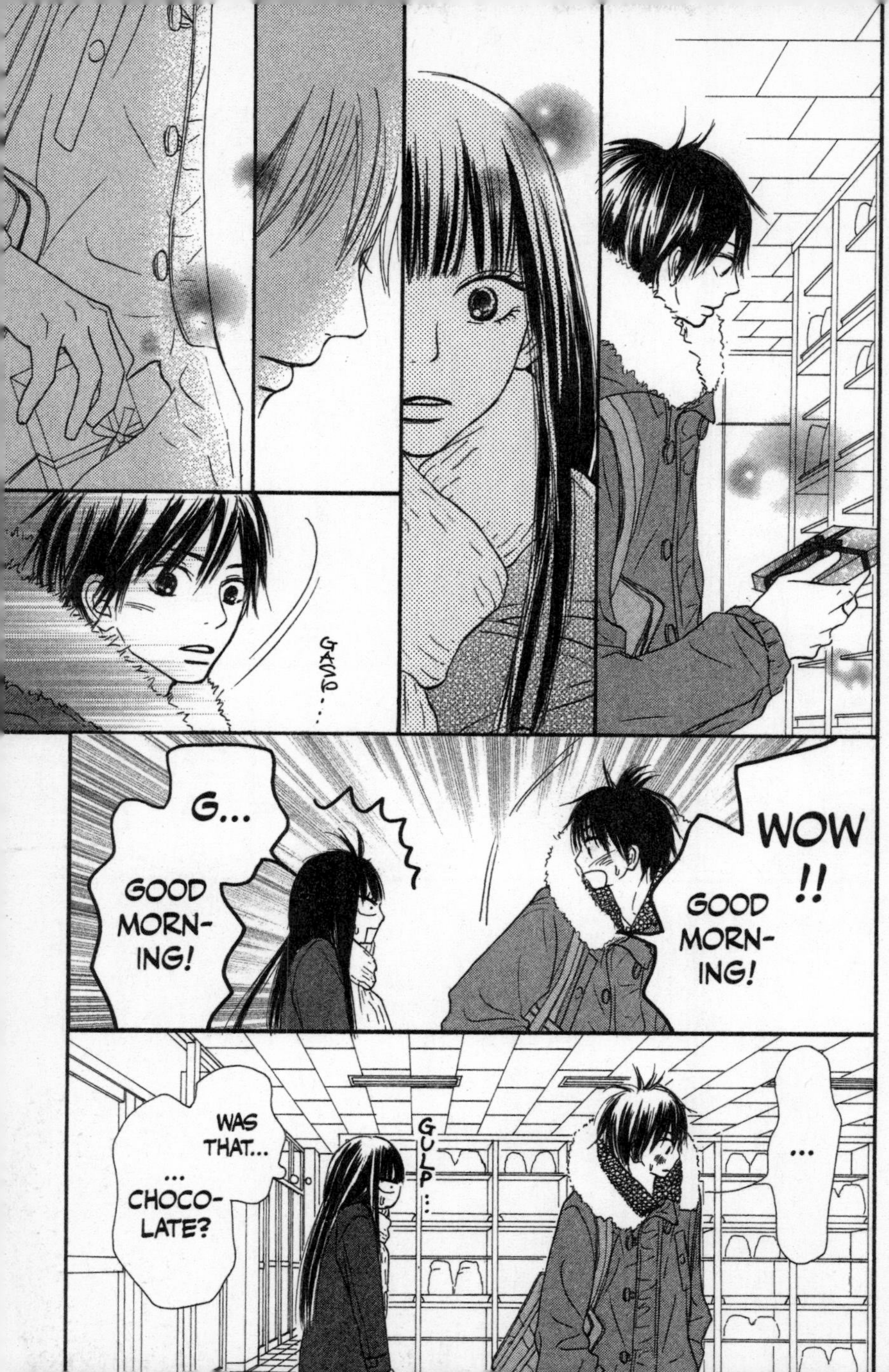
GASP...
WOW!!
GOOD MORNING!
G...
GOOD MORNING!
...
GULP...
WAS THAT...
...CHOCOLATE?

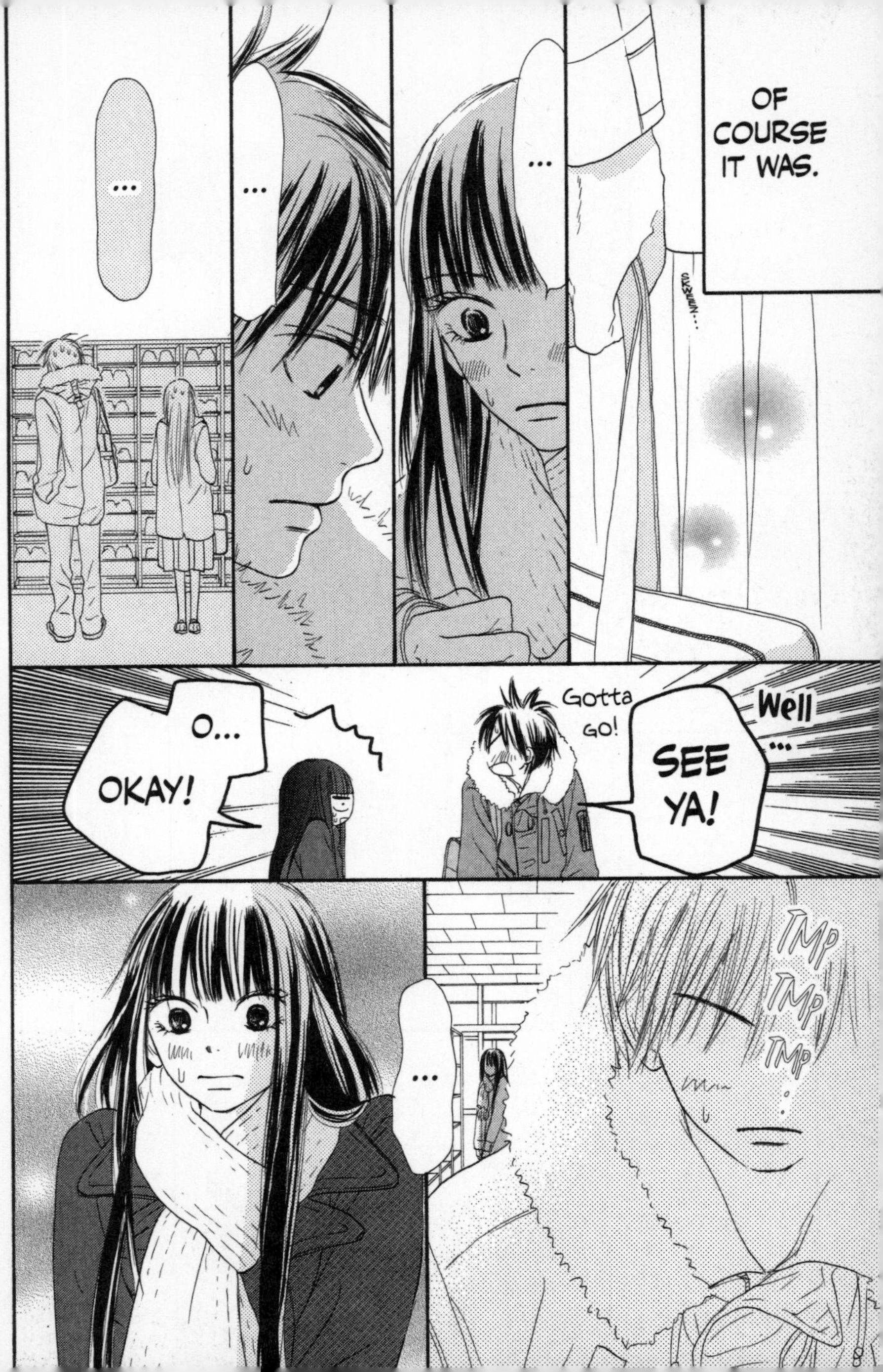
OF COURSE IT WAS.
SKWEEN...
...
...
...
Well ...
SEE YA!
Gotta GO!
O... OKAY!
TMP TMP TMP
...

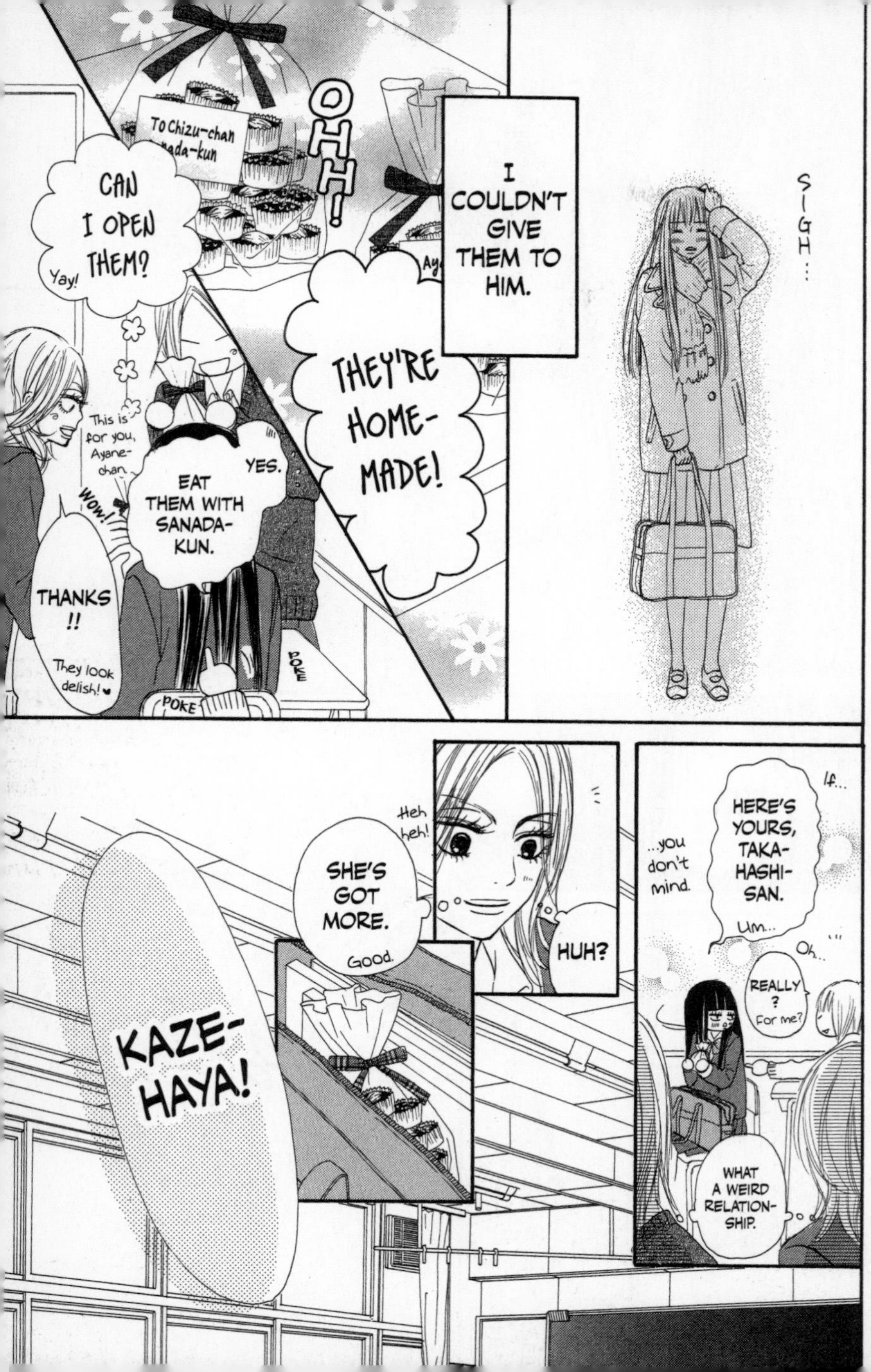
SIGH...
I COULDN'T GIVE THEM TO HIM.
OHH!
THEY'RE HOME-MADE!
To Chizu-chan
nada-kun
CAN I OPEN THEM?
Yay!
YES.
EAT THEM WITH SANADA-KUN.
This is for you, Ayane-chan.
WOW!
THANKS!!
They look delish!
POKE
POKE
If...
HERE'S YOURS, TAKA-HASHI-SAN.
...you don't mind.
Um...
Oh...
REALLY?
For me?
WHAT A WEIRD RELATION-SHIP.
Heh heh!
SHE'S GOT MORE.
Good.
HUH?
KAZE-HAYA!

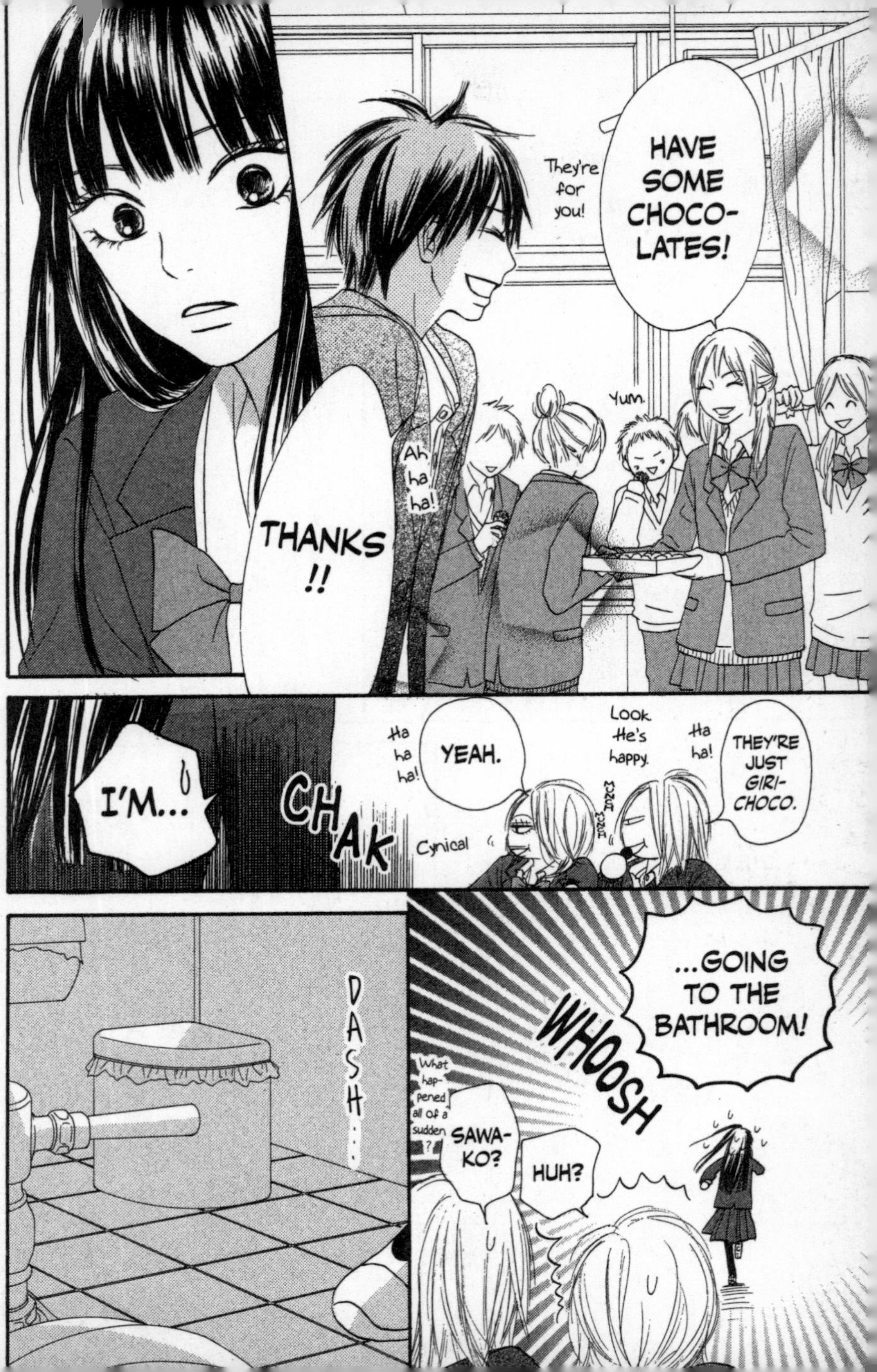
HAVE SOME CHOCO-LATES!
They're for you!
Yum.
Ah ha ha!
THANKS !!
THEY'RE JUST GIRI-CHOCO.
Ha ha!
Look. He's happy.
MUNCH MUNCH
YEAH.
Ha ha ha!
Cynical
CHAK
I'M...
...GOING TO THE BATHROOM!
WHOOSH
HUH?
SAWA-KO?
What hap-pened all of a sudden?
DASH...

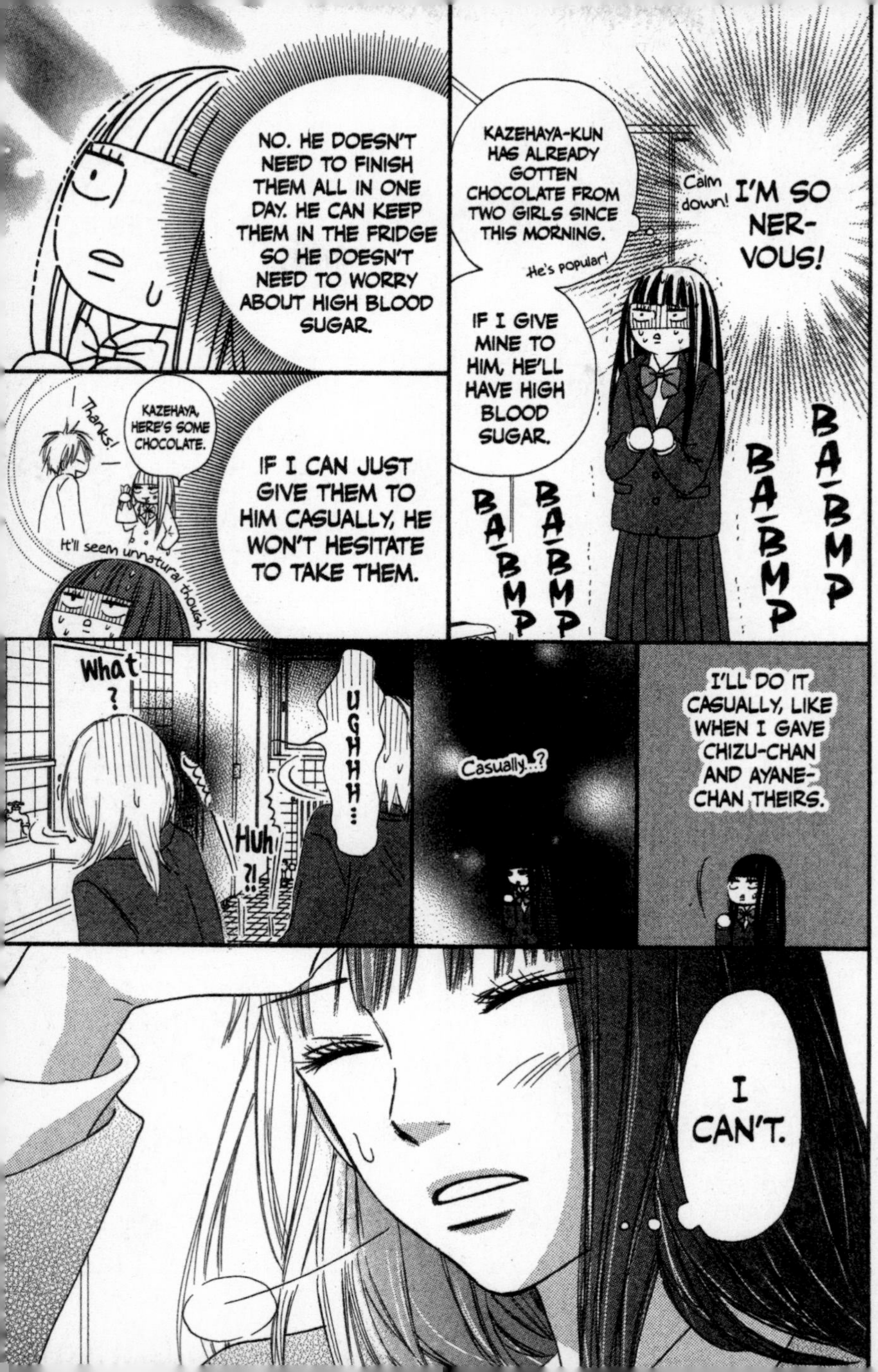
I'M SO NER-VOUS!
Calm down!
KAZEHAYA-KUN HAS ALREADY GOTTEN CHOCOLATE FROM TWO GIRLS SINCE THIS MORNING.
He's popular!
IF I GIVE MINE TO HIM, HE'LL HAVE HIGH BLOOD SUGAR.
BA-BUMP
BA-BUMP
BA-BUMP
BA-BUMP
NO. HE DOESN'T NEED TO FINISH THEM ALL IN ONE DAY. HE CAN KEEP THEM IN THE FRIDGE SO HE DOESN'T NEED TO WORRY ABOUT HIGH BLOOD SUGAR.
IF I CAN JUST GIVE THEM TO HIM CASUALLY, HE WON'T HESITATE TO TAKE THEM.
KAZEHAYA, HERE'S SOME CHOCOLATE.
Thanks!
It'll seem unnatural though
I'LL DO IT CASUALLY, LIKE WHEN I GAVE CHIZU-CHAN AND AYANE-CHAN THEIRS.
Casually...?
UGHHH...
What?
Huh?!
I CAN'T.

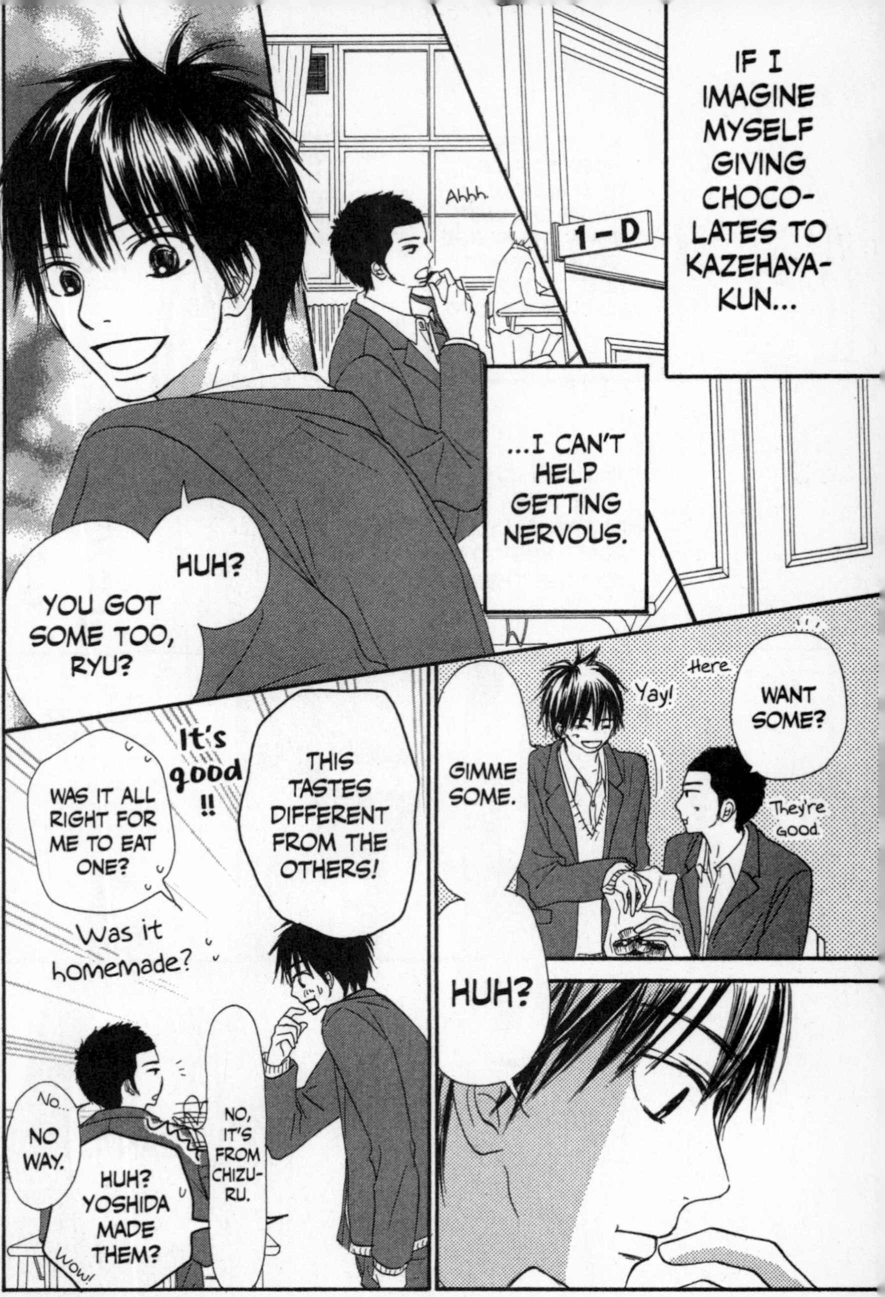

IF I IMAGINE MYSELF GIVING CHOCOLATES TO KAZEHAYA-KUN...
1-D
Ahhh
...I CAN'T HELP GETTING NERVOUS.
HUH? YOU GOT SOME TOO, RYU?
Here
WANT SOME?
They're good.
Yay!
GIMME SOME.
HUH?
THIS TASTES DIFFERENT FROM THE OTHERS!
It's good!!
WAS IT ALL RIGHT FOR ME TO EAT ONE?
Was it homemade?
NO, IT'S FROM CHIZURU.
HUH? YOSHIDA MADE THEM?
No... NO WAY.
Wow!

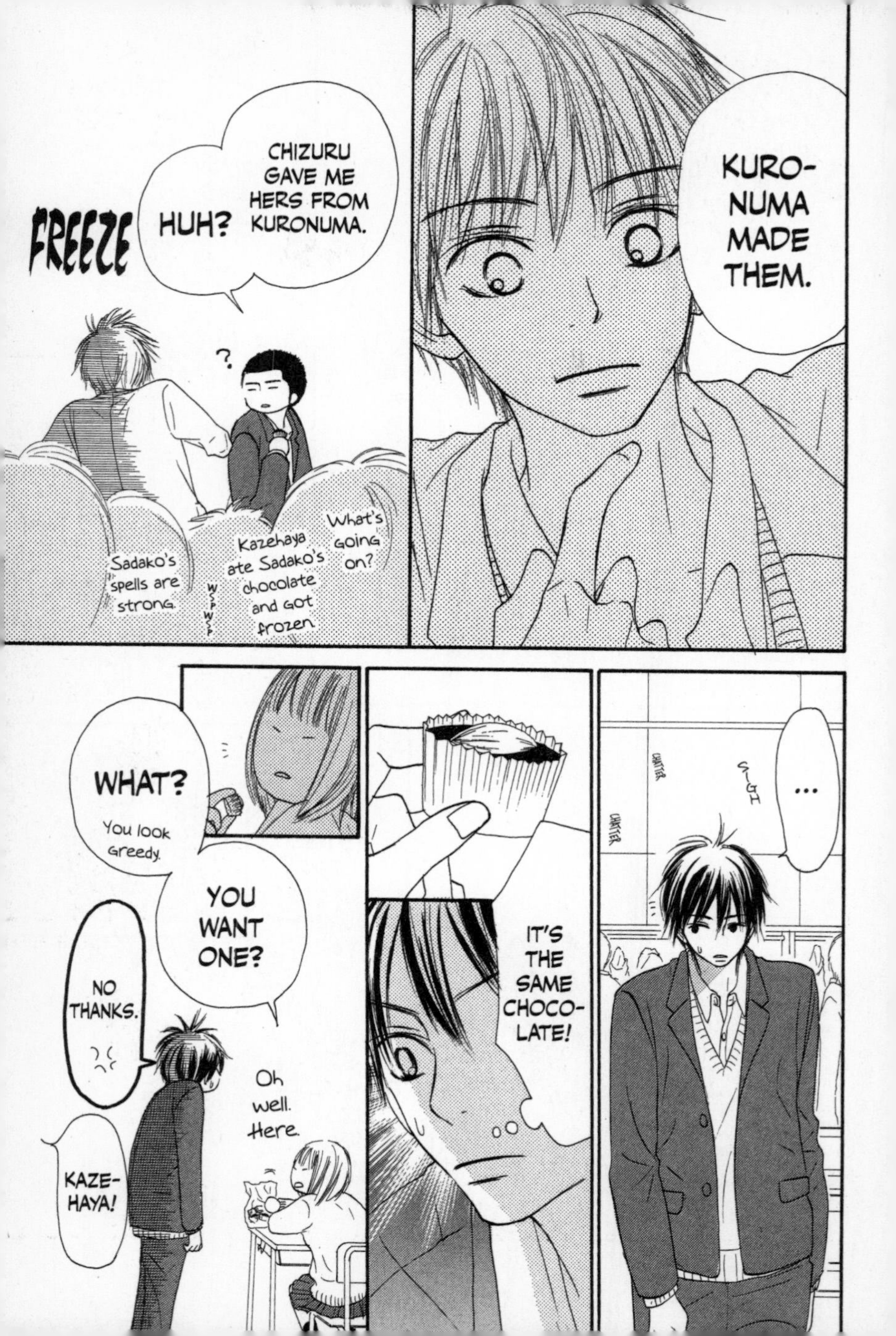
KURO-NUMA MADE THEM.
CHIZURU GAVE ME HERS FROM KURONUMA.
HUH?
FREEZE
?
What's going on?
Kazehaya ate Sadako's chocolate and got frozen
WSP WSP
Sadako's spells are strong.
...
SIGH
CHATTER
CHATTER
IT'S THE SAME CHOCOLATE!
WHAT?
You look greedy.
YOU WANT ONE?
NO THANKS.
Oh well. Here.
KAZE-HAYA!

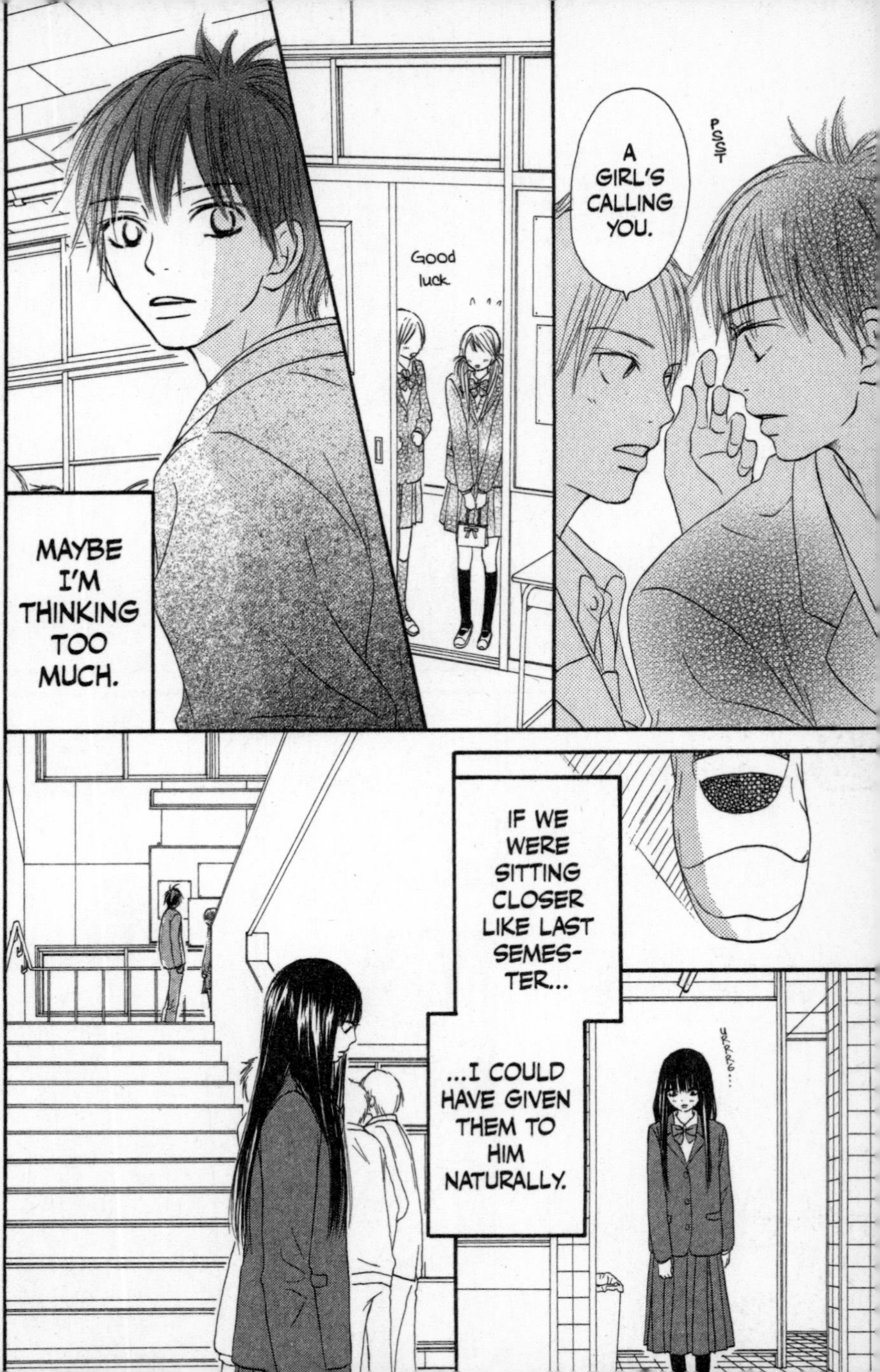
PSST
A GIRL'S CALLING YOU.
Good luck
MAYBE I'M THINKING TOO MUCH.
IF WE WERE SITTING CLOSER LIKE LAST SEMES-TER...
...I COULD HAVE GIVEN THEM TO HIM NATURALLY.
URRRG...

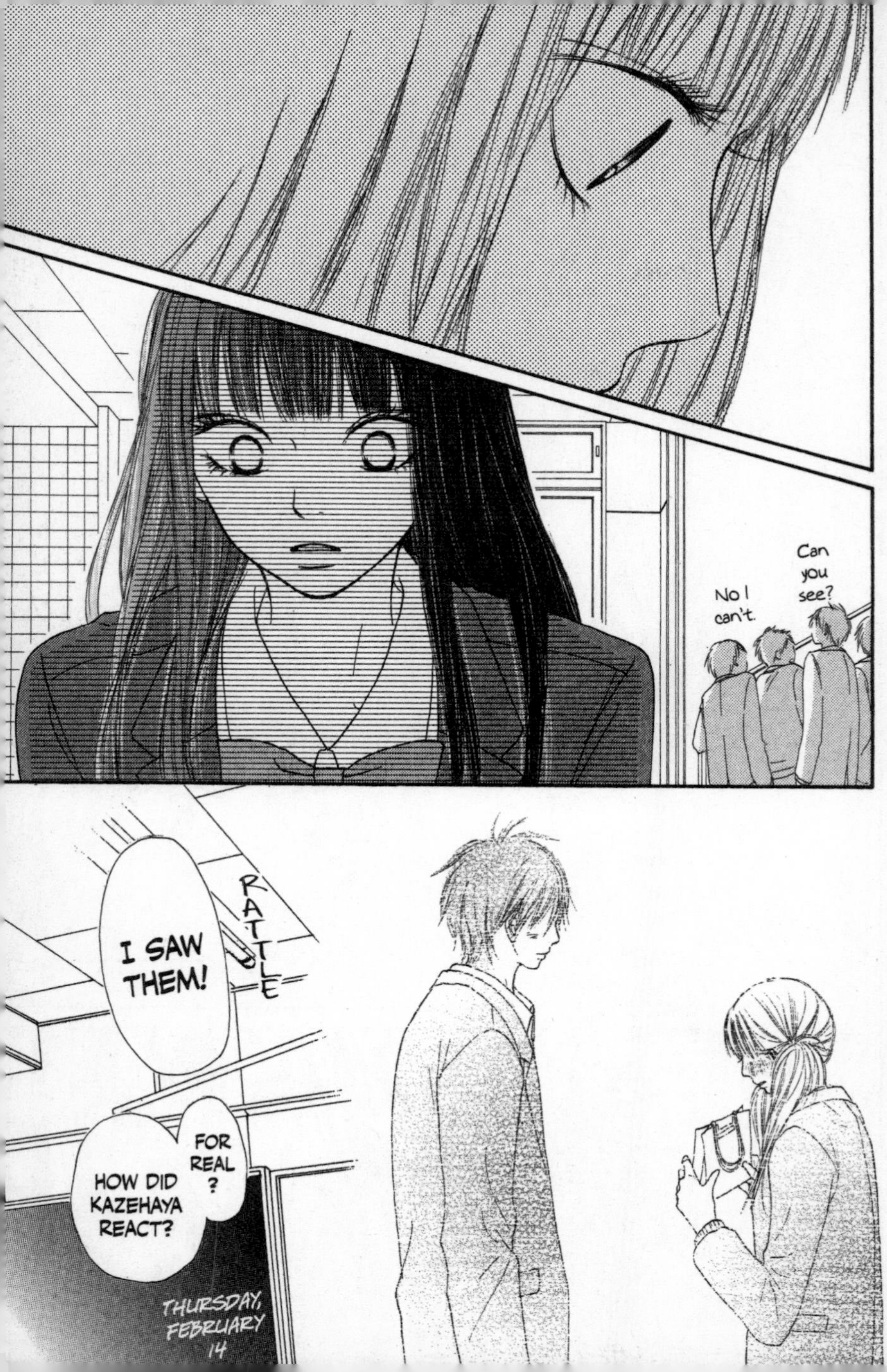
Can you see?
No I can't.
RATTLE
I SAW THEM!
FOR REAL?
HOW DID KAZEHAYA REACT?
THURSDAY, FEBRUARY 14

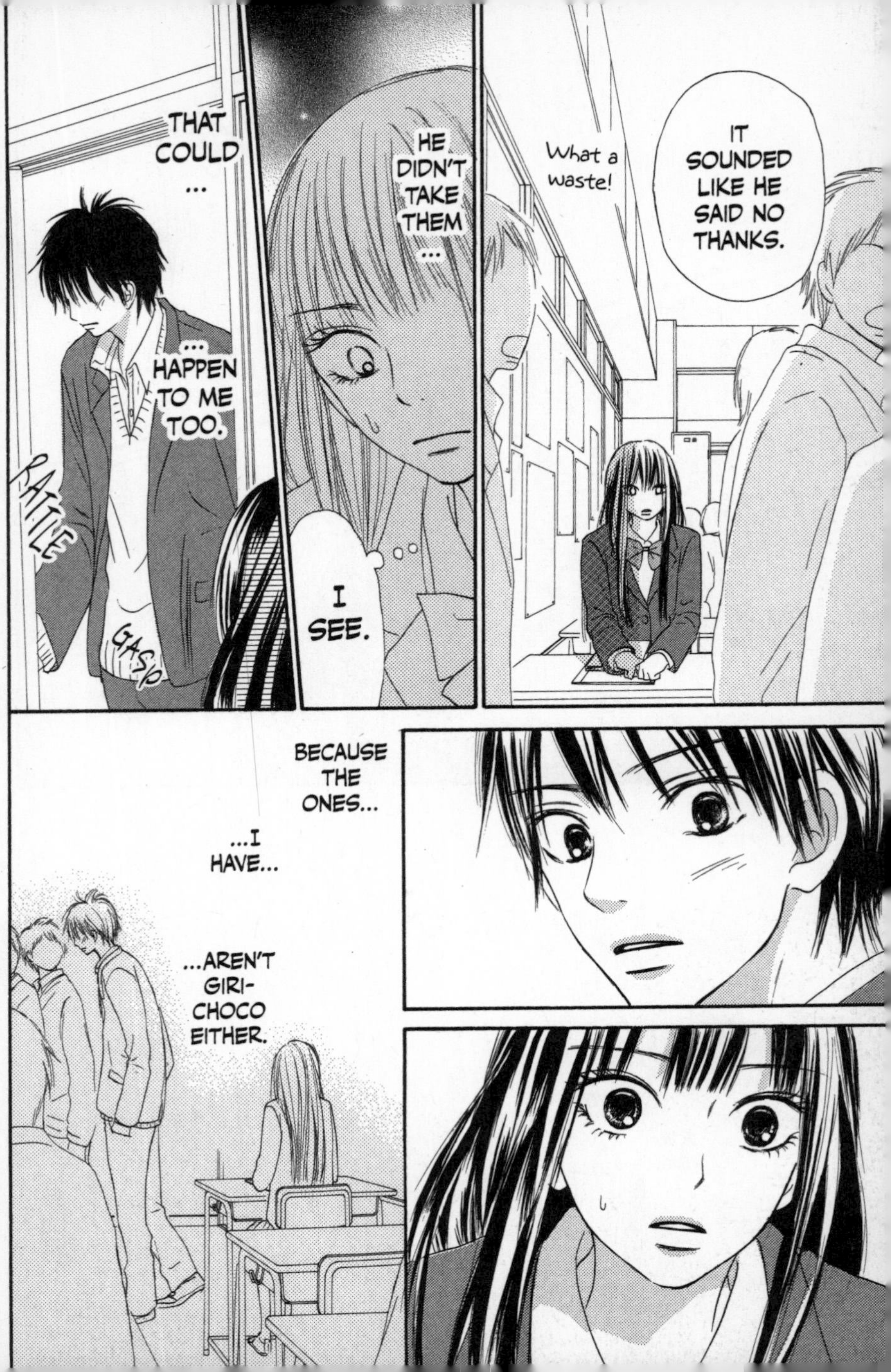
IT SOUNDED LIKE HE SAID NO THANKS.
What a waste!
HE DIDN'T TAKE THEM ...
I SEE.
THAT COULD ...
... HAPPEN TO ME TOO.
RATTLE
GASP
BECAUSE THE ONES...
...I HAVE...
...AREN'T GIRI-CHOCO EITHER.

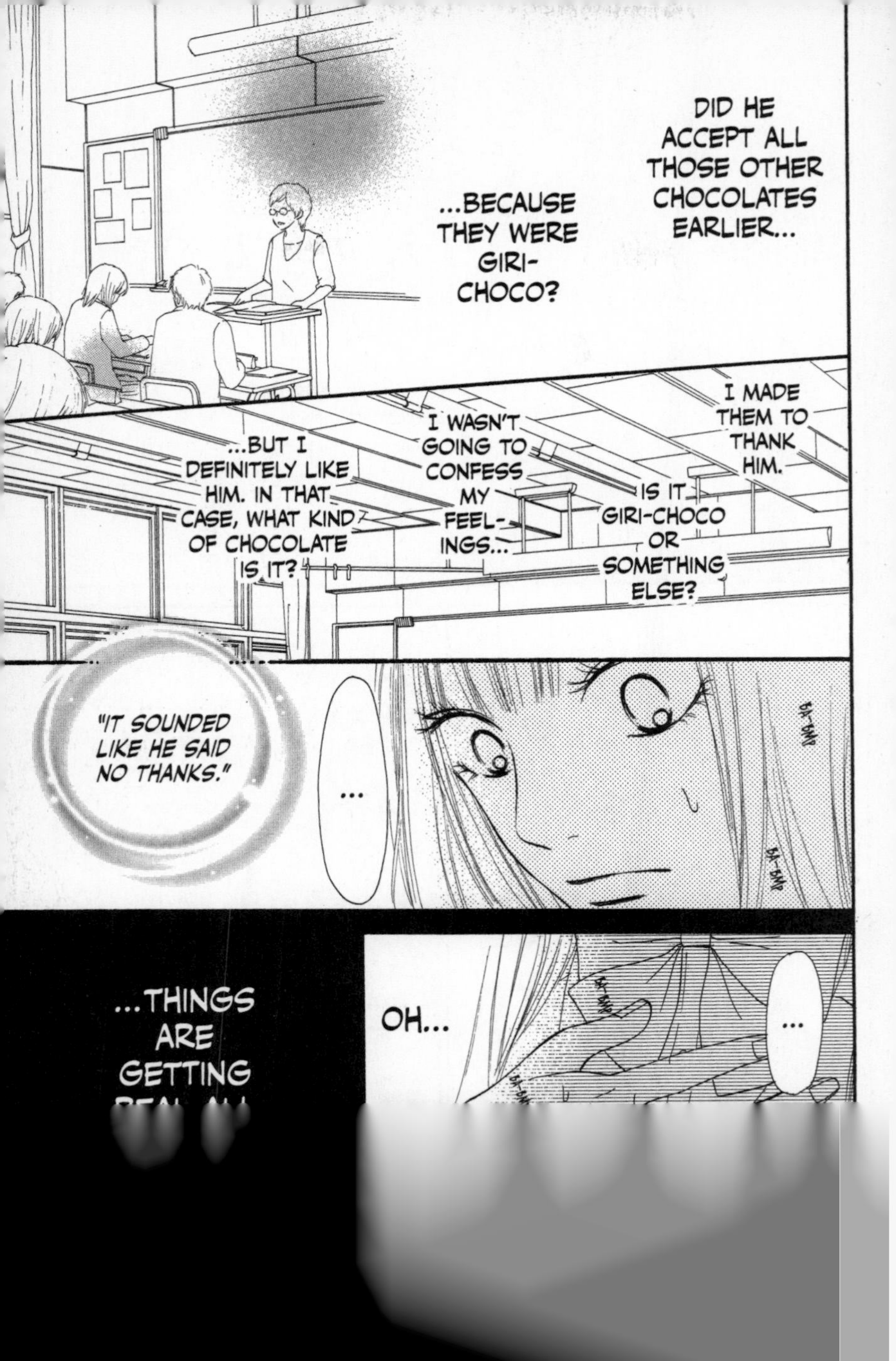
DID HE ACCEPT ALL THOSE OTHER CHOCOLATES EARLIER...
...BECAUSE THEY WERE GIRI-CHOCO?
I MADE THEM TO THANK HIM.
IS IT GIRI-CHOCO OR SOMETHING ELSE?
I WASN'T GOING TO CONFESS MY FEEL-INGS...
...BUT I DEFINITELY LIKE HIM. IN THAT CASE, WHAT KIND OF CHOCOLATE IS IT?
BA-BMP
BA-BMP
...
"IT SOUNDED LIKE HE SAID NO THANKS."
...
OH...
...THINGS ARE GETTING

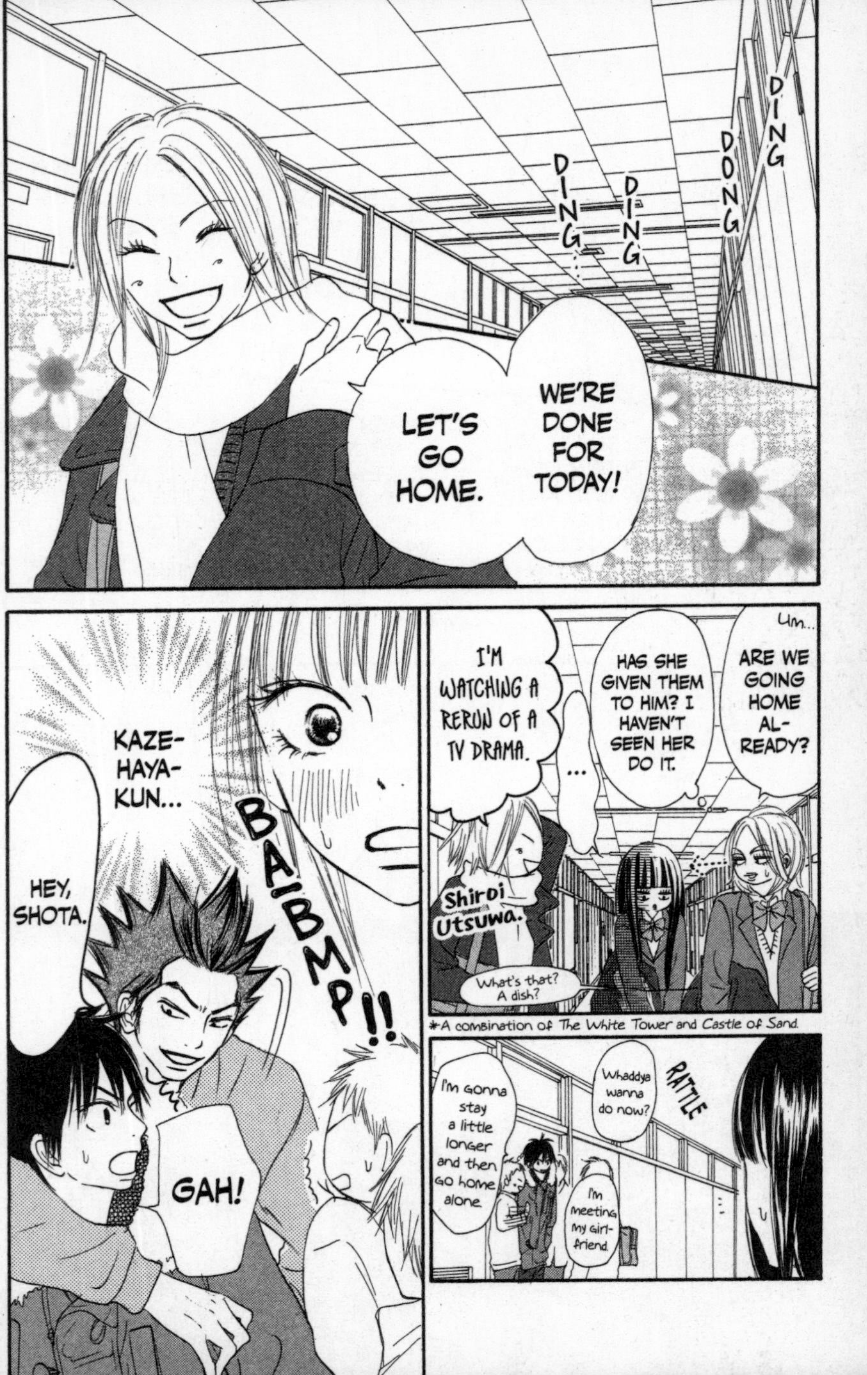
DING DONG DING
DING DING
WE'RE DONE FOR TODAY!
LET'S GO HOME.
Um...
ARE WE GOING HOME AL-READY?
HAS SHE GIVEN THEM TO HIM? I HAVEN'T SEEN HER DO IT.
...
I'M WATCHING A RERUN OF A TV DRAMA.
Shiroi Utsuwa.
What's that? A dish?
RATTLE
Whaddya wanna do now?
I'm gonna stay a little longer and then go home alone.
I'm meeting my girl-friend.
BABMP!!
KAZE-HAYA-KUN...
HEY, SHOTA.
GAH!
*A combination of The White Tower and Castle of Sand.

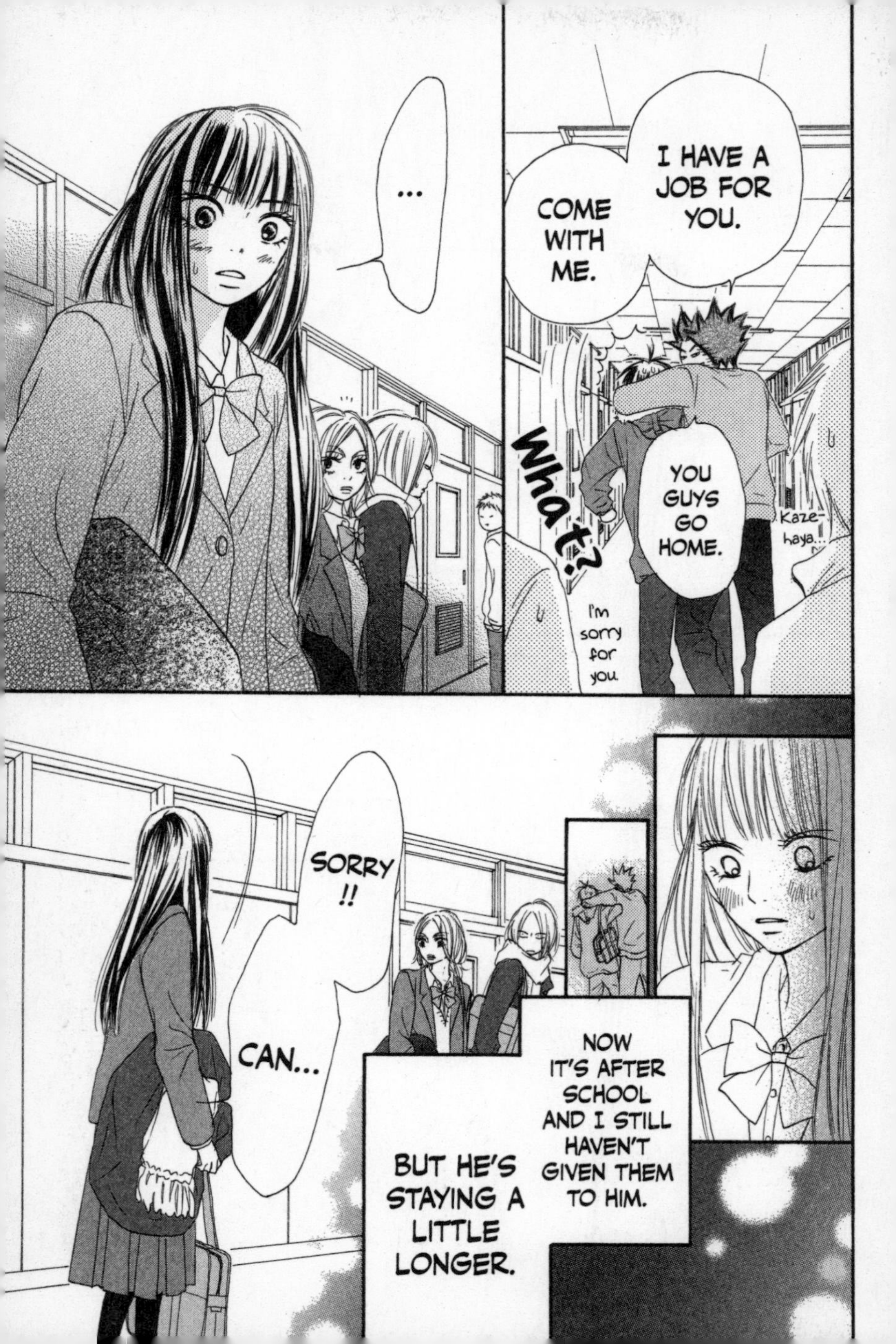
I HAVE A JOB FOR YOU.
COME WITH ME.
Kaze-haya...
YOU GUYS GO HOME.
What?!
I'm sorry for you.
...
NOW IT'S AFTER SCHOOL AND I STILL HAVEN'T GIVEN THEM TO HIM.
BUT HE'S STAYING A LITTLE LONGER.
SORRY !!
CAN...

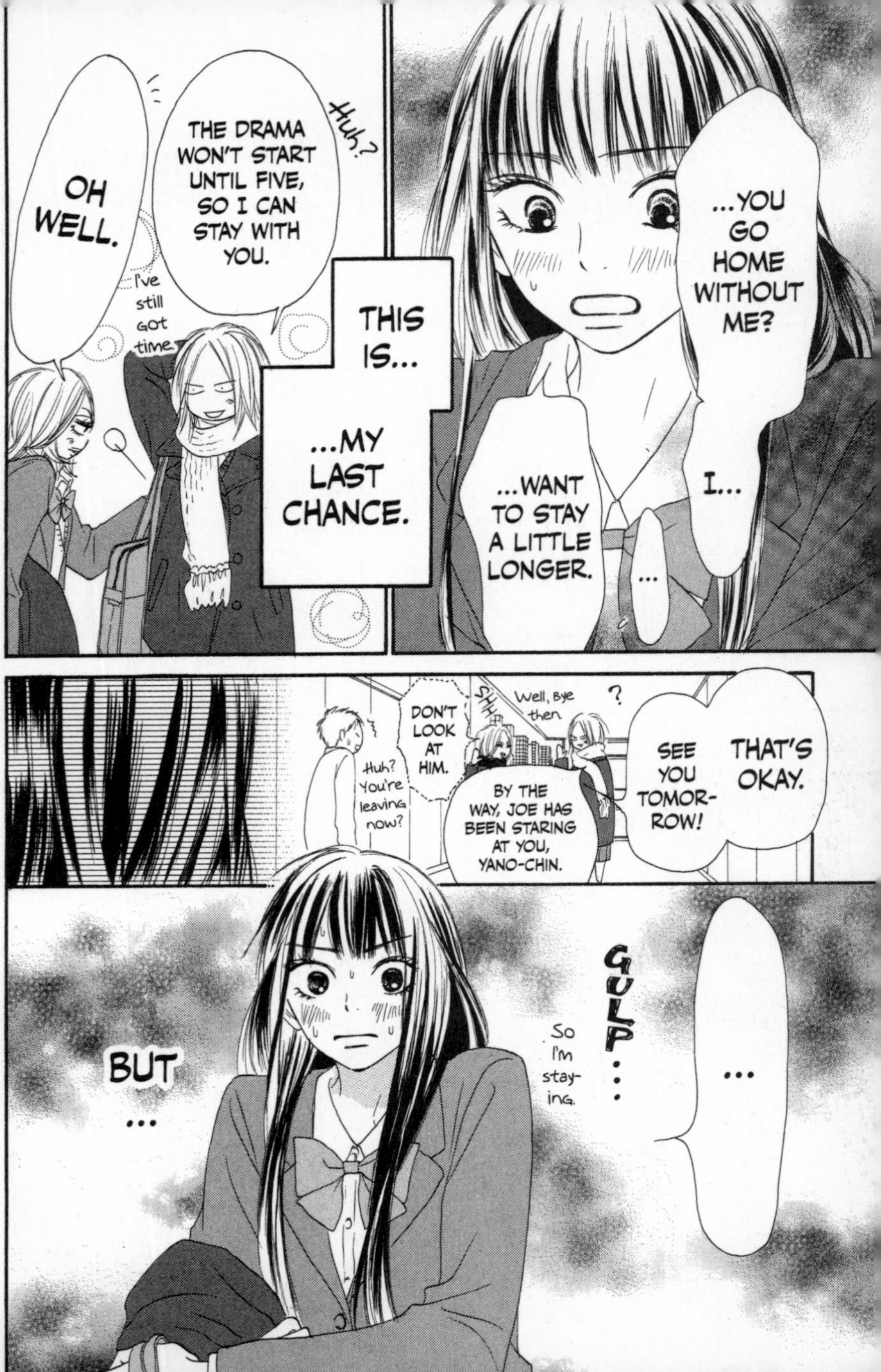
...YOU GO HOME WITHOUT ME?
I...
...
...WANT TO STAY A LITTLE LONGER.
THIS IS...
...MY LAST CHANCE.
Huh?
THE DRAMA WON'T START UNTIL FIVE, SO I CAN STAY WITH YOU.
I've still got time.
OH WELL.
THAT'S OKAY.
SEE YOU TOMOR-ROW!
?
Well, bye then.
SHH
BY THE WAY, JOE HAS BEEN STARING AT YOU, YANO-CHIN.
DON'T LOOK AT HIM.
Huh? You're leaving now?
...
GULP...
So I'm stay-ing.
BUT ...

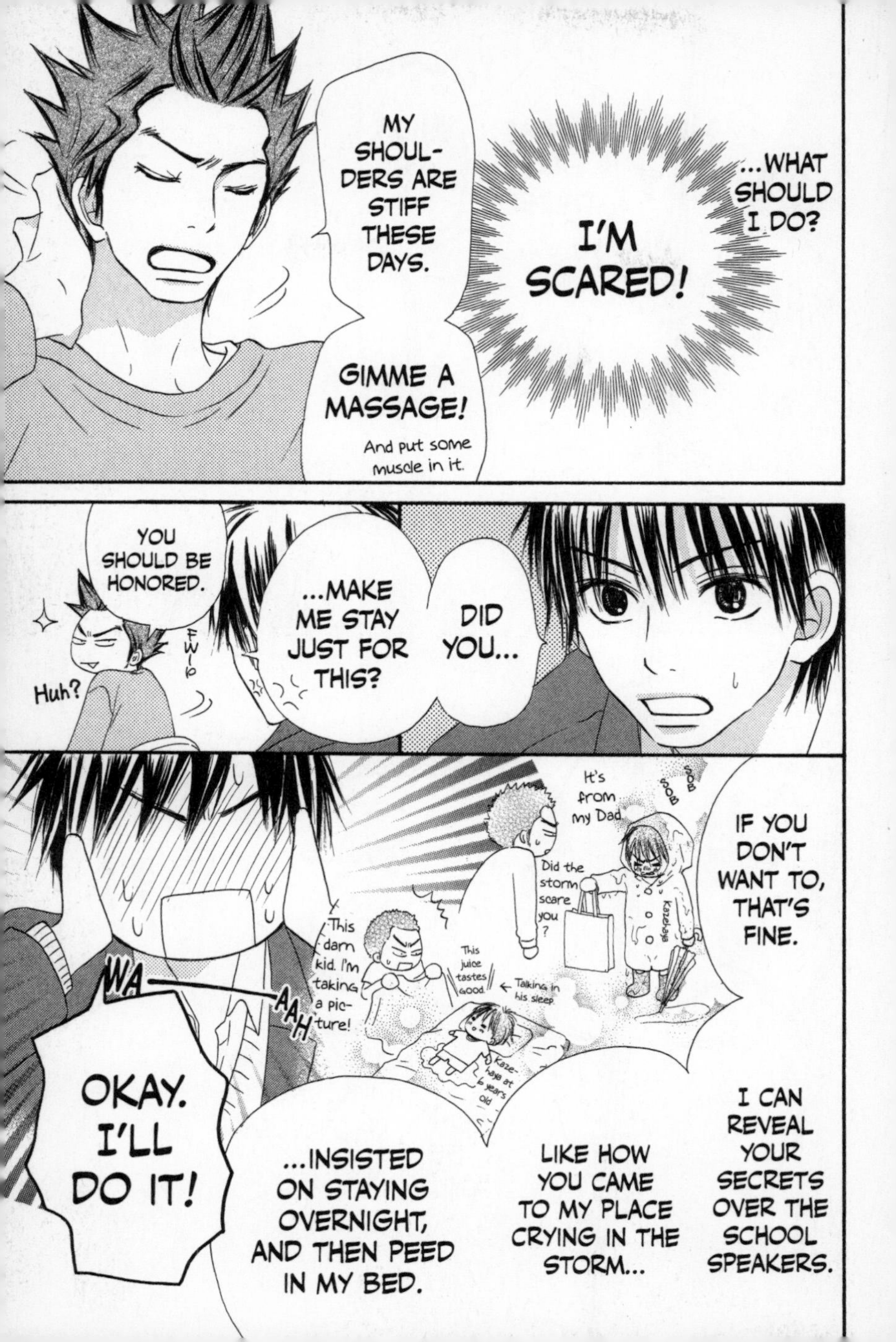
...WHAT SHOULD I DO?
I'M SCARED!
MY SHOUL-DERS ARE STIFF THESE DAYS.
GIMME A MASSAGE!
And put some muscle in it.
DID YOU...
...MAKE ME STAY JUST FOR THIS?
YOU SHOULD BE HONORED.
FWIP
Huh?
IF YOU DON'T WANT TO, THAT'S FINE.
I CAN REVEAL YOUR SECRETS OVER THE SCHOOL SPEAKERS.
LIKE HOW YOU CAME TO MY PLACE CRYING IN THE STORM...
BOO BOO
It's from my Dad
Did the storm scare you?
Kazehaya
This juice tastes good.
Talking in his sleep.
This darn kid. I'm taking a pic-ture!
Kaze-haya at 6 years old
...INSISTED ON STAYING OVERNIGHT, AND THEN PEED IN MY BED.
WA—AAH
OKAY. I'LL DO IT!

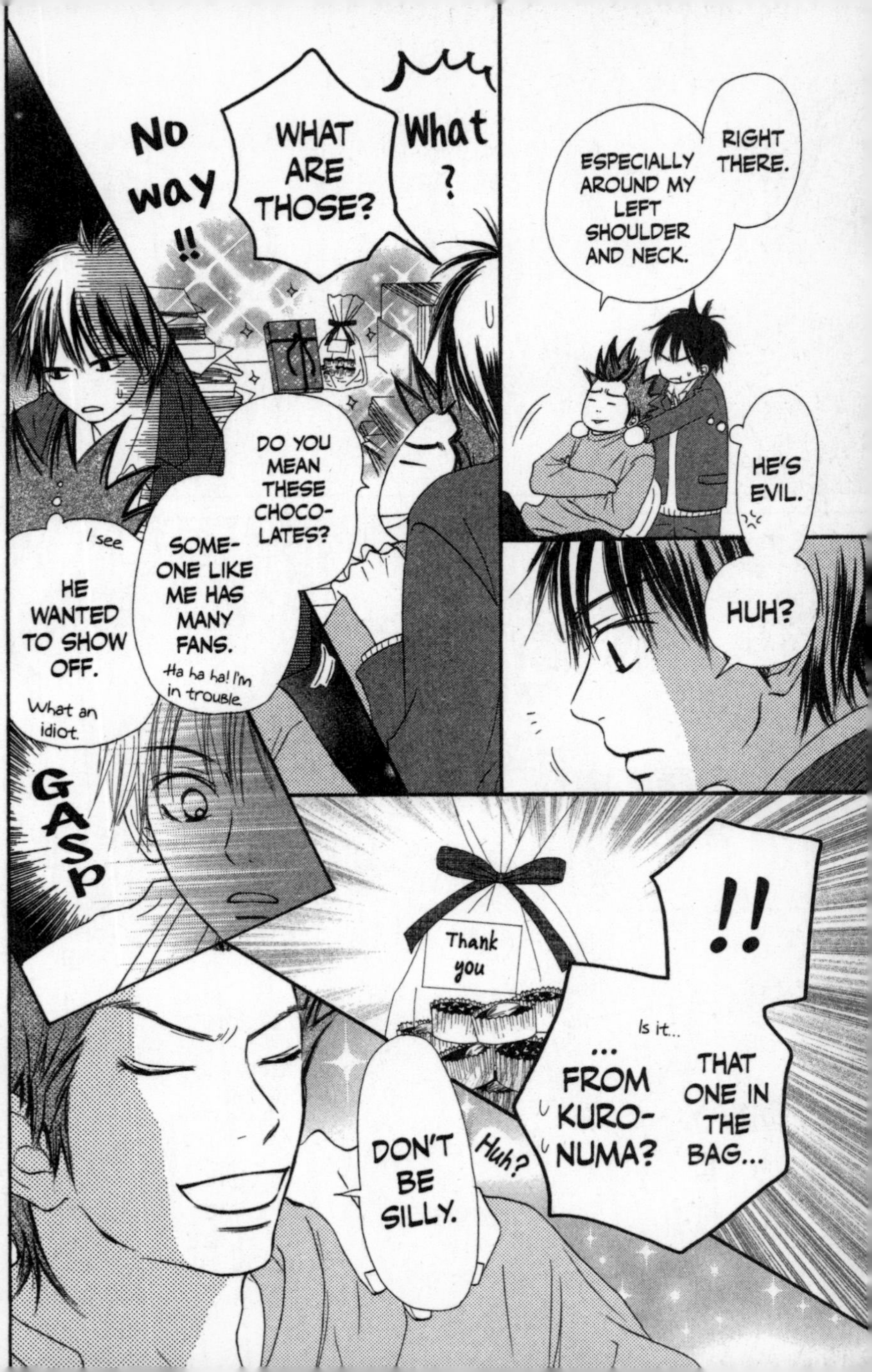
RIGHT THERE.
ESPECIALLY AROUND MY LEFT SHOULDER AND NECK.
HE'S EVIL.
HUH?
What?
WHAT ARE THOSE?
No way!!
DO YOU MEAN THESE CHOCOLATES?
SOMEONE LIKE ME HAS MANY FANS.
Ha ha ha! I'm in trouble.
I see.
HE WANTED TO SHOW OFF.
What an idiot.
GASP
!!
Thank you
THAT ONE IN THE BAG...
Is it...
...FROM KURONUMA?
Huh?
DON'T BE SILLY.

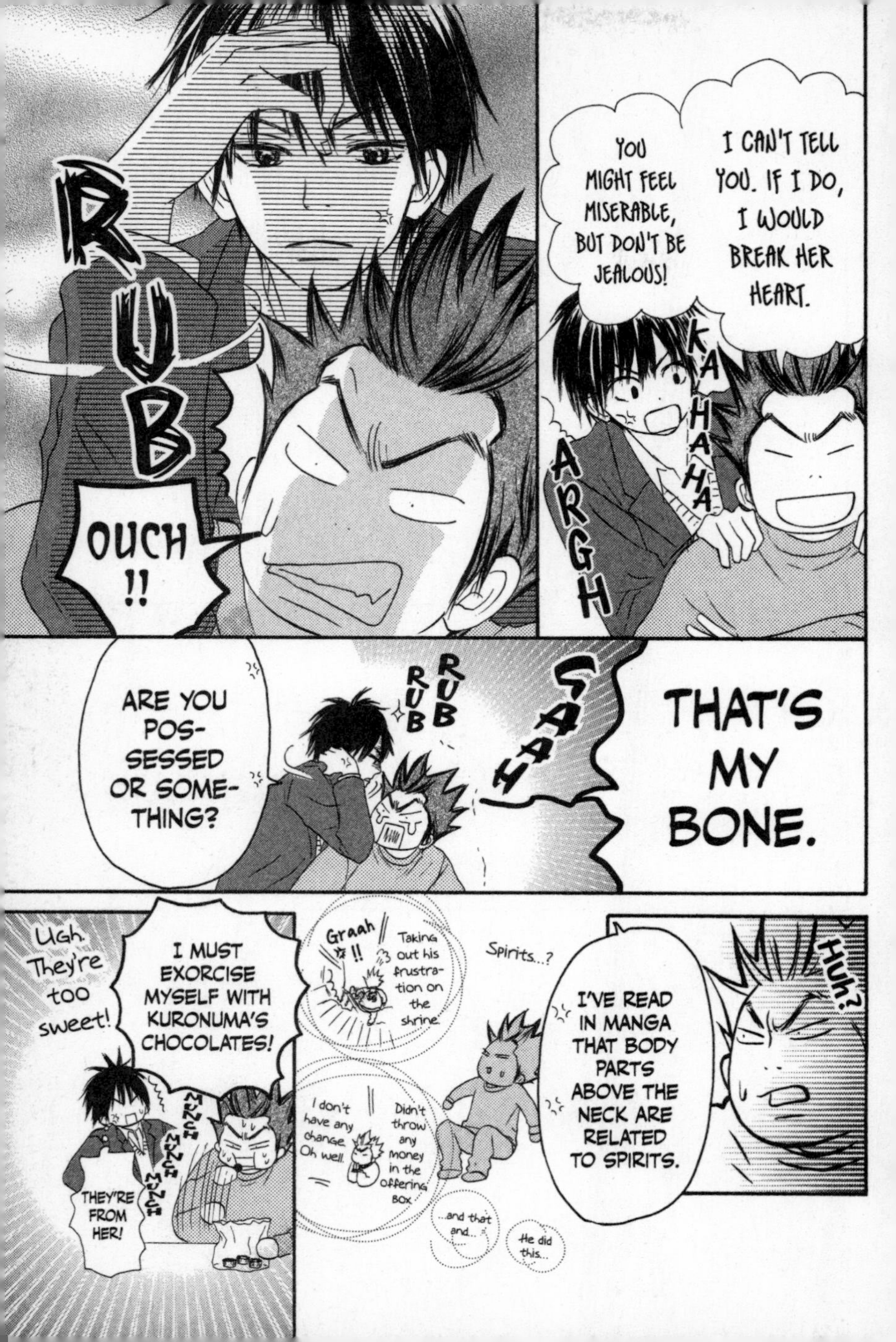
I CAN'T TELL YOU. IF I DO, I WOULD BREAK HER HEART.
YOU MIGHT FEEL MISERABLE, BUT DON'T BE JEALOUS!
KAHAHAHA
ARGH
RUB
OUCH!!
THAT'S MY BONE.
SAAAH
RUB RUB
ARE YOU POS-SESSED OR SOME-THING?
HUH?
I'VE READ IN MANGA THAT BODY PARTS ABOVE THE NECK ARE RELATED TO SPIRITS.
Spirits...?
Taking out his frustra-tion on the shrine.
Graah!!
Didn't throw any money in the offering box.
I don't have any change. Oh well.
...and that and...
He did this...
I MUST EXORCISE MYSELF WITH KURONUMA'S CHOCOLATES!
Ugh. They're too sweet!
MUNCH MUNCH MUNCH
THEY'RE FROM HER!

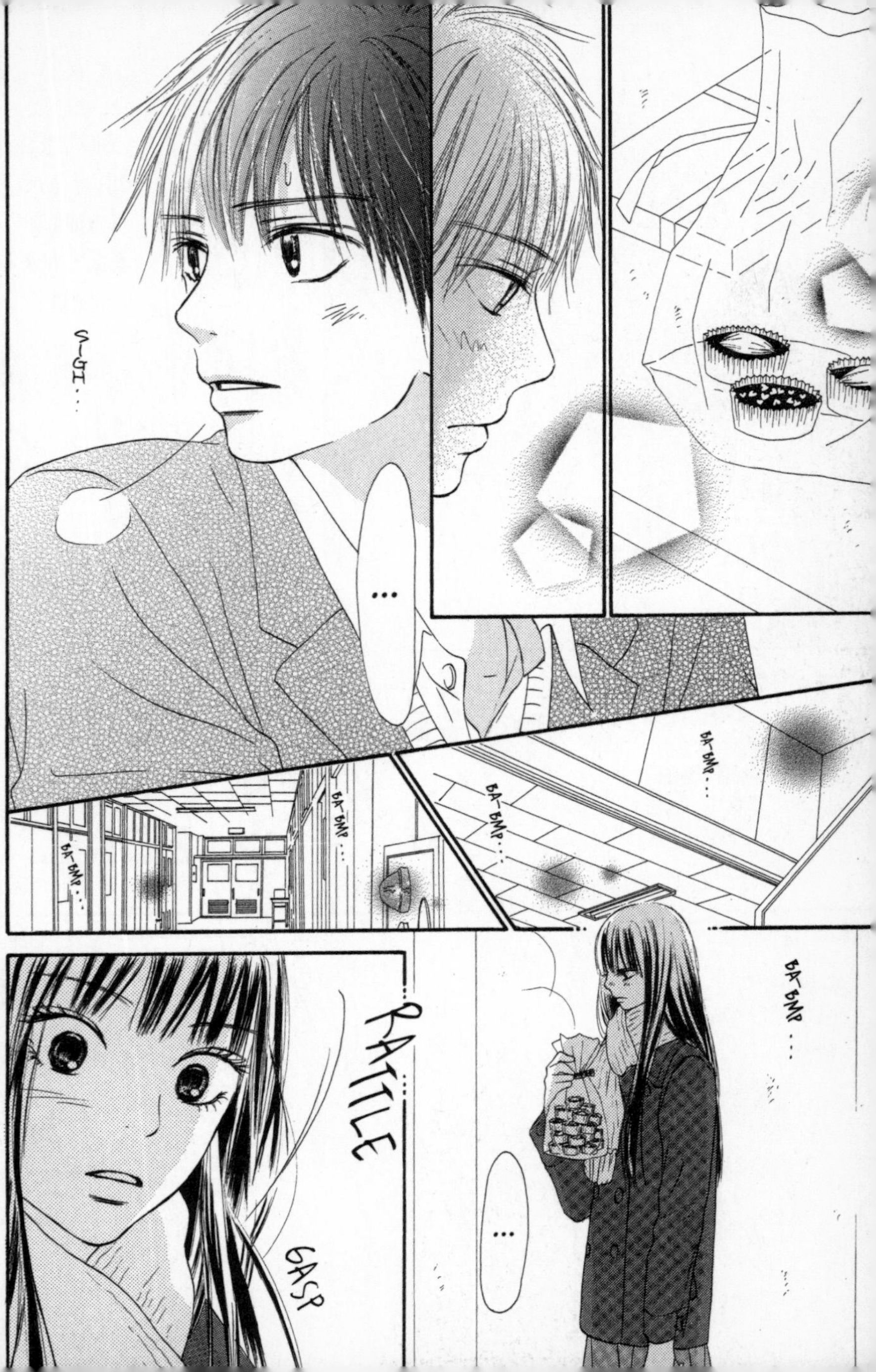

S-GH...
...
BA-BMP...
BA-BMP...
BA-BMP...
BA-BMP...
BA-BMP...
...
RATTLE
GASP

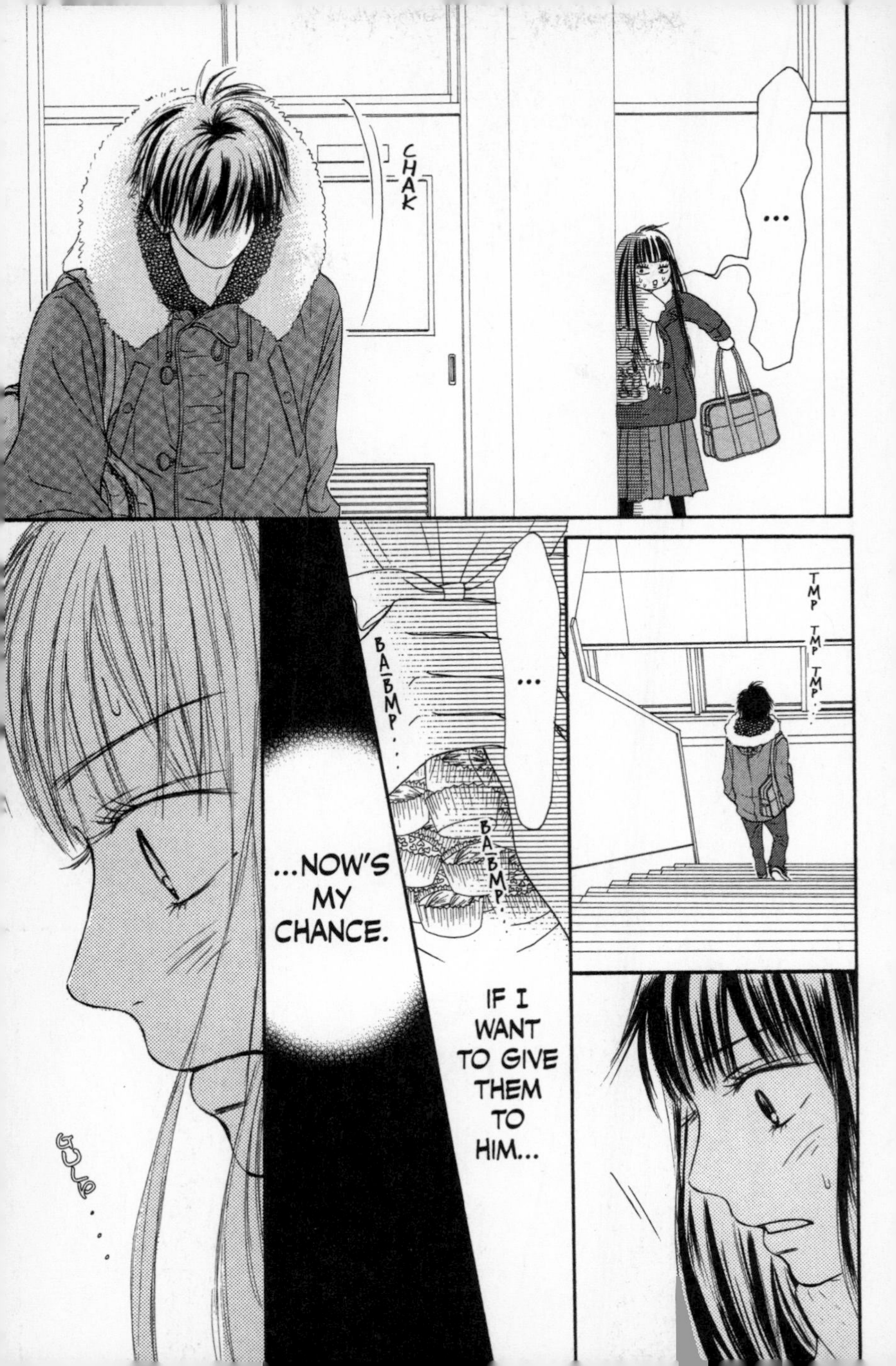
...
CHAK
TMP TMP TMP...
...
BA-BMP...
BA-BMP...
IF I WANT TO GIVE THEM TO HIM...
...NOW'S MY CHANCE.
GULP...

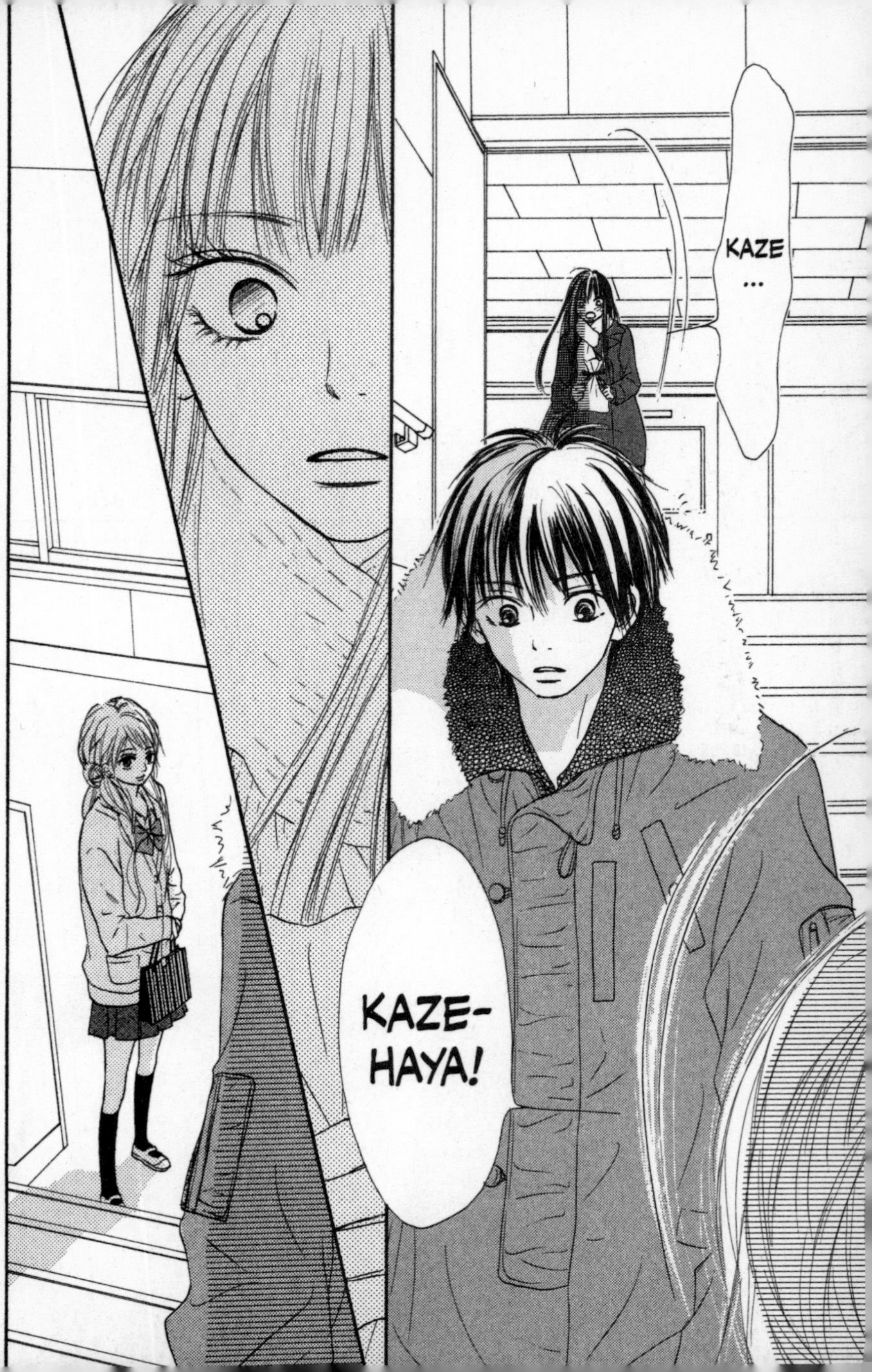
KAZE ...
KAZE-HAYA!

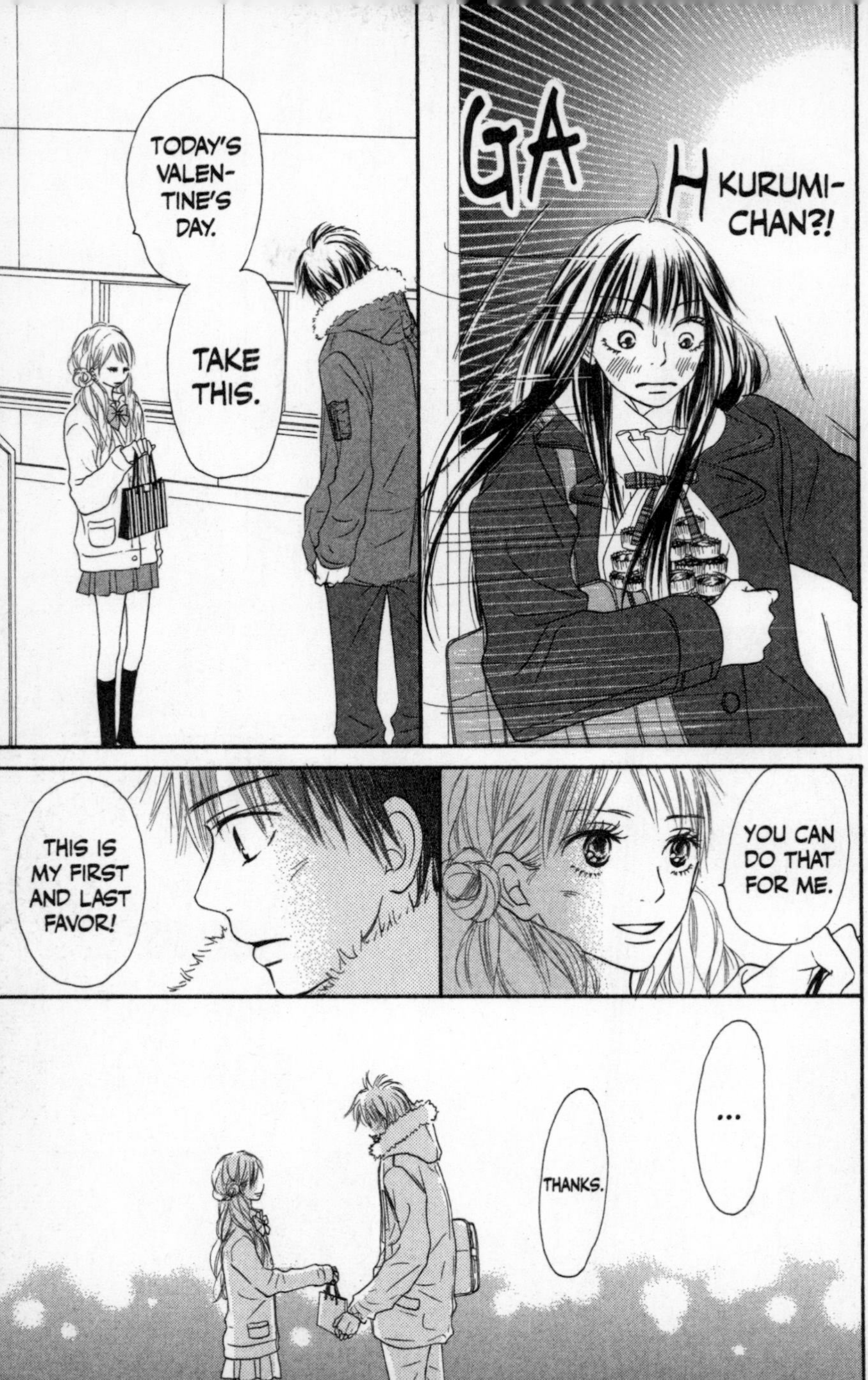

GA
H
KURUMI-CHAN?!
TODAY'S VALENTINE'S DAY.
TAKE THIS.
YOU CAN DO THAT FOR ME.
THIS IS MY FIRST AND LAST FAVOR!
...
THANKS.

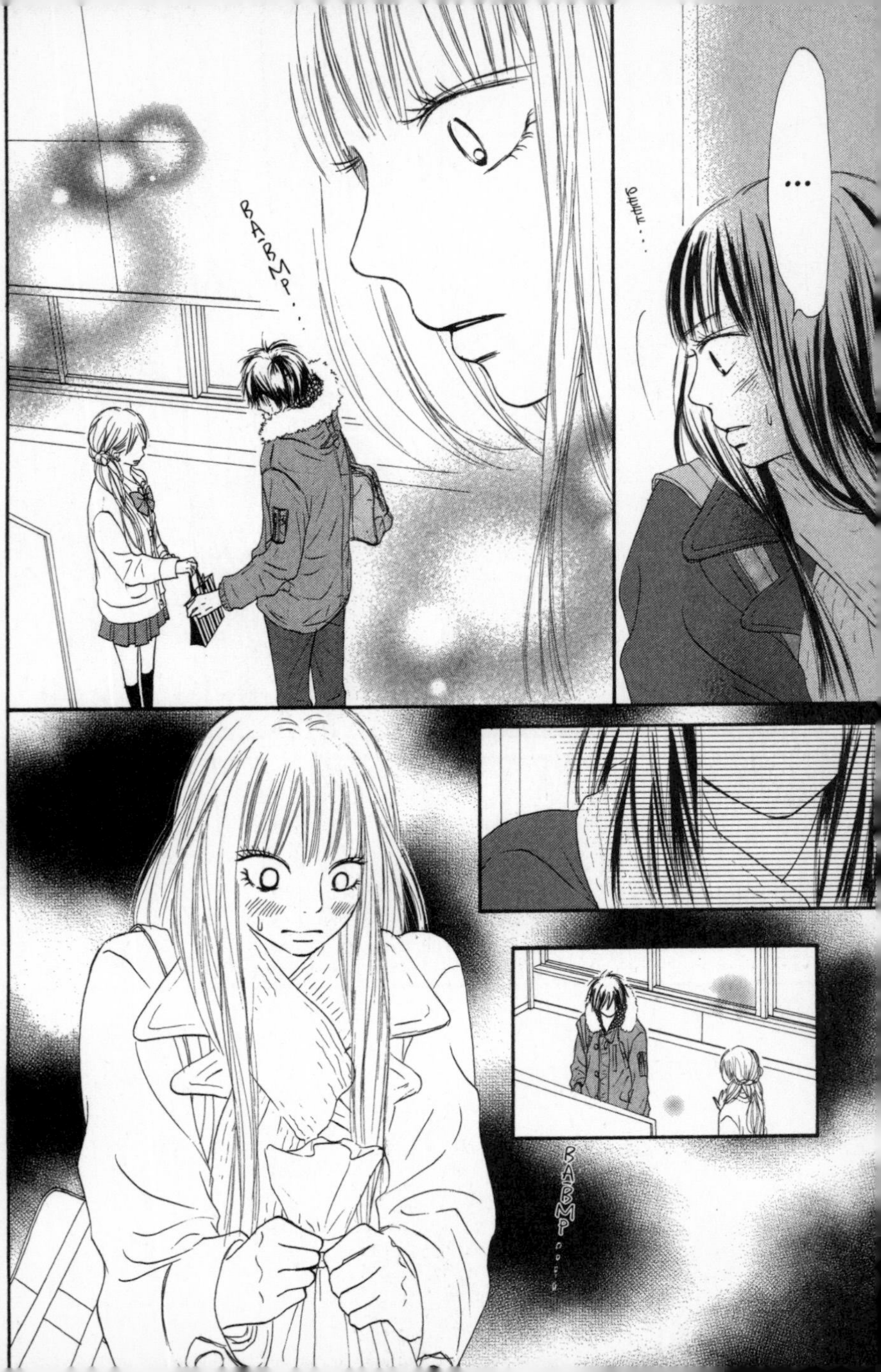
...
BA-BUMP...
BA-BUMP...

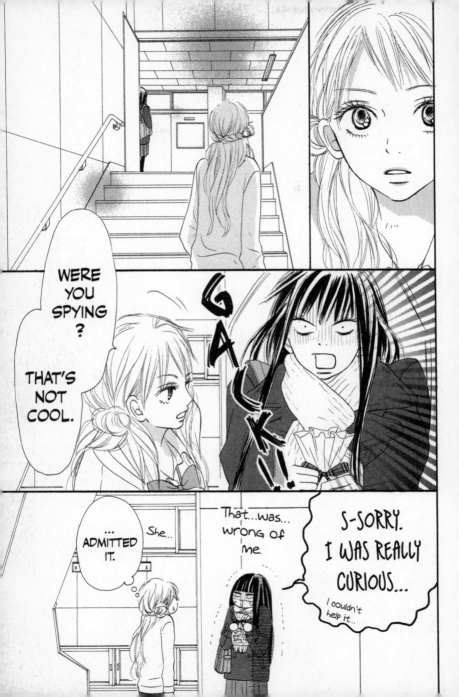

WERE YOU SPYING?

THAT'S NOT COOL.

GA K!

S-SORRY. I WAS REALLY CURIOUS...

I couldn't help it...

That...was... wrong of me.

She...

...ADMITTED IT.

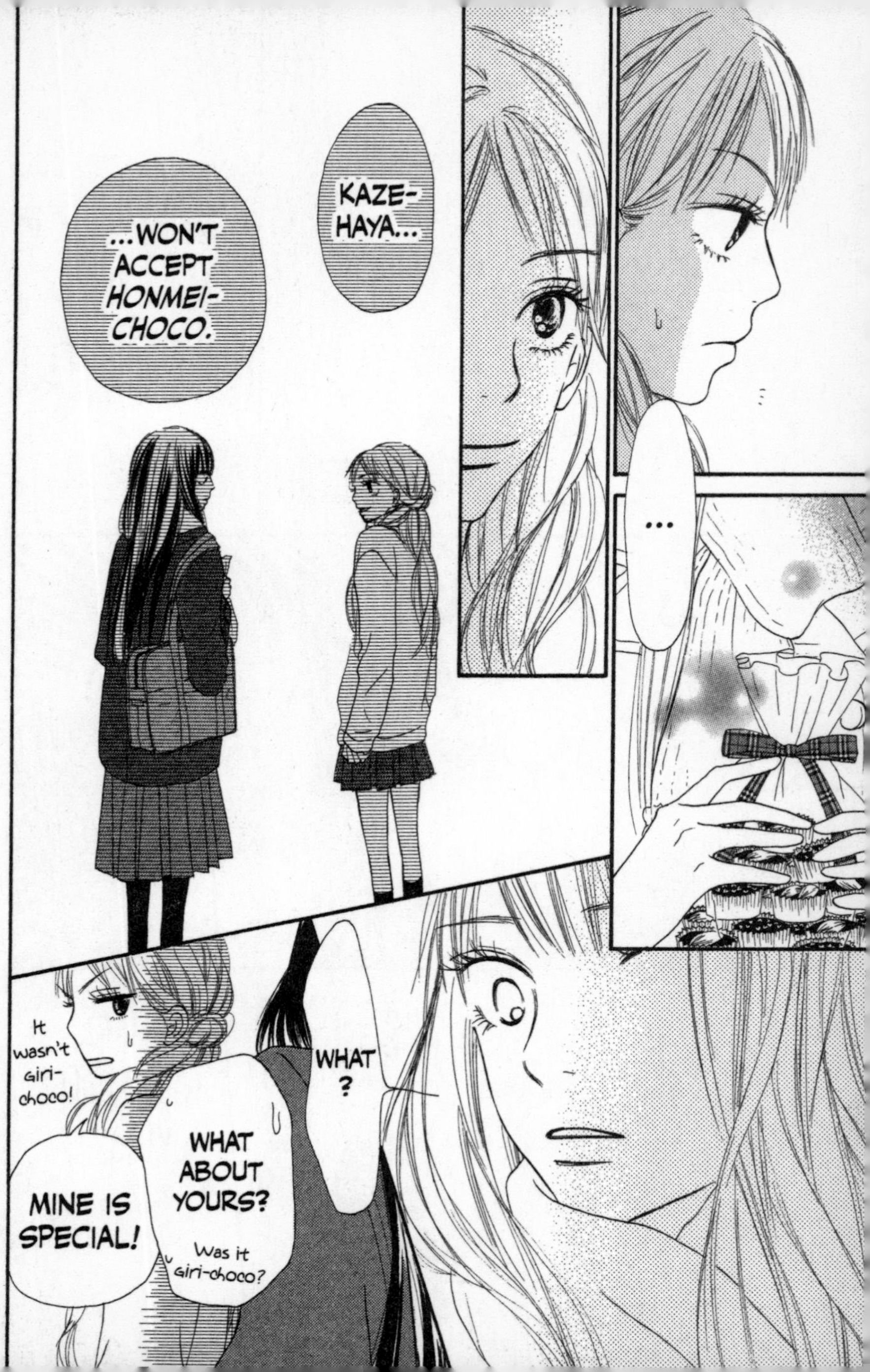
...
KAZE-HAYA...
...WON'T ACCEPT HONMEI-CHOCO.
WHAT?
WHAT ABOUT YOURS?
Was it giri-choco?
It wasn't giri-choco!
MINE IS SPECIAL!

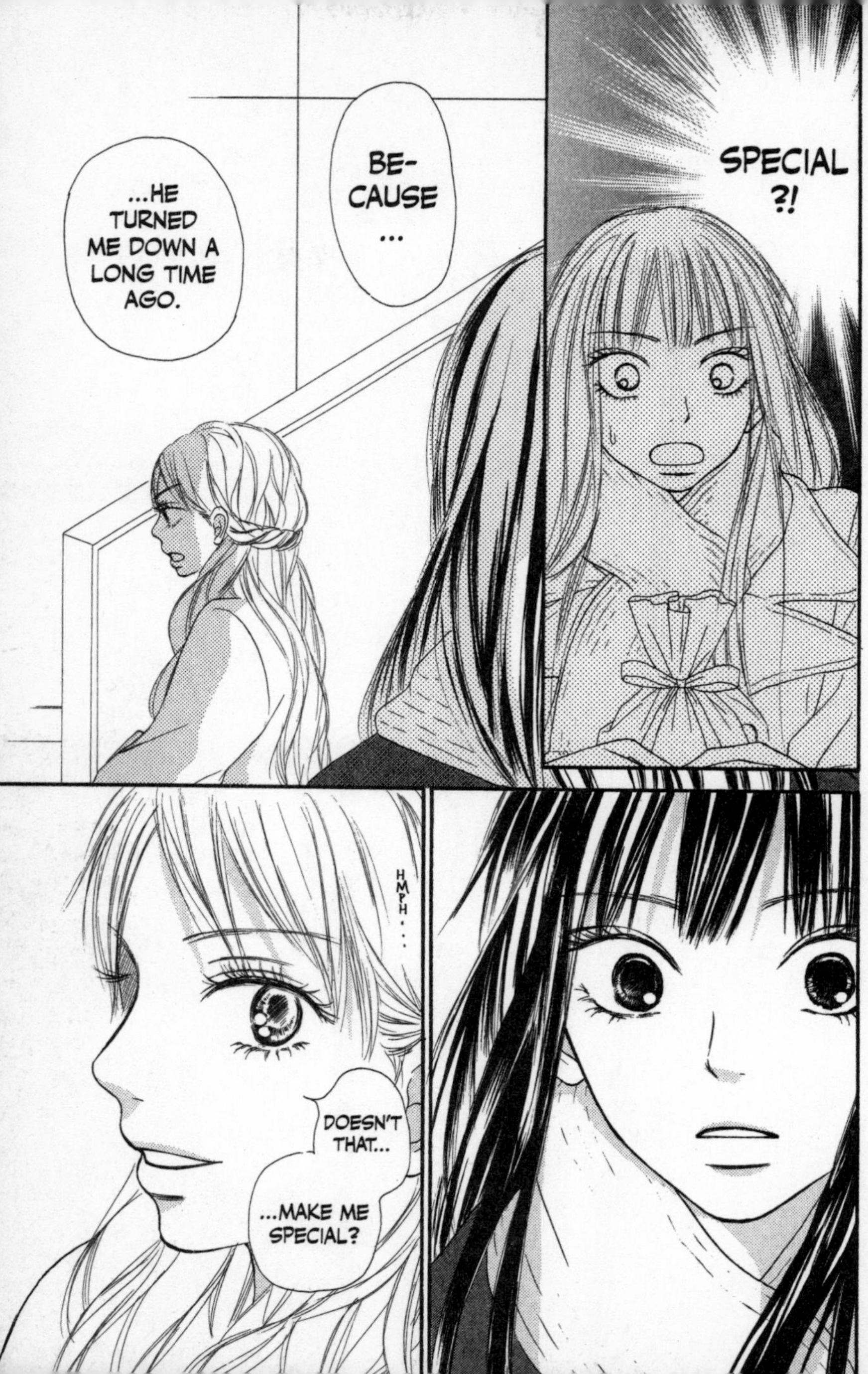
SPECIAL ?!
BE-CAUSE ...
...HE TURNED ME DOWN A LONG TIME AGO.
HMPH...
DOESN'T THAT...
...MAKE ME SPECIAL?

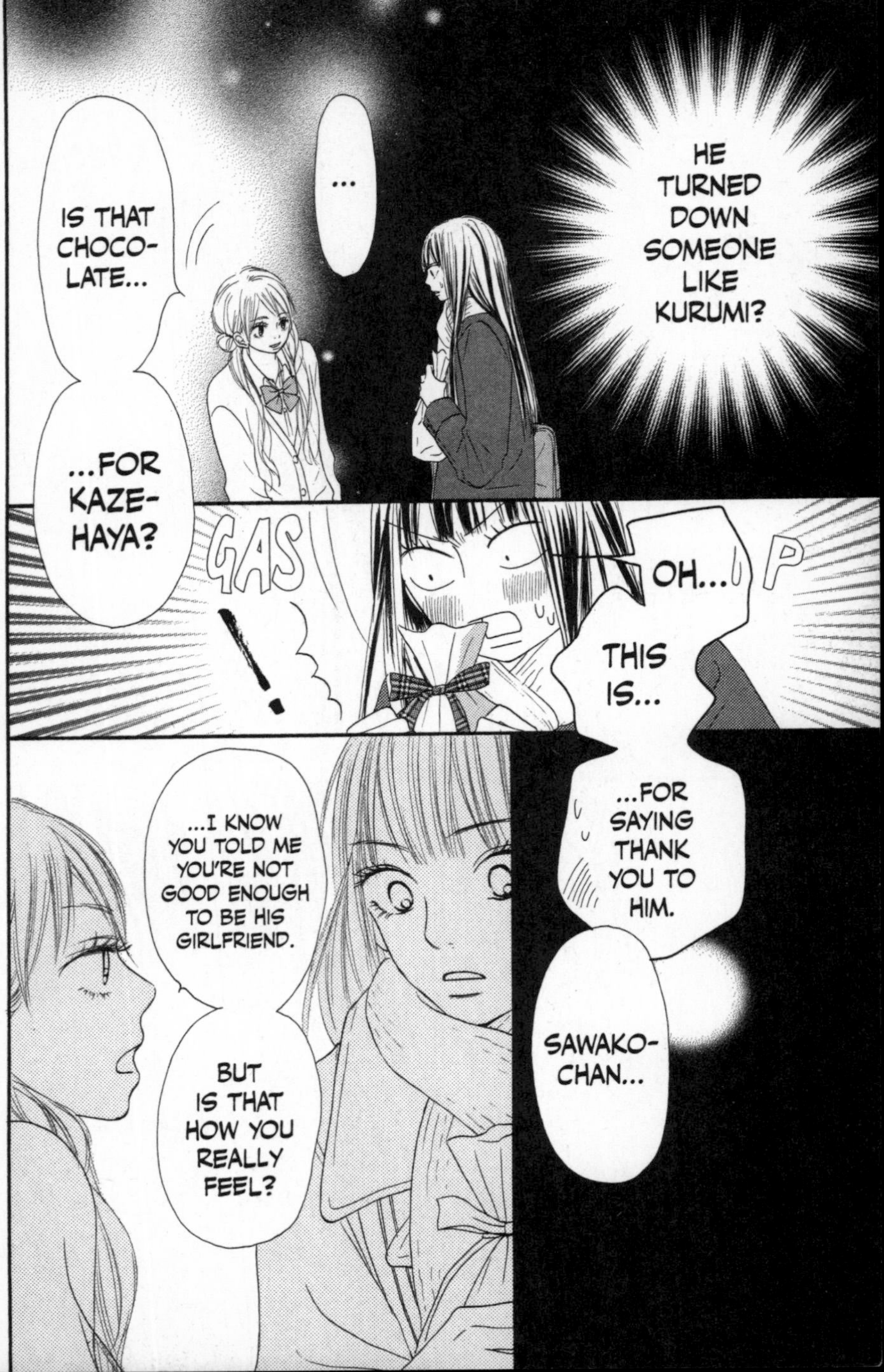
HE TURNED DOWN SOMEONE LIKE KURUMI?
...
IS THAT CHOCO-LATE...
...FOR KAZE-HAYA?
P
OH...
THIS IS...
GAS
!
...FOR SAYING THANK YOU TO HIM.
SAWAKO-CHAN...
...I KNOW YOU TOLD ME YOU'RE NOT GOOD ENOUGH TO BE HIS GIRLFRIEND.
BUT IS THAT HOW YOU REALLY FEEL?

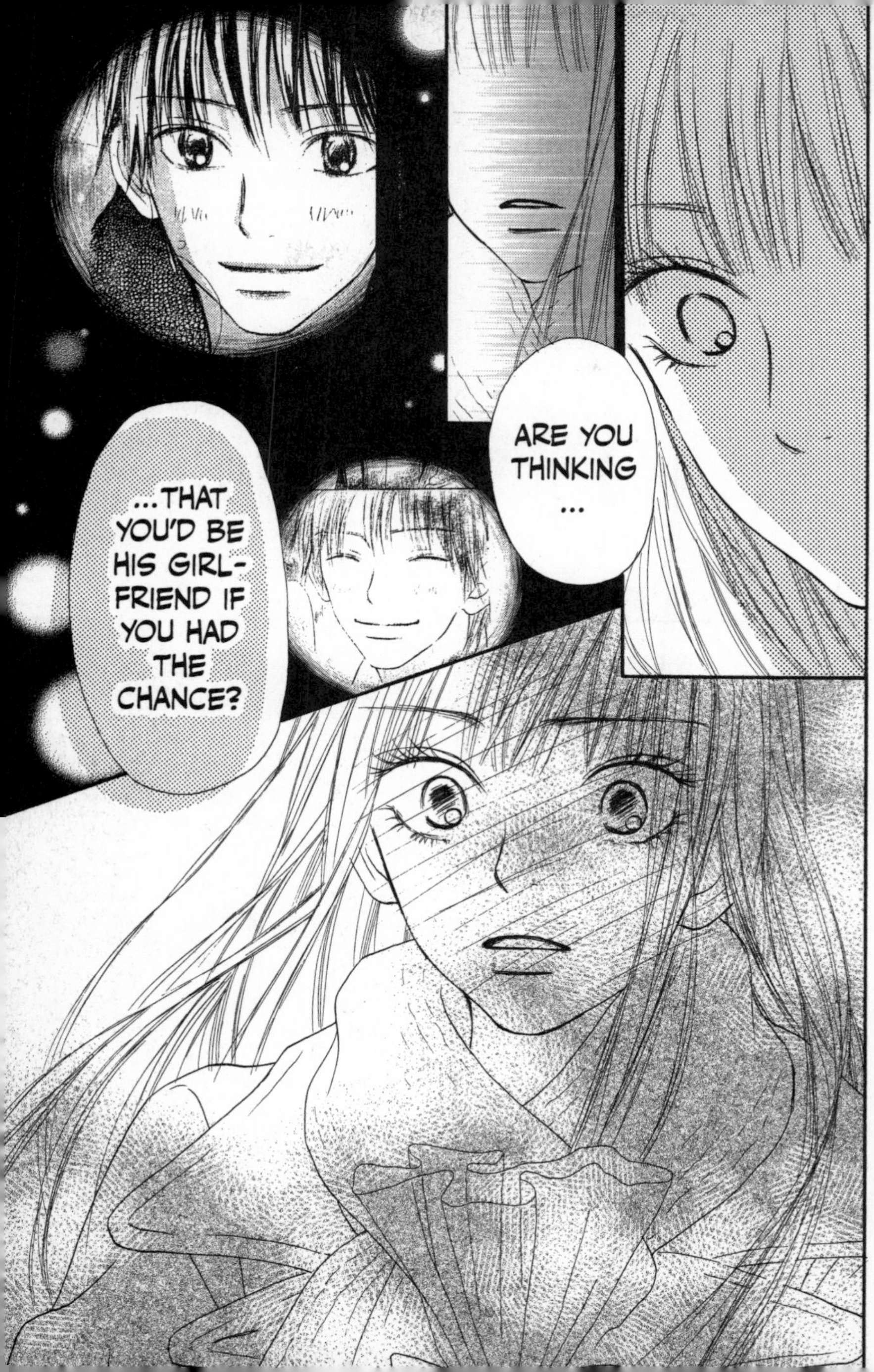
ARE YOU THINKING ...
...THAT YOU'D BE HIS GIRL-FRIEND IF YOU HAD THE CHANCE?

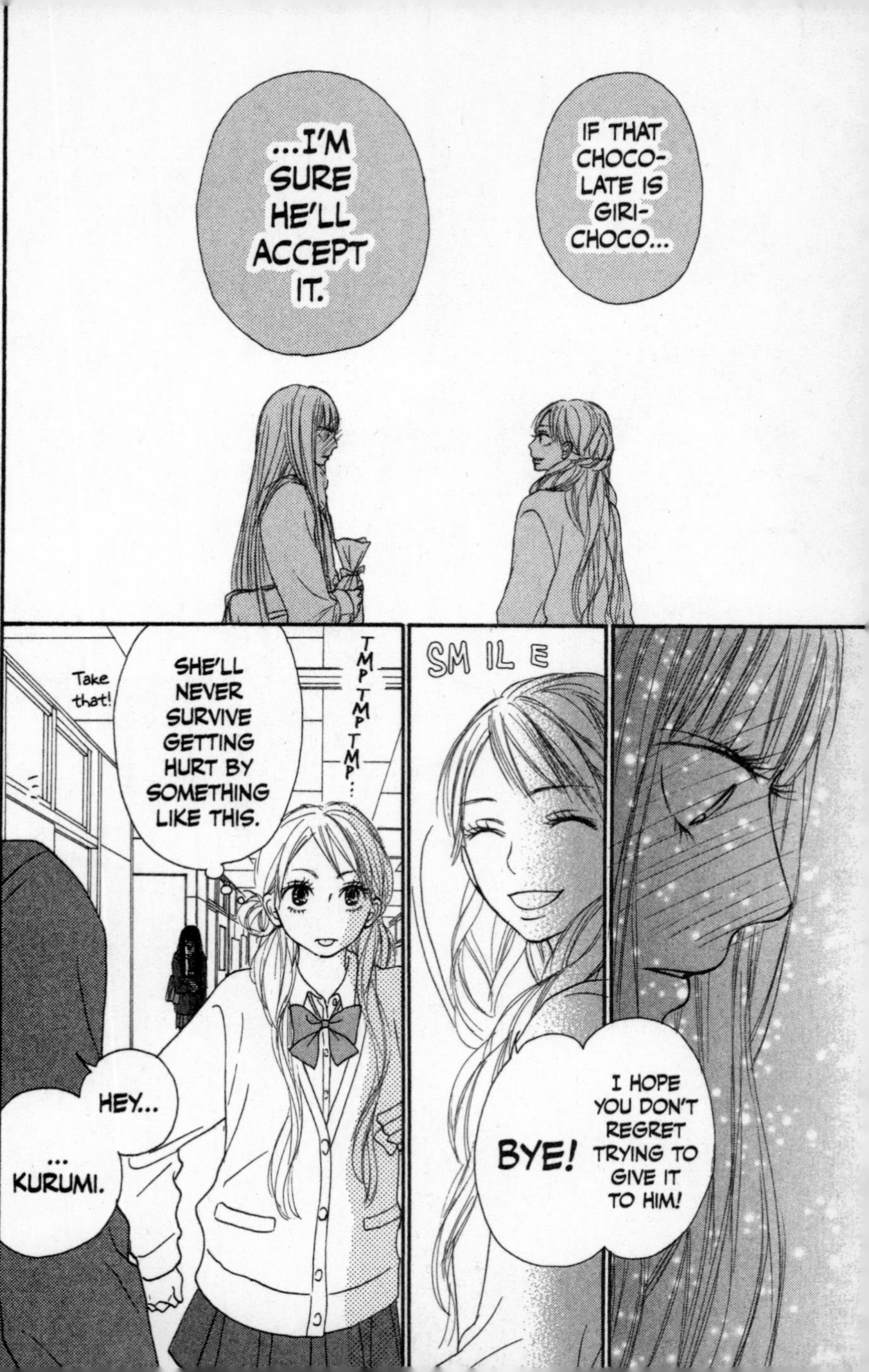
IF THAT CHOCOLATE IS GIRI-CHOCO...
...I'M SURE HE'LL ACCEPT IT.
SM IL E
I HOPE YOU DON'T REGRET TRYING TO GIVE IT TO HIM!
BYE!
TMP TMP TMP...
SHE'LL NEVER SURVIVE GETTING HURT BY SOMETHING LIKE THIS.
Take that!
HEY...
... KURUMI.

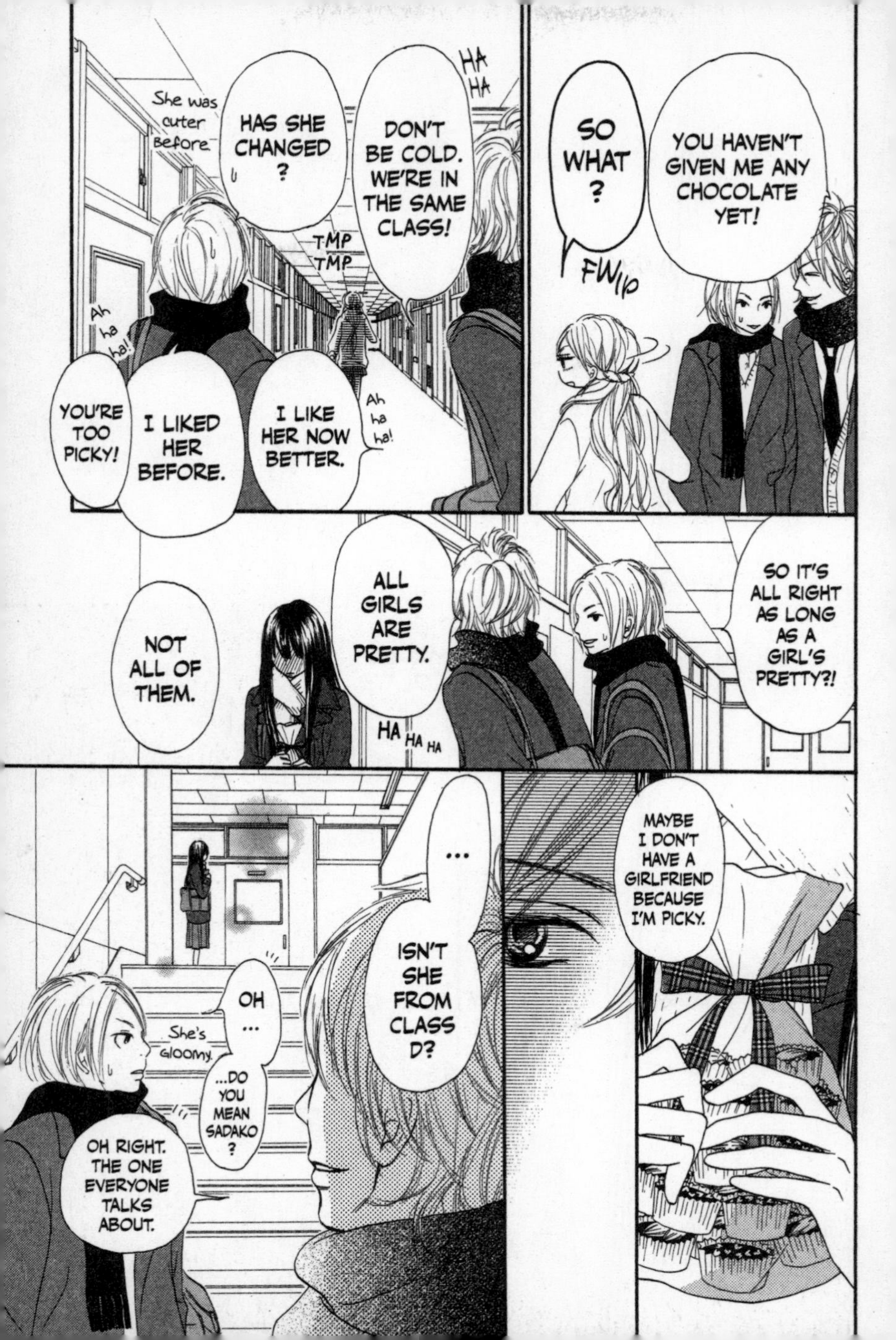
YOU HAVEN'T GIVEN ME ANY CHOCOLATE YET!
SO WHAT?
FWIP
HA HA
DON'T BE COLD. WE'RE IN THE SAME CLASS!
HAS SHE CHANGED?
She was cuter before
TMP TMP
Ah ha ha!
I LIKE HER NOW BETTER.
I LIKED HER BEFORE.
Ah ha ha!
YOU'RE TOO PICKY!
SO IT'S ALL RIGHT AS LONG AS A GIRL'S PRETTY?!
ALL GIRLS ARE PRETTY.
HA HA HA
NOT ALL OF THEM.
MAYBE I DON'T HAVE A GIRLFRIEND BECAUSE I'M PICKY.
...
ISN'T SHE FROM CLASS D?
OH ...
She's gloomy.
...DO YOU MEAN SADAKO?
OH RIGHT. THE ONE EVERYONE TALKS ABOUT.

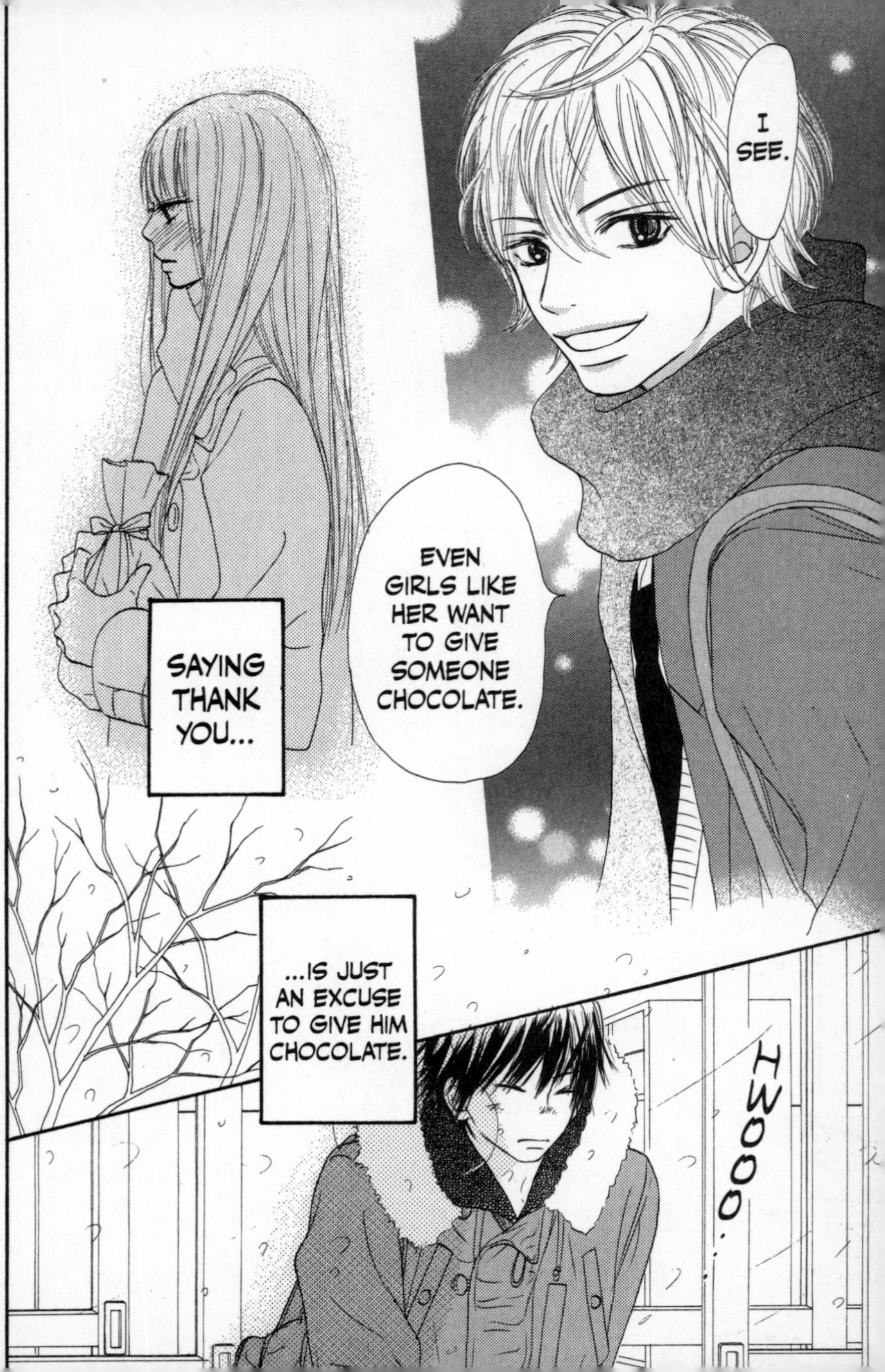
I SEE.
EVEN GIRLS LIKE HER WANT TO GIVE SOMEONE CHOCOLATE.
SAYING THANK YOU...
...IS JUST AN EXCUSE TO GIVE HIM CHOCOLATE.
HWOOO...

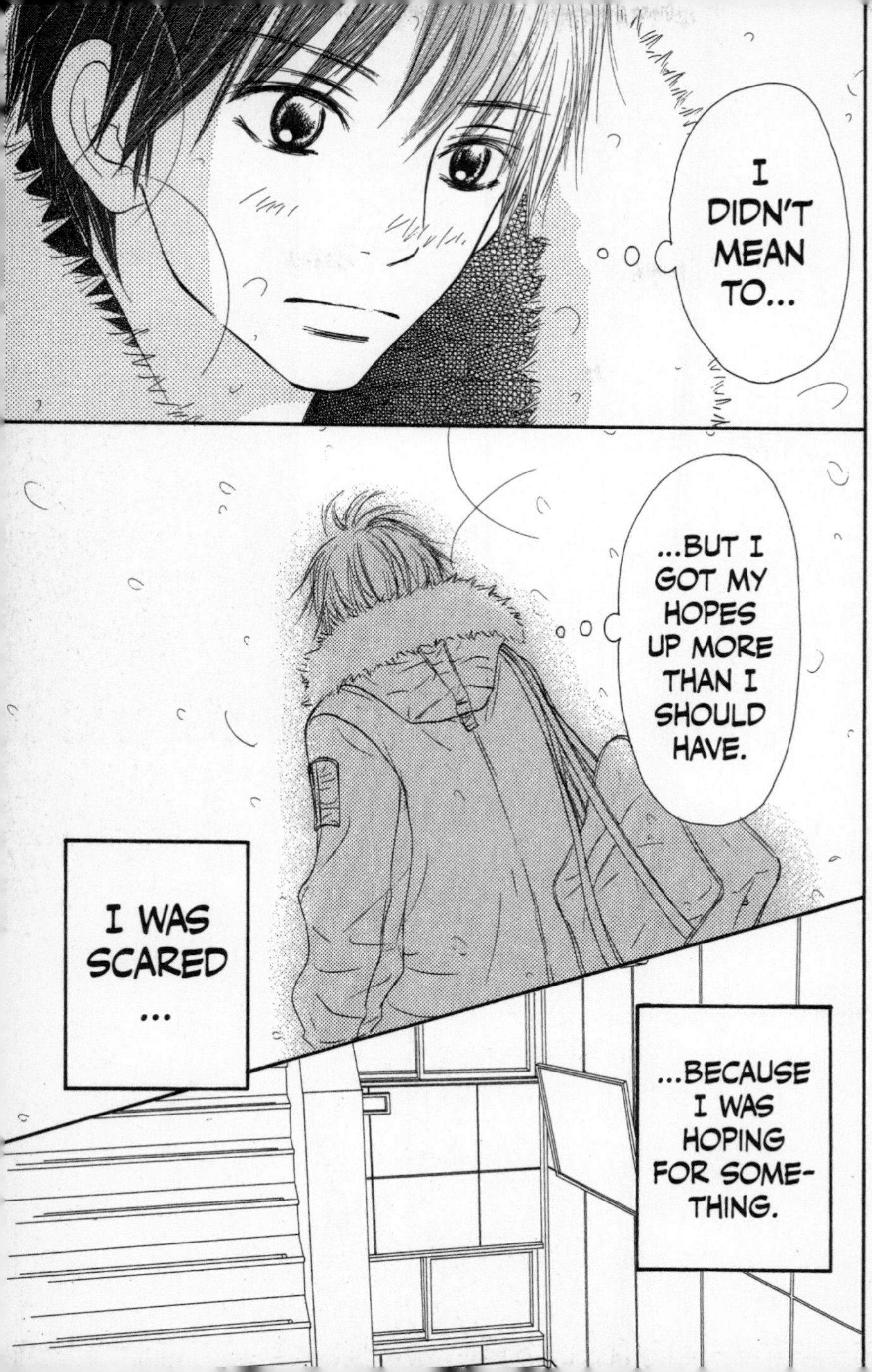
I DIDN'T MEAN TO...
...BUT I GOT MY HOPES UP MORE THAN I SHOULD HAVE.
I WAS SCARED ...
...BECAUSE I WAS HOPING FOR SOME-THING.

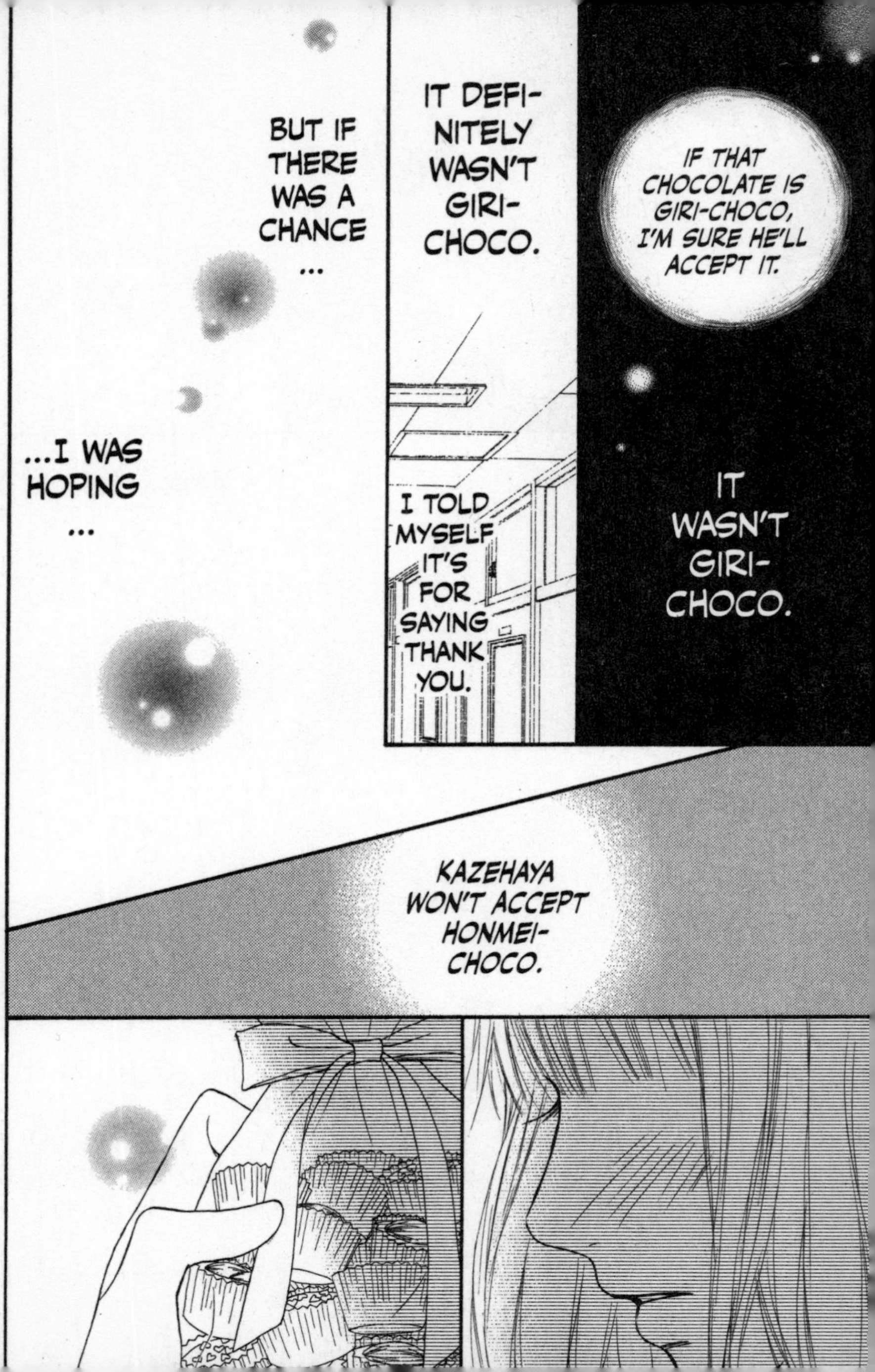
IF THAT CHOCOLATE IS GIRI-CHOCO, I'M SURE HE'LL ACCEPT IT.
IT WASN'T GIRI-CHOCO.
IT DEFINITELY WASN'T GIRI-CHOCO.
I TOLD MYSELF IT'S FOR SAYING THANK YOU.
BUT IF THERE WAS A CHANCE...
...I WAS HOPING...
KAZEHAYA WON'T ACCEPT HONMEI-CHOCO.

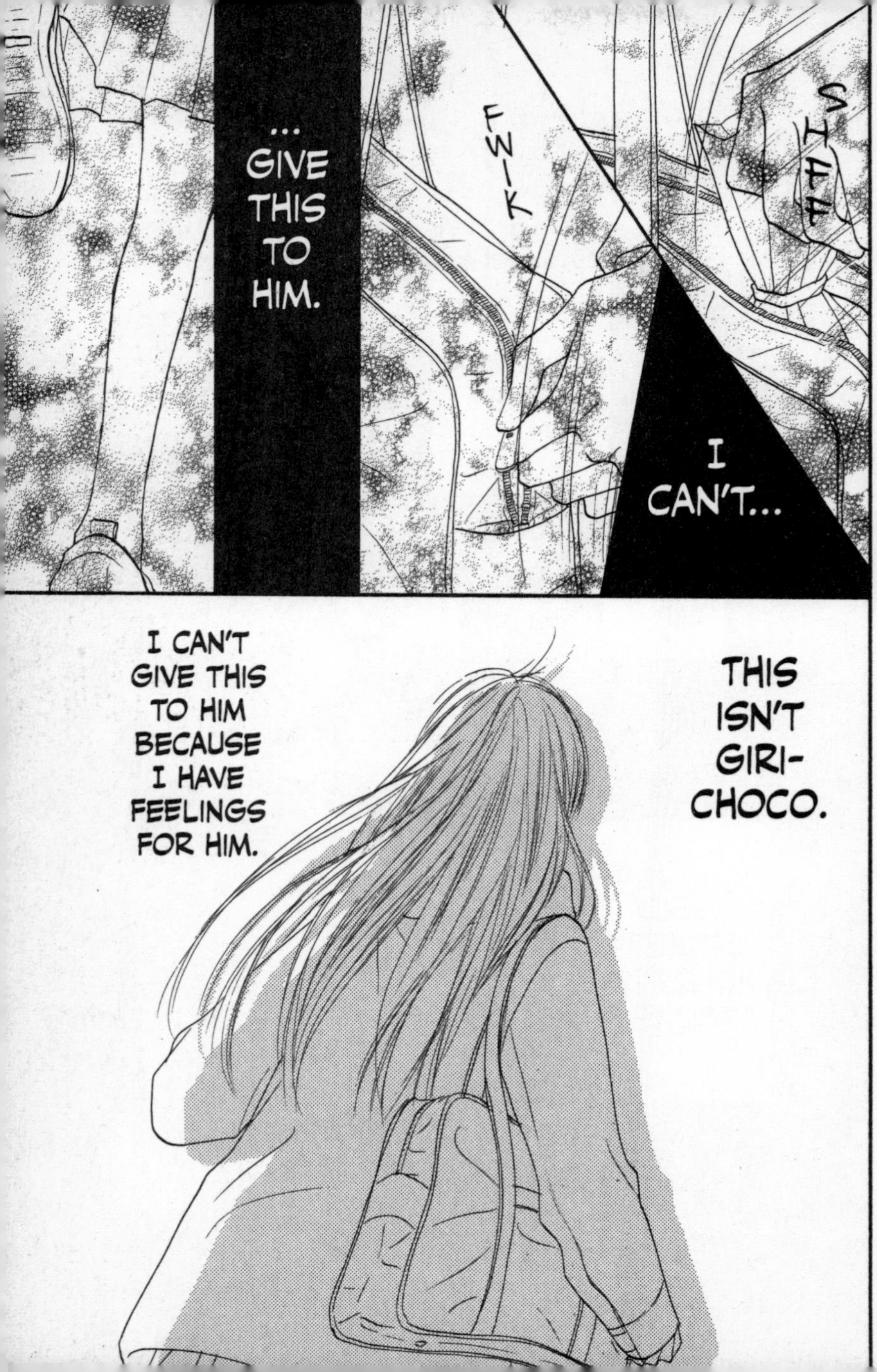
SHFF
I CAN'T...
FWIK
... GIVE THIS TO HIM.
THIS ISN'T GIRI-CHOCO.
I CAN'T GIVE THIS TO HIM BECAUSE I HAVE FEELINGS FOR HIM.

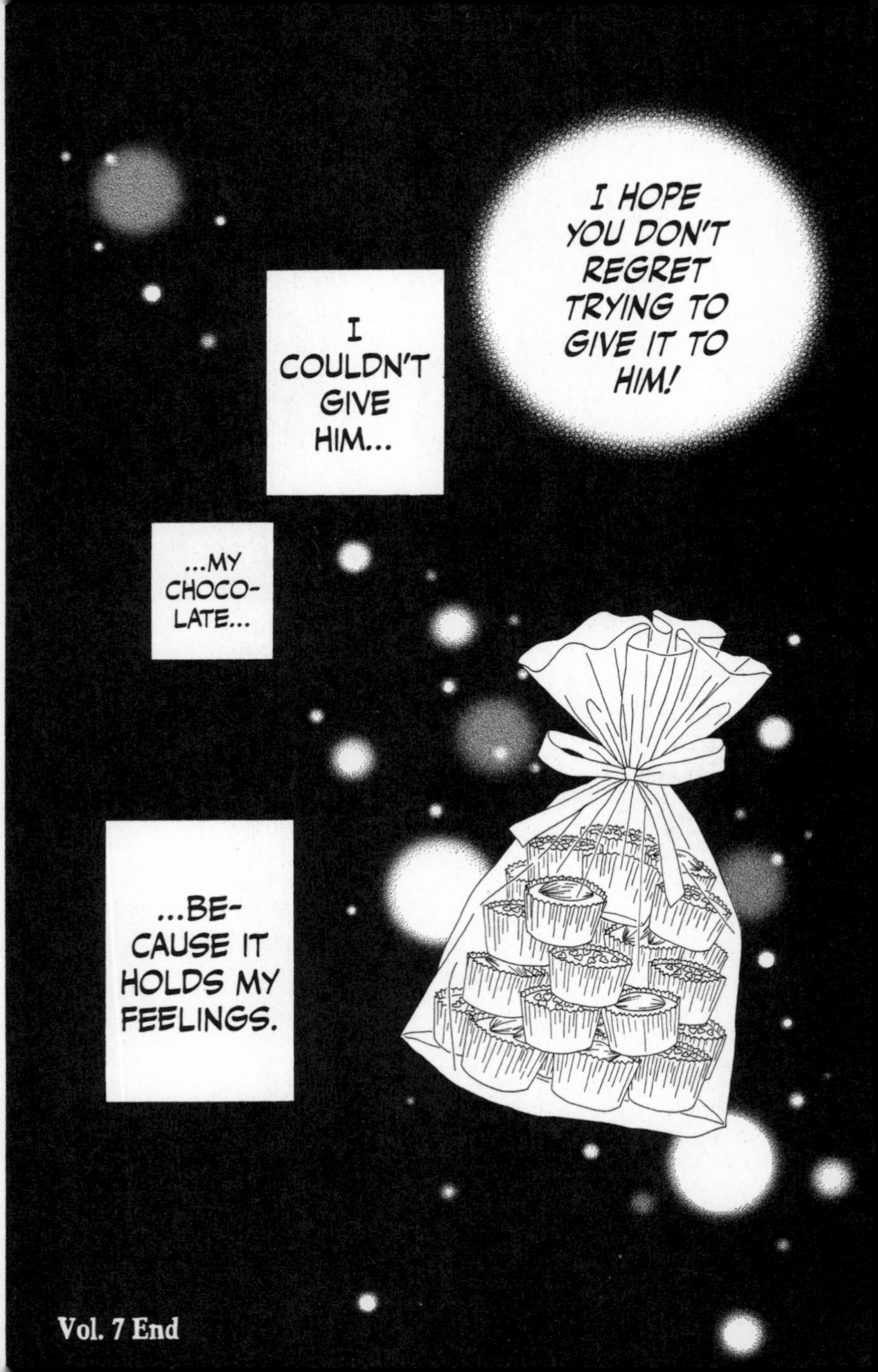
I HOPE YOU DON'T REGRET TRYING TO GIVE IT TO HIM!
I COULDN'T GIVE HIM...
...MY CHOCO-LATE...
...BE-CAUSE IT HOLDS MY FEELINGS.

Vol. 7 End

From me (the editor) to you (the reader).

Here are some Japanese culture explanations that will help you better understand the references in the *Kimi ni Todoke* world.

Honorifics:
When saying someone's name in Japanese, a suffix is often attached to indicate how familiar the speaker is with the person. Some are more polite and respectful, while others are endearing. Calling someone by just their first name is the most informal.
-kun is used for young men or boys, usually someone you are familiar with.
-chan is used for young women, girls or young children and can be used as a term of endearment.
-san is used for someone you respect or are not close to, or to be polite.

Page 19, "…when I turn 20!":
The legal age for drinking alcoholic beverages in Japan is 20.

Page 22, default address:
Phones in Japan use the phone number as the email address until you set your own.

Page 57, amazake:
A sweet drink made from fermented rice, often served warm with a pinch of grated ginger.

Page 89, Zashikiwarashi:
A deity who protects old traditional manor homes in Tohoku (the northern part of Honshu, the main island of Japan). Usually portrayed as a young girl with straight black hair and a kimono.

Page 116-117, fortunes:
Omikuji, or paper fortunes, are often available at shrines for a small fee. The levels range from *daikichi* (great luck) to *daikyo* (certain disaster).

Page 137, Valentine's Day:
Girls give chocolate to boys on Valentine's Day. A month later, on White Day, boys are expected to give gifts to the girls who gave them chocolates.

Page 144, giri-choco:
"Obligation chocolate," given to a girl's male classmates, friends and associates with no romantic intentions.

Page 157, possessed:
According to folklore, a stiff left shoulder could mean that you're possessed by a spirit.

Page 164, honmei-choco:
"True feeling chocolate," given to someone with romantic feelings.

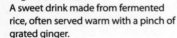

This is volume 7! This is the longest of my series so far. This unremarkable manga received a wonderful honor called the Kodansha Manga Award. Thank you to my fans who have been cheering for me. A lot will happen as the story progresses, so keep reading!

--Karuho Shiina

Karuho Shiina was born and raised in Hokkaido, Japan. Though *Kimi ni Todoke* is only her second series following many one-shot stories, it has already racked up accolades from various "Best Manga of the Year" lists. Winner of the 2008 Kodansha Manga Award for the shojo category, *Kimi ni Todoke* also placed fifth in the first-ever Manga Taisho (Cartoon Grand Prize) contest in 2008. An animated TV series debuted in October 2009 in Japan.

Kimi ni Todoke
VOL. 7

Shojo Beat Edition

STORY AND ART BY
KARUHO SHIINA

Translation/Ari Yasuda, HC Language Solutions, Inc.
Touch-up Art & Lettering/Vanessa Satone
Cover Design/Yukiko Whitley
Interior Design/Nozomi Akashi
Editor/Carrie Shepherd

KIMI NI TODOKE © 2005 by Karuho Shiina
All rights reserved. First published in Japan in 2005 by SHUEISHA Inc.,
Tokyo. English translation rights arranged by SHUEISHA Inc.

Printed in the U.S.A.

Published by VIZ Media, LLC
P.O. Box 77010
San Francisco, CA 94107

10 9 8 7 6 5 4 3 2
First printing, February 2011
Second printing, August 2011

www.viz.com

www.shojobeat.com

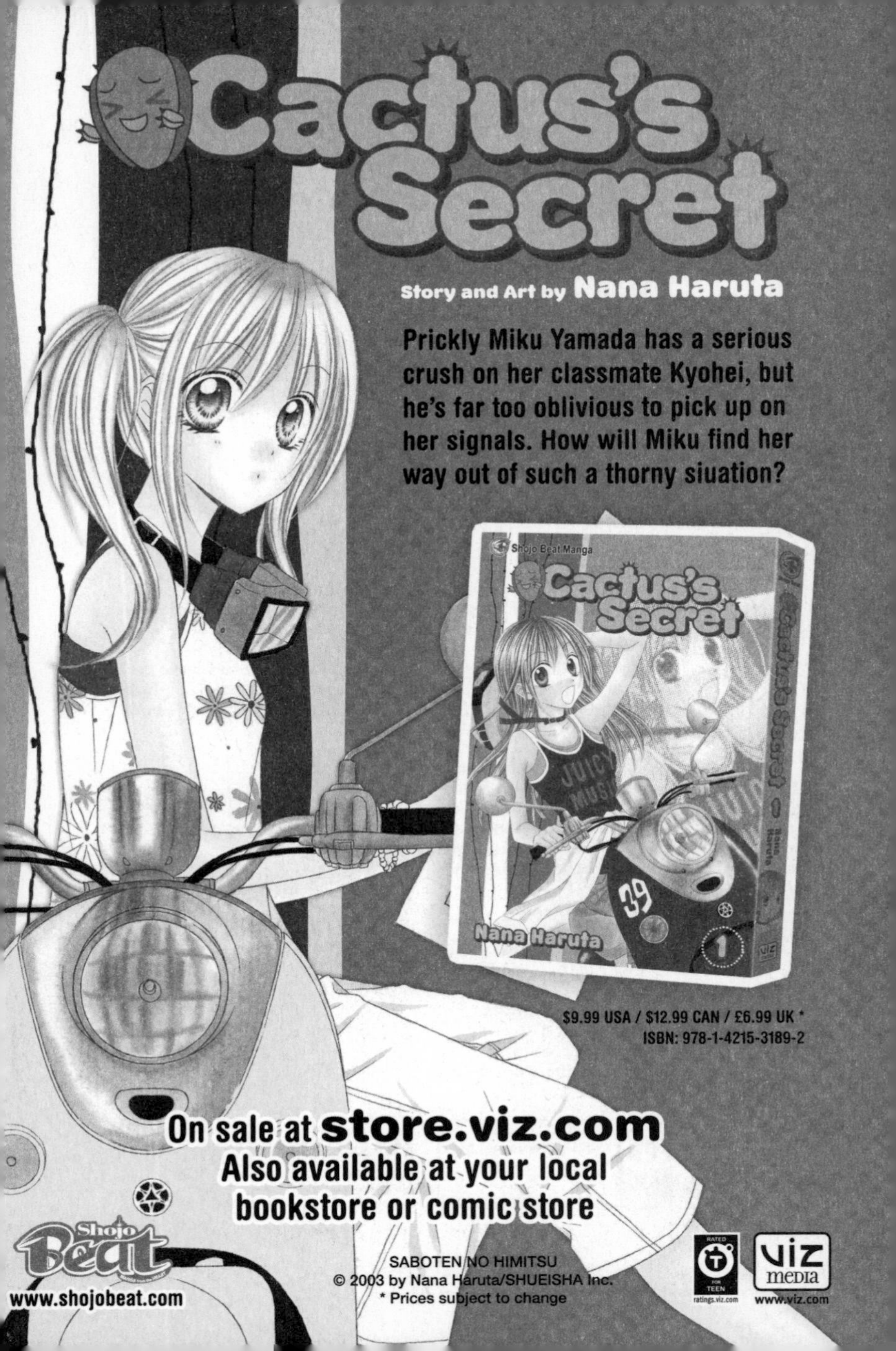
Cactus's Secret
Story and Art by Nana Haruta
Prickly Miku Yamada has a serious crush on her classmate Kyohei, but he's far too oblivious to pick up on her signals. How will Miku find her way out of such a thorny siuation?
Shojo Beat Manga
Cactus's Secret
Nana Haruta
1
$9.99 USA / $12.99 CAN / £6.99 UK *
ISBN: 978-1-4215-3189-2
On sale at store.viz.com
Also available at your local bookstore or comic store
Shojo Beat
www.shojobeat.com
SABOTEN NO HIMITSU
© 2003 by Nana Haruta/SHUEISHA Inc.
* Prices subject to change
RATED T FOR TEEN
ratings.viz.com
VIZ MEDIA
www.viz.com

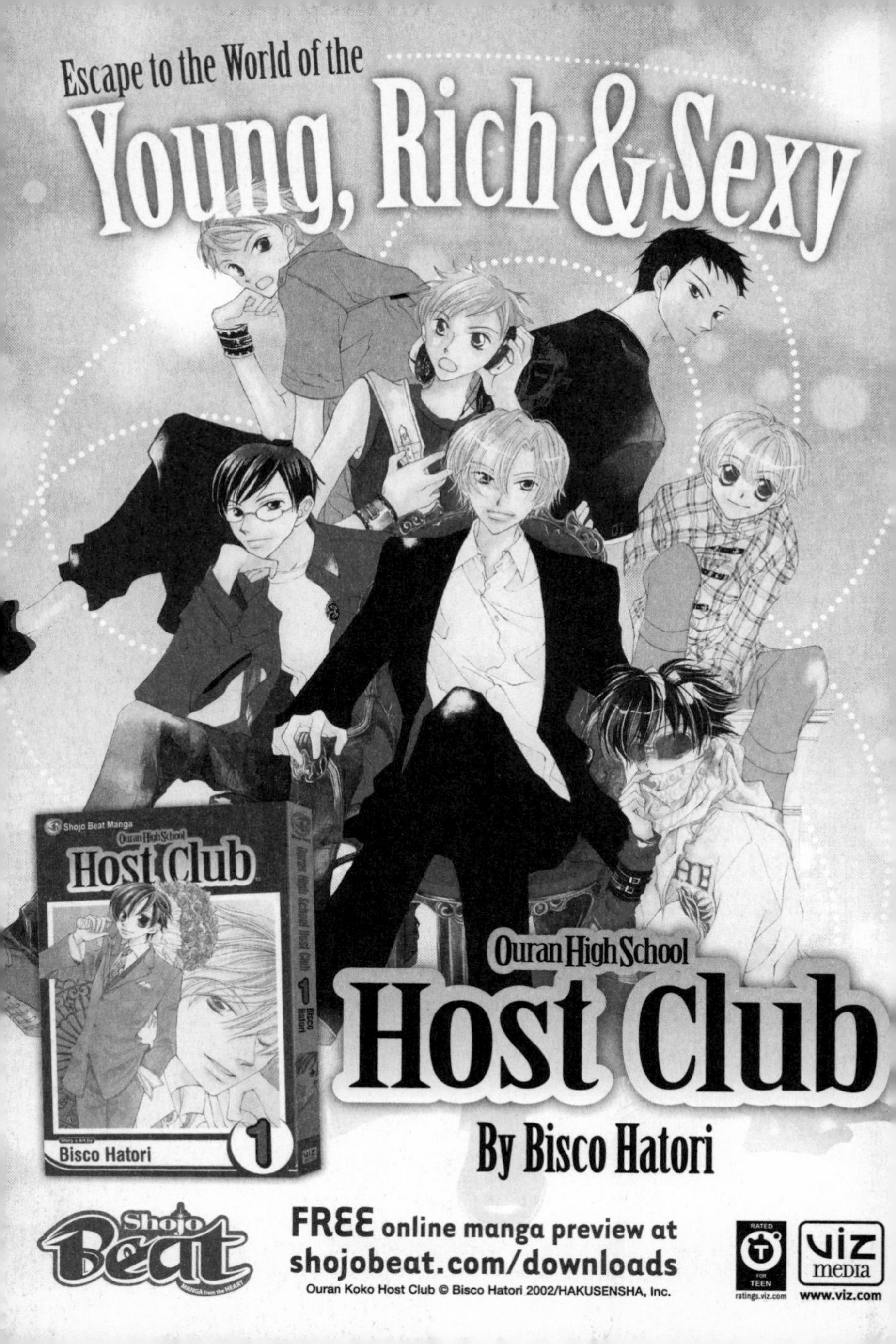
Escape to the World of the
Young, Rich & Sexy
Shojo Beat Manga
Ouran High School
Host Club
Ouran High School Host Club 1
Bisco Hatori
Story & Art by
Bisco Hatori
1
Ouran High School
Host Club
By Bisco Hatori
Shojo Beat
MANGA from the HEART
FREE online manga preview at
shojobeat.com/downloads
Ouran Koko Host Club © Bisco Hatori 2002/HAKUSENSHA, Inc.
RATED
T
FOR
TEEN
ratings.viz.com
VIZ
media
www.viz.com

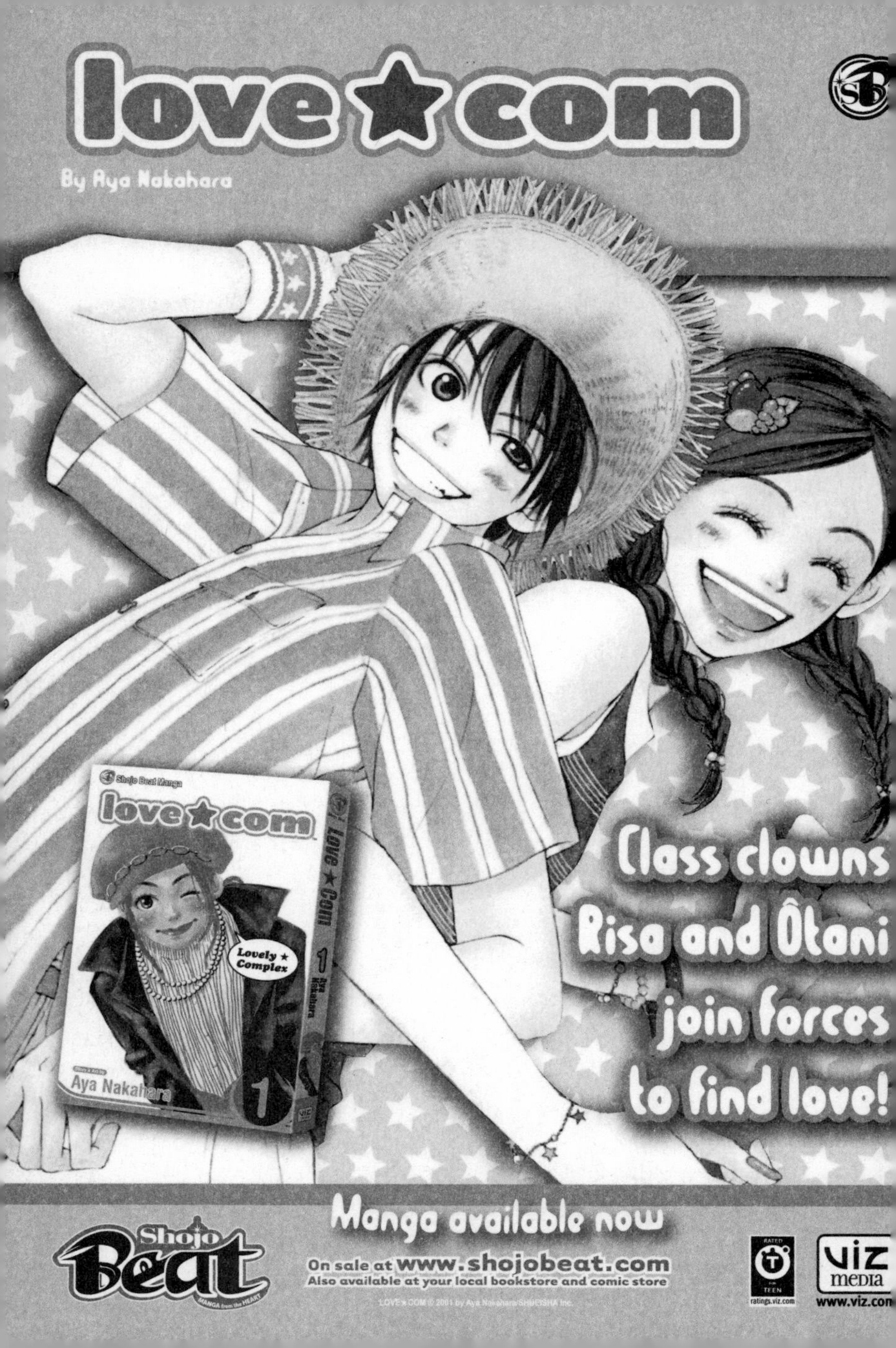
love★com
By Aya Nakahara
Shojo Beat Manga
love★com
Lovely ★ Complex
Aya Nakahara
Class clowns Risa and Ôtani join forces to find love!
Manga available now
Shojo Beat
On sale at www.shojobeat.com
Also available at your local bookstore and comic store
LOVE★COM © 2001 by Aya Nakahara/SHUEISHA Inc.
ratings.viz.com
VIZ media
www.viz.com